Teaching

Second Edition

Sharleen L. Kato, EdD, CFCS-HDFS

Professor and Director
Department of Family and Consumer Sciences
Seattle Pacific University
Seattle, Washington

Publisher
The Goodheart-Willcox Company, Inc.
Tinley Park, Illinois
www.g-w.com

About the Author

Sharleen L. Kato, EdD, loves teaching as well as learning. She is a Professor at Seattle Pacific University where she encourages students to become creative and successful. Dr. Kato has taught undergraduate students for over 25 years, and currently serves as the Family and Consumer Sciences Department Director. She holds a Doctorate in Education, a Master's in Human Ecology, and an undergraduate degree in Home Economics. Dr. Kato has served on the Bellevue Christian Schools Education Committee and Board of Directors, the Health and Wellness Advisory Committee for Seattle Public Schools, and education committees and task forces for Washington State Public Schools. Dr. Kato has published many books and articles, and has presented papers in the education field. She travels extensively—spending at least two weeks each year serving in an orphanage, school, teen home, and prenatal clinic in the Philippines. Dr. Kato is passionate about inspiring others to take on the challenge of becoming effective teachers.

Reviewers

The author and publisher are grateful to the following reviewers who provided valuable input to this edition.

Jan Dye
Family and Consumer Sciences Educator
Cedar Hill High School
Cedar Hill, Texas

Gina Freeland
Teacher
Ocean Springs High School
Ocean Springs, Mississippi

Cindy Grega
Teacher
Horizon High School
Scottsdale, Arizona

Mary Karlik
Family and Consumer Sciences Teacher
Garland High School
Garland, Texas

Elisa McIntire
Family and Consumer Sciences Educator
Elkins High School, Fort Bend ISD
Missouri City, Texas

Terri Michael
Teacher
Walnut Grove High School
Loganville, Georgia

Melinda Peterman
Teacher Trainer Program Teacher & Coordinator
Mesa High School
Mesa, Arizona

Erica Peyton
Family and Consumer Science Teacher
Arlington High School
Arlington, Tennessee

Jennifer Piotrowski
Teachers for Tomorrow Instructor
Chantilly Governor's STEM Academy
Chantilly, Virginia

Faria Nimmo P'Pool
Family and Consumer Sciences Teacher
Trigg County High School
Cadiz, Kentucky

Brief Contents

Contents

Features

Case Studies

Professional Tips

Perspectives on Teaching

The Complete Package for

Student Text—Print or Online

The student edition of *Teaching* is available in print or as an online text. This edition offers a clean, sophisticated design and logical organization the supports reading, comprehension, and application to enhance learning for the teachers of tomorrow.

Workbook

The Workbook includes a variety of activities for review and application of chapter concepts.

Online Student Center

The Online Student Center combines the online student text and workbook in digital format. Pages from the student text and workbook can be printed on demand. Students can complete the workbook activities online using embedded form fields and print or e-mail the results for grading. In addition, the Online Student Center includes video segments provided by expert educators to support text concepts and enhance learning.

Companion Website

The easy-to-navigate companion website provides multiple opportunities to increase comprehension and retention of key concepts. The website includes e-flash cards, interactive vocabulary games and activities, and interactive self-assessment quizzes.
www.g-wlearning.com/teaching/

Mobile Website

Students are able to study on the go with the mobile site. E-flash cards and interactive games help students review vocabulary terms. Interactive quizzes help students review chapter materials, assess comprehension, and prepare for quizzes and tests.
www.m.g-wlearning.com/0094/

both Students and Teachers

Online Instructor's Resources

The Online Instructor's Resources 6-year subscription provides 6 years of individual access to the classroom support materials used most often—all in one convenient location that can be accessed from anywhere. The Online Instructor's Resources includes Instructor's Resources, Instructor's Presentations for PowerPoint®, and Examview® Assessment Suite.

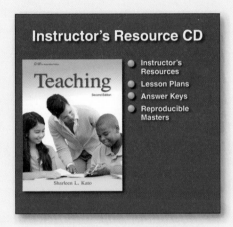

Instructor's Resources

Resources include daily lesson plans, answer keys, and reproducible masters.

Examview® Assessment Suite

Quickly and easily prepare and print tests with the Examview® Assessment Suite. With hundreds of questions in the test bank, you can choose which questions to include in each test, create multiple versions of a single test, and automatically generate answer keys.

Instructor's Presentations for PowerPoint®

Includes colorful presentations for each chapter to reinforce main ideas and terms. Content is presented by objective, and review questions are included for each chapter.

Promotes Learning Success

Unit 3
The Learner

Chapter 6—Understanding Human Development
Chapter 7—Middle Childhood: Growth and Development
Chapter 8—The Teen Years: Growth and Development

Event Prep
Community Service Project

Many Career and Technical Student Organizations (CTSOs) offer competitive events that include a community service project. An entire CTSO chapter typically carries out this type of project which often takes several months to a year to complete. There may be several parts to this type of event—written and oral. In addition, the event may also involve preparation of a display or portfolio. The CTSO chapter will designate several members to represent the team at the competitive event.

To prepare for a community service project, complete the following activities.

1. Read and analyze the event rules and guidelines the organization offers.
2. Select a theme for your chapter's community service project as a team.
3. Identify the target audience of the community service project. Your project may include businesses, schools, and community groups.
4. Decide on which roles the team needs. For instance, you may need a team captain, secretary, treasurer, and any other roles that are necessary to create and carry out the plan. Ask your instructor for guidance in assigning roles to team members.
5. Brainstorm with your chapter members. Use a decision-making planning process to develop a plan for your project. Create a project rationale, identifying the project goals and needs. What is the desired end result of this project? What are the benefits of supporting and completing the project? Identify tasks, budget if necessary, and ways to execute the plan.
6. This project will likely span the school year. During regular chapter meetings, have group members report on progress with the project. Create a draft report based on guidelines from your CTSO organization. Update and refine your group's written report, create necessary visuals or a portfolio until the project is complete. Include an analysis of the success of your project as part of the presentation.
7. Practice the presentation for the competitive event. Chapter members and the instructor can serve as judges during practice. Incorporate suggestions for refinement.

127

Event Prep

Presents information about Career and Technical Student Organization competitions that can help lead to career success.

Objectives

The objectives summarize learning goals for each chapter.

Reading Prep

Activities address literacy skills for college and career readiness.

Chapter 1
The Teaching Profession

Objectives

After studying this chapter, you will be able to

- **summarize** the qualities of effective teachers.
- **analyze** challenges related to teaching and how teachers meet them.
- **identify** the educational requirements for teachers at various levels.
- **summarize** other career opportunities for teachers outside schools, including administrative and support services and professional support services.
- **describe** employment opportunities and trends in teaching.
- **identify** the factors that impact school employment opportunities.
- **analyze** teacher salary and benefits.

Reading Prep

Arrange a study session to read the chapter aloud with a classmate. Take turns reading, alternating at each heading. As you read, take notes of any words you do not know. At the end of the chapter, discuss the list of words you do not know and ask for clarification.

Content Terms

extracurricular activities
curriculum
school-based curriculum
self-contained classrooms
abstract thinking
concrete thinking
collaborative learning
postsecondary education
technical schools
corporate trainers
curriculum developer
program director
developmental disabilities
parent educator
psychologist

Academic Terms

diversity
advocate
nonsectarian
paraprofessional
salary schedule

Terms

Content and *Academic* terms emphasized in the chapter help expand your teaching vocabulary.

At the Companion Website you can

- **Practice** terms with e-flash cards and interactive games
- **Assess** what you learn by completing self-assessment quizzes
- **Expand** knowledge with interactive activities

www.g-wlearning.com/teaching/

Study on the go
Use a mobile device to practice terms and review with self-assessment quizzes.

www.m.g-wlearning.com/0094/

4

Copyright Goodheart-Willcox Co., Inc.

Copyright Goodheart-Willcox Co., Inc.

5

Online Resources

Link to the text's Companion Website or Mobile Site to utilize activities that reinforce learning of chapter material.

Extends and Assesses Learning

Core Skills

Application activities link chapter content to various core skills such as reading, writing, speaking, listening, and research, along with technology applications and CTE College and Career Readiness Practice.

Vocabulary Activity

Includes activities to reinforce and enhance mastery of vocabulary.

Critical Thinking

Questions and activities develop and reinforce higher-order critical-thinking skills when learning and applying chapter concepts.

College and Career Portfolio

Introduces key portfolio development concepts and activities to apply them, helping students effectively showcase their best work examples.

Chapter 1 Review and Assess

Summary

- Effective teachers have individual personalities and talents, but share important qualities and personal characteristics.
- Teachers spend most of their time planning, presenting lessons, and evaluating learning, and may supervise extracurricular activities.
- Teaching is rewarding and fulfilling. Teachers observe students learn, grow, and change as they acquire the knowledge and skills essential to becoming valuable society members.
- Teaching is also challenging as caring teachers put in long hours of work under conditions that are not always ideal.
- Many societal problems affect students, requiring teachers to find creative, empathetic ways to meet their educational needs.
- The field of education holds many career options including traditional classroom teaching options from preschool through college levels, and in such areas as administration and administrative support and professional support services.
- Effective teachers are always in demand, although options vary by subject area and location.
- Teaching salaries vary but usually increase with experience and more education.

Review and Study

1. Contrast effective teaching qualities with effective personal characteristics of teachers.

2. How do state curriculums and school-based curriculums differ? What would supporters of each give as an advantage?
3. Name three rewards of teaching.
4. What are self-contained classrooms? At what level are these classrooms most common?
5. What is the difference between abstract thinking and concrete thinking?
6. What is collaborative learning?
7. List four types of teaching specialists.
8. Compare and contrast the duties of a corporate trainer with those of a cooperative extension educator.
9. Name four educational or societal trends that are likely to impact employment opportunities for teachers.
10. In addition to regular salaries, what types of benefits do most school districts provide for teachers?

Vocabulary Activity

11. Review the *content* and *academic* vocabulary terms at the beginning of the chapter. For each term, identify a word or group of words describing a quality, or an *attribute* of the term. Pair up with a classmate and discuss the similarities and differences in your list of attributes. Then discuss your list of attributes with the whole class to increase understanding.

Critical Thinking

12. **Make inferences.** Review the personal qualities of effective teachers on page 8 of the text. Choose at least four qualities, and use the text and other reliable

Copyright Goodheart-Willcox Co., Inc. 33

Unit 1   You—The Teacher of Tomorrow

resources to infer situations in which effective teachers use this quality. Discuss your inferences with the class.

13. **Analyze assets.** In teaching situations beyond the school environment, analyze why having a bachelor's degree and a teaching certification is an asset. Cite evidence from the text and other reliable resources to support your analysis.

14. **Evaluate factors.** Use the example in *Figure 1.12* and the Internet to research average teacher salaries in four states. Choose your own state, one that is similar in population, and two that are very different. Identify the years of the surveyed information and its source. Evaluate the factors that influence teachers' salaries. Then create a chart showing how average salaries compare. Post your chart to the class website. How does your evaluation compare to those of your classmates?

Core Skills

15. **Speaking, listening, and writing.** Ask an adult you know to describe the characteristics of his or her favorite teacher. What grade did the teacher teach? What impact did the teacher have on the person? Listen carefully and then write a summary of your conversation to share with the class.

16. **Technology application.** Go to the O*NET website and use the *Skills Profiler* self-assessment to help determine the skills and qualities you possess that apply to a teaching career. Analyze the results of the self-assessment. What skills and qualities do you possess that are assets in a teaching career? What improvements can you make if you have passion for a career in teaching? Write a summary of your findings.

17. **Reading and writing.** Access the United States Department of Labor *Bureau of Labor Statistics* website. Choose career profiles for two types of teachers. Demonstrate your writing skills by writing a one-page summary describing each type of teaching, typical working conditions, job outlook, and expected earnings and benefits.

18. **Research and speaking.** Think about challenges related to teaching that concern you most. Choose one. Research how teachers cope with this type of challenge. Give an oral report identifying the challenge you chose, summarizing your research findings, and explaining strategies you would use to try to meet the challenge.

19. **Research, speaking, and listening.** Use the text and reliable Internet resources to research teaching and training in nontraditional settings such as corporations; community outreach; non-profit clubs, organizations, and community groups; and government entities. Discuss teaching and training in these settings, citing reliable evidence about key aspects of these positions.

20. **Investigating, formulating, and writing.** Investigate education and training alternatives after high school for a career choice in education *administration and administrative support* program of study within your interest area. Use the Bureau of Labor Statistics, O*NET, or CareerOneStop websites to investigate education and degree plans for various occupations. Formulate and examine education and training degree plans for various occupations within education administration and administrative support. Write a summary of your findings.

34   Copyright Goodheart-Willcox Co., Inc.

Chapter 1   The Teaching Profession

21. **Investigating, formulating, and speaking.** Investigate education and training alternatives after high school for a career choice in *professional support services* program of study within your interest area. Use the Bureau of Labor Statistics, O*NET, or CareerOneStop websites to investigate education and degree plans for various occupations, and formulate and examine education and training degree plans for various occupations within education professional support services. Give an oral report of your findings for a professional support services career of your choice.

22. **Technology application.** Search an online job board or the newspaper classifieds for specific job postings found under the heading "education." How many of the listings include traditional elementary or secondary teaching positions? How many of the postings are advertising other related job openings? Create a table of your

findings to post to the school-approved class blog or website. Which education-related job posting surprised you and your classmates the most?

23. **CTE College and career readiness practice.** Calculate the potential savings from completing the first two years of a bachelor's degree program at a community college. Identify each school's name and location (city). Utilize college and university websites for information on schools in your state. Find the cost per semester hour or yearly tuition cost at each. Use 32 semester hours per year as your basis. Compare tuition costs for the following:

- four years at a state university
- four years at a private college or university
- two years at each, community college and a state university
- two years at each, community college and a private college or university

College and Career Portfolio

When you apply to a college or for a job or community service, you may need to tell others about how you are qualified for this position. A portfolio is a selection of related materials that you collect and organize. These materials show your qualifications, skills, and talents. These materials may be in the form of certificates of achievement, written essays on a number of design-related issues, and a transcript of your school grades and courses.

Two types of portfolios are commonly used: print portfolios and electronic portfolios (e-Portfolios).

A. Use the Internet to search reliable sources for print portfolio and e-Portfolio. Read articles about each type. Then briefly describe each type in your own words.

B. You will be creating a portfolio in this class. Write a paragraph describing which type of portfolio you prefer. What might be the benefit of creating both?

Copyright Goodheart-Willcox Co., Inc.   35

Features Capture Students' Attention

Case Studies

Scenarios with real-life insight focus on teaching issues and chapter concepts. *Let's Discuss* follow-up questions spark conversation and encourage students to engage with the content.

Perspectives on Teaching

Young teachers' reflections about their classroom experiences connect students to the world of teaching. *Analyze It* activities utilize critical-thinking skills and discussion.

Case Study

As a class, read the case study and discuss the questions that follow. After you finish studying the chapter, discuss the case study and questions again. How have your responses changed based on what you learned?

Annie is just beginning her junior year of high school, and is already feeling both the pressure and the excitement of things to come. People, especially relatives and her mom's friends, are starting to ask her what she would like to do after she graduates from high school.

Annie enjoys working with kids in an after-school community program, tutoring math and science—her strengths. She especially likes working in the tutoring program with at-risk kids as Annie herself may have been considered an at-risk kid. She is a minority, female, economically challenged, and the product of a single parent home. Despite the so-called odds, Annie has done well in school. She has good friends and when she puts in the effort, she does well academically. She knows that her favorite teachers, Ms. Swanson and Mr. Cho, along with her mom, have played big roles in her success. So much so, she is seriously considering becoming a teacher.

At the last extended family gathering, relatives questioned this interest. They thought that she should become a doctor—because of her interest in math and science—a field that doesn't interest her as much.

Let's Discuss

Discuss your reflections on how Annie might respond to the following:

- "I hear that teaching is really hard. Are you sure you want to do this?"
- "Will there be teaching jobs available by the time you finish college?"
- "What if you don't like teaching; will your degree be wasted?"

Why are you interested in teaching? Is it a love for children? Do you want others to love learning as you do? Perhaps a favorite teacher inspired you or had a significant impact on your life. Maybe you want to make a difference in the world.

6   Copyright Goodheart-Willcox Co., Inc.

Perspectives on Teaching

Li Shao is a Chinese-American kindergarten teacher. Today had been a heart-warming day in her kindergarten classroom. A new student joined the class who speaks very little English. The other students welcomed her with open arms, communicating in a way only kindergarteners can without words. As Li Shao pondered the day, her thoughts went back to her kindergarten experience.

Li Shao's Thoughts...

Today, I am a kindergarten teacher, but I can still remember being a kindergarten student. Because of my circumstances, starting school left a lasting impression.

My parents came to America from China as young adults. They spoke only Chinese in our home when I was young. They socialized with other Chinese people, so when I started kindergarten, I neither spoke nor understood English.

Of course, school was bewildering at first. I can remember standing back and watching the other children, trying to figure out what they were saying. Fortunately, children pick up new languages easily. My parents told me I began to learn English words and phrases rather quickly. Each day when I came home, I would play school with my younger brother and sister, teaching them what I had learned.

I was fortunate to have a wonderful teacher. She spent extra time helping me with the language, but she did much more than that. She made me feel special instead of different. She incorporated learning about China into many lessons. She even invited my mother to come and share some of our Chinese customs and foods with my kindergarten class. I never forgot that experience or my kindergarten teacher.

Today, many schools have special classes for students who do not speak English. My own experience taught me that a creative and caring teacher can make a real difference in students' lives. Each child needs acceptance and recognition. Acceptance and recognition do not just help them socially and emotionally. When children feel secure, they learn more, as well.

Analyze It!

After reading *Perspectives on Teaching*, analyze Li Shao's comment about caring teachers. "My own experience taught me that a creative and caring teacher can make a real difference in students' lives." Discuss points of evidence in the narrative that supports this statement. To extend this activity, interview a student who moved from another country and who did not speak English at first. How is this student's experience similar to or different from Li Shao's?

174   Copyright Goodheart-Willcox Co., Inc.

Professional Tips

Focus on concepts and issues related to teaching and workplace success. *Dig Deeper* activities encourage inquiry and analysis.

---

can help meet specific learning needs. With some games, the student competes against the clock, trying to complete a game within a given time period. Computer games often have more than one level, allowing students to progress to more difficult knowledge or skills.

When used appropriately, games can generate enthusiasm and increase learning. In choosing or constructing games, it is important to evaluate the type of learning involved, student appeal, initial cost or effort, and whether the time involved produces sufficient learning.

Cooperative Learning

Cooperative learning is a form of small-group learning in which students work together to achieve a common goal. The group is responsible for making sure all members participate, contribute, and learn. With effective use, cooperative learning is a highly effective learning technique.

Cooperative learning takes many different formats and is adaptable to most subject areas and age groups. The specific assignment requires careful planning. The teacher divides students into groups, usually of two to six students with diverse characteristics. The structure of the learning task encourages students to work together and to be responsible for each other's learning. At the same time, the teacher builds in **individual accountability**, or a way to assess each student's participation and learning. Group members share ideas and propose solutions. The group must resolve differences and work together to complete the assignment. The teacher acts as a facilitator, monitoring the groups to keep them on track, but not offering solutions.

Cooperative learning offers many advantages. The ability to work together in a group is an important life skill. Opportunities to work together build students' willingness to contribute, listen to and respect others' opinions, help one another, and negotiate differences. Self-esteem and responsibility improve, as well. Most students enjoy learning more when working with their peers.

Professional Tip

Collaboration

In the classroom, effective teachers execute a plan keeping in mind the specific subject matter learning and their students' longer-term success in their specific subject or learning area. In doing so, most teachers rely a lot on others for ideas. Professional teachers are collaborative. They cooperate with other teachers who work with similar students and with teachers in grades before and after. It may not always be evident on the surface, but they are team players. They work as a team with other teachers, aides, specialists, and administrators.

Dig Deeper

Take notice of the number of professionals that contribute to your own education. Inquire about how they find time to collaborate with one another. How do they facilitate communication? Discuss your findings with the class.

306   Copyright Goodheart-Willcox Co., Inc.

To the Student

This book has a simple title—*Teaching*. Teaching implies action. This is a book about how and why you should take action to become a teacher—not just any teacher, but a well-prepared, committed, engaging, skilled, effective, and creative teacher.

Additionally, this book is about educators who came before you, their motivations, and their accomplishments. These historical accounts will help you understand the business of education—how schools are funded, who is in charge, and how schools impact society.

Without students, schools would not exist. Students are energetic, engaging, curious, serious, challenging, and fun! As you consider a career in teaching, this textbook teaches you about students and how they change physically, intellectually, emotionally, and socially as they grow and mature. Understanding these dramatic changes in growth and development are key factors in learning how to teach.

While exploring the world of education today, you will learn what makes a teacher effective. For example, how can classrooms promote active learning? How do teachers plan for effective instruction? How can technology enhance and promote learning? What is assessment and how do teachers use it to evaluate and encourage learner achievement?

Will you learn how to teach? *Yes*. In this book, you will learn foundational skills in how to design an instructional plan, choose teaching strategies, and assess whether learning has taken place. Asking questions of experienced teachers will motivate and inspire you to learn more about how to become an effective teacher. As you observe teachers who know how to manage classrooms and create an effective learning environment for their students, you will learn more about what it takes to become a teaching professional.

Will you be a teacher when you finish this book? *No.* Becoming a teacher requires much more preparation. Becoming an excellent teacher requires experience and the lifelong desire to keep learning. This book will, however, inspire you and provide a road map for your exploration of the teaching profession. Remember, teaching requires action. Begin to take action toward your teaching career today!

Unit 1
You—The Teacher of Tomorrow

Event Prep
CTSOs and Competitive Events

Career and Technical Student Organizations (CTSOs) are valuable assets to any educational program. These organizations support student learning and the application of skills learned in real-world situations. There are a number of organizations from which to choose, depending on the program goals. Three that fit well with teaching and education are *Future Educators of America (FEA), SkillsUSA,* and *Family, Career and Community Leaders of America (FCCLA).* Participating in competitive events is a key aspect of membership in any CTSO. Participating in such competitions helps you expand your leadership skills and develop skills necessary for life and career. Scholarship opportunities are also available.

To learn more about competitive events, complete the following activities.

1. Talk with the local adviser or contact the organization well before the next competition. Review and decide which competitive events are best for you and your team.

2. Research the organization website to find *specific* information for the competitive events. Visit the site often because information can change frequently.

3. Select one or two events of interest and print the event information. Competitive events may be written, oral, or a combination of both. Discuss the events with your instructor or adviser.

4. Read all event guidelines closely, including the rubrics against which you will be judged. To avoid disqualification from an event, strictly follow the rules and regulations.

5. Because communication plays an important role in competitive events, carefully research which communication skills are required in the event you select. Research and practice are important factors to competition success.

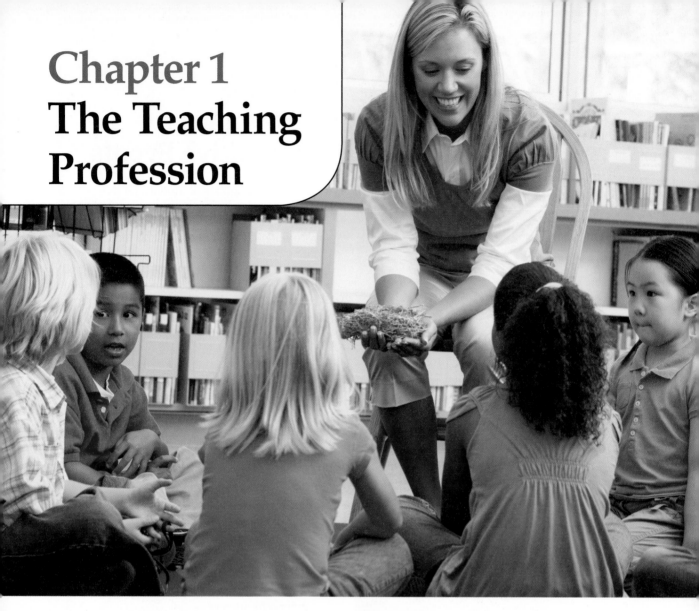

Chapter 1
The Teaching Profession

Content Terms

extracurricular activities
curriculum
school-based curriculum
self-contained classrooms
abstract thinking
concrete thinking
collaborative learning
postsecondary education
technical schools
corporate trainers
curriculum developer
program director
developmental disabilities
parent educator
psychologist

Academic Terms

diversity
advocate
nonsectarian
paraprofessional
salary schedule

Objectives

After studying this chapter, you will be able to

- **summarize** the qualities of effective teachers.
- **analyze** challenges related to teaching and how teachers meet them.
- **identify** the educational requirements for teachers at various levels.
- **summarize** other career opportunities for teachers outside schools, including administrative and support services and professional support services.
- **describe** employment opportunities and trends in teaching.
- **identify** the factors that impact school employment opportunities.
- **analyze** teacher salary and benefits.

Reading Prep

Arrange a study session to read the chapter aloud with a classmate. Take turns reading, alternating at each heading. As you read, take notes of any words you do not know. At the end of the chapter, discuss the list of words you do not know and ask for clarification.

At the Companion Website you can

- **Practice** terms with e-flash cards and interactive games
- **Assess** what you learn by completing self-assessment quizzes
- **Expand** knowledge with interactive activities

www.g-wlearning.com/teaching/

Study on the go

Use a mobile device to practice terms and review with self-assessment quizzes.

www.m.g-wlearning.com/0094/

Case Study

As a class, read the case study and discuss the questions that follow. After you finish studying the chapter, discuss the case study and questions again. How have your responses changed based on what you learned?

Annie is just beginning her junior year of high school, and is already feeling both the pressure and the excitement of things to come. People, especially relatives and her mom's friends, are starting to ask her what she would like to do after she graduates from high school.

Annie enjoys working with kids in an after-school community program, tutoring math and science—her strengths. She especially likes working in the tutoring program with at-risk kids as Annie herself may have been considered an at-risk kid. She is a minority, female, economically challenged, and the product of a single parent home. Despite the so-called odds, Annie has done well in school. She has good friends and when she puts in the effort, she does well academically. She knows that her favorite teachers, Ms. Swanson and Mr. Cho, along with her mom, have played big roles in her success. So much so, she is seriously considering becoming a teacher.

At the last extended family gathering, relatives questioned this interest. They thought that she should become a doctor because of her interest in math and science— a field that doesn't interest her as much.

Let's Discuss

Discuss your reflections on how Annie might respond to the following:

- "I hear that teaching is really hard. Are you sure you want to do this?"
- "Will there be teaching jobs available by the time you finish college?"
- "What if you don't like teaching; will your degree be wasted?"

Why are you interested in teaching? Is it a love for children? Do you want others to love learning as you do? Perhaps a favorite teacher inspired you or had a significant impact on your life. Maybe you want to make a difference in the world.

Teaching is an exciting profession. It requires patience and persistence. It requires an appreciation for **diversity**—the distinct and unique differences among people—and individuality. What makes teaching truly different from many other professions is the potential long-term effect that you can have on the lives of others (Figure 1.1).

Although being a student may have drawn you to teaching, sitting on the "other side of the desk" may be a far different reality than your expectations. You may wonder if you are up to the challenge. Can you manage a classroom full of students? Should you pursue a job with higher pay? Does the responsibility of the position concern you?

This class can help you to assess if teaching is the right career for you. You will

- learn about some aspects of teaching that you may not have considered
- have opportunities to try some of the tasks associated with teaching
- observe teachers and students

You may also take part in activities with children of various ages. Increasing knowledge, experience, and insight into your own goals and aptitudes better enables you to make an effective career decision.

Figure 1.1   A teacher can impact the lives of students for many years to come.

What Are the Qualities of an Effective Teacher?

Think about the teachers you have had throughout your education. Which were your favorites? Which ones taught you the most? What was it about these teachers that made them successful? Most likely, your favorite teachers were not all alike. Effective teachers come in many forms. They may be outgoing and dramatic, demanding and firm, soft-spoken and reflective, or reserved and quiet. Their approaches to life can differ greatly, too.

Although teachers may vary, effective teaching requires a common set of qualities. Effective teachers are able to motivate, inspire, and influence their students. They communicate well with both students and adults. They are able to convey their own enthusiasm for learning. In addition, effective teachers need to be well organized to deal with the planning, record keeping, and many administrative tasks that go along with the job. While there are many other key skills, these are some of the most basic.

Effective teachers have many personal qualities in common, as well. A brief list might include

- caring
- commitment
- courtesy
- honesty
- kindness
- patience
- responsibility
- tolerance

This list of personal characteristics is important in all teaching situations. What other qualities can you add to the list? Successful teachers respect their students, love learning, have high expectations for themselves and their students, and are adaptable.

What Happens in a Teacher's Typical Day?

Most of a teacher's day is spent designing and presenting classroom learning experiences. This is where creativity and knowledge of students' learning styles and abilities is necessary. As time permits and depending on class size, teachers may also work with students individually.

Teachers are responsible for assessing the learning of students. This involves grading assignments and evaluating student participation in class activities. These evaluations are summarized on report cards and at meetings with parents or guardians.

In addition to classroom activities, teachers coordinate with other specialists, which may include counselors, reading specialists, and speech therapists. They may supervise **extracurricular activities** (those before or after school) and other duties, as well.

Determining What to Teach

Do teachers teach whatever they want? No. **Curriculum** must be decided before teaching begins. Curriculum is the term that describes what schools teach. (*Curricula* is the plural form.) It includes all the courses taught and what is taught in each course, as well as how the courses are sequenced (Figure 1.2).

Who determines the curriculum? That depends. There are usually a number of influences. Each subject area has national curriculum standards developed by related national education organizations and state departments of education. While use of these is voluntary, they have significant influence. In addition, some states set curriculum standards for courses taught in the state. This helps make certain that students are ready to advance to the next level of courses, even if they move to another school. **School-based curriculum** is another alternative. Teachers are involved in making decisions about what is taught in their classrooms and schools. According to *advocates*— people who support or promote the interests of others—of school-based curriculum, local teachers can best design curriculum to meet the needs of students.

Figure 1.2   The established curriculum helps teachers determine what to teach.

Professional Tip

Maintaining Confidentiality

Did you ever receive an exam grade that you were less than proud of? Most people have. Grades are personal. If there is a breakdown in confidentiality, it often leads to embarrassment and disengagement in the learning process. Likewise, events that happen on school grounds must remain confidential unless safety issues surround the events.

Being a part of a school community, whether as a teacher or as a student helper, requires cautious and thoughtful behavior. This also includes actions in regard to record keeping and communication. It takes vigilance to maintain confidentiality. This is especially true about school events, and student behavior, achievements, and personal data. Teachers and administrative staff must use discernment, trust, and clear communication in regard to confidential issues.

Maintaining confidentiality protects students from harm. Take note of how your school maintains confidentiality. This includes informal communication between teachers and students, school behavioral issues, and grade reporting.

Dig Deeper

Use reliable online resources to further investigate confidentiality in schools. What factors influence confidentiality policies for schools? What information can be shared and what information cannot? How can you practice confidentiality in your daily life as you contemplate a teaching career?

The Rewards of Teaching

Many experienced teachers will tell you that teaching is inspiring, challenging, and as unique as each student. Every student presents an opportunity to the teacher. Since each has his or her own learning style and personality, the teacher's challenge is to determine how to best help each individual maximize learning.

Teaching is a career that does make a difference in the world, even though you might not feel it on a daily basis. Because learning takes time, seeing the effects of your efforts requires patience. Still, there are everyday victories. You help a young child deal successfully with conflict on the playground. A struggling student passes a tough test. A reluctant reader chooses three books from the library.

As a teacher, you observe your students change in many ways. You will see them grow physically as well as make strides emotionally and socially. Day-by-day achievements in learning will be among the meaningful changes you observe.

Most teachers agree that seeing students develop new knowledge, skills, and confidence can be the most rewarding part of teaching. There is great satisfaction in knowing that you played a significant role in that process.

The Challenges of Teaching

Is teaching always rewarding? Of course it is not! Every job has its challenges, and teaching is no exception.

Teachers work hard. They typically spend long hours outside of school preparing lessons and grading students' work. During vacations, they are often thinking ahead and planning. Updating their knowledge and skills takes additional time. Most teachers attend workshops or conferences. Many take classes toward a more advanced degree.

The working conditions in schools are not always ideal for teachers. Classes can be large and workloads heavy. Many school buildings are old. School districts vary in their ability to provide teachers with up-to-date textbooks, educational technology, and other learning aids.

Schools also reflect the problems of society. Poverty, alcohol and other drug abuse, and similar problems affect students. These factors can make teaching emotionally draining. Teachers must sometimes cope with disrespect, unruly behavior, and even violence in schools.

These and other problems are receiving careful analysis. The goal is to make schools safe and positive for both teachers and students. Effective teachers find strategies to help them cope with the problems they encounter.

Where Do Teachers Work?

You may think it is obvious that teachers work in schools. They may, however, work for a variety of employers, and some are self-employed. Both full-time and part-time teaching work is available. The following sections explore the nature of work in schools and some of the other settings in which teaching takes place.

Teaching in Schools

Since attending school is a requirement for children, schools are where most teachers work. Among schools, however, there is great variation. Schools range from preschools to colleges and universities. To add to the mix, some schools are small and some are large. Schools can be in rural areas, suburbs, or major urban areas. Most schools are *public* and funded by tax dollars, but there are also many *private* schools. Some of these are sponsored by religious organizations, while others are **nonsectarian** (not based on or affiliated with any religion). The purpose of all schools, however, is the same—to promote learning.

Schools are generally divided by grade levels. Figure 1.3 shows the most common designations, although variations are fairly common.

Figure 1.3	Common School Designations	
Level	Grades	Typical Student Ages
Preschool		2–4
Kindergarten		4–5
Elementary	Kindergarten—grades 4, 5, or 6	5–11
Middle school	Grades 5 or 6–8	10–13
Junior high	Grades 7–8 or 9	12–14
High school	Grades 9 or 10–12	14–18

Preschool and Prekindergarten Programs

Increasing numbers of children are enrolled in educational programs prior to kindergarten. Child care programs focus primarily on providing a safe, caring environment. Preschool and prekindergarten programs have a stronger educational focus than in the past. Preschool programs are generally for children ages two to four. Prekindergarten programs, where available, are for children—usually four-year-olds—who will be in kindergarten the following year. (Prekindergarten programs are often referred to as *pre-K*.)

Play is the main occupation of young children. It is also how they learn. Children learn language skills as they listen to and tell stories. Imagination and creativity develop as they pretend to be shoppers, pilots, and dogs. They build sandcastles and block towers (Figure 1.4). Children express themselves in paintings and songs.

Figure 1.4   If you enjoy working with young children, you might want to consider teaching in a preschool or prekindergarten program.

Preschool and pre-K teachers plan activities that build on children's curiosity and interest in play. Such activities require a thorough understanding of child development and experience with children. The activities help children develop the many skills they need for kindergarten and beyond. Children in preschool and pre-K programs also spend time in unstructured play, choosing their own play activities.

Requirements for leading preschool and pre-K programs vary. Many demand that teachers have at least an associate's degree in early childhood development and education, which generally requires two years of study and practice. Some, especially those linked to elementary schools, require a bachelor's degree from a four-year college or university.

Some states require certification by a nationally recognized authority, such as the Child Development Associate (CDA) designation from the National Association for the Education of Young Children. See Figure 1.5 for a description of the various academic degrees. Paraprofessional positions are also available for those with less education or experience. A *paraprofessional* works under the supervision of a more highly educated professional.

Figure 1.5	**Understanding Academic Degrees**		
The specific degree granted (such as BA vs. BS) depends on the student's area of study, program requirements, and the tradition of the institution granting the degree. Many other degrees exist. Note that an ABS (Associate of Baccalaureate Studies) degree is granted by community colleges to students who complete a program of study equivalent to the first two years of a four-year bachelor's degree. These students normally transfer to a four-year college or university as a junior.			
Degree	**Type of Institution**	**Years to Achieve**	**Typical Degrees**
Associate's	Community college	2	AA—Associate of Arts AS—Associate of Science ABS—Associate of Baccalaureate Studies
Bachelor's	University or four-year college	4	BA—Bachelor of Arts BS—Bachelor of Science
Master's	University or four-year college	1–2	MA—Master of Arts MS—Master of Science MEd—Master of Education
Doctorate	Some universities	3 or more	PhD—Doctor of Philosophy EdD—Doctor of Education

Elementary Schools

What do you remember about elementary school? Who were your best friends? Which grade did you enjoy most? Do any favorite teachers, field trips, or class projects come to mind? Did you lose your lunch money, miss the bus, encounter a bully, or struggle to learn long division? Elementary school is a time of great exploration, language development, social development, and the introduction of scientific and mathematical concepts.

Think about the tremendous developmental changes that occur between kindergarten and fifth grade. The physical, intellectual, social, and emotional differences between a child in kindergarten and an 11-year-old are enormous. In this time span, small children grow into preteens. They learn to read, compute, and tackle more complex information. They make friends and figure out how to handle disagreements. Children learn to deal with feelings and develop a sense of who they are. In these early years, students often have classroom experiences that affect their success or failure in school, work, and even their personal lives.

Most elementary school teachers teach in **self-contained classrooms**. This means the same teacher and group of students remain in one classroom for most of the day, with one teacher teaching most or all subjects. Elementary school classrooms are typically active and visually stimulating. Teachers use a variety of teaching ways to engage students in learning. Lessons may incorporate games, music, art activities, computer programs and other digital technologies, and visuals, as well as textbooks and teacher presentations. Most traditional elementary schools employ teachers who specialize in one grade level, although some school systems are structured so teachers instruct across several grades.

Middle Schools and Junior Highs

Most school districts provide older preteens and young teens with their own school campus or area. Schools recognize that students in these age groups have different needs. Middle schools usually include grades 6, 7, and 8, although some include grade 5 as well. Schools with a junior high system include students in grades 7 and 8 *or* 7, 8, and 9. Even if these students remain physically within the same building with children in earlier grades, their teaching and learning experiences change.

There are good reasons for these grade levels. Brain development in children in these grades encourages thinking at a higher level. Students think faster and more creatively. They can identify multiple solutions to problems and develop ability to think abstractly. **Abstract thinking** is in-depth thinking about ideas and concepts, such as justice or love. Students who think abstractly are interested in *why* things are as they are.

Abstract thinkers can also connect how they feel to what they think. In contrast, the **concrete thinking** of younger students focuses on facts and actual experiences.

Changes in student thinking and learning make the role of middle school and junior high teachers different from that of an elementary school teacher. Because older students study topics more in depth, most teachers specialize in teaching one or two areas, such as social studies or science or math. The transition to having several teachers during the day helps students move toward the system they will have in high school. Learning in the middle school or junior high often has less structure, incorporating more projects and activities. Students can be lively and creative. Because learning social skills is so important at this stage, **collaborative learning** offers a way for students to work in groups and solve problems together (Figure 1.6).

Developing responsibility for their own learning and conduct is an expectation for middle school and junior high students. Information and tasks are more complex. Students are encouraged to learn to structure their time and make plans, then organize and carry out the plans. Teachers help them systematically build these and other skills and habits needed for high school.

High Schools

High school brings new subject areas and greater opportunities for in-depth study and learning. General math gives way to algebra, geometry, and trigonometry. Students like you have five to seven different classes (and teachers) each day.

In high school, students take primary responsibility for their learning. It is not unusual to have homework in every subject every night, as well as long-term projects. If they do not understand concepts, teachers expect students to ask for help. More assignments require complex thinking skills, and students routinely practice solving problems by gathering and evaluating information.

High school teachers typically specialize in one subject or a group of related subjects. In small communities, however, teachers may

Figure 1.6 Learning collaboration skills is important for students in middle school and junior high.

have a more diverse teaching schedule. Teaching high school courses requires more content depth than teaching in earlier grades. Teachers must have at least a bachelor's degree from a four-year college or university and be certified to teach in their state. Training for high school teachers focuses more on their subject areas of choice.

Although they have curriculum guidelines, teachers usually have some flexibility in what and how they teach. Teachers determine how much to emphasize various topics and how to best present them. Which topics will they assign for papers? Is the most effective way for students to learn a concept through a teacher presentation, group discussion, lab experience, or combination of these and other techniques? These are among the many aspects managed by individual teachers (Figure 1.7).

High school teachers usually have other responsibilities in addition to teaching. They may monitor study halls, serve as advisors for school organizations, tutor, coach sports, and chaperone events. (Some responsibilities are part of their regular teaching duties, but they may receive extra pay for others.) Many teachers willingly help students outside class with such issues as choosing colleges or careers or dealing with personal concerns.

Figure 1.7   This high school anatomy teacher guides students working on a class project.

Postsecondary Education Programs

There are many opportunities for teachers in **postsecondary education**, which takes place after high school. Technical schools, community colleges, and four-year colleges and universities are the most common options.

Technical Schools

Technical schools offer programs that teach the specific skill requirements to begin working in a trade. Most courses directly relate to those skills. You may recognize technical schools by other names, such as trade schools, vocational colleges, business schools, technical institutes, or fashion institutes. There are technical colleges for a wide range of occupations, including culinary arts, Web design, nursing, graphic design, fashion design, mechanical, and medical skills. Programs of study are focused and generally shorter than college or university programs.

Although a college degree is often preferable, having relevant skills and experience is most important for teachers employed at technical schools. For example, to teach culinary arts, a teacher must have extensive knowledge and experience in the culinary field, often as a head chef.

Community Colleges

The purpose of community colleges is to focus on meeting the education and training needs of the communities they serve. Most offer two-year associate's degrees. Many also offer programs that lead to certification in such areas as respiratory therapy or welding. Some students attend a community college for their first two years of a four-year degree program, and then transfer to a four-year school. This requires close coordination between community colleges and the colleges and universities in their states to make sure courses will transfer. Students usually save considerably on educational costs under this plan.

Entrance to a community college is generally open to anyone with a high school diploma although requirements may vary. The student population tends to be quite diverse, with full-time and part-time students, recent high school graduates, adults, and even high school students taking classes for college credit (Figure 1.8).

Figure 1.8   Community college instructors work with a diverse population of students.

Adults may be going back for an education they never completed, improving skills for their present job, or studying for a new occupation.

Currently, there are over 1,100 community colleges in the United States. They serve almost half of the high school graduates each year. Because of the breadth of programs offered, many teaching positions exist. Most community colleges require a teacher to hold at least a master's degree (a two-year degree beyond the traditional four-year college degree). Because the student population varies greatly, teachers must prepare for working with students at various skill levels.

Four-Year Colleges and Universities

Colleges and universities are the traditional places for higher education. Although the terms are often used interchangeably (as in a "college education"), universities offer graduate degree programs. Colleges often offer degrees in one area. A university offers degrees in a variety of areas because it is actually comprised of a collection of colleges.

Students in colleges and universities complete general education courses plus classes specific to their area of specialization. *General education requirements* (or *core courses*) provide a broad background of knowledge. If you plan to become a high school social studies teacher, you would complete a variety of general education courses, social studies courses (such as American and world history, geography, political science, and government), courses in education, and a student teaching experience. This would lead to a bachelor's degree.

College or university teachers specialize in one particular area and teach a limited number of different courses. A doctorate degree (usually called a PhD or EdD) is a requirement for most professors, although many schools also have teachers with master's degrees. At this level, teachers must conduct research in their fields and do scholarly writing in addition to their teaching duties.

Other Opportunities in Education

Trained and skilled teachers do not always teach in the school system. Because education is vital to so many aspects of society, teachers find their skills in demand in other places as well. Opportunities are quite varied. A few examples are described here.

Business and Industry

Many businesses and industries provide education to their employees. **Corporate trainer** is another name for the teachers who provide this education. The types of education they offer depend on company needs (Figure 1.9). Some programs focus on technical work skills, but most seek to improve key personal skills such as motivation, effective communication, leadership, or team building. International companies may hire people to teach employees moving to other countries the languages they will need to know.

Large companies often employ corporate trainers as full-time employees. Others are self-employed or work for a company that specializes in providing corporate trainers on an as-needed basis.

Businesses may employ teachers for many other purposes. For example, a cruise line may hire a teacher to teach passengers on a cruise about the

Figure 1.9   A corporate trainer may be hired by a company to introduce a new computer program to its employees.

history of their destinations. Teachers provide classes or one-on-one instruction to children undergoing long-term treatment in hospitals. Whatever the challenge, basic teaching skills are simply adapted to fit the situation.

Adult and Community Education

In a society where jobs require up-to-date knowledge and skills, the need for adult education is ongoing. Literacy programs, for example, may focus on teaching adults to gain and improve reading skills or learn the English language. For those who did not get a high school diploma, *General Equivalency Diploma (GED)* programs can provide the equivalent of a high school diploma. Other programs provide general or specific job skills, and technical skills in areas such as computer training, or personal enrichment. Most professional degrees also require some level of continuing education in order to maintain or renew licenses.

Adult education teachers plan, deliver, and evaluate educational programs. Their roles are similar to elementary, middle school, high school, and college educators, but their audience is different. As other teachers do, they may use lecture, hands-on learning, computers and other forms of digital media, group work or team work, and projects to teach course content. They must stay informed and current in their teaching. As in all teaching, personal interaction between students and the teacher is important at all levels.

Adult education programs are often government funded. Some receive support through private funds and/or companies that must make a profit. Community colleges and universities may also provide adult education programs, although these do not normally lead to a degree. Because the field is so varied, career opportunities range from teaching one course to full-time positions. Adult education teachers also work in job-training centers, community centers, or any environment where training and education programs are a need.

Some teachers work for community organizations such as the Boys and Girls Clubs of America, summer camps, or park districts (Figure 1.10). Many organizations sponsor educational programs on topics of interest. These may range from gardening and cooking to religious studies. For example, a community group might sponsor defensive driving classes. Many music teachers find employment with religious organizations, providing music for services or organizing and leading musical groups such as choirs.

Figure 1.10 Some teachers work with students outside the classroom at summer camps and with youth organizations.

Cooperative Extension Service

Cooperative extension educators, or agents, are community teachers. They provide useful, practical and research-based information to individuals and communities. They also provide technical assistance to agricultural producers and small business owners.

It is common for cooperative extension educators to coordinate 4-H youth activities and to recruit, train, and develop community leaders. They are professional employees of state universities and receive support from the federal government. Their job duties are varied and include offering formal and informal educational outreach opportunities to community members.

Administrative and Support Services

Schools and educational organizations need staff to help the organization run smoothly. District administrators and school principals lead school communities with visionary leadership. They also manage or oversee daily activities. They are in charge of budgets, staffing, and legal compliance. They are often seen as the "face" of the school community and are placed in very public roles. But administrators cannot do it all themselves. Like teachers, district and school administrators need staff support to provide an optimum learning environment for students.

Supporting staff in educational organizations is called *administration and administrative support*. People working in these careers mainly work behind the scenes assisting administrators and teachers with the ultimate goal of helping students learn. Essentially, they help lead, manage, and support the instructors (Figure 1.11). These professionals must also be comfortable working with many people, as a learner, leader, and team member.

Figure 1.11 Support staff, such as this technology assistant, work with teachers to enhance student learning.

Sample Occupations

Schools and universities could not efficiently function if only instructors were present. Administrative support help manage daily job duties involved in an educational organization. Administrative support comes in many forms. Examples of administration duties include deciding what will be taught, training and supporting teachers or instructors, and measuring the effectiveness of teaching and student learning. These professionals also lead and manage other educational activities within the organization. Professionals in administration and administrative support roles have at least an associate's degree. Many positions require a higher degree, such as a bachelor's or master's degree. Examples of job titles in administration and administrative support include curriculum developer and program director.

Curriculum developer. Before a school year or course begins, school districts decide, develop, and plan the information that teachers will teach to students. Curriculum describes the material and content taught in a school or program. Curriculum includes all the courses taught in a program of study and the material taught in each course.

A **curriculum developer**, or an *instructional coordinator*, helps develop course content in a program of study or specific course. Curriculum developers stay informed of educational standards set at national, state, and district levels. They ensure the curriculum meets educational standards and will prepare students for the next course or level of education. Curriculum developers may recommend the purchase of instructional materials, such as textbooks, teaching aids, learning equipment, and technology.

Curriculum developers are also responsible for training instructors. This may include training them on how to use materials effectively in the classroom. Curriculum developers may also attend and lead sessions relating to new research, teaching strategies, or other new developments within the field. They may also observe a classroom and provide feedback to the instructor for improving teaching methods.

Program director. A **program director** oversees the mission, goals, and programs of an organization, such as a child care center. Program directors develop programs, organize how they are run, and evaluate the program's progress and success. They hire caregivers, instructors, and supporting staff, and provide orientation and training (Figure 1.12).

Figure 1.12 As part of the management role in a child care center, the program director is responsible for hiring and supporting staff.

This is a supervisory position that requires a combination of educational expertise and experience. Most program directors also work with state and federal agencies to secure grants, maintain health and safety regulations, and stay up-to-date with current developments relating to their program.

Teaching specialists. In addition to regular classroom teachers, most schools also rely on teachers who play special roles. In elementary school, you may have had separate teachers for music or physical education. Perhaps in middle school, specialty teachers taught Spanish or Chinese once a week. *Reading specialists* typically work with students who have difficulty with that key skill. Their training involves learning to identify specific reading problems and help students progress.

Special education teachers also fall into the category of teaching specialists. They work with students who have special learning needs. They use various techniques to help students learn. After carefully considering the needs, strengths, and weaknesses of each individual student, teachers develop a plan of action for student success. A team of teachers and specialists (including a social worker and psychologist) along with parents or guardians often work together to develop these plans.

Many special education teachers work with students who have mild to moderate learning disabilities. These students typically spend most of their day in regular classrooms. Some special education teachers assist students with specific disabilities in speech, hearing, sight, or language. Often they work with regular classroom teachers to adapt their teaching for these students. Others help children with emotional problems that impact learning.

A few special education teachers work with students who have **developmental disabilities**—a group of conditions (physical, intellectual, or behavioral) that can severely impact learning. Developmental disabilities appear before age 18 and usually last a lifetime. With these students, teachers work on both basic literacy skills and life skills (Figure 1.13). Life skills can include social skills, self-care skills, and job-related skills for high school students.

Career and technical education (CTE) teachers. These teachers instruct and train students to work in a wide variety of careers.

Figure 1.13 For children who have developmental disabilities, special education teachers focus on basic literacy skills and skills for daily living.

They assist students in exploring career interests and connecting what they learn in the classroom with what they encounter in the real world. CTE teachers help students know what to expect when dealing with employers.

Career and technical education covers many career pathways. For example, in trade and industrial fields, it includes training as automotive technicians, carpenters, and electricians. Career preparation in family and consumer sciences may include early childhood education, food production, hospitality management, apparel, and interior design. Career and technical education teachers also prepare students to work in the health occupations field, in public safety and security, and other technical areas. Career and technical education teachers teach in middle schools, high schools, and two-year colleges.

Coaching, sports, and fitness programs. Many schools and universities also have coaches for specific sports and physical activities. Coaches are responsible for training students in the rules, practices, and strategies of a particular sport. They provide athletic training and nutritional advice. They ensure safety practices are being followed and maintained. Coaches also support athletes and help students develop their strategies and skills. Specialized coaches manage a particular team, such as basketball, football, or volleyball.

Most communities have opportunities for people of all ages to learn and play sports as well as to assist others in improving their physical fitness (Figure 1.14). Sports and fitness programs depend on

Figure 1.14   A fitness instructor motivates people to reach fitness goals.

people such as coaches, athletic trainers, athletic directors, aerobics instructors, camp directors, and recreation specialists. Sports and fitness teachers must have knowledge and experience, although a college degree is not always required. These educators must be able to motivate others to learn and to accomplish goals. They may work as coaches or trainers in a private gym. Others may be self-employed as coaches and trainers.

Knowledge and Skills

To work in any career within the administration and administrative support pathway, professionals use a variety of knowledge and skills. They have foundational skills in addition to the skills needed to work in the education and training industry. They are also comfortable working closely with others, managing staff, and recognizing legal and political factors relating to job duties and the organization.

Many careers in the administration and administrative support pathway involve management and leadership. Administration professionals supervise and/or train instructors or caregivers within an educational institution. This requires knowledge of the most up-to-date research, teaching strategies, educational standards, technology, and health and safety practices. They must not only be aware of recent trends and development, but also know how to incorporate new knowledge into their organization. They enjoy lifelong learning. Administration professionals enhance the learning environment and motivate learners. They also support and motivate the instructors.

Administration and administrative support professionals are also aware of legal, cultural, and political factors that are relevant to the organization. Many laws and regulations are involved in educational settings. Administration professionals are informed of these laws. They are also culturally knowledgeable and comfortable with diversity. They address political concerns and may create new rules and regulations to better ensure the organization continues to run smoothly.

Professional Support Services

There are many professional supporting roles within the field of education. These jobs are often creative and flexible, providing invaluable support to education and training systems. For example, audio-visual and multimedia collections specialists help secure and maintain electronic resources. Adaptive physical education specialists work with students who are challenged with mobility issues. Similar to administration and administrative support, many of these jobs are highly specialized.

Sample Occupations

Job titles in the professional support services pathway include parent educator, school and career counselor, speech-language specialist, and children's librarian. All of these occupations require a degree. To become a parent educator, a bachelor's degree is required. Other occupations within this pathway typically require more than a bachelor's degree.

Parent educators. Some school districts, hospitals, places of worship, and other community organizations provide parent educators. **Parent educators** come from a variety of backgrounds and offer training and encouragement to parents. They may facilitate discussion among parents of newborns (Figure 1.15). They may organize playgroups that focus on good parenting skills. They may offer classes on how to communicate with teens. Parenting coaches can share knowledge and skills while offering encouragement and a community for parents to interact and ask questions.

Figure 1.15 Parent educators work in a variety of settings, offering training and encouragement to parents.

School and career counselors. Counselors are an important type of support professional. *School guidance counselors* help students learn social skills, solve issues, cope with personal crises, and make education and career decisions. They can help students determine their interests, aptitudes, and abilities, and decide which courses they need to take to follow a specific career path.

Career counselors help people make career decisions by leading them through the process of choosing and preparing for a career. They often offer assistance in completing résumés and preparing for interviews. Career counselors may work in colleges or government career centers. Entrepreneurial opportunities are available for those who wish to work in private practice.

School counselors must be certified in all states. In addition, a master's degree is often a requirement for certification or licensing as a counselor.

School psychologists. A **psychologist** studies human behavior and mental processes and develops theories to explain why people behave the way they do. Psychologists conduct studies and research to help understand and predict human emotions, feelings, and behavior. They look for patterns of behavior or cause-and-effect relationships between events.

School psychologists work with students' emotional, social, and learning needs. They commonly have certain areas in which they specialize. Psychologists may work as part of a health care team to improve a student's overall health and well-being within the school setting.

Becoming a psychologist requires considerable time and commitment as psychologists must earn a doctoral degree. It usually takes between four and eight years of post-high school full time study to complete a Ph.D. Some graduate programs require completion of a master's degree (2–3 years) before acceptance into a doctoral program. Others combine the master's and doctoral degrees. Graduate programs include required coursework, comprehensive examinations, and a dissertation or project at the doctoral level.

Speech-language specialists. Communication is critical to learning. Some children struggle with speech. They may stutter, struggle to form sounds and words, or have trouble hearing or understanding language. When a child struggles with speech or language disorders, it affects their learning. *Speech-language specialists* are trained to diagnose and provide treatment that helps each individual student. They work closely with the student's doctor, family, and teachers to address the speech or language challenge at all levels.

Children's librarians. Libraries and other learning resources are an important part of every school. Librarians specialize in books and other online materials that can enhance learning. They order books, maps, computer software, and other visual materials that boost learning. *Children's librarians* specialize in resources for young children (Figure 1.16). Other librarians specialize in meeting the needs of older children, teens, or adults. In addition to remaining current in what is available and desirable, they offer reading sessions or story times, teach reading or research skills, and help students navigate computer software or Internet resources.

Knowledge and Skills

Occupations in the professional support services pathway require highly specialized knowledge and skills plus these personal qualities—creativity, patience, and caring. These professionals must be able to work well with students, teachers, family members, and other professionals in the community one-on-one or in a group setting. They must have the desire to contribute to a student's success. Providing support services and then evaluating outcomes is critical in order to enhance the student's learning and environment. An undergraduate degree is usually desired for professional support careers and often a master's degree is a requirement.

Figure 1.16 Offering reading sessions and story times is just one of the roles of a children's librarian.

Employment Opportunities and Trends

Will there be a need for teachers by the time you are ready to teach? Yes! There will always be a need for talented teachers. Education is the key to a successful society. Children need to be educated to be contributing members of society. Adults need to learn new skills and deepen their knowledge. In fact, predictions indicate that over the next 10 years, the United States will need over two million new teachers in schools alone.

Why is there a need for more teachers? First, many current teachers are reaching retirement age soon. Second, there is a national movement for educational reform. Many people believe that having more teachers with exceptional training will help students get a better education.

What kinds of teachers will be in need? It depends. Some subject areas are in greater demand, including math and science. There is also a great need for more teachers who speak a language in addition to English. *Bilingual education* (teaching in two languages) is growing in many parts of the country. Teachers who have the skills to teach in two or more languages, as well as those who teach children with disabilities, will be in great demand.

Teacher shortages already exist in some geographic areas, inner-city schools, and rural schools. In addition, population growth is likely to be greater in some states than others. Consequently, teachers who are able to relocate may have an advantage over those who are not.

If you desire to teach, develop the knowledge, skills, and passion that will make you a great teacher. Teachers are always in demand.

Teacher Salaries and Benefits

Teacher salaries vary considerably. Location, amount of education, years of experience, and additional responsibilities are among the variables that impact teacher salaries and are typically spelled out on school **salary schedule**—a chart or table that shows the progression of employee wages over time (Figure 1.17). Public school salaries tend to be higher than those of private schools, especially nonprofit private schools.

Schools usually pay teachers extra wages for some out-of-class activities, such as coaching and advising clubs and activities, such as student council. In addition, since most schools have more than two months of vacation in the summer, teachers often take part-time jobs to boost their income or use this time for continuing education.

For teachers who complete additional education, there is often an increase in pay. A four-year college or university degree is a requirement for school teachers. To encourage teachers to stay current in their field, however, many districts offer a higher salary for taking additional classes or obtaining an advanced degree, such as a master's degree.

Figure 1.17	Sample Salary Schedule for Certified Teachers			
Years of Experience	Bachelor's Degree (annual salary)	Bachelor's Degree + National Board Certification (annual salary)	Master's Degree (annual salary)	Master's Degree + National Board Certification (annual salary)
0	$32,300	$33,280	$34,550	$36,400
1	$32,480	$33,460	$34,740	$37,080
2	$32, 675	$33,655	$34,925	$37,405
3	$32, 860	$33,840	$35,115	$37,850
4	$33,900	$34,030	$35,300	$38,120
5	$34,350	$37,425	$37,650	$40,100
6	$35,200	$37,625	$37,850	$40,350
7	$35,400	$38,050	$38,650	$40,615
8	$35,450	$38,250	$39,050	$41,100
9	$35,600	$38,450	$39,860	$41,610
10	$37,900	$40,875	$41,000	$43,680
24	$44,200	$47,490	$47,950	$51,150
25	$46,200	$49,660	$49,990	$53,500

*Averages for teacher salaries vary from state to state and school district to school district and increase over time. It is important to note the progression or increase in teacher salaries based on their years of experience and professional degrees and certifications.

Although public schools provide benefits that vary by district, most offer the following additional benefits:

- health insurance
- retirement savings plans
- leaves of absence, paid or unpaid
- various other benefits, including travel expenses to attend meetings or reimbursement for the cost of additional education

Some public school districts, in an effort to attract top teaching candidates, offer additional incentives such as signing bonuses. A few offer home-loan assistance and tax breaks for teachers living within the school district.

Public schools receive funding from tax dollars. In good economic times, they may have extra money to spend. When the economy takes a downturn, their budgets tighten. Eliminating some programs and positions helps compensate for fewer funds. Still, teaching is one of the most basic occupations, and flexible teachers can find many ways to use their skills.

Perspectives on Teaching

Arianna laid the stack of student papers on her desk and sat down. (She had only been a middle school English teacher for six months.) It was a beautiful spring afternoon. The windows were open, letting in the fresh breeze. Arianna felt a sense of satisfaction. As usual, she was spending a few minutes of reflection on her day before leaving school, noting what had gone well and what changes she might make in the future.

Today had been a successful day. The students stayed reasonably focused, and there were no major concerns for that particular school day. She even had time to have a couple of one-on-one conversations with students about some of their personal matters. As she regrouped, her thoughts turned toward her speaking engagement tonight at her high school. Just four years earlier she had graduated, having completed a teaching academy program.

Arianna's task this evening was to speak to students about the field of education. She wondered how she could possibly convey to her audience just how much she had learned during this short time. She wanted to share an honest account of what it was like to be a teacher, including both the positive and negative experiences. As her thoughts went back to when she first decided to be a teacher, the words she would say this evening took shape in the following way:

Arianna's Thoughts...

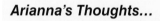

In high school, I was quite confident about my decision to go to college and major in education. I wanted to be a middle school teacher and work with children in those awkward, frustrating preteen years of self-discovery.

I applied to the university's teacher education program and was accepted. Even though my goal was to teach middle school, my certification would be to teach all subjects from kindergarten to grade 9. Consequently, I worked with children of various ages as part of my teacher education training. I also had to choose two areas of specialization. I chose English and social studies. I really enjoyed the classes, as well as observing and working with children.

When it came time to complete my student teaching, I was placed at a middle school in the city. The first day I walked in, I realized that

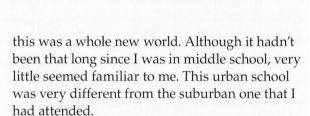

this was a whole new world. Although it hadn't been that long since I was in middle school, very little seemed familiar to me. This urban school was very different from the suburban one that I had attended.

My feelings must have been obvious. When my supervising teacher asked me what I thought of my first day, I told her that everything seemed chaotic. I said that I didn't feel that I would be able to relate effectively to students with such diverse backgrounds. She asked me what had led me to teaching and what my career goals were. I told her of my dream of teaching young teens. Fortunately, she was very understanding. She reminded me that all preteens are basically similar, and that I was focusing too much on exterior differences. She assured me that this would be a challenge, but that it was one she was sure that I could meet. She reminded me just how many these students needed enthusiastic teachers who cared about them. She predicted that I would learn from them, as well as about them. It was at that moment I decided to prove that I could be an inspiring teacher.

Before I started teaching, I thought anyone could be a good teacher. I was going to touch young lives and be everyone's favorite teacher. Students would come to me and share their secrets. I would prepare and deliver meaningful lessons that would change lives. In the summers, I would travel the world. No one told me what teaching was really going to be like. These are the things I never knew.

I never knew that I would spend infinite evenings planning lessons that would be met by rolling eyes, groans, and complete apathy. I never knew that in the rare case that a new lesson went off brilliantly, the fire alarm would sound and the rest of the class time would be lost forever. I never knew how many homework assignments could be "lost." I didn't realize that I would often feel more stress over giving a failing grade to a student than the student receiving it. I didn't know that students wouldn't always give me the respect I thought all teachers deserved (even though I was known for my silly teacher impersonations when I was in middle school).

I now know the exhilaration of creating a lesson that leaves students buzzing as they leave the room. I know how it feels to work in an atmosphere with other intelligent and like-minded staff that pull together and help one another. Back then, I didn't know how appreciative I would be when a holiday card was laid on my desk or when a "thank you" escaped a smiling face. I didn't know how I would learn to laugh at myself. I now know that I laugh when I trip over an electrical cord in front of 30 13-year-olds.

No one told me that I would be haunted at night by a conversation with one of my many students who have traumatic home lives. Take Eli for example. His mother overcame a drug addiction, but couldn't find a job that paid enough for basic expenses. She and Eli ended up living on the streets. I didn't find out about Eli's situation right away. It became apparent over time. I know I can't solve all my students' problems, but I have seen that listening to and encouraging them are gifts I can give. During breaks, I find myself wondering how "my kids" are doing.

Most of all, I did not know that I would feel so needed. I have discovered that teaching happens in one-on-one relationships. Often, I'm teaching my students that they are capable and able to learn. I try to convey why reading, writing, and communication skills are so important by making my lessons connect with their lives.

My life is so varied. No two days are the same. No two students are the same. My days are filled with planning lessons, grading assignments, following through on discipline issues, and keeping up on individual student needs. As a first-year teacher, I am creating every learning activity from scratch. Sometimes, I'm so busy living each day that I forget why I became a teacher—because I care deeply about cultivating minds and spirits. There aren't many people who get to witness these profound changes in people on a daily basis.

My life is very full and satisfying. All things considered, teaching is a lifestyle and a career choice that is right for me.

Analyze It!

After reading *Perspectives on Teaching*, analyze Arianna's comment about her decision to teach. "Before I started teaching, I thought anyone could be a good teacher." Cite evidence from Arianna's narrative that either supports or does not support this statement. Discuss your points of evidence with the class.

Chapter 1 Review and Assess

Summary

- Effective teachers have individual personalities and talents, but share important qualities and personal characteristics.
- Teachers spend most of their time planning, presenting lessons, and evaluating learning, and may supervise extracurricular activities.
- Teaching is rewarding and fulfilling. Teachers observe students learn, grow, and change as they acquire the knowledge and skills essential to becoming valuable society members.
- Teaching is also challenging as caring teachers put in long hours of work under conditions that are not always ideal.
- Many societal problems affect students, requiring teachers to find creative, empathetic ways to meet their educational needs.
- The field of education holds many career options including traditional classroom teaching options from preschool through college levels, and in such areas as administration and administrative support and professional support services.
- Effective teachers are always in demand, although options vary by subject area and location.
- Teaching salaries vary but usually increase with experience and more education.

Review and Study

1. Contrast effective teaching qualities with effective personal characteristics of teachers.

2. How do state curriculums and school-based curriculums differ? What would supporters of each give as an advantage?

3. Name three rewards of teaching.

4. What are self-contained classrooms? At what level are these classrooms most common?

5. What is the difference between abstract thinking and concrete thinking?

6. What is collaborative learning?

7. List four types of teaching specialists.

8. Compare and contrast the duties of a corporate trainer with those of a cooperative extension educator.

9. Name four educational or societal trends that are likely to impact employment opportunities for teachers.

10. In addition to regular salaries, what types of benefits do most school districts provide for teachers?

Vocabulary Activity

11. Review the *content* and *academic* vocabulary terms at the beginning of the chapter. For each term, identify a word or group of words describing a quality, or an *attribute* of the term. Pair up with a classmate and discuss the similarities and differences in your list of attributes. Then discuss your list of attributes with the whole class to increase understanding.

Critical Thinking

12. **Make inferences.** Review the personal qualities of effective teachers on page 8 of the text. Choose at least four qualities, and use the text and other reliable

resources to infer situations in which effective teachers use this quality. Discuss your inferences with the class.

13. **Analyze assets.** In teaching situations beyond the school environment, analyze why having a bachelor's degree and a teaching certification is an asset. Cite evidence from the text and other reliable resources to support your analysis.

14. **Evaluate factors.** Use the example in *Figure 1.12* and the Internet to research average teacher salaries in four states. Choose your own state, one that is similar in population, and two that are very different. Identify the years of the surveyed information and its source. Evaluate the factors that influence teachers' salaries. Then create a chart showing how average salaries compare. Post your chart to the class website. How does your evaluation compare to those of your classmates?

Core Skills

15. **Speaking, listening, and writing.** Ask an adult you know to describe the characteristics of his or her favorite teacher. What grade did the teacher teach? What impact did the teacher have on the person? Listen carefully and then write a summary of your conversation to share with the class.

16. **Technology application.** Go to the O*NET website and use the *Skills Profiler* self-assessment to help determine the skills and qualities you possess that apply to a teaching career. Analyze the results of the self-assessment. What skills and qualities do you possess that are assets in a teaching career? What improvements can you make if you have passion for a career in teaching? Write a summary of your findings.

17. **Reading and writing.** Access the United States Department of Labor *Bureau of Labor Statistics* website. Choose career profiles for two types of teachers. Demonstrate your writing skills by writing a one-page summary describing each type of teaching, typical working conditions, job outlook, and expected earnings and benefits.

18. **Research and speaking**. Think about challenges related to teaching that concern you most. Choose one. Research how teachers cope with this type of challenge. Give an oral report identifying the challenge you chose, summarizing your research findings, and explaining strategies you would use to try to meet the challenge.

19. **Research, speaking, and listening.** Use the text and reliable Internet resources to research teaching and training in nontraditional settings such as corporations; community outreach; non-profit clubs, organizations, and community groups; and government entities. Discuss teaching and training in these settings, citing reliable evidence about key aspects of these positions.

20. **Investigating, formulating, and writing.** Investigate education and training alternatives after high school for a career choice in education *administration and administrative support* program of study within your interest area. Use the Bureau of Labor Statistics, O*NET, or CareerOneStop websites to investigate education and degree plans for various occupations. Formulate and examine education and training degree plans for various occupations within education administration and administrative support. Write a summary of your findings.

21. **Investigating, formulating, and speaking.** Investigate education and training alternatives after high school for a career choice in *professional support services* program of study within your interest area. Use the Bureau of Labor Statistics, O*NET, or CareerOneStop websites to investigate education and degree plans for various occupations, and formulate and examine education and training degree plans for various occupations within education professional support services. Give an oral report of your findings for a professional support services career of your choice.

22. **Technology application.** Search an online job board or the newspaper classifieds for specific job postings found under the heading "education." How many of the listings include traditional elementary or secondary teaching positions? How many of the postings are advertising other related job openings? Create a table of your findings to post to the school-approved class blog or website. Which education-related job posting surprised you and your classmates the most?

23. **CTE College and career readiness practice.** Calculate the potential savings from completing the first two years of a bachelor's degree program at a community college. Identify each school's name and location (city). Utilize college and university websites for information on schools in your state. Find the cost per semester hour or yearly tuition cost at each. Use 32 semester hours per year as your basis. Compare tuition costs for the following:

- four years at a state university
- four years at a private college or university
- two years at each, community college and a state university
- two years at each, community college and a private college or university

College and Career Portfolio

When you apply to a college or for a job or community service, you may need to tell others about how you are qualified for this position. A portfolio is a selection of related materials that you collect and organize. These materials show your qualifications, skills, and talents. These materials may be in the form of certificates of achievement, written essays on a number of design-related issues, and a transcript of your school grades and courses.

Two types of portfolios are commonly used: print portfolios and electronic portfolios (e-Portfolios).

A. Use the Internet to search reliable sources for print portfolio and e-Portfolio. Read articles about each type. Then briefly describe each type in your own words.

B. You will be creating a portfolio in this class. Write a paragraph describing which type of portfolio you prefer. What might be the benefit of creating both?

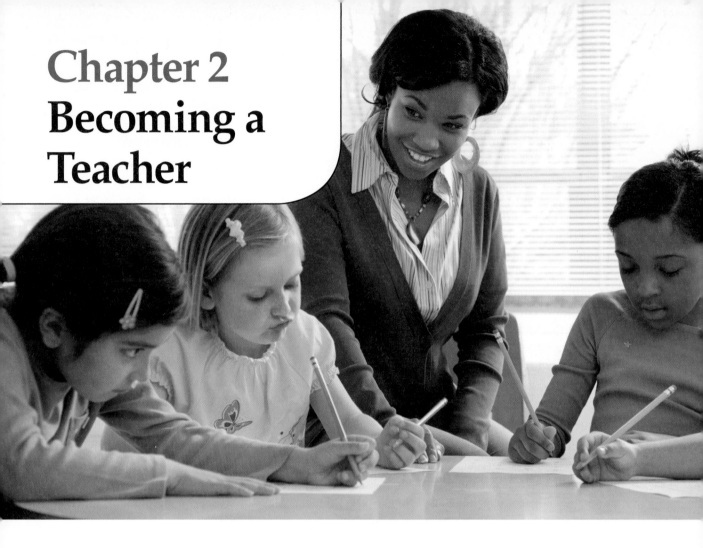

Chapter 2
Becoming a Teacher

Content Terms

teaching academies
teacher education programs
job shadowing
service-learning
prerequisite course
proficiency test
student teaching
cooperating teacher
certified teacher
teaching license
philosophy of teaching

Academic Terms

grants
reciprocal agreements
career goal
analogy
personal portfolio
artifacts
articulate

Objectives

After studying this chapter, you will be able to

- **identify** the steps to becoming a teacher.

- **compare** ways of gaining experience with children while in high school.

- **analyze** the requirements for admission to a teacher education program.

- **develop** a personal career goal.

- **create** an initial personal portfolio for teaching to use throughout the class.

- **generate** your philosophy of teaching.

Reading Prep

As you read the chapter, record any questions that come to mind. Note where the answer to each question can be found: within the text, by asking your teacher, in another book, on the Internet, or by reflecting on your own knowledge and experiences. Pursue answers to your questions.

At the Companion Website you can

- **Practice** terms with e-flash cards and interactive games

- **Assess** what you learn by completing self-assessment quizzes

- **Expand** knowledge with interactive activities

www.g-wlearning.com/teaching/

Study on the go

Use a mobile device to practice terms and review with self-assessment quizzes.

www.m.g-wlearning.com/0094/

Case Study

As a class, read the case study and discuss the questions that follow. After you finish studying the chapter, discuss the case study and questions again. What have you learned about developing a philosophy of teaching statement?

Can teaching and baseball combine into one career? Andrew hopes so. Andrew is now a senior and is applying to colleges with the hopes of beginning a degree program in elementary education. His dream is to become a certified teacher, to coach Little League® baseball, and eventually, to start a school for at-risk kids that combines a love for sports with a love for learning. He knows that these are big dreams and he wants to make sure that he chooses a university program that will help him achieve these goals. The program he is most interested in is at his state university. As part of the application process, Andrew must write his *philosophy of teaching* for admittance into the School of Education within the university.

Let's Discuss

- What is a philosophy of teaching statement?
- What should Andrew consider including in this statement to make him stand out from other applicants and yet be authentic?

You are considering teaching as a career although that may seem to be years into the future. In reality, you need to begin the process now. The goal of this chapter is to help point you in the right direction. Learning about the steps to take to reach your goal and what you can accomplish while you are still in high school are instrumental in becoming a teacher.

What if you change your mind along the way? Changing your mind is okay, too. Through your experiences, you may decide you still want to teach, but perhaps a different level or subject. Gaining this valuable insight is vital to a successful career. If you decide that teaching is not for you, you can explore another career path knowing more about your interests and abilities. Virtually everything you learn along the way will serve you well, regardless of the career you eventually choose.

What Are the Steps to Becoming a Teacher?

What does it take to become a teacher? It depends. Specific teacher preparation standards vary by state and by the level of teaching, although the same general steps are involved across the country.

The class you are taking provides you with an excellent start. As you begin the process of exploring the teaching profession, you will gain helpful experience and begin to build the skills you need to be a successful teacher.

Step 1: High School Preparation

High school is the best place to start the process toward a career in teaching. Setting your goals and working systematically toward them is a real advantage over students who begin later. The actions you take now really do have a major impact on your future.

Maximize Your Educational Opportunities

As a student, you are in a school setting every day. You have years of experience as a student. More high schools are offering students the opportunity to explore careers in teaching through special career exploration classes or programs. Some of these programs, or **teaching academies**, help high school students to explore the teaching profession through classes, observations, and hands-on experiences. The class you are taking now may be such a program.

Make the most of your high school educational experience. Choose challenging high school courses, and commit to doing as well in them as possible. Why is this so important? First, the knowledge you gain serves as a solid basis for your college career. Every course gives you insight into a new subject area. In addition, a strong academic record makes you a better candidate for the college or university of your choice and admittance into a teaching program.

In subjects that come more easily for you, you may choose to help others learn the material. There is an old saying, "If you really want to know a subject well, try teaching it to someone else." When you have difficulty with a class or particular topic, ask for help. The experiences you gain mirror that of your future career.

Observe Your Teachers

Take the opportunity to observe your teachers (Figure 2.1). It is your chance to see how a variety of teachers work. Notice how they interact with students. What are their particular teaching styles? How do they adapt material for different levels or interests? What are their class rules and procedures? How do individual teachers earn the respect of their students? Be sure to note your observations for future reference.

Utilize your own teachers as resources about teaching. Ask what led them to teaching and their specific career paths. What advice would they give to someone interested in the profession? Most will be happy to share their knowledge and experiences with you.

Explore College Programs

Begin now to gather information about colleges and universities that offer teacher training, or **teacher education programs** (or *teacher preparation programs)*. Many schools have such programs, but some are more highly regarded than others. Your high school guidance staff can be an excellent source of information. Ask your

Figure 2.1   As a student, you have a great opportunity to observe teachers every day.

teachers for their recommendations. Search online to find possible schools and learn more about them. This will help you decide which schools interest you most and might be a good fit for you.

When you narrow your list of potential colleges and universities, visit their websites to learn about their entrance requirements and the courses you would take. Try to visit the colleges or universities at the top of your list during your junior year. Send applications for admission to colleges in the fall of your senior year.

Guidance counselors also have a wealth of information. For example, if the cost of college is a concern, ask for information about financial aid. Colleges and universities award scholarships on a basis of academic excellence or other criteria. Some **grants** are available, usually for those who show real economic need. Grant money does not require repayment. Student loans are usually available at low interest rates with repayment over a longer time period than normal loans. Your guidance counselor can help you figure out options for financial aid possibilities and other options for coping with educational expenses.

Gain Experience and Improve Your Skills

While in high school, gain as much experience working with children of various ages as you can. Why gain experience now? You have opportunities now that are different from those open to you later in life. Working with children can help you make a better decision about whether teaching in an elementary or secondary school is a good career choice for you. In addition, colleges and universities look favorably on applicants who have shown community involvement. There are many ways you can gain experience in teaching and working with children.

Job shadowing. In many high school teaching programs, students have the opportunity to visit a classroom and job shadow a teacher. In **job shadowing**, you follow a person on the job for a few hours, a day, or even longer to experience what the person's career typically involves. Job shadowing has many benefits. It can give you valuable insight into the person's daily tasks, activities, and interactions with others. Seeing a professional in action helps you identify the skills you need. You may also have the opportunity to discuss the experience with the person you are shadowing and ask questions.

Since job shadowing is only a short-term activity, you might try to shadow a variety of people in careers of interest to you. You could, for example, spend time with teachers at different grade levels or perhaps a special education teacher or a reading specialist. In addition to what you learn, each experience offers you a new professional contact. Sometimes teachers and counselors arrange for job shadowing, but you can also make arrangements to do so yourself.

Figure 2.2 Serving as a volunteer offers you an opportunity to work with students of varying age levels and abilities.

Volunteering. Volunteering is an excellent way to actually interact with children. Volunteers do much of the important work in communities without payment or wages. Once you become aware of needs, you are likely to find many opportunities. You can learn more about children of different age levels. You might volunteer to help with an after-school program at an elementary school. You could become a tutor in a youth program or get involved in programs such as Cub Scouts or Brownies. You could help coach a sport. Summer camps, child care programs, Special Olympics (Figure 2.2), and community recreation programs all benefit from enthusiastic and committed volunteers.

Short-term projects are also an option. You might help with an elementary school fundraiser, set up a school's art fair, or help a middle school group with a car wash. Volunteering can give you valuable leadership experience. In essence, teachers are those who lead others in learning.

All volunteer experiences, even those that do not involve children, can help you improve the skills you need for success in college and a career. You may assist with planning, carrying out, and evaluating activities. Volunteer activities typically require creativity and problem-solving skills, and offer opportunities to work with people of different backgrounds and ages. Dedication to your volunteer job, even if it is inconvenient, strengthens your sense of commitment. Every experience teaches you much and helps you stretch and grow as a productive citizen.

Volunteer work can also be a valuable addition to your résumé. In addition, some of the adults with whom you work may be willing to act as references, attesting to your character, commitment, and work.

Service-learning. A special type of unpaid volunteer effort, or **service-learning**, combines classroom learning with meaningful hands-on experience to meet community needs. Service-learning projects require analyzing needs, learning related information, planning a way to help, following through, and evaluating the experience.

For example, a child development class might look into the problem of injury and death rates among young children involved in vehicle accidents. Research might show that many child safety seats lack proper installation, while others may have active recalls. The class might work with an agency such as the American Red Cross to organize a safety-check day. Parents of young children could bring their vehicles to school to have the child safety seats checked. In addition, the class might prepare an information sheet on child safety to give to parents who attend the safety check day. Both the parents and students would evaluate the experience.

A service-learning project such as this enhances learning, fills a community need, and helps students see that they can make a difference (Figure 2.3). If your school does not have a service-learning program, talk to your teachers about establishing one.

Part-time work. Part-time work is another way to gain experience with children while still in high school. Child care centers, recreation programs, and after-school care programs are just a few of the places that hire part-time or summer staff. Your interest in teaching, related classes you have taken, and any volunteer experiences would help make you a good candidate.

Figure 2.3 By combining your volunteer efforts and a service-learning project, you can gain valuable experience to improve your leadership and work skills while helping others.

There are many opportunities for learning more about the field of education through actual experience with children. Take advantage of as many as possible to test your interests and boost your skills. Whom would you be interested in job shadowing? What volunteer opportunities exist in your community? Does your school have service-learning projects? Perhaps you can find a part-time or summer job related to your career goal. Whatever your choices, they will enhance your learning and your life.

Step 2: College Preparation and Teacher Training

To teach in kindergarten through high school, requires a bachelor's degree. This degree, or an *undergraduate degree*, generally takes four years to complete. It is usually either a bachelor of arts (BA) or bachelor of science (BS), depending on your college major and the course requirements you have met.

Colleges and universities have individual requirements for admission to teacher education programs. Some require students to wait until their junior year of college to apply. By this time, students have completed most of their general education or core courses, and the teacher education program can better evaluate applicants.

Entrance requirements into teacher education programs often include personal interviews, prerequisite courses, a minimum grade point average, and proficiency tests. A **prerequisite course** is one that students must complete before entering a program or prior to taking a higher-level course. **Proficiency tests** measure skill and knowledge in a subject area. Teacher education candidates or majors may be required to pass proficiency tests in subjects such as reading, writing, and math. All classes teachers teach require integration of these skills. Many programs ask applicants to list related experiences they have had working with children.

Professional Tip

Responsibility in Action

It is easy to see why dependable teachers are so greatly valued. You have no doubt witnessed many. Responsible teachers are committed 100 percent of the time in all situations, relationships, and actions. They do not blame someone else when things do not go exactly as planned. When working on a team, responsibility means giving their all even if one team member does not do the same. They earn respect from others, a reputation for accomplishment and trustworthiness, and as a result, feel more in control of their own destiny.

Analyze It!

How does added responsibility make you feel more in control? When does it make you feel less in control? What are some opportunities in your home, school, or work life where you can share responsibility today?

Elementary and secondary education students must complete course work related to education. Some courses provide background about education as a profession and how schools function. Others help students learn specific teaching strategies and classroom management techniques. Students focusing on elementary education also take courses to prepare them to teach all subject areas. Students preparing to teach for middle grades and high school, study one or two subject areas in much more depth, such as science or physical education.

Step 3: Classroom Experiences and Student Teaching

An important part of preparing to become a teacher is gaining necessary experience. As part of course requirements for teacher education students, most classes require working with children or teens. Students may observe, help a teacher, tutor students, teach a lesson, or be involved in some other capacity. There are real advantages to this practice. Teacher education students gain more experience, improve their skills, and see how they like various aspects of teaching.

Teacher education culminates in a **student teaching** experience. This experience involves placement of student teachers in public or private school classrooms to immerse themselves in the practice of teaching. There, they have at least one **cooperating teacher**—a classroom teacher who supervises and mentors the student teacher. A professor at the college or university oversees the student teaching experience. All states require teacher education programs to include a student teaching experience.

Student teachers begin by observing in the classroom. By the end of their experience, which usually lasts one semester, they are often taking over for the cooperating teacher while under his or her supervision. This includes planning and teaching material, assigning work, evaluating and assessing learning, and interacting with parents and school personnel.

Step 4: Gaining Certification

Teaching kindergarten through high school requires certification in the state where teachers want to teach. A **certified teacher** is one who has met the state requirements for teacher preparation. Typically, this includes having a bachelor's degree or higher, successfully completing an approved teacher education program (including student teaching),

Figure 2.4 After successfully completing your student teaching, earning a bachelor's or advanced degree, and meeting state requirements, you can become a certified teacher.

and any other state requirements (Figure 2.4). In many states, students can complete a bachelor's degree and approved teacher education program within four years. Some states, however, require one or two years of education courses after completing a bachelor's degree.

A certified teacher receives a **teaching license** or teaching certificate from his or her state. This official document verifies for schools that the person is qualified to teach at specific grade levels or in particular subject areas. For example, teachers have a license to teach at the early childhood level, the elementary grades, the middle grades, or secondary school. A teaching license may also list a specific subject area qualification, such as music. Not all private schools require teachers to have a teaching license, but most do.

College and university teacher education programs usually correlate to the licensing requirements of their state. What if you plan to teach in a state other than where you go to college? It is important to know the specific requirements of the state in which you will be teaching as early as possible. You can work with your advisor to develop a plan. States often have *reciprocal agreements* with some other states regarding teaching licenses or certifications. This means that they agree to honor teaching credentials issued in another state with which they have an agreement.

States issue teaching licenses for a specific time period. At the end of this period, teachers must renew their licenses. States typically require teachers to document additional education or training for license renewal. Some require teachers to eventually obtain a master's degree, such as a Master of Education. This is a graduate degree and requires the equivalent of one or two years of full-time course work. Many teachers begin working on their master's degrees part-time shortly after they begin teaching.

If your goal is to teach at the college level, you may need to complete a master's degree to teach at the community college level. This degree is usually not in education, but in a particular subject area or specialization. To teach at a four-year college or university, a doctoral degree may be a requirement. This, too, is usually in a specialized area.

Getting Started

Now that you have seen the big picture, where do you begin in your quest to become a teacher? Taking the class you are in is your best guide to exploring the teaching field. Observe what you see around you. Look for examples of effective teaching and learning. Take advantage of every opportunity for learning and gain experience working with different age groups.

There are several other keys to beginning the path toward teaching: defining your career goal, creating a personal portfolio, and developing a philosophy of teaching. Together these will help you get started on the path to a successful teaching career.

Set a Career Goal

Dreams rely on chance. Goals take concerted effort (Figure 2.5). Your life's dreams, however, can become your life's goals. How can you make your dream of becoming a teacher—and others—reality?

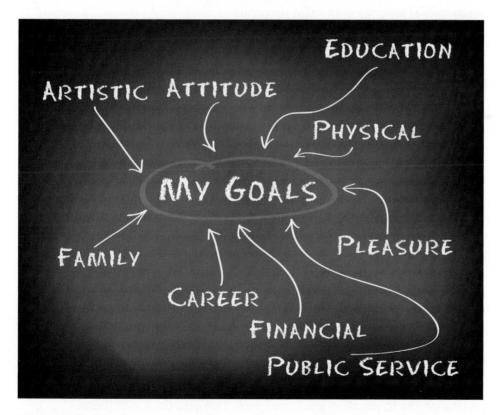

Figure 2.5   You have many other goals to consider when setting your career goal.

Think seriously about what subjects and age group you want to teach. These are two important questions in understanding your desire to become a teacher. First, think about what you would like to teach. Do you have a passion for a particular subject? Some people love a single subject area such as biology or art. Others like to teach in all basic areas, including reading, writing, science, and math. Is your desire to teach young children, those in middle grades, younger teens, older teens, or young adults?

When you know what you want to achieve, you are more likely to achieve it. Use your personal answers to the "what" and "who" questions as a basis for writing a career goal, a **career goal**—a clear, concise statement of what you want to become in life. Write down exactly what you want to accomplish in specific terms. Perhaps your goal is to be a third grade teacher. Maybe you want to teach in a rural school. How will you feel when you accomplish this goal? Although you may modify your goal later, having a career goal helps you move forward with your career plans and education.

Your career goal forms the foundation for identifying interrelated goals that help you achieve it. For example, to become that third grade teacher, you might set the goal of gaining admittance to a particular university with an excellent teacher education program.

Use the **analogy** (a comparison of two unlike things for similarities) of a tree as you think of the process of achieving your career goal. Your main career goal is the trunk while your related goals, such as acceptance into the university of your choice, are the main branches. For each of those, identify the specific steps you need to achieve them. These steps are like smaller branches off the main ones. You can identify even more specific ways to achieve these goals. In this way, you have a series of very specific goals to meet that connect you to your main goal, giving you have a path to follow.

Next, outline the steps to take to complete each goal. If you want to get into a particular university with an excellent teacher education program, figure out what you need to do to gain acceptance and be able to attend. Perhaps you need to improve your grades, apply to the university early in your senior year, and develop a plan for paying for the cost of your education. Determine the specific actions to take to achieve each of these steps. For example, to improve your grades, you may commit to writing down each assignment, doing your homework as soon as you get home (with your cell phone off), and studying an extra hour each day. Then reevaluate your strategy at the end of each month and modify it if your grades are not improving. Consider possible roadblocks or challenges to meeting your goal. How can you deal with these?

Does setting a career goal seem overwhelming? It does not have to be. Begin your career planning today. Consider what you can do today, this week, this month, or this year to help you move toward your goal.

Perhaps you can begin by searching the Internet for information about college or university teacher preparation programs. Find a volunteer or paid work experience. Maybe you can have a conversation with one of your teachers about his or her career path. Now is a good time to set goals, enjoy your experiences, and be open to the changing world around you. See Figure 2.6 for an example of one student's career plan. How will yours look?

Create a Portfolio

Artists, photographers, architects, designers, and writers commonly use professional portfolios as a way to showcase their abilities and work. In other words, a professional portfolio serves as an expanded visual résumé. A written *résumé* simply lists a person's accomplishments, skills, and experience, but a *professional portfolio* adds visual evidence to support it.

Anyone can use a portfolio, and its use is becoming increasingly common in education. Now is the time to start developing a personal portfolio for teaching. A **personal portfolio** is an organized collection of materials and information that shows how personal knowledge, skills, and attitudes have developed over time. It can be adapted to serve as a professional portfolio when you are ready to enter your career field. Developing a portfolio may be a requirement for this course. Even if it is not required, you will find it very helpful.

Figure 6	Sample Career Plan
High School	• Gain experience working with children and youth • Job shadow • Take a career exploration course • Meet with guidance counselor and discuss interests • Look for college teacher preparation program • Apply to colleges • Choose college program that best meets your needs
College	• Meet with guidance counselor and enroll in courses • Job shadow • Gain additional experience working with children and youth • Complete necessary coursework • Complete student teaching • Graduate
Last Year or After College	• Apply for certification • Conduct job search

Your portfolio is a personal collection of materials and reflections that illustrate your learning, accomplishments, strengths, and best work. These examples show what you have learned over time.

Think of your portfolio as an opportunity to keep track of your learning. Use it to display and record items that showcase your developing skills and abilities. These may include **artifacts**, or items such as projects or papers you prepare for class, examples from a related volunteer activity, and academic and other awards, just to name a few. As you add items to your portfolio, it reveals how your knowledge, thinking, and skills are growing. Your portfolio also serves as a source of personal reflection, much like a visual journal.

Characteristics of Effective Portfolios

Effective portfolios share several common features. As you prepare and evaluate your own, keep the following in mind:

- *Portfolios have a clear purpose.* Remember that the purpose of your teaching portfolio is to record and highlight your experiences and abilities that identify you as a good candidate for teaching. It is not simply a scrapbook about your life.

- *Portfolios reflect uniqueness.* Your abilities and experiences are not the same as anyone else's. Because of this, your portfolio should be original. You may choose to include different artifacts than others in your class. You might, for example, include photographs, certificates, descriptions of your work with children, and evidence of your personal leadership experiences.

- *Portfolios show progress.* Your portfolio is not just a random collection of things. Think carefully about what to include. Identify and date each item. For each, you also need to include a thoughtful statement about why the item is meaningful and what it demonstrates. These statements, along with the changing quality of your work, show how your thinking, understanding, and skills have evolved. For example, you might include the first lesson plan you developed for your teaching class, along with a paragraph about what you learned from the experience.

    Later, you may add other teaching materials that you have developed. The differences in their quality and your thoughts about them show how you have progressed from your earlier efforts. Remember that portfolios evolve over time, but they should be current. You may remove some items (or store them elsewhere) as you add new ones and progress in your professional preparation.

- ***Portfolios reflect professionalism.*** An effective portfolio is well-organized, neat, and easy to understand (Figure 2.7). One of the most common methods of organizing a portfolio is to use a three-ring binder with tab dividers. Make the pages interesting, but professional. Even the paper you choose, the way you arrange items, and the lettering you use say something about you.

  Make sure that what you have written is accurate, clear to the reader, and grammatically correct. To be effective, a portfolio must be error-free. Proofread carefully several times. It is a good idea to ask at least two people to review your portfolio before you turn it in for a class or use it for another purpose.

Figure 2.7 Present your portfolio in a professional, organized manner in a binder or case that protects your artifacts.

What Should You Include in Your Portfolio?

Even though portfolios vary, there are several documents that are often part of a personal teaching portfolio. If you are preparing this as a class project, your teacher will give specific guidelines. The following are some items to include in a portfolio:

- basic information about yourself, including your name and year in school

- an essay focusing on your career goals and personal interests

- projects, assignments, or examples from experiences that display your skills

- journal entries about your experiences related to teaching

- a list of the courses you have taken in high school

- a list of community activities, including any community service

- information about any jobs you have had

- academic recognition, such as letters, certificates, or honors

- information on leadership positions you have held or demonstrated

- documentation of special skills, such as foreign language or exceptional computer skills

Throughout this text, you will find ideas for developing a portfolio. Look for the *College and Career Portfolio* section at the end of each chapter. In addition, artifacts and reflections from many of the other activities may be good items to include in your portfolio.

Using Your Portfolio

As you move through high school, your learning experiences multiply. It is easy to lose track of what you did and the importance of individual activities. A portfolio allows you to keep the important components of your career goals in an organized format. Recording how you changed, or grew, or what you learned from the experience each component represents, shows meaningful reflection and documents the significance of each milestone.

If you are creating a portfolio as a part of a teaching course or academy program, your portfolio may count as part of your final grade. You might use materials from your portfolio if you apply for a part-time job. Colleges and universities often use portfolios to assess students' levels of knowledge and experience when they apply to teacher preparation programs. Starting a portfolio in high school helps you build a solid professional foundation that can move with you through your college career.

Electronic Portfolios

Preparing your portfolio in an electronic format is an alternative to an actual physical one (Figure 2.8). There are benefits to this option. With an electronic portfolio, or *e-portfolio*, you can easily store information on a computer hard drive or storage device, transport materials, and access them with minimal effort.

With traditional portfolios, items included in the portfolio can be lost. Materials also take up a lot of space and must be stored in boxes, notebooks, binders, or files. By scanning or taking digital photos of objects, you can preserve their images. A portfolio in electronic form can be shared electronically. Electronic portfolios also serve to demonstrate the creator's computer skills. Just be sure the technology used is compatible and accessible to the viewer. Remember, some people prefer to be able to see and touch the actual items in a portfolio.

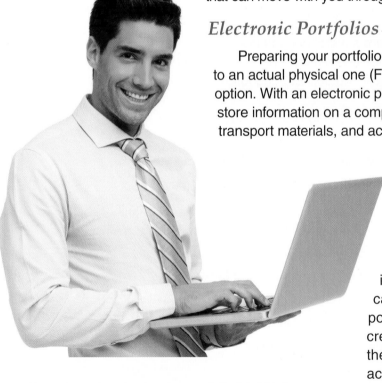

Figure 2.8 An electronic portfolio highlights your education, skills, and teaching experience in a manner that is convenient to send to potential employers at a distance.

Develop Your Philosophy of Teaching

Teachers and student teachers often receive questions about their philosophy of teaching. A **philosophy of teaching** is a personal statement about your thoughts, views, and values as they relate to teaching.

As a high school student interested in the teaching profession, you already have ideas about the characteristics and qualities of good teaching. What do you think a classroom environment should be like? How should teachers and students relate to each other? Ideas and opinions such as these form your philosophy of teaching.

Why do you need a statement about your philosophy of teaching? The process of developing such a statement helps you think seriously about your current ideas and beliefs (Figure 2.9). Your statement gives others insight into what is important to you. The courses you take and experiences you have are likely to have an impact on your thinking.

Figure 2.9 Developing your philosophy of teaching takes careful thought.

You can update or rewrite your statement to reflect these changes. This, too, is a sign of growth. You can use your philosophy of teaching statement when you apply to a college teacher preparation program. Eventually, you may use it when you apply for your first teaching position.

The most difficult part about writing a philosophy of teaching is to **articulate** your thoughts, or put them into words. Starting with questions often makes writing your thoughts easier. Use the questions in Figure 2.10 to start your thinking.

When writing your statement, use language that everyone understands, rather than words you think impress others. The format is up to you. You may decide to write in the form of a story, use relevant quotations, include visuals, or use a question/answer format. It is usually best to use a first-person or "I" perspective. Keep your philosophy statement short. As a student, two or three paragraphs are sufficient.

Giving serious thought to your goals, career, and personal objectives pays off in the long run. Such thinking helps you identify what you want to put your time and effort into achieving. It also provides a means of assessing when you have reached your goals and objectives.

Figure 2.10   Developing Your Philosophy of Teaching

The following questions can help you in developing your personal philosophy of teaching. Think about each of them, and jot down your thoughts. Your philosophy statement may include some, but not necessarily all, of these points.

- Why do you want to teach?
- What characteristics make a teacher effective?
- How do students learn?
- What is an ideal classroom?
- What should the relationship between teacher and student be?
- What motivates students to learn?
- What should be the primary goal of a teacher?
- Who is the best teacher you have ever known? What made him or her so special?
- What is the most important role of a teacher?

Chapter 2 Review and Assess

Summary

- Specific teacher preparation standards vary by state, although the same general steps are involved in becoming a teacher across the country.

- High school is an excellent time to begin exploring the field of teaching and gaining experience in working with children and people of all ages.

- Job shadowing, volunteering, service-learning, and part-time work in relevant positions can help you gain experience in working with children.

- A bachelor's degree, along with successfully completing an approved teacher education program including student teaching, is required to teach in kindergarten through high school.

- A teaching license verifies a person's qualifications to teach specific grade levels or subject areas in his or her state.

- Setting a career goal and outlining steps to achieve that goal are an important beginning to a journey toward teaching.

- A personal portfolio offers an organized collection of materials and information to show how personal knowledge, skills, abilities, and attitudes change and develop over time.

- A philosophy of teaching is a personal statement of thoughts, beliefs, and values as they relate to teaching.

Review and Study

1. List four steps to becoming a teacher.
2. What are three advantages of taking challenging courses while in high school?
3. What is job shadowing? Name a benefit of job shadowing.
4. How are volunteering and service-learning similar and different?
5. Name three possible requirements for entrance into college or university teacher education programs.
6. What is the role of a cooperating teacher during a student teaching experience?
7. What is a certified teacher? Why is the purpose of certification?
8. Explain why setting a career goal is important.
9. Name four characteristics of effective portfolios. Give an example of each characteristic.
10. What is a philosophy of teaching statement? List two reasons why you need it.

Vocabulary Activity

11. Review the *content* and *academic* terms at the beginning of the chapter. Work in small groups to locate small images online that visually describe or explain each of the terms. To create flashcards, write each term on a note card and paste a printout of the image that describes or explains the term on the opposite side of the card.

Critical Thinking

12. **Predict outcomes.** Review the text and other reliable sources to identify criteria teacher education programs typically used to evaluate students applying to the program. Predict why the criteria may indicate probable success in the program and as a teacher.

13. **Analyze evidence.** Why is certification for teachers important for each of the following groups: states, schools, parents, and students? In teams, create a four-column table. Label each column with one of the groups. Then list as many reasons as you can for each group in the correlating column. As a class, compile team lists and analyze the responses. What are the top reasons indicating the importance of teacher certification?

14. **Draw conclusions.** The author cites that many people use professional portfolios to showcase their abilities and work. Draw conclusions about how your personal portfolio can become the foundation of a professional portfolio as you pursue a career in teaching.

Core Skills

15. **Research and speaking.** Observation is a key skill for those who want a career in teaching. You may observe teachers, children of various ages, and educational programs. Work in groups to research what it takes to be a good observer. Consider how to prepare, what to do during the observation, and how to follow up afterward. Give a group report of your findings.

16. **Technology application.** Search online for colleges and universities that offer a major in education. Create a spreadsheet that records the following information:

- type of degree offered (elementary education, K-8, secondary education, etc.)
- number and cost of credits required/tuition
- cost of commuting to or residing on or near campus
- availability and types of scholarships
- your ranking of this program

17. **Research, writing, and speaking.** Use the Internet or college catalogs to locate a college or university in your state that has a teacher education program. Find out when students may apply to the program. Choose one level of teaching (early childhood through high school) and research the number and types of classes required and the length of the student teaching experience. Prepare an oral report of your findings to share with the class. Include the website for the school in your report.

18. **Research and speaking.** Research the requirements for teacher certification or licensing in your state. What education and training is required? How many years is the license valid? What, if any, requirements must teachers meet to renew the license? What categories of teaching licenses does the state issue (for example, kindergarten through grade 6 or high school math)? Share your findings in a brief oral report to the class.

19. **Writing.** Write a concise career goal based on your current interest in teaching. Be sure to include specific information on the type of position in which you are interested.

20. **Writing.** With the text as your guide, write your initial *philosophy of teaching statement* in two or three paragraphs. Ask your teacher for feedback, and then revise your statement. Save your philosophy of teaching statement in your *College and Career Portfolio* and review or revise it periodically throughout this course.

21. **CTE College and career readiness practice.** You have almost decided that teaching is the career for you. After researching the educational requirements, you think it is a good fit with your personal and career goals. You feel, however, you are missing the first-hand experiences needed to totally commit to teaching. Locate a teacher at a school in your area who is an expert in the area you want to teach. Arrange to job shadow or work with this person as a mentor while pursuing your career. How can you benefit by having such a mentor in your life?

College and Career Portfolio

Before beginning to collect information for your portfolio, it is helpful to know the components to include in your portfolio. It is also important to identify the clear purpose of your portfolio and write an objective for what you want to accomplish.

A. Create your checklist to use an ongoing reference as you create your portfolio throughout this class. Follow the guidelines on pages 50–51 of the text to formulate your list.

B. Decide on the purpose of your portfolio. Are you creating a portfolio for temporary or short-term employment, a career, and/or college application?

C. Conduct research on the Internet to locate articles about writing objectives. Also, look for articles that contain sample objectives for creating a portfolio.

D. Write an objective for creating your portfolio to use in applying for a job or to a college. Include statements for both a print portfolio and an e-portfolio.

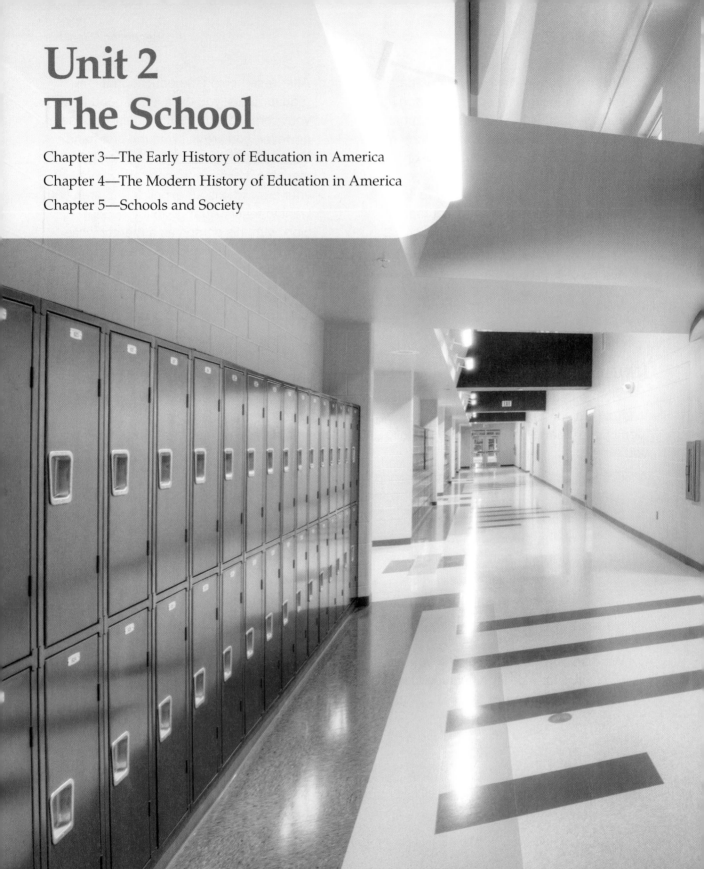

Unit 2
The School

Event Prep
Public Speaking

Public speaking is a competitive event or part of a competitive event you might enter with your Career and Technical Student Organization (CTSO). This allows you to showcase your organizational skills along with verbal and nonverbal communication skills in making an oral presentation. Public speaking is generally a timed event. You will have time to research, prepare, and practice before attending the competition.

To prepare for a public-speaking event, complete the following activities.

1. Read the rules and guidelines your organization provides. Note the topics from which you may choose to make a speech.

2. Locate the rubric or scoring sheet for this event on your organization's website.

3. Confirm whether you can use props or visuals as part of your presentation. Determine how much setup time the guidelines permit.

4. Analyze the rules to confirm whether the judges will ask questions of you or whether you will need to defend a case or situation as part of your speech.

5. Make notes on index cards about important points to remember and use them to study. You may be able to use your notes during the presentation depending on the guidelines for your event.

6. Practice your presentation! Be sure to introduce yourself and the topic of your presentation, defend your position on the topic with supporting evidence, and conclude with a summary.

7. Ask your instructor to serve as competition judge when you practice your speech. In addition, you might also have a student audience listen and give feedback.

8. Keep practicing until you are comfortable and can give your speech without flaw.

Chapter 3
The Early History of Education in America

Content Terms

apprentice
dame schools
hornbook
common schools
normal schools
McGuffey's Readers
Montessori Method
career and technical education

Academic Terms

Oregon Trail
Industrial Revolution
Progressives
disposable income
quotas

Objectives

After studying this chapter, you will be able to

- **identify** examples of how education during the American Colonial Period reflected local culture and beliefs.

- **summarize** changes in the preparation, roles, and status of teachers over time.

- **infer** how educational opportunities changed from colonial times forward.

- **analyze** how key people in early education reform responded to concerns of the time.

- **summarize** how education developed in your community.

Reading Prep

Arrange a study session to read the chapter with a classmate. After reading each section independently, stop and tell each other what you think the main points are in the section. Continue with each section until you finish the chapter.

At the Companion Website you can

- **Practice** terms with e-flash cards and interactive games
- **Assess** what you learn by completing self-assessment quizzes
- **Expand** knowledge with interactive activities

www.g-wlearning.com/teaching/

Study on the go

Use a mobile device to practice terms and review with self-assessment quizzes.

www.m.g-wlearning.com/0094/

Case Study

As a class, read the case study and discuss the questions that follow. After reading the chapter, revisit the discussion questions. Have your answers changed? If so, explain how.

Ben's class is visiting an assisted-living home for elderly residents as a part of his high school history class. He and his classmates are supposed to engage the residents in conversation as a way of practicing oral-history data collection.

Ben shares his interest in pursuing a career in teaching with one of the residents, William, who is in his 90s. William was a teacher, school principal, and also served as a district superintendent during his working years. Cognitively, William is functioning well and the conversation between he and Ben is lively and rich. Stories about his memories of being a student, his own students, colleagues, and community expectations abound. Ben gleaned a wealth of information and looked forward to continuing his relationship with William in the future.

Let's Discuss

- Predict what might William have shared about the influences on the state of education in his youth.
- What might William have shared about the influences on the state of education during his early career?

Have you ever wondered how schools came to be the way they are today? Who decided which subjects should be taught? Where did textbooks originate? Has school attendance always been required? In the next two chapters, you will learn more about the history of schools in America. That history is divided into periods characterized by historical events and social trends that significantly affected education.

The early history of education in America formed the foundation for things to come. From the influx of the first immigrants to the Great Depression, a system of free public education by qualified teachers developed. Education had to adapt to a significantly changing world.

Looking back is more than an interesting exercise in history. The development of American schools from their earliest roots helps explain much about today's schools. As you read, think about how people in your own community were educated through time. In every period, society, history, and government shaped the availability and quality of education. The education students receive also impacts society, events of the time, and government institutions.

The American Colonial Period (1600–1776)

European migration to what would later become the United States began in the seventeenth century. In education, the time period between about 1600 and 1776 is known as the *American Colonial Period* of education.

What motivated Europeans to come to a new land? Their reasons varied. Some were seeking economic opportunity. Many were looking for greater religious freedom. The motivation for others was the idea that they could produce a better society. Some were simply adventurers.

Educational opportunities here were as varied as the motives for immigrating. They reflected the beliefs and circumstances of the immigrants. While some similarities existed, options for education also differed by location, since there was no overall educational system.

At first, most education took place in the home. Those parents, who were able, taught their children basic reading and arithmetic skills. Daily life and work provided many additional opportunities for the practical learning needed for adulthood. Even after schools began to be established, they were available mainly in well-populated areas.

The schools that did exist were primarily for elementary grades. A few universities and colleges, including Harvard University and the College of William & Mary, were founded during this period. Very few students, however, had the opportunity to attend them. Most older children worked on their family farms or businesses. Others, including some girls, learned a trade in an *apprenticeship*. An **apprentice** is someone who learns a skilled trade by watching and helping an expert in that trade. In early America, some apprentices worked without pay for an agreed period in exchange for their learning (Figure 3.1).

Figure 3.1   Working as an apprentice in a blacksmith shop was a way to learn a skilled trade in early America.

Most colonists in the New England colonies (Massachusetts, Connecticut, New Hampshire, and Rhode Island) came from England. The majority of them were Puritans. This religious group believed in the importance of religious education and valued each person's ability to read the Bible. They viewed schools as a way to reach those goals and also to teach basic skills for farming. Education was a way to safeguard their beliefs and way of life. As early as 1642, Massachusetts enacted a law requiring every town to establish a school, although towns did not always follow this law.

In the middle colonies (New York, New Jersey, Pennsylvania, and Delaware), people came from a number of different backgrounds. Many emigrated from Ireland, Scotland, Holland, and Germany, as well as England. Because their backgrounds were more diverse, there was no one common school system. Instead, cultural groups developed their own schools. The Quakers, a religious group from England that settled around Philadelphia, believed that everyone should be educated and were tolerant of others' religious beliefs. They established the first school there that welcomed all, regardless of religion or race. Quaker schools were open to girls, African Americans, and Native Americans.

Social and economic class divisions were more rigid in the southern colonies (Virginia, Maryland, North Carolina, South Carolina, and Georgia), and education was not considered a function of government. Sons of wealthy plantation owners received a formal education that prepared them for college in the colonies or Europe. Plantations were geographically separated; so many boys were educated at home by tutors. The middle class was much smaller in the southern colonies than in other areas. Middle-class and poor children, especially girls, had fewer opportunities for formal education. Enslaved people (slaves) were only taught skills that were useful to their owners.

Dame schools also existed in the colonies. Students were taught by women in their own homes. Parents paid a fee for their children to attend. Such schools were open to both boys and girls.

The Role of Teachers

Throughout the colonies, teachers ranked just below religious leaders in importance. Both groups of men were better educated than the general population. Both were expected to teach and to act as examples of moral behavior.

Serving as a role model brought with it many expectations. Teachers could not drink, smoke, date, or marry. Regular church attendance was required, along with participation in civic events. Teachers were expected to be industrious and honest. A teacher routinely cleaned the school and often visited the sick or performed other charitable acts to set a good example.

School Curriculum

In most schools, teaching focused on basic reading, writing, simple math, and religion. Some students were educated beyond elementary school, although few formal schools existed. In the middle and New England colonies, training was available for trades, such as shoemaking. Sons of wealthy parents often learned Latin, Greek, and more advanced math. Those in the South also studied astronomy for navigation and plantation management skills.

In addition to basic skills, girls learned sewing and other home management skills. Girls from wealthy households sometimes had the opportunity to study literature and learn poetry, in addition to their basic subjects.

Books were rare and expensive. Schools used hornbooks for instruction. A **hornbook** was a flat wooden board with a handle. A sheet of paper—usually containing the alphabet, a prayer or two, and Roman numerals—was pasted on the board (Figure 3.2). Since paper was scarce, a thin, flat piece of clear animal horn was attached to cover and protect the paper. Hornbooks were used widely throughout the colonies until the 1800s when books became less expensive.

Figure 3.2 Since paper was scarce, hornbooks were used throughout the colonies.

The American Early National Period (1776–1840)

The second period of education began with the American Revolution. People of the time believed they could make a better society and were eager to try out new ideas.

During the *American Early National Period*, America was still primarily a rural nation. Most children grew up on farms or in small towns and expected their adult lives to be much like those of their parents.

Change occurred more quickly in cities. Their populations were more diverse, and people freely shared and discussed new ideas. Educational changes began in cities, eventually spreading to rural areas.

During this time, educators came to believe that people could improve their lives and society through the use of reason. People able to think critically would be able to find rational solutions for problems. Schools were seen as a vehicle for making a better society.

As America continued to grow and prosper as an independent nation, the ideas and traditions of Europe had less of an influence. Education was the way to promote the new nation's ideals of freedom and liberty. Religion played less of a role in education. Instead, growing communities focused on teaching skills to help students enter fields such as agriculture, business, and shipping.

Benjamin Franklin and Thomas Jefferson were two influential political leaders of the time. They also helped to shape the development of schools during this period.

Benjamin Franklin

Benjamin Franklin was one of the most important early leaders in the colonies, urging independence from England (Figure 3.3A). He signed the Declaration of Independence and the Constitution. In addition to serving as a politician, he was well respected as a scientist, writer, and inventor.

Curious about everything, Franklin experimented with all sorts of scientific concepts, from electricity to the common cold. He believed that understanding science helped people understand people and societies. He read every book he could find. Wanting others to have this opportunity, Franklin began the first public library.

Benjamin Franklin also worked to expand educational opportunities. He started a secondary school, or academy, in Philadelphia that offered a broad range of subjects, including practical ones. The school was open to anyone who could pay the tuition and attend, regardless of their religious beliefs.

Because of Benjamin Franklin's influence, schools to this day teach good citizenship. Public schools are available to everyone and teach a wide variety of subjects. Although Franklin himself was primarily self-educated, he had a lasting impact on how the American education system developed.

A   **B**

Figure 3.3   Benjamin Franklin (A) and Thomas Jefferson (B) were important leaders during the American Early National Period. What did each provide to American education?

Thomas Jefferson

Many consider Thomas Jefferson, the third president of the United States, one of the most brilliant individuals in history (Figure 3.3B).

He was a politician, an architect, a philosopher, an inventor, a farmer, and a writer. His interests were limitless, and his accomplishments were vast.

Jefferson also played a major role in establishing the current American educational system. He believed that education was the key to making the newly formed democracy a success. If common people were well educated, they could take part in democratic government, and it would thrive. Others countered his views. Alexander Hamilton, for example, believed only those who were wealthy and educated were suited to rule.

Jefferson introduced legislation to divide counties in Virginia into smaller districts that were responsible for education—a public system of education. He wanted to make sure that elementary schools were available without cost. While he was only partially successful, in the next century, his dream became the way America's public schools were organized. Another of Jefferson's major educational achievements was the establishment of the University of Virginia.

The Role of Teachers

During the American Early National Period, teachers continued to be positive models of good citizenship for their students. They were expected to be involved, making the community a better place through both church participation and effecting change in community issues. Teachers taught that citizenship involved obeying laws and rules and respecting authority.

School Curriculum

Schools continued to teach the basics of reading, writing, and math, along with Christian principles and citizenship (Figure 3.4). Students learned Greek, Roman, and English history, and now American history, as well. Educational opportunities, however, remained limited, especially in less populated areas.

Professional Tip

Dressing like a Professional

As you have the opportunity to go into a classroom, whether to shadow a teacher or tutor, be sure to dress professionally. Does professional dress mean wearing a suit? No, professional dress means dressing appropriately and communicating a sense of cleanliness, good grooming, and awareness of self and culture. Professional attire does not draw attention to yourself, but gives you confidence to perform the job well.

For teachers, their job is to teach. Appropriate and modest dress and appearance can foster respect. Inappropriate dress and appearance can distract both the wearer and those around them. It makes a difference in how others perceive you. You have heard of making a good impression through dress and appearance. Professionals seek to make a good impression every day. Teachers should arrive at work looking the part.

Dig Deeper

Use reliable print and Internet career resources to investigate professional attire for teaching. How do these resources support the author's views on professional attire? Do you agree or disagree? How do you think teachers should dress? Should there be dress and grooming guidelines? Why or why not? Cite sources to support your opinion.

Figure 3.4   In a typical classroom from the American Early National Period, slates and chalk were often used instead of paper.

Wealthy boys went on to study Greek, Latin, and English grammar plus advanced math, geography, literature, and science in preparation for university entrance. If girls received additional education, it was often through a tutor at home or in schools designed specifically for girls. Education, at that time, was mainly limited to those of European ancestry.

The American Common School Period (1840–1880)

The *American Common School Period* in education extended from 1840 to 1880. These years marked events that significantly altered the American way of life. In the 1840s, the **Oregon Trail** was opened—the only practical route for people to emigrate from Independence, Missouri to the western United States, primarily Oregon and California. After discovery of gold in California, the expansive west gave many people new hopes and dreams of finding their fortune and starting a new life. Labor-saving devices, including sewing and washing machines, gave people more time for other interests and pursuits.

Throughout the 1850s, the country moved closer to the internal split of the Civil War. Some Americans realized the injustice of slavery and worked actively to end it. In the South, slavery was a great economic influence. In the 1860s, the Civil War claimed many lives in both the North and South. Ultimately, the freeing of slaves and the triumph of the Union cause altered American life.

At the beginning of the American Common School Period, most American children received minimal schooling, if they received any at all. By the end of the period, education—including free public education for many—was much more widely available. One reason for the improvement in educational opportunity and quality was the influence of Horace Mann.

Horace Mann

Horace Mann served as the first secretary of the State Board of Education in Massachusetts. In this role, he made an impact on education nationally, as well as in his state.

Mann worked hard to establish free, public education for every boy and girl in Massachusetts. He believed that everyone had the right to an education. The first public state-supported schools were called **common schools**, giving the same education to people from different levels of society.

Horace Mann tried to improve and standardize schools. One key innovation was the establishment of teacher-training schools called **normal schools**. (The term "normal school" reflected the hope that through teacher training, all schools would become *normalized*, or similar, to each other to improve quality.)

Mann advanced education in other ways, as well. He successfully advocated the establishment of free libraries. He increased state funding for public schools by using state taxes to pay for education. This provided money to raise teachers' salaries and improve educational materials and equipment (Figure 3.5).

Because taxpayer dollars were the source of school funding, Mann believed schools should be nonsectarian. They should not teach any specific belief system. His reasoning was that people should not be required to pay (through taxes) for education that might teach religious principles contrary to their own religious beliefs. Since the country was overwhelmingly Christian at the time, however, morality based on general Christian principles was still taught.

Other states copied Horace Mann's efforts. Many of his ideas are still part of today's educational system.

Figure 3.5   Early American school buildings were often one-room schoolhouses.

African-American Education

In the years before the Civil War, very few enslaved African-Americans were able to read and write. Most who learned did so in secret. Laws existed in many places in the South prohibiting the education of African-Americans. Whites feared that education would lead to rebellion.

Former slaves in northern states faced tremendous obstacles to education, both social and economic. Not many African-American schools existed, and Quaker schools were among the few other schools that allowed African-American students to attend. In addition, African-Americans, as a group, usually struggled with very low wages. Children often found work as soon as they were old enough to do so.

After the Civil War, there was a real effort by many to improve educational opportunities. Educated African-Americans set up schools. Some northern churches sent missionaries to the South to start schools. It was then that the first African-American colleges were founded, including Howard University and Spellman College for women. At the same time, there was real debate among African-Americans about what type of education was best.

Many of these efforts were short-lived. All were hampered by the fact that most schools remained strictly segregated. African-American schools lacked the funds to provide a truly equal education for those who attended.

The Role of Teachers

At the beginning of the American Common School Period, the country was still primarily rural. Most children were educated at home or in small country schoolhouses where one teacher taught all grades (Figure 3.6). Teachers in these schools were paid by community members. Often, their salaries were quite low. It was not that education was not valued, but running schools was expensive, and people had little money to spare.

Because of Horace Mann's impact on education, teachers trained in normal schools were better prepared to teach. To gain entrance to a normal school, applicants had to take a test to show they had been properly educated. As a result, people had higher expectations of teachers' knowledge and teaching abilities. More women enrolled in normal schools and entered the teaching profession. This provided an opportunity for them to make a living on their own.

Figure 3.6 In Early American schools, classrooms looked much like this and had few resources.

School Curriculum

The American Common School Period brought more change in *how* subjects were taught than in which subjects were taught. Significant changes included the establishment of kindergartens in public schools, the use of McGuffey's readers, and the passing of the Morrill Act of 1852.

Kindergarten

Friedrich Froebel, a German educator, developed the idea for kindergarten. He believed that young children learned best through play. Although his ideas were not widely adopted in Germany, American educators were interested in the concept.

The intention of the first kindergarten classes established in America was to help poor children succeed in school. Using Froebel's ideas, songs and games were used in schools. His creative and social approach to learning worked well with young children. Educators and parents noticed the success of his methods. In the 1870s, public schools began to offer kindergarten programs. Prior to this time, young children did not attend school until they were about seven years of age.

Today, play and social interaction are still the foundation for educational programs for young children. Preschoolers and kindergarteners have opportunities to choose their own activities, express their creativity, and interact with one another. This helps expand and reinforce their learning.

The McGuffey's Readers

Textbooks became much more widely available during the American Common School Period. Reverend William Holmes McGuffey was asked to write a textbook series on reading for primary students. This was the beginning of the **McGuffey's Readers**, a series of books widely used in schools across the country (Figure 3.7). The books taught moral lessons along with reading, spelling, and other subjects. A reading story, for example, might show the importance of being honest or kind. Subsequent McGuffey's Readers taught other subjects, such as history, biology, botany, literature, and speech, along with lessons on proper behavior. Because they were used in so many schools, the McGuffey's Readers contributed to the standardization of American education.

Figure 3.7   As one of the best known readers of the nineteenth century and into the twentieth century, the McGuffey's Readers helped transform and standardize education in America.

The Morrill Act

In 1862, the Morrill Act, also known as the Land-Grant College Act, gave federal land to establish colleges in every state. These colleges were to provide practical education in agriculture, home economics, and other useful professions to people from all social classes. Land-grant colleges made higher education available to Americans nationwide. Many well-known universities of today began as land-grant colleges. A second Morrill Act in 1890 expanded the system.

The American Progressive Period (1880–1921)

The American Progressive Period in education bridged the nineteenth and twentieth centuries. The United States had been divided by, but survived, the Civil War. Women were gaining more rights. European immigrants poured into the nation's cities. At the same time, the Industrial Revolution continued to change the nature of both work and society. The **Industrial Revolution** was a period of complex economic, technological, and social change in America and worldwide. It was marked by a transition from home-produced goods and use of hand tools to innovative, technological advances in manufacturing processes involving power-driven machines.

The Progressive Era was a time of business expansion and reform in the United States. Members of this reform movement called themselves **Progressives**. They wanted to regulate big business that often took advantage of both workers and consumers. Corrupt government officials were another target. Progressives wanted to make America a better and safer place to live, and education had a key role to play (Figure 3.8).

Figure 3.8   This is a typical school building built in 1897.

Between 1880 and 1920, half of the rural population in America abandoned farming and moved to towns and cities to find work. In addition, over 15 million new immigrants came to the country, most from Ireland, Italy, and Eastern Europe. They, too, settled primarily in cities. The Industrial Revolution held the promise of work for many. Urban areas, however, quickly became overcrowded. Many of the new city dwellers lacked education, practical skills, and financial resources. Few social, charitable, educational, or government services were available to help these people meet basic needs. Poverty and disease became widespread.

Those who did find work in factories found their lives profoundly changed during that time. Work hours were long. Working conditions were often hazardous. Many children worked alongside their parents, limiting their educational opportunities. Urban schools quickly became overcrowded, and conditions in the schools were poor.

Progressives expected to make the world a more democratic place. They fought for better pay for women. They passed laws reducing the number of hours children could work in factories. By 1920, all states had laws requiring children to attend elementary school. Many policies and institutions from the Progressive Era remain central to American life today.

Segregated Education

Schools during the American Progressive Period were still highly segregated. African-American children attended separate public schools that received less funding. Educational materials were scarce and inferior, often the castoffs from the "white" schools. African-American teachers could only teach in African-American schools, and they received significantly lower pay than their counterparts.

The Role of Teachers

During the American Progressive Period, teachers were considered professionals. Teacher preparation programs in colleges replaced normal schools. More emphasis was placed on educational theories. Teachers were well trained and qualified to both run a classroom and teach a variety of subjects.

Many teachers grew unhappy with the emphasis on standardization. They wanted more freedom in the classroom. As a result, the first teachers' labor union formed to protect the working rights of teachers. The union fought to improve the pay, status, and working conditions of teachers.

During the Progressive Period, women entered the workforce in greater numbers. Many became teachers, and a few rose to positions as school principals. By the end of the Progressive Period, women had achieved the right to vote. Many believe that this change was a direct result of women's presence in classrooms.

School Curriculum

Progressives believed that schools should focus on students more as individuals. Many felt that the curriculum was too standardized. They felt that students should be encouraged to think critically and independently, rather than simply memorize information and accept facts. These changes were significant for education. Progressives believed that citizens trained to think and question would work to clean up corrupt city governments, improve working conditions in factories, and create better living conditions for those who lived in poverty. Schools could set students on this path. For example, a science class might focus on the need for water sanitation.

One notable change during this era was the opening of thousands of public high schools. In 1880, there were only about 800 such schools. This movement allowed students to continue their education and prepare for a career, even if they were not attending college. A high school diploma became more important in finding a job.

John Dewey

John Dewey, an educational philosopher, psychologist, and writer, was a leading voice for progressive education during this time. His influence on what was taught and how it was taught was not to be underestimated.

Dewey believed that classrooms were too rigid and inflexible, and did not adapt to the needs, interests, and abilities of individual students. Like Progressives in general, he believed that schools should place a greater emphasis on the development of problem-solving and critical-thinking skills. He saw these skills as a means of improvement of society.

Dewey promoted the link between learning and experience. He believed that students learned best through real-life activities that linked new information to previous experiences. He also believed social interaction—working together on projects and discussing topics—aided learning. Other educators, influenced by his work, began focusing on the role of the teacher as guiding learning, rather than simply providing information. You can see evidence of John Dewey's theories in today's educational system.

Maria Montessori

Maria Montessori, Italy's first female doctor, tried to find ways to help children who had difficulty learning. The students with whom she worked had medical conditions that may have kept them from learning. The teaching program she developed had a significant impact on young children during the American Progressive Period. Her program remains well-recognized and accepted today (Figure 3.9).

Montessori believed that young children are capable of great discovery and have motivation to explore the world. She believed that sensory experiences should come before learning to read and write. The educational program Maria Montessori developed is known today as the **Montessori Method**.

Figure 3.9   This contemporary Montessori kindergarten classroom carries out the educational philosophy of Maria Montessori.

How is it different? The Montessori Method considers all of a child's needs, not just intellectual needs. Montessori classrooms are stimulating environments. There are many opportunities for large- and fine-motor development and sensory exploration, along with language, science, art, geography, and math. Children direct their own learning with teachers as their partners. Teachers encourage children to judge their own progress and choose their own interests.

Career and Technical Education

The Smith-Hughes Act of 1917 established federal funds to support vocational education (now called *career and technical education*). **Career and technical education** prepared (and still prepares) students for the many career opportunities in specific trades and occupations where skilled workers were needed. The funding provided greatly influenced the spread of the career and technical classes in public high schools.

The 1920s and the Great Depression Era (1921–1940)

Following World War I, many Americans turned away from concerns about political reform. America was the most industrialized country in the world, and economic prosperity and growth were strong. The influence of the Progressive movement in education, however, continued throughout this period.

The economic prosperity of the 1920s increased the size of the middle class. More people had *disposable income*, money to spend on things they wanted, not just needed. Americans became consumers, rather than producers, of their own consumable goods. The introduction of the automobile became the stimulus for industrial growth in the nation. Consumer credit issues surfaced for the first time as credit became more widely available, so consumer education became a need.

There were concerns about the rate of immigration. *Quotas* (government limits) were set on the number of immigrants allowed in the country.

Many economists believed the economic prosperity would continue. Few had concerns when, on October 14, 1929, the New York Stock Market crashed. That day, known as Black Thursday, caused an economic panic that put the country into the Great Depression.

Impact of Economy on Schools

In good economic times, schools expand both in number and what they offer. This was true during the 1920s. In hard economic times, schools had to respond to lost revenue. During the Great Depression of the 1930s, the situation for schools was bleak (Figure 3.10). Public schools faced a shortage of cash, since many citizens were unable to pay their taxes. Some school districts ceased to operate while others shortened the school year. Decreases in or elimination of teacher pay was common, and course offerings cut back to basic subjects.

For families finding it difficult to keep their children fed and dressed, there often was not enough money for books and school supplies necessary to attend school. Many were simply unable to attend. Children who could work often did so to supplement the family income.

The federal government stepped in to help. Funds helped support some schools to hire teachers and purchase supplies. With federal money, schools began offering free hot lunches for children. As part of the program to employ others, better schools were built in some communities.

Figure 3.10   This is a Great Depression-era classroom. How does it compare to the classrooms of today?

By the end of the 1930s, the Great Depression was starting to ease. Families were trying to get back on their feet. Social institutions, including schools, were also working to recover from a decade of hardship. Americans were focusing inward. Rumblings in Europe, however, would eventually lead to the beginning of yet another world war.

"Dick and Jane" Readers

In spite of the Great Depression, in the early 1930s, a new set of reading textbooks for beginning readers began publication. Often known as the "Dick and Jane" books, these books taught basic reading skills with simple stories about a family (Figure 3.11). From the 1930s to the 1960s, over 85 million students used these textbooks. As with the McGuffey's readers before them, their widespread use helped standardize education.

Come down, Dick.
Come and see.
See the big, big mother.
See the funny little baby.
Puff is my baby.
Puff is my funny little baby.

36

37

I see the big mother.
I see the little baby.
Look, Jane.
See the big father.

Figure 3.11   The simple family stories about Dick and Jane were used to teach basic reading skills to millions of students in America.

Chapter 3 Review and Assess

Summary

- The type and availability of education varied much by region and local population during the American Colonial Period, with education primarily focused on the basics of reading, writing, and math, along with religion.

- In the American Early National Period, many believed that education could prepare citizens to participate in a democracy, make the economy grow, and society to succeed.

- Benjamin Franklin and Thomas Jefferson were significant contributors to educational innovations of the American National Period.

- During the American Common School Period, schools became more standardized, and the first formal teacher training programs were established.

- The American Progressive Period occurred about the turn of the twentieth century with a push for educational reforms to improve society. Immigrants and people from rural areas moved to cities to find work, overwhelming schools.

- Progressives believed that education was the place to start teaching citizens to create better living conditions.

- In the 1920s, after World War I, Americans enjoyed economic prosperity and educational reforms continued.

- Education, like other aspects of life, was pared back to basics during the Great Depression of the 1930s.

Review and Study

1. List at least four sources of education during the American Colonial Period.

2. Name three ways schools changed during the American Early National Period.

3. What did Thomas Jefferson believe about education and what role did he play in establishing the current American educational system?

4. Identify the subjects commonly taught during the American Early National Period.

5. Contrast common schools with normal schools.

6. Who developed the idea for kindergartens? What was the intended purpose of the first kindergartens in America?

7. Who were the Progressives, and what did they believe about the importance of education?

8. What beliefs did Progressives hold about school curriculum?

9. Name two of the educational changes advocated by John Dewey.

10. List four key features of the Montessori Method.

11. What was the purpose of career and technical education?

12. How did the Great Depression impact schools? How did the federal government help?

Vocabulary Activity

13. Read the text passages that contain each of the *Content* and *Academic* terms listed at the beginning of the chapter. Then write the definition of each term in your own words. Double-check your definitions by rereading the text and using the text glossary.

Critical Thinking

14. **Analyze roles.** Reread the content about the roles of teachers in America during the *Colonial Period*, the *Early National Period*, the *Common School Period*, and the *Progressive Period*. In small groups, analyze the roles of teachers across these periods. What are the similarities and differences? What trends in teacher roles do you see across these periods? Discuss your team's analyses with the class.

15. **Make inferences.** One-room schoolhouses with one teacher responsible for all grades developed in rural areas with limited populations. A few of these schools still exist. If you were teaching in such a school now, infer how technology could help you manage to teach students at so many different levels. Discuss your inferences with the class.

16. **Analyze evidence.** Reread the text regarding the education of African Americans prior to the Civil War and throughout the *American Common School* and *Progressive Periods*. Analyze how educational opportunities for African Americans changed during these periods of American history. Write a summary of your findings.

Core Skills

17. **Writing.** After reading the chapter, create an annotated time line—post Civil War to 1940—identifying significant events in public education in the United States. Save a copy of your time line for later research.

18. **Listening, speaking, and writing.** Arrange an oral history interview with someone who was in school before 1940. Ask details about the schools the person attended, what they learned, how teaching and learning compared to that of today, how information was presented, a typical day's schedule, and what life was like at that time. After the interview, write a summary using actual quotations where appropriate. Identify what you learned from the experience.

19. **Technology application.** Create a digital presentation that depicts the life and times of one of the historic periods described in this chapter. Include verbiage in bullet form that summarizes events contributing to changes in education. Locate images to support your descriptions, being sure to cite your sources.

20. **Research and writing.** Choose two of the following key people in the early history of education to research: Benjamin Franklin, Thomas Jefferson, Horace Mann, or John Dewey. Use the text and reliable resources to investigate historical, societal, cultural, and political factors surrounding these individuals that influenced their thinking about education. Write a brief report to share on the class website or blog.

21. **Research and speaking.** The Morrill Act is linked to the establishment of land-grant colleges and universities. Use the Internet to research more information about the original purpose of these schools. Identify a land-grant school in your state and find out whether it still carries out any of its historical purposes. What is the current relationship between land-grant colleges and universities and the Cooperative State Research, Education, and Extension Service (CSREES)? What services does CSREES provide? Give an oral report of your findings to the class.

22. **CTE College and career readiness practice.** Use your reading and interpreting skills to understand more about Maria Montessori and the Montessori Method still in existence today. Interpret what factors influenced Montessori's philosophy for schools and how children learn. What teaching/learning methods are foundational to the Montessori Method? What are the teacher preparation requirements? Report your findings and interpretations to the class in an organized oral report.

College and Career Portfolio

As you collect items for your portfolio, you will need a method to keep items clean, safe, and organized for later assembly. A large manila envelope works well to keep hard copies of documents, photos, awards, and other items. Three-ring binders with protective sleeves offer another way to store your items. A box large enough for full-size documents works well, too. Group similar items together and label the categories. For instance, store sample documents that illustrate your writing or computer skills together. Clip notes to the documents to identify each item and why you included it in your portfolio.

A. Select a method for storing hard copy items you will be collecting for your portfolio. (A later activity will address where to store electronic copies.)

B. Write a paragraph that describes your organizational plan for storing and label items. Refer to your plan each time you add items to your portfolio.

Chapter 4
The Modern History of Education in America

Content Terms

Project Head Start
bilingual education
illiterate
back-to-basics movement
educational standards
national standards
competency-based education
standardized tests
charter school
programs of study

Academic Terms

baby boom
Holocaust
Cold War
civil rights movement
global economy
accountability

Objectives

After studying this chapter, you will be able to

- **identify** links between key federal education legislation and perceived threats to national security or prosperity during the 1940s and 1950s.

- **summarize** the impact of the civil rights movement on American education, citing examples of ways this movement prompted improved educational opportunities for other groups.

- **evaluate** the impact of educational reforms of the 1970s and 1980s on teachers and students.

- **identify** how educational changes in the 1990s and 2000s continue to shape education today.

Reading Prep

After reading each section (separated by main headings), stop and write a three- to four-sentence summary of what you just read. Be sure to paraphrase and use your own words.

At the Companion Website you can

- **Practice** terms with e-flash cards and interactive games

- **Assess** what you learn by completing self-assessment quizzes

- **Expand** knowledge with interactive activities

www.g-wlearning.com/teaching/

Study on the go

Use a mobile device to practice terms and review with self-assessment quizzes.

www.m.g-wlearning.com/0094/

Case Study

As a class, read the case study and discuss the questions that follow. After reading the chapter, revisit the discussion questions. Have your answers changed? If so, explain how.

Britta just found out who her lead teacher would be for her student teaching placement. Mr. Lee had quite a reputation as a well-respected and loved teacher. The school principal referred to him as a "master teacher." When Britta met him, her first reaction was "but he is so old!" She expected her lead teacher to be much closer in age—especially when hearing how well-liked he was—and had hoped that the two of them would become friends.

Discouraged but hopeful, she decided to find out more about Mr. Lee's background. During their first meeting, she discovered that he went to college in the 1970s and began teaching in 1980. He reminisced about all the changes he had seen in education during his career—some good, some very challenging. Although eligible for retirement, he chose

to keep teaching because he loved seeing and helping a new generation of teens achieve their learning goals.

Let's Discuss

- What changes might Mr. Lee have shared about the influences on the state of education during his career?

- In what areas might Mr. Lee serve as a mentor to Britta?

- How might Mr. Lee and Britta create a strong teaching team together?

Why are math and science so important? Why do you take so many exams? When did schools start offering classes in languages other than English? Why did it take so long for schools to become desegregated? Who decides what should be taught in schools? In this chapter, you will learn the answers to these questions as you read about the history of schooling in America from the 1940s up to today.

In the previous chapter, you learned about American education from the settlement of the colonies through the Great Depression of the 1930s. These beginnings shaped the structure and the role of the educational system that exists in the United States today. This chapter provides an overview of education from 1940 to the present. What happened during these more recent decades has had a direct effect on the policies, procedures, and issues of education today.

During every era, historical events and changes in American life impact expectations of the educational system and the public's perception of it. New initiatives are tried, then revised and made in reaction to perceived problems. Presidential beliefs and priorities determine their degree of federal involvement in education. Some presidents have believed in the importance of shaping educational policies, while others believed this should be left up to the states. During some periods in history, international conflicts or major problems within the country may deflect attention away from educational concerns.

American Education During the 1940s and 1950s

The first half of the 1940s was dominated by World War II. Production of war-related material, from tanks to uniforms, helped pull the country out of the Great Depression. Thousands of young men left each month to fight the war overseas. This created job vacancies in factories, offices, and classrooms. These positions were filled by women and African-Americans. Both of these groups also had expanded roles in the military during the war. Never before had so many women worked outside of the home.

With the end of World War II (1945), the troops flooded back into civilian life (Figure 4.1). They looked forward to returning to normal life, but they, and society, had changed. Many war workers had to give up

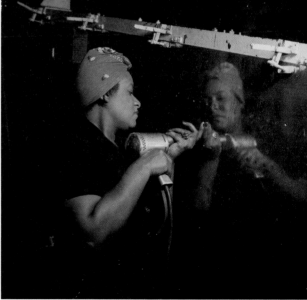

Figure 4.1   During World War II, women and African-Americans filled many workplace roles in factories, business, and education.

their jobs for veterans. Other soldiers took advantage of what was known as the *GI Bill*, federal legislation that included money for veterans to attend college or train to learn new skills. Young people married in record numbers. The result was a surge in the birth rate over the next years. This is often known as the **baby boom**.

After the war, neither African-Americans nor women were willing to again accept the lower status they held during the prewar years. They had proven their capabilities in the workplace and in the armed forces. Long-held ideas began to change. Photographs and stories of the **Holocaust**—the mass slaughter of European civilians, especially those of Jewish descent by the Nazis during World War II—made people more aware of the tragic effects of prejudice. These changes aided the subsequent *civil rights movement*.

The period after World War II was a time of new ideas and technology. As factories stopped producing products for the war effort, consumer goods finally became more available. There were new options in housing, home technology, fashion, and even food. Industries grew, jobs were available, and Americans were hopeful. It was also a time of social and political conservatism and a fear of the spread of communism.

Education was not immune to this era of change. The children of the baby boom began to enter the public school system. Their sheer numbers resulted in the need for more schools and teachers. In addition, world events and social change had significant impact on American education.

Keeping America Competitive

In the late 1940s after World War II, tensions and competition increased between the Soviet Union on one side and the United States and its allies in Western Europe on the other. While no actual fighting broke out, this came to be known as the **Cold War**. This standoff continued for decades.

Both America and the Soviet Union had programs to develop and test missiles. Americans were alarmed when the Soviets launched the first satellite, Sputnik, in 1957. There was a fear that the Soviets' emphasis on math and science in their schools was giving them a technological advantage that could later translate into a military advantage.

In 1958, Congress passed the *National Defense Education Act*. This made money available to improve scientific equipment for public and private schools and to provide college scholarships and student loans. It encouraged schools to strengthen their math, science, and foreign language instruction. Schools responded by requiring students to take additional math and science courses. Foreign language programs were improved. Homework requirements increased in an effort to spur learning.

Brown vs. the Board of Education

In the early 1950s, many schools in America were still racially segregated based on "separate but equal" policies. Yet, African-American schools still were not equal in funding. Educational materials were inferior and usually outdated. African-American teachers were only allowed to teach in African-American schools, and they received significantly lower pay. School buildings were often in disrepair.

In 1954, the Supreme Court agreed to hear the case of *Brown vs. the Board of Education of Topeka, Kansas*. The court ruled that racial segregation of schools violated the Constitution because segregated schools were, by nature, unequal. As a result, public

Figure 4.2   As a result of a Supreme Court ruling in the 1950s, public schools were ordered to desegregate.

schools were ordered to desegregate (Figure 4.2). Some districts did so. Others used delaying tactics.

Although school desegregation has gone through many phases since 1954, this initial Supreme Court ruling was critical to the civil rights movement. The **civil rights movement**—a social movement in the United States led primarily by African-Americans and their supporters—sought to gain equal rights regardless of race. The push to integrate schools was the most radical, and potentially influential, aspect of the movement.

Behaviorism

Chapter 3 described a variety of learning theories, including B. F. Skinner's behaviorism. Behaviorism is the belief that how a person behaves is determined by that person's experiences. Skinner's book *Science and Human Behavior* was published in 1953.

Figure 4.3   Education in the 1940s and 1950s focused on controlling the classroom environment and experiences.

Many educators embraced Skinner's theory during the 1950s. They believed that by controlling the classroom environment and experiences, they could produce educated, well-behaved students (Figure 4.3). Appropriate behavior and achievement were rewarded. For example, young students were often given gold star stickers when they performed well. Punishments were also common. This way of approaching learning was widely accepted, and influenced American education for decades.

American Education During the 1960s

The 1960s were a time of change. Those born during the baby boom were becoming teenagers and young adults. Many in this new generation questioned the conservatism of the 1950s and challenged the values, policies, and way of life of older adults.

The sixties were a decade of contrasts. They began with the optimism of newly elected President John F. Kennedy. Neil Armstrong walked on the moon in 1969. However, it was also the decade America became involved in the Vietnam War. John Kennedy, Dr. Martin Luther King, Jr., and Robert Kennedy were all assassinated.

The civil rights movement was especially active during this period. Its leaders favored peaceful methods, such as sit-ins and marches, to protest discrimination. In 1963, more than 200,000 people of all races marched in Washington, D.C. in support of civil rights. They heard Dr. Martin Luther King's famous "I Have a Dream" speech.

The civil rights movement spurred other groups to work for their own equality. These included women, Hispanic Americans, Native Americans, and people with disabilities. Like African-Americans, all had been discriminated against in various ways.

The 1960s were a time of educational innovation. Schools and teachers had the freedom to try creative ideas in an effort to improve education. On the national level, the most significant changes affected students who were disadvantaged economically or educationally.

The Civil Rights Act

Although the Supreme Court decision in 1954 called for an end to segregation, many schools, especially in the south, were slow to comply. Even a decade later, many African-American children were still being educated both separately and unequally.

The *Civil Rights Act of 1964* formally outlawed segregation in the United States public schools and public places. School districts were ordered to end segregation. They were called to "undo the harm" segregation had caused by racially balancing schools. Federal guidelines were issued. However, some school districts continued to stall, and problems remained.

The Elementary and Secondary Education Act

President Lyndon Johnson, who succeeded President Kennedy, pushed for wide-ranging reforms with his "War on Poverty" and "Great Society" programs. The *Elementary and Secondary Education Act of 1965* sought to improve the schools most in need. Federal education dollars were given to school districts based on the number of poor children enrolled. This was a major boost to struggling schools and helped equalize educational opportunities.

Project Head Start

Project Head Start, still in existence today, also began in 1965 during the Lyndon Johnson administration. Its purpose was to help preschool children from low-income families develop the skills they needed for success in kindergarten and beyond (Figure 4.4). Students who begin with a good start in school are less likely to experience academic problems later.

Some Head Start programs are coordinated with other social programs. They may, for example, provide all-day child care. These programs provide a positive, high-quality environment for preschool children. Today, the program is open to more families and serves hundreds of thousands of children each year.

Figure 4.4   This contemporary Head Start classroom is in existence today because of legislation passed in the 1960s to provide a high-quality educational environment for children affected by poverty.

American Education During the 1970s

During the 1970s, America had many foreign and domestic preoccupations. On the international front, after years of protests, the Vietnam War finally drew to a close. President Nixon visited the communist countries of the Soviet Union and China. At the end of the decade, United States citizens were killed and held as captives in the American Embassy in Iran.

At home, America was changing, and people faced many concerns. The divorce rate rose, and the number of single parents increased. Overall, there were significantly more women in the workforce in a broader range of jobs. An oil crisis sent prices soaring and created shortages. There was a push for conservation and finding alternative sources of energy.

Unemployment went up during the 1970s. So did prices as inflation hit home. People had less disposable income and were less willing to spend on education. Many schools suffered from inadequate funding.

Desegregation and Busing

The civil rights movement continued to push for equality. Desegregation at the school level had not solved unequal education. The problem stemmed partially from the tradition of neighborhood schools. By choice or lack of opportunity, neighborhoods tended to be divided by race. That meant that schools often had little racial diversity and those with primarily minority populations often had inferior facilities and lacked sufficient, up-to-date educational materials.

School districts were mandated to look at desegregation at the larger district level, rather than just school by school. This led the way to forced integration. School districts assigned students to schools in proportions that would achieve integration and bused them to those schools.

This plan certainly was not without controversy. Many families of all races objected to having children forced to take long bus rides to schools outside their neighborhoods (Figure 4.5).

Congress voiced the opinion that busing was not the issue, and that desegregation was not necessarily the answer to making schools equal. Injustices still existed, even in desegregated schools. The issue of inequality would continue for years.

Figure 4.5 Busing was a controversial plan aimed at achieving desegregation in public schools.

Bilingual Education

Amid the controversy over school busing, the Supreme Court ordered that a group of Spanish-speaking students be granted **bilingual education**. That is, classes would be taught in two languages, both English and Spanish. In 1971, the Supreme Court ordered the joining of two school districts in Texas, one that had primarily Spanish-speaking students and the other mostly English-speaking. The Court found that language was a barrier for equal education. All students were taught both Spanish and English.

In 1974, the Supreme Court acknowledged the problems students face when they have limited English skills. The Court ordered schools to provide basic English language classes for children who had limited English skills. This ruling was based on the difficulty Chinese students were facing in San Francisco.

Gender Equity

The Civil Rights Act affected education in many ways. It stimulated a variety of subsequent laws that provided equal opportunities for other groups. For example, in 1972, *Title IX* or the *Equal Opportunity in Education Act* was passed. It prohibited discrimination based on gender in all programs and activities receiving federal financial assistance. If a school, even a college, receives federal funds, every program and activity must be open to all, regardless of gender. One impact of this act was opening sports, even those formerly designated for boys only, to girls. The overall influence of the law, however, was much more far-reaching.

Tradition and discrimination had long limited the career options of women. This began to change in the 1960s and 1970s. Prior to that time, nursing and teaching were the two professions most available to women. It was unusual for women to enter professions dominated by males, such as law and medicine. Even when women held comparable positions, they were usually paid considerably less than men. Due to the combination of job options and pay discrepancies, in 1970, women earned 59 cents for every dollar earned by men. In 1978, more women than men enrolled in college for the first time.

Professional Tip

Showing Respect

Professionals treat their colleagues and supervisors with respect. Many new professionals make the mistake of not acknowledging their place in the workplace organization. Even the most casual and unstructured organizations have hierarchies. They may just be more difficult to identify. Be sure you fully understand an organization's hierarchical structure when employment begins. Whether it is another professional, a customer, or your boss, you will be the one who benefits by understanding the importance of *deference*, or showing respect. Even more importantly, show respect to your students. When you model respect to your students, gaining their respect will be much easier for you.

Dig Deeper

What is your definition of respect? Compare your definition of respect to the definitions of *respect* and *deference* in the dictionary. How does your definition compare? To whom do you show respect to in your daily life? In what ways do you practice showing respect? Write a short essay on the importance of showing respect to post to the class website or blog.

Children with Disabilities

In 1975, Congress passed the *Education for All Handicapped Children Act*. For the first time, it guaranteed a free public education for children with disabilities. Further, it mandated that the education provided for each child be appropriate and take place in the least restrictive environment. Parents were to be involved in decisions about their child's placement.

Previously, most children with disabilities had been segregated in special classrooms. With this legislation, children are able to spend part or all of their school day in regular classrooms (Figure 4.6).

Figure 4.6   In 1975, Congress passed legislation that guaranteed free public education for children with disabilities.

American Education During the 1980s

During the 1980s, there was less national emphasis on education. President Ronald Reagan believed the federal government's role in education should be reduced. His vice president, George H. W. Bush, who succeeded him, held similar views.

The 1980s were a time of growth and prosperity for some people, but the gap between rich and poor widened. Consumerism was at an all-time high. Buying on credit was a way of life for many. Those born during the baby boom had reached adulthood and many were raising families of their own. The families of baby boomers, on average, had fewer children. There were more single-parent families as the divorce rate rose. In addition, two-income families were more common than in previous decades as women gained more career opportunities.

The Back-to-Basics Movement

In 1983, a report called *A Nation at Risk* was published by a federal government agency. The report asserted that America's competitive edge was at risk. It said that the United States was falling behind other countries in business, science, and technology. There was concern that creative innovations in schools in the 1960s and 1970s had left many students lacking a good foundation of basic knowledge and skills in reading, writing, and math.

A number of indications of this gap were cited. American students fell behind students of other developed countries in math and science scores. College graduates were scoring lower on general knowledge tests than in prior years. The military reported that recruits had poorer reading and writing skills than the previous generation. Millions of Americans were **illiterate**, meaning they could not read or write.

There were calls for school reform. Many Americans believed that schools again needed to emphasize reading, writing, and math, leading to the **back-to-basics movement**. Critics of the movement believed that students needed more than basic reading, writing, and math skills to succeed in a complex world.

American Education During the 1990s and Beyond

The 1990s were about technology. The Internet changed the way people communicated, received information, shopped, and conducted business. It played a key role in education, as well.

The economy was booming and unemployment was at an all-time low. At the same time, the United States became involved in conflicts around the world, including in Bosnia and the first Gulf War.

The first decade of the twenty-first century brought new challenges to the United States. After the terrorist attacks in New York and Washington, D.C. on September 11, 2001, the United States went to war in Afghanistan and Iraq. At home, the economy seemed strong, with rising real estate values and high consumer spending, much of it on credit. In 2008, however, a financial crisis began that plunged the country into a period of financial uncertainty. Some financial institutions failed. Jobs were lost as spending slowed.

What was striking about this financial crisis was how quickly it spread around the world. It confirmed the existence and impact of the *global economy*. Finance, international corporations, and trade link the economies of nations around the world—particularly those of major countries. For example, computer links made it possible to move many of a business' functions to any country with an educated, but less expensive, workforce.

The Computer Revolution

With computers such an integral part of education today, it is hard to believe that they played a minor role in learning until the development of smaller versions (very large by today's standards) in the 1980s. It was not until the mid-1990s that most classrooms were equipped with a single computer.

Figure 4.7 Computers, digital tablets, and other forms of digital media are essential learning tools in classrooms of today.

As more educational programs were developed and the price of computers declined, they became more available. It was the development of the Internet and search engines that turned computers into the powerful and essential learning tools of today. The ability to use computers skillfully soon became a key career skill. Today education, as well as information, is readily available via computer and other digital media (Figure 4.7). This makes learning available at a time and place convenient to the student.

Educational Standards and Accountability

State governments and local school districts largely control the public educational system. Consequently, there has always been much variation in what is taught at various grade levels, in different courses, and in individual schools. Uniformity was promoted by state curriculum guidelines and textbooks used in schools across the nation. Beginning in the 1980s, the call for more demanding and uniform educational standards grew louder. *Standards* are agreed-on levels of quality or achievement. **Educational standards** refer to guidelines defining what students at various levels should know and be able to do.

In 1991, Congress established the National Council on Education Standards and Testing (NCEST). This group began asking questions. What should be studied? How should learning be measured? What standards of performance should be set?

In addition, teacher associations for various subject areas (such as history, physics, math, and others) voluntarily began to develop standards for what should be taught in school. They answered the questions about what should be studied and how it should be measured. They also set standards for performance in their subject areas. These are commonly referred to as **national standards**.

Teaching toward standards is often called **competency-based education**. That is, schools teach toward students demonstrating mastery and achievement of specified knowledge and skills in subject areas. Many people who support standards believe that they provide an objective way of evaluating student learning. Many who object to standards believe that real learning and creativity is lost and the only gain is memorization of facts.

In 1999, President Clinton made it clear that the role of the federal government was to establish guidelines for achieving excellence in education. Individual states would establish specific standards and objectives, testing to evaluate whether standards were met, and ways to measure whether schools met the standards. Although this seemed like a reasonable plan, it soon became complicated by politics.

Setting standards naturally led to the question of how to measure whether or not students had met the standards that had been set. There was a move toward educational **accountability**—measurable proof that schools and teachers were providing high-quality education. Beginning in the 1990s, many states began using standardized tests to measure success.

Standardized tests are designed to give a measure of students' performance compared with that of a very large number of other students. For example, they may measure reading comprehension skills of third-grade students across the country.

Standardized tests serve a variety of purposes in addition to measuring student achievement. They are useful to compare different groups of students or schools. They can help educators make decisions about which teaching programs are working and which are not. They can report on an individual student's progress.

Goals 2000

During the 1990s, most Americans were feeling the impact of the back-to-basics movement. After wide distribution of the report, President George H.W. Bush and the nation's governors set six educational goals to reach by the year 2000. These goals, along with two additional goals added by Congress, gained wide approval and Congressional support in the *Goals 2000 Act of 1994* (Figure 4.8). Implementation of these goals, however, was up to the states and local school districts. Translating the goals into specific plans took time, and there was little opportunity to remedy complex problems within the last years of the twentieth century.

Figure 4.8	National Education Goals

By approving the *GOALS 2000: Educate America Act*, Congress reaffirmed the six National Education Goals agreed to by the nation's governors under the leadership of Governor Clinton and then-President George H.W. Bush in 1990. In the Act, which passed with strong bipartisan support in 1994, Congress also added two goals—one on teacher learning and one on parent partnerships. Every major parent, education, and business group endorsed the National Education Goals and GOALS 2000 across the country. The goals stated the following:

By the year 2000
- All children in America will start school ready to learn.
- The high school graduation rate will increase to at least 90 percent.
- All students will leave grades 4, 8, and 12 having demonstrated competency over challenging subject matter including English, mathematics, science, foreign languages, civics and government, economics, the arts, history, and geography, and every school in America will ensure that all students learn to use their minds well, so they may be prepared for responsible citizenship, further learning, and productive employment in our Nation's modern economy.
- Students from the United States will be first in the world in mathematics and science achievement.
- Every adult American will be literate and will possess the knowledge and skills necessary to compete in a global economy and exercise the rights and responsibilities of citizenship.
- Every school in the United States will be free of drugs, violence, and the unauthorized presence of firearms and alcohol and will offer a disciplined environment conducive to learning.
- The Nation's teaching force will have access to programs for the continued improvement of their professional skills and the opportunity to acquire the knowledge and skills needed to instruct and prepare all American students for the next century.
- Every school will promote partnerships that will increase parental involvement and participation in promoting the social, emotional, and academic growth of children

Figure 4.8 The *Goals 2000 Act of 1994* tried to remedy complex problems in education.

No Child Left Behind Act

In January 2001, just three days after taking office, President George W. Bush announced his plan for educational reform. The *No Child Left Behind Act* was passed later that year. The goal of this act was to improve the performance of schools in the United States. Important components of this act included increased accountability, more choices for parents when choosing schools for their children, and an increased focus on reading.

The underlying premise of the act was the belief that high expectations and goals would result in success for all students. One of the most controversial features was the expectation that every child should meet state standards in reading, math, and science. One method of measuring achievement was the use of standardized tests at specific grade levels. Standardized tests and other measures of evaluation were encouraged. The receipt of federal educational funds was tied to school performance. Schools demonstrating success in meeting high standards would receive more money. Parents would have the opportunity to move their children from low-achieving schools to higher-achieving schools.

While few argued with the need for higher achievement, many expressed concerns about the provisions of the *No Child Left Behind Act*. Some pointed out that the characteristics of students and funding levels varied widely among schools. Those schools starting with a higher percentage of students already behind grade level would have difficulty meeting the goals, especially if their funding was poor. There were complaints that teachers were encouraged to spend much of their time specifically preparing students for the standardized tests at the expense of other content information and educational experiences.

One impact of the *No Child Left Behind Act* was an increase in the variety of school options. In some states, more charter schools were established. A **charter school** is a public school that operates with freedom from many of the regulations that apply to traditional public schools. Charter schools often use innovative teaching practices. Each has a charter that establishes the school's mission, goals, students served, programs, methods of evaluating programs, and ways to measure success. Parents must specifically choose to send their children to charter schools.

Not all states have approved charter schools. Proponents believe parents need choices and competition among schools will improve public education. Opponents worry about schools becoming competitive in nature, and leaving some students behind. Others worry that experimental methods will not work or that long-established, traditional public schools will see reductions in funding.

Competing in the Global Economy

Schools play a crucial role in preparing future workers with the necessary skills to compete in a global economy. In the United States, even before the financial crisis, many jobs formerly performed by American workers had shifted abroad. Part of the reason was that wages and benefits in the United States were higher than those of other nations. The availability of many highly educated workers was also a major factor. In many countries around the globe, students and societies see education as their best hope for a better life.

With falling math and science scores and many students not completing high school, there has been real concern that the United States may lose its competitive edge. It may be one of the countries that fall behind economically. The most important factor in remaining competitive in a global market is having a skilled and well-educated workforce (Figure 4.9). This is the job of schools. As in earlier times, there has been debate about how education must change to meet these challenges.

Figure 4.9   Preparing workers to compete in the global economy is a current challenge faced by educators.

Career Clusters

Since a skilled workforce is a key to prosperity, one essential goal of education is to prepare students to succeed in the workplace. The United States government partnered with business and industry professionals, colleges, trade schools, and high schools to discuss how to help students prepare for successful careers. Based on predictions that today's students will change careers a number of times during their working life, the group developed a system of career clusters.

Career clusters are a framework of 16 general career areas or categories (Figure 4.10). Each career cluster has a range of *career pathways*—or subcategories of related career options. By developing the essential knowledge and skills identified through industry validation for a cluster, students can pursue a variety of career options within the cluster and its pathways. Educators can use career clusters and pathways to design and create curriculum. They also develop **programs of study**—rigorous sequences of career and technical and academic courses—to prepare students for successful transition from high school to postsecondary education/credentialing and employment.

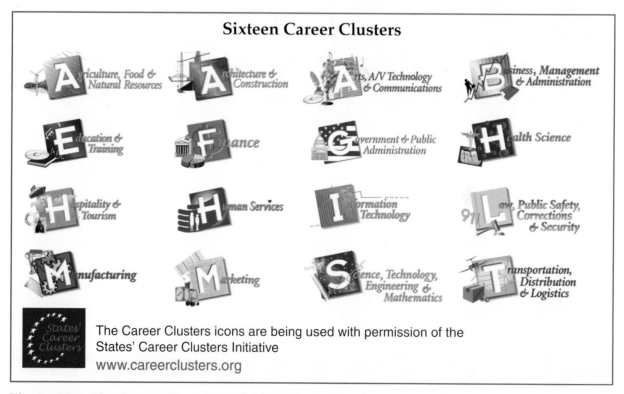

Sixteen Career Clusters

Agriculture, Food & Natural Resources

Architecture & Construction

Arts, A/V Technology & Communications

Business, Management & Administration

Education & Training

Finance

Government & Public Administration

Health Science

Hospitality & Tourism

Human Services

Information Technology

Law, Public Safety, Corrections & Security

Manufacturing

Marketing

Science, Technology, Engineering & Mathematics

Transportation, Distribution & Logistics

The Career Clusters icons are being used with permission of the States' Career Clusters Initiative
www.careerclusters.org

Figure 4.10   The Career Clusters model lists the 16 areas that include a variety of career options.

Chapter 4 Review and Assess

Summary

- During the 1940s and 1950s, World War II and the Cold War with the Soviet Union impacted education. African-Americans and women who assumed new jobs during the war wanted to retain their improved status.

- The Cold War prompted increased emphasis on American education, especially science, technology, and foreign languages.

- In the 1950s, Skinner's theory of behaviorism made punishments and rewards common tools in American schools.

- The 1960s brought demands for change. *The Civil Rights Act* became law. A war on poverty was declared and schools began focusing on meeting the special educational needs of children living in poverty.

- In the 1970s, educational issues focused on equity and the continuing desegregation of schools, bilingual education, and education for children with disabilities.

- In the 1980s, concern deepened over students' perceived lack of basic knowledge and skills fueled by a government report titled *A Nation at Risk*.

- In the 1990s and well into the 2000s, concerns about America's international competitiveness continued to affect education.

Review and Study

1. How did events of the World War II era spur the development of the civil rights movement?

2. What was the purpose the National Defense Education Act?

3. What was the result of the Supreme Court ruling in the case of *Brown vs. the Board of Education*?

4. What is the purpose of the Project Head Start program? List one possible reason that it is still in existence.

5. Explain the intended purpose of busing. Why was it unpopular with many families?

6. Summarize the *Education for All Handicapped Children Act*.

7. Explain what prompted the back-to-basics movement. What subjects were considered basic?

8. Contrast the use of computers in education from the 1980s to today.

9. What is the link between educational standards and accountability?

10. Name three important components of the *No Child Left Behind Act*.

11. What is a charter school?

12. What is a program of study?

Vocabulary Activity

13. With a partner, use the Internet to locate photos or graphics that depict the *Content* and *Academic* terms at the beginning of the chapter. Print the graphics or use presentation software to show your graphics to the class, describing how they depict the meaning of the terms.

Critical Thinking

14. **Analyze effects.** The text states that as the children of baby boomers began entering the public school system, the result was the need for more schools and teachers. In teams of two, use the text and additional resources to investigate and analyze the effects of this influx of students on the educational system. Share a brief report of your findings in class.

15. **Analyze reasoning.** The *Elementary and Secondary Education Act of 1965* gave more federal education funds to schools with higher enrollments of children from low-income families. The *No Child Left Behind Act* imposed penalties on under-performing schools, many of which had large low-income populations. Use the text and other resources to analyze the reasoning behind each approach's attempt to improve education for low-income students. Which method appears to be most effective? Discuss your answer, citing evidence to support your conclusions.

16. **Identify evidence.** Review the descriptions of major educational issues and changes since 1980. Which has had the greatest impact on your education? Cite specific text evidence to support reasons for your choice.

17. **Infer.** The civil rights movement continued to impact education, including bilingual education. Use the text and other reliable resources to make inferences about historical, societal, cultural, and political trends or issues that influenced bilingual education. How do these trends or issues continue to impact bilingual education today? Write an essay summarizing your inferences.

18. **Evaluate evidence.** Read the text passage on the *No Child Left Behind Act* in the text. Cite text evidence of benefits and controversies surrounding this act. Write a summary of your conclusions.

Core Skills

19. **Writing.** After reading the chapter, create an annotated time line—from the 1940s through the 2000s—identifying significant events in public education in the United States.

Combine it with the time line you started in Item 17 of Chapter 3. Save a copy for later research.

20. **Technology application.** Create a digital poster showing significant events in the civil rights movement's push for equal education. Use the text and other resources to identify events. Note reasons why it took so long to deal with this complex issue. Upload your digital poster to the class website or blog to share with the class.

21. **Reading and speaking.** Review the text and research other reliable resources on gender equity as related to the *Equal Opportunity in Education Act*. How did this act change not only education but other areas of society, too? How did it open doors for women in education and careers? Give an oral report of your conclusions to the class.

22. **Writing.** Identify one aspect of your education that relies on computers or other forms of digital media. How would it have differed before computers were widely available in schools? Write a paragraph summarizing your response.

23. **Research and speaking.** Use the Internet to research, access, and print an example of national or state standards for a particular subject area and level (such as health education, grades K–4). How are the standards organized? Are they written in language that is clear enough that teachers would know what to teach and how to evaluate learning? Do you think teachers are limited to teaching only what is in the standards? What questions do you have about this process? Discuss your responses with the class.

24. **Writing and speaking.** Often concerns about education focus on math and science knowledge and skills. Write an

essay making a case for the importance of at least three other types of knowledge and skills that you think are essential to career success in a global economy. In class, discuss what role courses preparing students for careers such as child care, building trades, and agriculture have in schools today and should have in the future.

25. Research how much and what type of impact a new president can have on education. Consider the status of existing laws, government policies, funding of programs, and new legislation. What roles do Congress and the Supreme Court play in educational policy?

27. **Technology Application.** Do a search for videos, apps, and computer games that are marketed toward early readers. Evaluate three items.

- How does technology change how children are educated?

- Is the presence of technology a distraction or an enhancement to a young learner? Why?

- Do these toys and games meet the educational needs of primary school children? Are they stimulating? Are they interactive? Do they promote a love of learning?

28. **CTE College and career readiness practice.** Attempts to change education have very real consequences for students' lives. Choose two educational reforms. Research the main implications of these reforms on the classroom experiences of students. Use your research to write fictitious accounts of the experiences of two students. In the first, show how one reform positively changed the life of a student. In the second, relate how the other reform negatively impacted the student's life.

College and Career Portfolio

Arrange to interview a teacher or administrator who has been in education for a number of years. The purpose of the interview is to understand someone's personal experience in dealing with changes in the field of education. Prepare questions prior to the interview to determine what shifts in education the person has seen, the effects of those changes on teachers and students, and any patterns of change the person has identified over time. Take accurate notes. If possible, and with the person's permission, record the interview. Write a summary of the interview, including what you learned and your personal thoughts about educational change. Add the document to your portfolio.

Chapter 5
Schools and Society

Content Terms

spending per pupil
school funding gap
achievement gap
corporate-education partnership
zero tolerance policy
expulsion

Academic Terms

at risk
mentor
intimidation
cyberbullying
conflict resolution

Objectives

After studying this chapter, you will be able to

- **analyze** the organization and control of education in your state.

- **summarize** how public schools are governed and funded.

- **identify** examples of how schools and communities interact and share resources.

- **summarize** societal problems that impact schools and learning, along with possible solutions.

Reading Prep

Read the chapter title and tell a classmate what you have experienced about the topic or already know about the topic. Write a paragraph describing what you would like to learn about the topic. After reading the chapter, share two things you have learned with a classmate.

At the Companion Website you can

- **Practice** terms with e-flash cards and interactive games
- **Assess** what you learn by completing self-assessment quizzes
- **Expand** knowledge with interactive activities

www.g-wlearning.com/teaching/

Study on the go

Use a mobile device to practice terms and review with self-assessment quizzes.

www.m.g-wlearning.com/0094/

Case Study

Read the case study and questions that follow. After reading the chapter, revisit the discussion questions. Have your answers changed? If so, explain how.

Melissa was tired of hearing about it and tired of witnessing it among her peers. Bullying had become epidemic in her rural community and although it had been dealt with within the school walls, it was subversive off school grounds. Even more so, bullying in social media through unkind, threatening, or aggressive postings was rampant. Melissa had heard this termed *cyberbullying* in national news reports. It was not as if her peers did not know it was wrong. School officials had held emotionally impactful school assemblies and had enacted a "no tolerance" policy on school grounds. But it seemed to Melissa that bullying behavior had only escalated outside the school walls.

Let's Discuss

- Should schools monitor after-school activities? Why or why not?
- If so, how can school officials be involved in reducing cyberbullying?
- Should bullying education be focused on bullies, those who are bullied, or both? Why?
- How might Melissa approach school and/or district officials with her concerns?
- How might Melissa personally deal with this social issue among her peers?

Schools are tools a society uses to help its children acquire the knowledge, skills, and values they need to carry society forward. As such, schools both reflect a society and shape it.

Around the world, countries understand the power, influence, and importance of education. Many countries put great emphasis on improving educational opportunities as a way to boost the economies of their nations and the lives of their citizens. In other countries, leaders have used educational policies for their own motives. Some have tightly controlled education, restricting what could be taught. By regulating access to information, they sought to limit dissent. In other countries, education—or quality education—is available only to those who can afford to pay for it.

How does the United States compare to other countries? Its educational system is not based on a national system, which has real advantages and disadvantages. However, less uniformity also results in variations related to quality and opportunity. American schools rank well compared with other nations in some regards, and not so well in others. This fuels the push to do better (Figure 5.1).

As in schools everywhere, American schools and learners are influenced by problems the country as a whole faces. In order to help students learn as effectively as possible, they must find ways to deal with such problems. Caring and creative teachers help to do this every day.

Who Is Responsible for Schools?

In the United States, millions of students are enrolled in public schools. Who is in charge of their education? Control of public education actually falls under three levels of government: individual state governments, local communities, and the federal government. Each plays a different role. The scope and degree of their control varies.

In the United States, powers that are not assigned by the Constitution fall under the jurisdiction of individual states. The Constitution does not specifically address education. Consequently, states have primary control of public education.

Figure 5.1   The power, influence, and importance of education are recognized by countries around the world.

This chapter focuses on education from kindergarten through high school, often abbreviated as K–12. All states also have public colleges and universities. These, however, are controlled and funded separately from the K–12 system.

State Governments' Role

Each state has its own method of organizing and controlling K–12 education. However, there are some similarities. Although their names and titles may differ, almost all states have the same following key people:

- *The legislature*. The state legislature passes laws and makes major decisions related to education. The state government also decides how much it will spend each year for education and identifies the source of those funds.

- *The state board of education*. The job of the state board of education is to provide leadership in educational policymaking. It promotes state education standards and advocates for equality of access to schools. Most importantly, the state board of education advocates for continued citizen support and public funds. Members of the state board of education may be appointed or elected.

- *The superintendent of public instruction (or commissioner of education)*. In most states, one person, usually an elected official, acts as the link between the state legislature and the state board of education. This person serves as a spokesperson for the state legislature and communicates expectations to the state board to execute.

- *The state department of education*. This agency is responsible for the operation of schools within a state. It performs many essential functions. For example, it is the state department of education that certifies teachers. It allocates money to school districts and checks that they follow state and federal regulations.

Local School Districts' Role

Early in the nation's history, local school districts were formed to organize and run local schools. Today, states are still divided into school districts. These districts have direct responsibility for providing education for the students within their boundaries.

As with state government, there is organizational structure at the local level, dividing responsibilities for schools in the district. The most common structures follow.

The School Board

This group of elected people sets policies and makes decisions about how schools within the district should be run (Figure 5.2). Some school boards oversee education from kindergarten through high school. Other boards may oversee a specific level of education, such as the high schools in a district.

The school board works with the school administration to set the vision for the school district. It controls or approves school curriculum (the courses taught), funding, and other policies that affect local schools. The board determines the budget and issues financial reports. It negotiates contracts with employee unions and oversees hiring practices and decisions.

School boards hold regular meetings that are open to the public. The agendas for these meetings must be publicly posted in advance. School board meetings generally include an opportunity for citizens to express opinions. In many communities, board meetings are broadcast on television.

The District Superintendent

For each school district, a district superintendent acts as the connection between the school board and the individual schools. The district superintendent acts much like the president of a company. The superintendent answers to the school district board much as a company president answers to the board of directors. The superintendent makes sure that schools carry out the school board's policies.

Figure 5.2   Members of school boards are elected to make decisions about how schools in their districts function.

School Administrators

Individual schools utilize administrators to oversee daily operations. In each school, a principal acts as the top executive with the help of assistant principals in larger schools. Other key personnel, such as deans and department heads, have specific responsibilities and provide administrative assistance to the principal.

School principals set the tone for their schools. They are responsible for carrying out day-to-day activities. They oversee a budget for the money allocated by the school district board for their school and provide leadership for curriculum development and educational updates.

School principals hire (with school board approval) and supervise teachers. They advise, support, and provide professional growth opportunities to foster teaching excellence. They visit classrooms to make sure that educational goals are being met (Figure 5.3).

School principals also spend time with parents, students, and community representatives. They act as the spokesperson for the school. They also deal with difficult issues, such as those related to discipline and personnel.

Figure 5.3   As part of their responsibilities, principals supervise and evaluate teachers, providing support and encouragement for excellence in teaching.

The Federal Government's Role

Although the states play the primary role, the quality of the nation's schools is also a concern of the federal government. The federal government has a compelling interest in making sure that its citizens receive a good education and become productive members of society.

Over the years, Congress has passed federal legislation to assist states in providing quality education for all students. As you learned in the previous chapter, sometimes legislation focuses on a particular group, such as students from low-income families or those with disabilities. Other times, legislation is passed in response to perceived problems, such as the United States falling behind in math and science education.

These programs generally come with federal funds if the states and local school districts follow the specified legislative guidelines. States must comply in order to receive these supplementary funds. Many school districts express concern that they do not receive sufficient reimbursement for many programs mandated by the federal government.

The United States Department of Education originated in 1867 with the job of collecting information on education. Today, the head of the department, the secretary of education, sits on the president's cabinet. The agency's mission is to ensure quality education for all children. It establishes priorities, focuses national attention on these priorities, and collects data to see how schools are achieving them. It evaluates what educational programs work most effectively. The agency also acts as a watchdog to prevent discrimination in schools.

Professional Tip

Rules and Expectations

School rules may not be the most fun topic of conversation on the first day of school, but there is a reason why teachers and school administrators present these rules and expectations. It is really all about *safety*. It is about helping everyone develop the same understanding about safety in the school. It is a matter of reducing conflict, stress, and fear when unexpected or undesirable happenings occur. Thus, it is important for all students, parents, staff, and community members to follow procedures and the protocols expected at their school.

Whether they include expectations for personal behavior or emergency procedures, true education professionals embrace the corporate school identity and values. They model them for their students.

Dig Deeper

Take a moment to review the rules, expectations, and guidelines for behavior at your school. Which ones most impact personal safety? How?

Private Schools and Homeschooling

Not all K–12 education takes place in public schools. Throughout the country, private schools educate about six million students. In addition, countless more students participate in homeschooling.

Private schools are quite varied. Many are associated with a specific religion. Students learn about religion and moral behavior along with reading, math, and other academic subjects. Many religious private schools are open to students of other faiths. Other private schools do not have a religious foundation. Examples may be one that offers an advanced course of study, more individualized attention, or have a specialized purpose, such as a military school or one for students with *autism spectrum disorder*.

Private schools do not receive public funding. Instead they depend on tuition and private support, such as donations and grants. A few private schools operate as for-profit companies.

Private schools are also free from many laws that govern public schools. They set their own policies. For example, they are not required to hire certified teachers, although most do. They are not required to accept every student.

In recent decades, more parents are choosing to homeschool their children. That means they are responsible for determining what their children will study, preparing and teaching lessons, and evaluating or assessing learning. Quality homeschooling takes a major commitment of time and effort. Some parents rely on textbooks and published materials, while others develop their own materials. At times, some use Internet courses, especially for more advanced subjects. State laws regarding homeschooling vary, but many have little oversight.

Funding for Education

In the United States, every child has the right to a free public education in grades K–12. Of course, the process of education is actually quite expensive. School districts must pay salaries, purchase books and materials, and build and maintain buildings. State governments, local school districts, and the federal government all contribute toward the cost of education. Sometimes private funds are also available. The proportion varies somewhat, but the pie graph in Figure 5.4 shows the average split of educational funding.

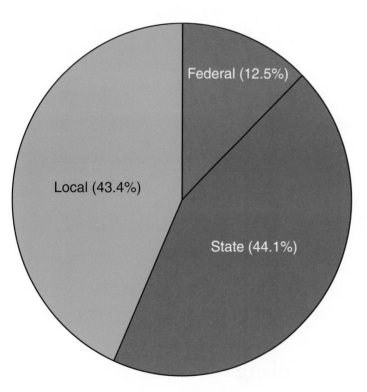

Federal (12.5%)

Local (43.4%)

State (44.1%)

Source: U.S. Department of Education

Figure 5.4 Funding for education is often allocated as indicated here.

State Funding

Each state determines how to fund its own educational system. Most states use taxes—generally sales taxes and income taxes—for the state portion of educational costs. The state pays the largest share of education expenses, with local funding a close second. Educational spending varies from state to state.

Local Funding

Local dollars also make up a substantial portion of educational funding. Local funding comes from the community, usually from a portion of local property (real estate) taxes. Some districts have a higher educational tax rate than others, even in neighboring districts. These differences are often due to building projects, such as the need for new schools, or special programs a district offers.

The use of property taxes to fund schools is often controversial. When property values increase rapidly, property taxes can rise sharply. For many people, such as retirees on fixed budgets, escalating taxes can cause real hardship. In addition, the use of property taxes means everyone, even those without children attending school, pay taxes for education. In contrast, those who rent or lease housing do not directly pay property taxes. Districts with large businesses or industries within their borders may collect large amounts of property taxes from those, often giving homeowners lower taxes for education. These and other issues have led some districts to look for other sources of income, such as sales taxes.

Federal Funding

Because of the federal government's interest in making sure its citizens are well educated, it contributes money to states for use in education. This is termed *national* or *federal funding*. Designation for these funds is usually for specific special programs. Common examples include Project Head Start, providing school lunches for low-income students, and remedial reading programs. Federal funding, however, provides less than 10 percent of the total money needed to operate schools.

The federal government has been involved in providing supplementary financial support for education for many years. The *Elementary and Secondary Education Act of 1965* made federal money available to schools with low-income students to help equalize educational opportunities. The *Carl Perkins Vocational and Technical Education Act of 1984* helped fund career and technical education, while the *No Child Left Behind Act of 2001* used federal money to help schools close the gap in student achievement among schools.

Figure 5.5 Federal funds for education are often linked to specific education legislation.

In addition to linking funds to major education legislation, the federal government often includes further funding to support education in its annual budget (Figure 5.5). The intention of these funds, however, is never to cover basic educational costs, which are the responsibility of states and communities.

Private Funding

Some private funding is available for education. For instance, some private charitable foundations award grants to schools for special projects or to help solve problems related to the goals of the foundations. In addition, individuals and groups help schools. For example, a civic group might raise funds to buy safety equipment or new band uniforms.

The Problem of Unequal School Funding

With the enormous costs involved in education and varying characteristics of students and schools, it is no surprise that school funding raises many issues. One of the most controversial is the gap in school funding among school districts. The amount of spending per pupil for education varies greatly from district to district. This is true not only when states are compared to one another, but also between school districts within the state. **Spending per pupil** refers to the average amount of money a school district spends to educate one student for one year. This figure is often used to compare school funding.

While the quality of a child's educational experience depends on various factors, schools that have more money can provide more teachers, materials, services, and opportunities. In one recent year, the spending per K–12 pupil in one state ranged from about $5,000 to over $18,000.

What causes these differences? One major factor is the use of local property taxes as the primary source of local funding for schools. School districts with lower property values have difficulty generating income for schools. Districts that include higher-priced homes and businesses often have higher local funding.

Unfortunately, school districts with lower levels of income from property taxes tend to be in urban areas. The schools in these districts often have a higher proportion of students who are from low-income families and need a higher level of services. This challenge, often called the **school funding gap**, is not easy to solve. Some states and school districts are changing the way they allocate funds to schools. They take into account how many students in a school need extra educational services and provide some additional funding for these students. This method does not equalize spending, but it narrows the gap among schools somewhat. Many of these same schools also have lower test scores and higher dropout rates. This **achievement gap**, or the differences in learning and graduation rates among schools, often correlates to differences in school populations and funding. Opponents of plans to change funding argue that additional spending does not necessarily translate into improved academic achievement.

Communities and Schools

Schools have long been a focal point for communities (Figure 5.6). That remains true today. Citizens take pride in the accomplishments of students and schools, from spelling bee champions to winning sports teams. Even those people without children in school may attend school programs or run for a position on the local school board. Positive school-community relationships benefit both sides. When they are strained, both the schools and communities lose.

Figure 5.6   The reciprocal relationships between schools and their communities help meet the educational needs of students.

Parents and Schools

Parents are the community members most closely tied to schools. They want their children to receive the best possible education. Some even base decisions about where they live on the reputation of the schools in a particular area.

Effective schools usually have good relationships with parents. They encourage teachers to communicate with parents on an ongoing basis, not just when problems arise. They create opportunities for parental involvement. Parents can serve on committees, participate in parent-school associations, help with sports and activities, or volunteer in many other areas. When parents are involved with schools, they are more likely to be strong supporters of education.

Business and Industry Links

The businesses and industries in a school district also care about education. They need potential workers who have the knowledge, skills, and attitudes needed for successful employment. A capable local workforce is important to a community's economy. In addition, companies that recruit workers from outside the area are more likely to attract good people if the school system is highly regarded.

Businesses and industries can be important partners in developing and maintaining effective schools. Company leaders can help schools design or upgrade programs related to business and industry by identifying the types of skills workers need in the future. Sometimes a group of business professionals join together to raise money to pay for a specific school improvement project.

Occasionally, businesses, especially large corporations, enter into an expanded and more formal relationship with a school, or a **corporate-education partnership**. The business essentially "adopts" a school and may help it in a variety of ways. Sometimes the business plays a significant role in working with the school to improve facilities or educational opportunities or offer grants for worthy projects (Figure 5.7). Corporate employees may be allowed time to volunteer at the school, including during working hours. There are many ways such a partnership can work to benefit both schools and the community.

Figure 5.7   With corporate-education partnerships, businesses often make contributions to improve school facilities such as this playground.

Schools and Community Resources

Schools depend on community resources to help educate and serve their students. In turn, schools can share some of their resources with community residents.

Although schools have personnel and services to help students with some learning-related problems, other problems require different types of assistance. School counselors and administrators may refer students and their families to community social services for appropriate support.

Other community facilities and organizations also help support teaching and learning. For example, public libraries typically have more resource materials than school libraries. Museums and other community resources offer ways to expand learning beyond the classroom. Some schools benefit from links to area colleges or universities. These offer their expertise, while the schools may serve as student teaching sites for college students studying to become teachers. Other times, schools and colleges develop programs to offer more advanced courses for students still in high school. Career and technical programs at secondary and postsecondary levels often coordinate course curriculum at each level so that students can transition smoothly from one level to the next.

Many K–12 schools offer programs outside of the school day to benefit citizens. They may provide adult education classes, open their facilities for community groups and recreational activities, or offer before- or after-school care for students with working parents. Schools sometimes buy supplies from local businesses. This practice, along with teachers' salaries, helps pump school tax dollars back into the community. There are many ways schools and communities can support and strengthen one another.

Social Problems Affect Schools

Because schools reflect the communities where they are located, they are not immune to societal problems. These can impact students' learning to a significant degree.

Unfortunately, many problems are serious and difficult to solve. Schools must work to minimize them in order to maximize learning. Students caught up in these difficulties are much more likely to fail academically or to drop out. The negative effects of these problems may also directly impact the education of students who do not experience them. The situations and problems of their classmates take time away from learning. Schools that are most effective in minimizing the impact of social problems on learning find that it takes the efforts of everyone—administrators, teachers, students, parents, and the community—to truly make a difference.

This section highlights some of the most common of the serious problems affecting education today. As you learn more about them, think about how they have influenced your experiences as a student and those of others in your school. Also consider how you might best respond to them in a teaching situation.

Poverty

The majority of Americans living in poverty are children. Such children face a long list of challenges that can impact their learning. For example, they are more likely to have inadequate nutrition and suffer from hunger. Limited access to health care means they are sick more often or have untreated conditions, such as poor eyesight. The living conditions of these children may make it difficult to get adequate rest. They are less likely to have books or computers at home. Because of a lack of resources, children living in poverty are less likely to have had enriching life experiences, such as travel and museum visits.

Children from families living in poverty are among those labeled as *at risk*. What does this mean? Basically, students or groups who are **at risk** have characteristics or experiences that make them more likely to fail academically.

Children become aware of social and economic status differences at a very young age. Students who are poor often struggle with emotional security and self-esteem issues. School may not feel like a welcoming environment, and they may develop negative attitudes toward learning and school.

Older students living in poverty have similar disadvantages. Access to computers and other technology, however, also becomes more of a concern. Finding a time and place to do homework may be difficult for students living in poverty. High school students may feel responsible for providing additional income for their family members. Some may be the sole providers for their families.

Families who live in poverty often move from place to place. Some are homeless. Without a permanent address, children may not be eligible to register for school or may change schools often. When school changes occur often, children lose friendships and relationships with teachers. There may have no place to study or to sleep. Learning is difficult when feelings of embarrassment, worry, anger, or fear limit concentration.

What Can Schools Do?

Education provides the best opportunity to break the cycle of poverty. Today, a high school diploma is the minimum needed to find employment, and most jobs require more advanced education or training. Those who fail to finish school are unlikely to be able to provide adequately for themselves in the adult world.

Schools need to draw on diverse resources to help students living in poverty succeed in school. Some have made school the place where students and families can find the various types of help they need for stability. The school works with social-service agencies and refers families to the services they need. These may range from helping parents find job training or housing assistance to signing students up for free meals and providing them with clothing (Figure 5.8). In addition, schools closely monitor individual students' progress to help keep them on track. Tutoring is available for students who need it. Community members may act as *mentors* to students. A **mentor** is an adult expert who commits to a long-term relationship with a student to provide support, guidance, and help. Often, having a caring relationship with another adult helps students see their strengths and set goals for the future. Many schools also find that getting students involved in school activities helps keep students in school.

Figure 5.8   Providing nutritious meals at school helps meet children's physical needs, which can lead to success with learning and achievement.

Violence

As violence escalates in society, it becomes more prevalent in schools as well. It is not just actual incidents of violence, but also fear regarding safety, which hinder teaching and learning.

Violence is pervasive in the media. Students watch it on television, see it in movies, hear about it in songs, and participate in it when playing video games. It is not surprising that violence spills over into schools. Children learn by example, mimicking what they see and hear. All too often, students also experience some form of violence in their homes or neighborhoods. It may be verbal abuse, fights, or gang activity. There is special concern about the impact of violence and fear of violence on schools and learning. When a person lives in fear or is intimidated, it is difficult to concentrate on learning. Some students become withdrawn.

Others have increased school absences. For teachers, dealing with violence takes time away from teaching.

Violence exists in many forms. It ranges from name calling to *intimidation* (real or implied threats) to physical violence. Sometimes violence is random in nature. Other times, a specific individual or group is targeted. In all cases, far more people than the individuals involved are affected. Some of the most common areas of violence in schools include the following:

- **Bullying and intimidation**. Someone steals a child's lunch money on the way to school, while others keep another from sitting in a certain row on the school bus. Others still, spread false rumors about other students. Bullying and treating someone in an intimidating way are common problems in schools. Bullies usually direct their behavior toward weaker, younger, or less resourceful persons.

    Bullying and intimidation are usually physical or verbal in nature. **Cyberbullying**—or intimidation through e-mail, social networking sites, and texting—continues to be a growing problem (Figure 5.9).

- **Sexual and racial harassment**. Similar to bullying, one person or a group tries to intimidate someone. Sexual harassment can take many forms, including unwanted touching, comments, rumors, and pictures. The victim usually feels uncomfortable and unsafe. Sometimes such harassment leads to sexual abuse or rape. Similarly, racial harassment takes many forms, too, but the root of such harassment is a person's race, color, or ethnic background. It, too, can precede more violent attacks.

- **Physical violence**. For some students, physical fights are the only way they know how to resolve conflict or to release frustration and tension. They need to learn alternative methods of resolving conflicts. Incidents of violence against students and teachers are all too common in schools.

Figure 5.9   Teachers who observe bullying and cyberbulling, or are made aware of it by others, have a responsibility to intervene immediately.

Unfortunately, the presence of weapons in schools, as well as in society, makes it easy for disagreements to become even more violent. Some students who carry weapons say they do so for self-protection. For others, weapons are a symbol of power or status. Others carry weapons specifically to threaten or intimidate classmates or teachers.

Gang activity adds significantly to problems of violence. Although only a small percentage of students actually belong to gangs, violence and crime escalate significantly in areas where gang activity occurs.

What Can Schools Do?

Schools must develop programs that combine maximizing safety with working to change circumstances that make violence seem like a reasonable option. Parents and communities need to be involved in these efforts in order for them to be effective.

Most schools have established zero tolerance policies regarding violent behavior. A **zero tolerance policy** means that the prohibited behaviors and actions will not be tolerated—no exceptions. In zero tolerance policies, expulsion is usually the only acceptable result. **Expulsion** means that a student no longer has the right to attend school for a specified period of time.

In addition, schools may use other measures to minimize violence. For example, where weapons are an issue, schools may install metal detectors at building entrances. Other schools have eliminated permanent lockers and require students to carry see-through bags to transport their personal items. Dress codes are another way to combat the effects of gang activity. Security personnel and security cameras are common on many campuses.

School administrators and teachers must establish strict standards and expectations for nonviolent behavior. Such policies go beyond forbidding physical fights. Other policies include any form of intimidation.

Changing attitudes is the other key. This means creating an atmosphere where tolerance, acceptance, and fairness are valued. Students must learn nonviolent alternatives for dealing with anger and frustration. *Conflict-resolution* skills can help students learn how to state their needs, negotiate, and collaborate. Students must be encouraged to break their informal code of silence. When they stand up for their own safety, campus crime and violence decrease.

Many communities support school antiviolence policies by promoting public awareness campaigns. Partnerships with community agencies that enhance school resources and activities are also effective. By partnering with local law enforcement, fire and police departments can help schools deal with safety issues more efficiently. This includes education, response, mental health resources, and identification and monitoring of potential threats.

Figure 5.10 Combined efforts of peers, school, parents, and community members can help teens make healthful choices about sex as their bodies are changing and maturing.

Sexually Active Students

As their bodies change, young teens become more aware of their sexuality (Figure 5.10). They become sexually curious. Some teens become sexually active, often because they think "everyone" else is. (The actual number of teens who are sexually active is fewer than half.) Others, realizing the risks involved in sexual activity or because of personal values, decide to delay sexual relationships.

As with violence, media's coverage of sex seems astounding. The media is often at odds with parental, community, and even personal values.

Teens who are sexually active usually know the risks, including unplanned pregnancy, HIV-AIDS, and other sexually transmitted infections. Even so, American teens have one of the highest rates of sexually transmitted infections of any developed countries. Teen pregnancy rates have been rising. In spite of teens' beliefs, the chances of contracting a sexually transmitted infection or becoming pregnant can be quite high. Both can have devastating effects for a student's future.

Treatments are available for sexually transmitted infections (STIs), but not all STIs have cures. For instance, HIV-AIDS can result in early death. Pregnancy brings with it enormous long-term responsibilities for both the mother and father. Many teen parents drop out of school to care for their child. This involves physical and financial responsibilities. Teen parents can often experience a life of poverty. Those teen parents who stay in school are more likely to experience academic challenges because of their increased responsibilities. Even though the responsibilities of teen parents are many, those who finish their education are in a better position for success in life than those who do not.

What Can Schools Do?

Schools have taken several approaches to stem premature sexual activity and its effects. Some focus on helping younger students develop positive self-esteem and decision-making skills. Students learn how to resist peer pressure. Involving peers and older students as part of these efforts can increase their effectiveness.

Schools often involve parents and the community in efforts to reduce teen sex, infection, and pregnancy. Health and social service agencies can share their expertise. Some schools offer health services on campus.

Supporting pregnant and parenting teens is another way to keep students in school. Some schools help teens find social services, monitor their academic progress, offer parenting classes and child care options, and arrange for a mentor or counselor to provide ongoing support. Such efforts can pay off in terms of the career opportunities for the parents and the parenting skills they need to successfully raise a child of their own.

Alcohol and Other Drugs

Student use of alcohol and other drugs are real problems. Use of these substances can adversely affect learning. It can also have devastating personal consequences.

Alcohol is illegal for minors for a reason. Even in small amounts, it can impair judgment and create learning challenges. In larger amounts, it can cause blackouts. Longer-term heavy alcohol use can cause permanent changes to the brain that hinder learning and achievement. Students who drink alcohol often have difficulty learning, especially students who drink on a regular basis. A drinking-related car crash or sexual encounter can have life-altering results that can jeopardize a teen's whole future. There is a strong link between substance abuse and a rise in violence.

The use of illegal drugs or misuse of prescription or over-the-counter drugs can lead to similar consequences. Responding to a "just try it once" dare can quickly become an addiction. Research shows that adolescents are more likely to become addicted than older drug users. A family history of any type of addiction adds to the risk. Parental supervision and discussions between parents and students are among the most effective means of minimizing these problems.

What Can Schools Do?

Parental communication, management, and discipline can reduce the risk of substance abuse. Peers often play a part in encouraging substance abuse. However, they can also be among the best deterrents. Active groups, such as Students Against Destructive Decisions (SADD), help teens take ownership of the problem and work toward solutions.

How Can Teachers Make a Difference?

Teachers are in a unique position when it comes to helping students who find themselves facing significant problems. Because they interact with students on a daily basis, teachers are often the first to see signs of difficulty.

Figure 5.11 Teachers are in a unique position to provide support in a warm, caring, and safe environment for students facing problems and challenges that impact learning and achievement.

Addressing problems as quickly as possible improves students' chances of getting back on track. Problems often snowball the longer they go on, and learning losses accumulate if students are preoccupied with the difficulties of their lives. Personal or social and academic problems often go hand in hand.

How can teachers identify students in trouble? The symptoms can vary greatly. They include aggression, violence, irritability, and a decrease in interest in grades and school activities. Changes in behavior, such as irregular school attendance, social withdrawal, or depression can also be clues.

After identification of problems, teachers can provide warm and caring relationships with both students and their parents or guardians (Figure 5.11). Sometimes it is the home environment that makes it difficult for students to concentrate on school. Teachers can help students and families by linking them with school and community resources.

Other effective techniques for helping students cope with difficulty also benefit the whole class. These include the following:

- having high expectations for all students
- encouraging ambitious but realistic goals
- providing consistent class routines
- making learning meaningful and linked to the real world
- providing students with opportunities to help others
- communicating respect and caring
- showing a willingness to listen
- being even-tempered
- having conflict management and mediation skills
- conveying a sense of hope and optimism
- suggesting positive choices and alternatives

As students work through their difficulties, teachers can help them remain focused on learning. Creative teachers can find ways to incorporate important life skills and issues into any subject. With an education, students have choices. Without one, their options are even more limited.

Chapter 5 Review and Assess

Summary

- Schools are institutions that society uses to prepare the next generation and keep the society strong.

- In the United States, responsibility for schools officially belongs to *states* that often transfer some duties to *local* school districts. The federal government also plays a role, primarily through legislation.

- While states vary somewhat in how they handle education, it is generally the legislature that passes laws, determines policies, and funds education.

- At the state level, the board of education, superintendent, and department of education translate the legislature's guidelines into policies and procedures for schools.

- States pay for basic school funding through state taxes, with local taxes making up a major share of the cost.

- The federal government makes some money available for carrying out education programs and specific educational initiatives.

- Good relationships among schools and parents, business and industry, and the community, benefit everyone.

- Societal problems impact schools and often negatively affect student learning.

- Schools that partner with parents and their communities are more successful in minimizing the impact of societal problems.

- Teachers play a vital role in helping individual students overcome obstacles, gaining the education and skills needed for future success.

Review and Study

1. Why do states have primary responsibility for education?

2. Compare the roles of the state superintendent of public instruction and a district superintendent.

3. Indicate who is responsible for each of the following: (A) allocating money for individual schools; (B) certifying teachers; (C) recommending which teachers to hire; (D) determining how money will be spent within a school; (E) deciding how much money will be spent for education within a state.

4. Identify one drawback of relying on property taxes for the local portion of school funding.

5. What may cause differences in per pupil spending from one school district to another within a state?

6. Why do effective schools usually have good relationships with parents?

7. What does it mean when students are described as *at risk*? How can mentors help?

8. What are zero tolerance policies? Why are they used?

9. Why is parental involvement a key to reducing the risk of drug and alcohol use among students?

10. List five techniques teachers can use to help students cope with problems and challenges.

Vocabulary Activity

11. On a separate sheet of paper, list the content and academic vocabulary terms at the beginning of the chapter. Next to each term, write words that relate to each of the terms. With a partner, discuss how these words are related to the vocabulary terms.

Critical Thinking

12. **Analyze differences.** Sometimes those accused of bullying say that they are only teasing others. Analyze the differences between bullying and teasing. What might be the effects of each? How can bullying disrupt learning for the person who experiences bullying? Discuss your thoughts in class.

13. **Identify evidence.** Think about the issues surrounding school funding gaps and the *solution* of giving schools with students who require a higher level of services more funding. With a partner, create a T-chart. Label the left column "Valid Arguments for the Solution" and the right column "Valid Arguments against the Solution." Cite valid arguments *for* or *against* the solution in the appropriate column using the text and other reliable resources for evidence. Share your evidence with another pair and then the class.

14. **Make inferences.** Some experts believe that by strengthening students' self-esteem and decision-making and communication skills, the students can avoid many difficulties. Make inferences as to why these particular skills are identified as crucial. Do you agree with experts' assessment? Why or why not? Post your thoughts on the school-approved class website or discussion board.

Core Skills

15. **Research and writing.** Create an annotated graphic illustration showing the structure of the U.S. educational system for pre-K through grade 12 and beyond. Cite evidence from the text and other reliable resources noting the structure of local school districts, state governing bodies that influence education, and the influence of federal government. Use a school-approved digital application to create your illustration in a format you would use to teach this information to the class. Post your illustration to the class web page or blog to discuss your findings with classmates.

16. **Research, math, and writing.** Research how school funding and per pupil spending is determined in your school district or community. Review narrative, charts, tables, and graphs to determine formulas used to allocate funds for schools. Write a summary of your findings to share with the class.

17. **Speaking and writing.** Select one of the societal problems the chapter discusses or another problem that impacts your school. Investigate how the presence of the problem affects the learning of students who do not experience it directly. Interview administrators and teachers for their perspectives on the problem and solutions they think are viable. Write a summary of your findings.

18. **Speaking and listening.** Interview a teacher to discuss how he or she responds to students who are dealing with problems. Develop a set of questions to use for the interview. After the interview, discuss your findings in class. Compare and contrast the teacher's responses to the author's suggestions in the text.

19. **Technology application.** Conduct an online search of urban newspapers for articles that pertain to current issues in education. When conducting your search, be sure to select cities or urban areas that represent different states or geographic areas of the country. What are the concerns, issues, or trends? What issues are the same among geographic areas? How do they differ? Why might they differ? How might educational funding play a part in solutions for these issues? Use presentation software to create a digital report of your findings to share with the class.

20. **CTE College and career readiness practice.** Presume you are a middle school teacher in your local school district. Your interpersonal skills—your ability to listen, speak, and empathize—are great assets in working with students and helping them achieve academic success. You recently learned that one of your students, Lily, and her mother are living out of their car—and nutritious meals are few and far between. How can you use your interpersonal skills to help Lily and her mother meet their basic physical needs? How can you offer support and guidance to Lily to encourage her academic success?

College and Career Portfolio

You may create both a print portfolio and an e-portfolio for this class. You have already decided how to store hard copy items for your print portfolio. Now you need to create a plan for storing and organizing materials for your e-portfolio. Ask your instructor where to save your documents. This could be on the school's network or a flash drive of your own. Think about how to organize related files into categories. For instance, school transcripts and diplomas might be one category, while awards and certificates are in another. In addition, another category might be teaching resources or lesson plans. Next, consider how to name your files. The names for folders and files should be descriptive but not too long. This naming system is for your use. Later, you will decide how to present your electronic files for viewers. Do the following:

- Create a folder on the network drive or flash drive in which to save your files.
- Write a paragraph describing how you will name the subfolders and files in your e-portfolio.
- Create the subfolders with which to organize your files, using the naming system you developed.

Unit 3
The Learner

Event Prep
Community Service Project

Many Career and Technical Student Organizations (CTSOs) offer competitive events that include a community service project. An entire CTSO chapter typically carries out this type of project which often takes several months to a year to complete. There may be several parts to this type of event—written and oral. In addition, the event may also involve preparation of a display or portfolio. The CTSO chapter will designate several members to represent the team at the competitive event.

To prepare for a community service project, complete the following activities.

1. Read and analyze the event rules and guidelines the organization offers.

2. Select a theme for your chapter's community service project as a team.

3. Identify the target audience of the community service project. Your project may include businesses, schools, and community groups.

4. Decide on which roles the team needs. For instance, you may need a team captain, secretary, treasurer, and any other roles that are necessary to create and carry out the plan. Ask your instructor for guidance in assigning roles to team members.

5. Brainstorm with your chapter members. Use a decision-making planning process to develop a plan for your project. Create a project rationale, identifying the project goals and needs. What is the desired end result of this project? What are the benefits of supporting and completing the project? Identify tasks, budget if necessary, and ways to execute the plan.

6. This project will likely span the school year. During regular chapter meetings, have group members report on progress with the project. Create a draft report based on guidelines from your CTSO organization. Update and refine your group's written report, create necessary visuals or a portfolio until the project is complete. Include an analysis of the success of your project as part of the presentation.

7. Practice the presentation for the competitive event. Chapter members and the instructor can serve as judges during practice. Incorporate suggestions for refinement.

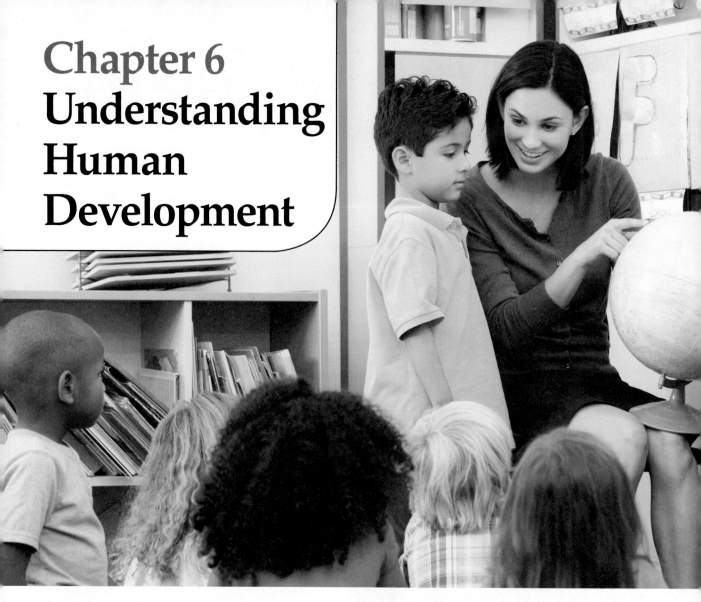

Chapter 6
Understanding Human Development

Content Terms

growth
development
physical development
gross-motor skills
fine-motor skills
cognition
cognitive development
social-emotional development
developmental theories
behaviorism
classical conditioning
operant conditioning
constructivism
experiential learning

Academic Terms

sequence
genetics
context
cognizant
Socratic learning
virtue

Objectives

After studying this chapter, you will be able to

- **distinguish** between growth and development.
- **identify** the main types of human development.
- **develop** examples that illustrate principles of development.
- **define** a developmental theory.
- **apply** developmental theories to real-life situations.
- **analyze** how developmental theories impact teaching.

Reading Prep

As you read the chapter, put sticky notes next to the section about which you have questions. Write your questions on the sticky notes. Discuss the questions with your classmates or teacher.

At the Companion Website you can

- **Practice** terms with e-flash cards and interactive games
- **Assess** what you learn by completing self-assessment quizzes
- **Expand** knowledge with interactive activities

Companion
G-W Learning

www.g-wlearning.com/teaching/

Study on the go

Use a mobile device to practice terms and review with self-assessment quizzes.

Mobile
G-W Learning

www.m.g-wlearning.com/0094/

Case Study

As a class, read the case study and discuss the questions that follow. After reading the chapter, revisit the discussion questions. Have your answers changed? If so, explain how.

It has been perplexing Lexi for the last few weeks. She has been observing a gifted or "pull out" class in the local elementary school this semester. The room is full of energy as the kids work on their robotics project that will be submitted to a district-wide competition at the end of the year. The classroom is unusually busy today as the kids are excited about their new ideas and findings, as well as preparing for the guest speaker who will be joining them today and for the field trip to a manufacturing plant tomorrow. These are definitely bright, academically gifted children! Lexi wonders how these kids became so excited about learning and tackling a high-level project such as this. As she got to know the kids, she learned that they come from very diverse family backgrounds. Lexi poses several questions to her friends. How would you respond?

Let's Discuss

- How can two children, with very different backgrounds, both be so cognitively gifted?

- Which matters most, nature or nurture?

- How does the classroom environment play a part?

- Which theories might best be applied to this situation?

A six-year-old is very different from a 13-year-old. Both are different from an infant or an adult. Why? Life is a process of growth and development. **Growth** refers to physical changes in size, such as gains in height and weight. Most growth occurs during the first 20 years of life. **Development** relates to growth. It is the gradual increase in skills and abilities that occurs over a lifetime. While each person progresses in an individual way, the stages of development are similar for almost everyone. Babies learn to walk, talk, and feed themselves. Children learn to jump, tell a joke, and spell. Human development occurs throughout the lifespan.

Areas of Development

There are four main types of development. These are physical, cognitive (or intellectual), social, and emotional. Social and emotional development are intertwined, and they are often referred to together as social-emotional development. During each stage of life, a person's physical, cognitive, and social-emotional development can be identified.

Physical Development

The rapid physical growth of the first years of life is matched by amazing strides in physical development. **Physical development** involves advances in physical abilities. A newborn cannot change position, but a two-year-old can run. Many individual developmental steps make this change possible. Random movements of the newborn's legs and arms add strength. The infant eventually becomes strong enough to roll over. Crawling follows. Next, the baby learns to stand upright and finally takes a few steps. It takes months of walking practice for steadiness and coordination to improve, and then running is possible.

Many other aspects of physical development are happening at the same time. These are often referred to as *motor skills*, since they depend on increasing strength and coordination of muscles. **Gross-motor skills**, such as walking and throwing, depend on development of the large muscles, including those in the arms, legs, back, and shoulders. **Fine-motor skills**, such as picking up objects and eating with a spoon, depend on development of the small muscles such as those in the hands and wrists (Figure 6.1). Beyond infancy, physical development continues, but the skills and abilities become more complex.

Figure 6.1   Physical development during the first years of life is dramatic. Self-feeding is a fine-motor skill that depends on the development of the small muscles of the fingers, hands, and wrists.

Cognitive Development

Humans are able to think. Thinking takes many forms. You *know* your locker combination. You *sense* what is happening around you. You *memorize* facts for a test and try to recall them when taking a test. You *organize* your thoughts to write a paragraph. These and other processes involving thought and knowledge are called **cognition**. The way people change and improve in their abilities to think and learn throughout life is **cognitive development**, or *intellectual development*.

Similar to physical skills, cognitive abilities increase gradually. Consider your math skills as a first grader, an eighth grader, and now. Your skills have improved dramatically over that time span. As a result, the way you receive instruction math has changed, too. Your current teachers assume you have mastered the most basic concepts. As time progresses, they present more difficult concepts and expect you to do more independently by reading your textbook and solving homework problems.

With increasing understanding of how the brain develops and works, scientists are providing new insights into cognitive development. The development of connections between nerve cells in the brain is a key component to cognitive development at all stages of life. Brain connections grow and strengthen with new experiences and repetition of familiar ones. For example for an infant, the faces of parents and other primary caregivers become familiar because the infant sees these people most often. After a few months, the sight of these people may be rewarded with a smile of recognition. Later, the names of those caregivers may be among the first words the child speaks.

Social-Emotional Development

Social-emotional development includes the areas of relationships and feelings. Individuals must learn social skills and how to care about others. They must develop both self-confidence and self-esteem. For example, learning self-control is an important skill for kindergarteners. Students learn to wait their turn, form a line, and listen while the teacher gives instructions.

At each stage of development, social and emotional challenges increase. Children must develop new skills to deal with increasing independence of childhood, such as the more complex social situations of adolescence, establishing an identity, adult relationships, parenting, careers, retirement, and the other challenges of life. How well individuals meet those challenges depends on the skills they develop early in life and how well they are able to adapt them to new situations (Figure 6.2).

Figure 6.2   As teens encounter new situations, they rely on social-emotional developmental skills to deal with complex life issues.

Principles of Human Development

It is the nature of human beings to try to figure things out. Observations about human development go back to the beginning of recorded history. The research continues, but the following include some of the basic principles that explain what is already known:

- Development is relatively orderly.
- Development is a gradual, continuous process.
- Development is interrelated.
- Development varies among individuals.

Development Is Relatively Orderly

Development occurs in a predictable and orderly manner—a *sequence* of steps that consistently follow one after another. Children learn sounds, then words. Eventually, they learn the letters of the alphabet and that these can be combined to represent words. Each of these steps must occur before children can read. Teachers use their knowledge of how development progresses to design effective learning strategies appropriate to the age of their students.

Development Is a Gradual, Continuous Process

Most developmental changes happen gradually and are apparent over time. A three-year-old may learn to ride a tricycle while a six-year-old masters the more difficult skills needed to ride a bike. A teen refines these skills and uses them, along with additional knowledge and judgment, to learn to drive a car. An adult driver typically has fewer accidents than a teen because years of practice and experience have improved his or her skills.

Development Is Interrelated

Most development is not solely physical, cognitive, social, or emotional. Acquiring new skills typically requires gains in several of these areas. Think about what it takes to become a skilled basketball player. You need physical stamina, coordination, and endless practice to be able to hurl the ball precisely into the hoop from any angle on the court. It also takes cognitive development to learn plays and to figure out those of your opponents. You must be able to judge the potential success of a shot. Socially, teamwork is required as is the ability to "read" the intent of the player you are guarding. You will note the body language and expressions of other players. Emotionally, you must have confidence, decisiveness, and perseverance. It takes all of these aspects of development, and more, to play well.

Figure 6.3 Development varies among individuals—even identical twins are unique in their development and life experiences.

Development Varies Among Individuals

Although development is orderly and predictable, each individual's progress is unique. That is because so many factors affect development. No two people—even twins raised together—have exactly the same experiences (Figure 6.3). Each individual faces life-changing experiences and responds to them based on his or her personality, knowledge, and prior experiences. Everyone grows and changes at a different rate and on a slightly different time schedule.

Theories of Development

You are waiting in the checkout line at the store when a small girl in front of you starts screaming. Your natural reaction is likely to try to figure out what caused the outburst. Is the child in pain, or is this a temper tantrum? Did her dad just tell her that she had to put back the candy bar she picked up? The screaming continues. You listen for the father's response. Will he handle the situation well? Your opinions about why the situation occurred and how well the parent responded are based on your current knowledge and past experiences.

Researchers also analyze behavior and development to better understand how and why it occurs. They may have more knowledge and experience and use more scientific methods, but the process is much like your own. They observe people, perform experiments, and consider earlier research studies. Then, they formulate their own explanations about why people act and behave the way they do and how they change over time. These are called **developmental theories**.

Why should you, as a future teacher, learn about developmental theories? While these are theories, not proven facts, they can be very useful. They can help you better understand what students are capable of doing and why. Instead of relying only on your own limited personal experiences and observations, understanding developmental theories will give you a broader picture. This knowledge can make you a better teacher.

Professional Tip

Respect and Dignity

Each child is an individual. Although each may present typical developmental milestones, "typical" can only be viewed in general terms, not independently. Good teachers know this. They take an interest in each and every child. They treat each child with respect and dignity. They do not make assumptions but develop a caring relationship, while maintaining professionalism. They understand that the better they know a student, the more influence they will have on them. Often this includes getting to know and offer professional support to the child's parent or caregiver. And it is not just about their students' present learning, knowing each student can impact his or her attitude toward life in general. Take the opportunity to observe a parent, caregiver, or teacher interact with a group of children. Then discuss the following.

Dig Deeper

- How is each child treated differently?
- Is the differential treatment most likely due to developmental stage, temperament, relationship, or a combination?
- Do you agree with the appropriateness of the differential treatment observed?

The developmental theories summarized in this chapter are just a brief overview of the many that exist. They are, however, the ones that have had a real influence on teachers and teaching. As you read about them, evaluate how their conclusions match your own life experiences, and think about their potential impact in the classroom.

Heredity Versus Environment

The most basic debate about influences on development is that of the relative importance of heredity versus environment. Consider two classmates sitting in class waiting for their turn to read aloud. Andre is shy and reserved. He is nervous about reading in front of the class. His classmate Bryson is bursting with energy and can hardly wait for his turn to read. When Bryson's turn comes, he speaks loudly and confidently, even when he stumbles over words. Were Andre and Bryson born that way? Was Andre taught to be shy by his shy parents, or is it a natural part of who he is? If Andre was born with a tendency to be shy, would he have been more outgoing if raised in Bryson's family rather than his own?

This question has been debated over and over again. Is it *nature* (heredity) or *nurture* (environment)? In other words, are a person's personality traits, abilities, skills, and tastes a result of **genetics** (what they were born with) or a result of their environment (a person's surroundings and the people in it)? Most researchers today will answer "both." It is not a matter of which, but how large a part, each plays. How much did heredity affect Andre's shyness or Bryson's outgoing personality? How much did the people around them have an effect on them? Did their own experiences affect each child?

The challenge for researchers is that heredity and the environment interact in complex ways. The genes a person has at birth have far-reaching influence. They carry a person's biological inheritance that determines basics such as hair and eye color. Genes also impact intellectual potential and much more.

Genetic predisposition even influences the kind of environment a person seeks. For example, Bryson is sociable and outgoing. He enjoys being with people. He loves to be around friends so much that when none are around, he seeks one out. He makes friends quickly. In short, what children experience in any environment is a personal response between their own genetic makeup and environment. A shy child, however, *can* become a more outgoing person.

No single gene determines a particular behavior. Behaviors, like all complex traits, involve multiple genes that are affected by a variety of environmental factors. Genes do influence human development, but they are just part of the story. Just because a person has the genetic makeup to have a trait, it does not necessarily mean that a particular trait will develop.

How does environment influence development? A person is shaped by his or her individual experiences. Social and emotional traits are affected by the environment, but physical traits and cognitive abilities are, too. For example, infants who are held and cared for develop more connections between brain cells. The same is true of children who grow up in a stimulating environment.

The term *environment* applies to many aspects of life. Some aspects influence development more than others do. As you read about those listed here, think about how your experiences shape your life. Also consider the impact your own words and actions have on others.

Family

Families often have the greatest effect on human development. It is in families that infants gain their first experiences with the world through the care and attention they receive. The bond between parent and child is the most basic. Most children learn how to interact with others within the family. Not surprisingly, research studies suggest that the quality of the home environment is especially important to children's development, and that these influences are very complex. Parents impact all aspects of development—physical, cognitive, social, and emotional. In addition, parents guide children's moral development.

Effective parenting techniques and providing a stimulating home environment are consistently associated with better outcomes for children. These qualities are not dependent on having an advanced education or a high income. Parents who lack effective parenting skills can learn them. Doing so is the best gift that they can give their children (Figure 6.4).

Researchers continue to study how and why families affect various aspects of development. Sibling relationships, the impact of being an only child, birth order, and the emotional climate of the home are a few areas of study for researchers.

Peers

Although families have the greatest social influence on children's early development, the impact of peers increases during later childhood and adolescence. The ability to make and maintain friendships as well as attaining, social power and status, acceptance, and belonging all affect social and emotional development. Peers offer equal status, a relationship that does not exist in child-adult relationships. Peer relationships remain important to development throughout life.

Figure 6.4   Parents have an impact in all areas of their children's development.

Community

Where a person lives also influences development. Behaviors that are modeled by others in neighborhoods and communities can impact the behavior and career expectations of its residents. Some researchers see a relationship between feelings of self-worth and how people perceive their environment and their feelings of self-worth. Some communities have more cultural opportunities than others. Schools are also part of communities. The culture of a school, the expectations conveyed to its students, and the abilities and attitudes of its teachers have an impact on students.

Media

Teachers hear it all the time—students mimicking television characters, reciting lines from performances, or singing ad jingles. Media messages are everywhere, and they have been blamed for many negative social problems in our society. Researchers know that no two people experience the same media message in exactly the same way.

How a person interprets a message and the effects of the message depend on things unique to that person's life. These can include age, related experiences, values taught in the home, and media education. Media messages can be positive or negative influences. Their effect may not be immediately apparent (Figure 6.5).

Figure 6.5   All forms of media can have positive or negative influences on development. How can viewing violent images over time impact children?

A child who watches a superhero fight may mimic the actions immediately while playing. Repeatedly viewing violent images over time can have long-term effects.

Health

Health influences development in a number of ways. Some diseases and illnesses may interrupt the normal development of a person. For example, a mother who abuses alcohol or other drugs may have a child that will have a lifetime of developmental delays. A child with autism may have difficulty in forming close friendships, and may have limited or delayed speech. A child with a chronic illness may miss more days from school and have difficulty with schoolwork.

The availability of health care can also influence development. When children receive regular checkups, developmental problems are likely to be detected and responded to promptly. This precaution often limits the impact of potential complications.

Nutrition and Physical Activity

Everyone, especially children and teens, needs nutritious food and adequate exercise for normal physical growth, development, and functioning. Lack of proper nutrition affects cognitive development, therefore limiting learning and productivity. Poor nutrition and lack of exercise can also impact social and emotional development. For example, children and teens that are overweight are more likely to have poor self-esteem. Due to the fact they are overweight, they may be teased or find it difficult to develop social relationships.

Behaviorist Theories

One of the earliest theories in development is behaviorism. **Behaviorism** is a theory based on the belief that individuals' behavior is determined by forces in the environment that are beyond their control. According to behaviorists, how people behave (their thoughts, feelings, and actions) depends on what they have learned through experience, rather than genetics or free will. In the debate of heredity versus environment, behaviorists believe that environment wins.

According to behaviorists, infants come into the world as "blank screens." The behaviors people exhibit are a direct result of their experiences in life. If eight-year-old Tyler is a bully on the playground, it is assumed he learned that behavior.

Pavlov's Classical Conditioning

One of the earliest behavioral experiments was conducted by a Russian researcher named Pavlov. He noticed that a dog naturally salivated at the sight of food. Pavlov began to ring a bell each time he fed the dog. Eventually, if the bell was rung, the dog salivated, even if no food was given to the dog. This response is an example of **classical conditioning**—the theory that behaviors can be associated with responses.

Can classical conditioning occur without specific training? Behaviorists say it can. For example, a parent who is afraid of bugs may unknowingly pass that fear along to their child. Perhaps the parent takes a loud deep breath or communicates alarm at the sight of a bug. If that happens repeatedly, the child is likely to acquire the same fear. You have probably experienced classical conditioning in your own life. Do you have a favorite song that makes you feel happy when you hear it because it reminds you of a positive experience (Figure 6.6)? All of our experiences, whether positive, negative, or neutral, can affect our emotions, attitudes, and behaviors.

Figure 6.6   All life experiences can affect emotions and behaviors. What aspects of classical conditioning can you see in your own life?

Skinner's Operant Conditioning

When you have a pleasant experience, such as receiving a compliment, you internalize the experience as positive. B. F. Skinner was a researcher well known for identifying this basic principle. This principle is called operant conditioning. **Operant conditioning** is when people tend to repeat behaviors that have a positive result or are reinforced. If your teacher praises you for your history project, you may decide that you like history. If you repeatedly get high grades on tests and projects, you may decide that you are good at history.

Skinner found that to make new behaviors permanent, the reinforcements (positive experience) are to be removed gradually, and in unpredictable patterns. Sometimes the behavior is reinforced, but not at other times. Even if you get an occasional lower grade in history, you still believe that you are good at the subject and try harder each time you are assigned a project. Your behavior has been changed. Behaviorists call this "learning."

It is easy to see why operant conditioning became so popular in American education. Providing continuous positive reinforcement when a new skill or behavior is learned, followed by gradual removal of the reinforcement, is believed to result in a permanent behavioral change. Negative reinforcement, or punishment, can reduce unwanted behaviors.

You have probably observed the effects of behaviorism when working with children. Encouraging children's efforts, modeling positive behaviors, and maintaining a positive attitude can have a very real effect on the behavior of children.

Bandura's Social Cognitive Theory

Is it really that simple? Imagine that you are babysitting several active young children. They are arguing over toys, whining, complaining, and hitting one another. Despite all your encouragement, modeling of appropriate behaviors, and having a positive attitude, the children will not behave. If all it takes is simple positive reinforcement and punishment, why do children not learn and behave after rewards for positive behavior and punishment for negative behaviors? If behaviorism really works, why does behaviorism fail to control behaviors in adults?

Albert Bandura argued that people are very different from Pavlov's dog. He stated that people are much more complex. He believed that people of all ages observe and imitate the behaviors of others, regardless of rewards and punishments involved. People are affected by rewards and punishments, but their reactions to them are filtered by their own perceptions, thoughts, and motivations. Bandura called this *social cognitive theory*.

Figure 6.7   Social cognitive theorists believe learning to share is an act of kindness children learn by observing others.

Social cognitive theorists believe that a child who observes a kind act may imitate it (Figure 6.7). This kind act may be shared with a classmate. A teen may tackle a tough geometry problem by imitating a teacher. However, the same experiences will not have the same result on every person. Each person's response is based on personal reactions and how the individual processes information. A child who observes aggressive behavior may become a bully or a person who avoids conflict. It all depends on the individual.

Piaget's Cognitive Theory

While many researchers were celebrating behaviorism, some began looking for a theory that would better explain the differences in how people think throughout the stages of life. One of the most well known researchers in this area was Jean Piaget, a Swiss researcher.

Piaget's observations led him to identify four stages of cognitive development. His studies showed that at any stage of life, thinking skills of individuals are similar. At each new stage, individuals incorporate new experiences into what they know based on skills they have developed earlier in previous stages. Figure 6.8 summarizes Piaget's findings.

Figure 6.8	Piaget's Stages of Cognitive Development	
Stage	**Age**	**Description**
Sensorimotor	Birth to 2 years	Babies begin to learn about the world through their senses. At first, learning relies on reflexes but more purposeful movement later enhances learning.
Preoperational	2 to 7 years	Toddlers and young children communicate through language. They recognize symbols and learn concepts. Both hands-on experiences and imaginative play are keys to learning.
Concrete operational	7 to 11 years	Children in this stage learn to think logically. They can make generalizations, understand cause and effect, group and classify items, and suggest solutions to problems.
Formal operational	11 years and older	Children master both logical and abstract thinking during this stage. This includes making predictions and considering "what if" questions.

By carefully documenting the thinking skills of many people at various ages, Piaget improved the understanding of how cognitive skills develop over time. Young children base their thinking on what they know through their senses. Their experiences are limited. Therefore, when Shana, age three, thinks that the moon is following her, it is a logical conclusion. This type of thinking will change with her gaining further knowledge and experience.

Although many researchers have added to the understanding of how thinking occurs, Piaget's four stages of cognitive development remain important. His theory helps teachers understand how children learn and develop, and explains why they need continuous exposure to experimentation, discovery, and first-hand experiences.

Bruner's Constructivist Theory

Learning is active and students learn best when they can learn in *context*. Context includes past experiences, knowledge, and current reality. They take new knowledge and interact with it by forming hypotheses, testing it, and making decisions on whether or not to add it to their learning. Bruner, a developmental theorist, calls this theory **constructivism**.

Teachers have all seen it before. Learning is challenging for students who are *not* willing and able to learn. Lack of readiness and ability may come from many sources. For example, not having an adequate breakfast, preoccupation with a distracting event, or fear and anxiety are examples of environmental factors that can alter a student's readiness to learn.

According to Bruner, instructors must be concerned about the context for learning. Effective teachers are **cognizant** (knowledgeable and mindful) of the challenges students face. They do everything in their power to remove barriers and find ways to present content to students in ways that are appropriate to their current state of understanding. Learning should add to previous learning, much like the growth rings of a tree. In other words, it is from previous learning that people acquire and build new knowledge.

Much like the physical development of a young child who learns to roll over, creep, crawl, stand, and then finally walk, learning must be presented at the right phase developmentally and must build on previous knowledge and skills. A child may not have to learn every single step, but sequential learning "fills in the gaps" toward more complex learning.

Bruner encouraged teachers to help their students discover new learning for themselves by actively dialoging together. Often termed **Socratic learning**, sharing dialogue between a teacher and students is part of constructivism. Using this method, the teacher asks probing questions. Students answer these questions with additional questions as the discussion progresses, with the goal of further understanding and expanded knowledge (Figure 6.9). Of course, the level of dialogue must be developmentally appropriate to the learners' cognitive and social abilities.

Vygotsky's Sociocultural Theory

Many researchers have challenged Piaget's theory, especially his belief that humans learn primarily through experimentation with objects. They point out the importance of human interaction as well as a person's social and cultural environment. Through the generations, older people pass knowledge on to younger people.

Lev Vygotsky, a Russian theorist, believed that children are social beings and develop their minds through interactions with parents, teachers, and other students. He believed that this social interaction is critical to cognitive development.

Figure 6.9   The dialogue occurring among these students and their teacher is an example of Socratic learning.

When Tasha's teacher shows her how to fold and cut out a paper heart, Tasha may later repeat her teacher's instructions to herself. Through this and many other interactions, Tasha will learn to be more skilled at problem solving.

Kolb's Experiential Learning Theory

Sometimes people learn best by doing. According to Kolb, **experiential learning** takes place when students actually experience and then reflect on their learning. Kolb used the example of learning to ride a bicycle. Instead of talking about it, watching others, or discussing bicycle skills, most people do best when they experience sitting on a bike, pedaling, and then reflecting on what went right and wrong. Students can then try again, building on their next new experience and reflecting on the changes.

According to Kolb's theory, experiential learning does not have to result in only gaining new skills. It can also result in new ways of thinking. Scientific experiments are also a type of experiential learning. Traveling to a different culture is a type of experiential learning, especially if self-reflection is encouraged.

Kolb's theory describes four elements of experiential learning. These include having a concrete experience, observation and reflection, formation of a hypothesis, and finally testing the hypothesis. Learned knowledge and skills add to students' existing body of knowledge and skills influencing how they process future new experiences.

Erikson's Psychosocial Theory

Erik Erikson was one of the most influential developmental researchers of the twentieth century. His focus was on the development of personality. According to Erikson's *psychosocial theory*, personality development occurs during eight stages of life. At each stage, people face, and must successfully resolve, a psychological or social conflict. If they do not, their unsuccessful resolution will affect future stages of their development (Figure 6.10).

During the first stage, a baby must resolve the conflict of trusting or not trusting others. The baby's sense of trust is built on learning that crying consistently results in being fed and comforted. Developing this sense of trust as an infant allows the child to develop other trusting relationships in life. Of course, a child also must gradually learn to meet his or her own needs.

According to Erikson's psychosocial theory, other stages follow. In early childhood, for example, preschoolers learn to develop initiative by carrying out plans or taking advantage of others. For example, Claire, age three, wants her younger sister and neighbor to play school with her.

Figure 6.10	Erikson's Psychosocial Developmental Stages	
Stage/Age	**Task**	**Description**
Infancy (Birth to 1 year)	Trust versus mistrust	Babies learn about trust from their caregivers who meet their needs, including food, attention, physical contact, interaction, and safety. When needs are not met, they perceive the world as an unpredictable place.
Toddler (1 to 3 years)	Autonomy versus shame and doubt	Toddlers learn self-help skills, such as feeding, toileting, dressing, and undressing and, as a result, increase confidence. Toddlers who lack control or independence may experience shame and doubt. Some caregivers punish toddlers for not doing things "right" while they are still learning new skills. This can undermine confidence.
Early childhood (3 to 6 years)	Initiative versus guilt	Through discovery and exploration, young children learn about the world and their place in it. They learn what is real and what is imaginary. They learn to take initiative to claim their place in the world. Too much criticism and punishment can result in feelings of guilt and shame.
Middle childhood (6 to 12 years)	Industry versus inferiority	Children develop competency both at school and at home. They develop a sense of self and confidence from becoming competent in the outside world. If they or others consistently compare them negatively against others, feelings of inferiority can surface.
Adolescence (13 to 18 years or older)	Identity versus role confusion	Preteens and teens begin to understand and experiment with a number of different roles. A task during this stage is to integrate multiple roles such as sister, daughter, student, athlete, friend, and employee. If a central, or core, identity is not established, role confusion exists.
Young adulthood (18 to 40 years or older)	Intimacy versus isolation	During later adolescence and early adulthood, close relationships form. These relationships should involve sharing oneself emotionally. Success in this stage depends on success in earlier stages. Failure to establish intimacy results in emotional or psychological isolation.
Middle adulthood (40 to 65 years)	Generativity versus self-absorption	Adults in middle adulthood begin to place emphasis on assisting others and improving the next generation. This can be done in many ways, including parenting, teaching or training others, or passing on cultural values. Failure to do so leads to self-absorption.
Older adulthood (65 years and older)	Integrity versus despair	In the last stage of life, adults review their life and reflect on its meaning. If people are satisfied with their life, there is a sense of integrity. Without it, despair may emerge as the end of life approaches.

She wants to be the teacher, and they are to be her students. They go along with her plan, but once she becomes bossy, they lose interest. It is important for Claire to take the initiative to carry out her plan to play school, but at the same time, she has to learn to make the game enjoyable for the other children.

During their elementary school years, children must master social and academic skills, such as making friends and learning to read. These are examples of skills that are important throughout life. Erikson calls this conflict "industry versus inferiority." Children who are unable to keep up with their peers feel inferior, or less important. This may hinder later development.

During the teen years, individuals must resolve the conflict of identity versus role confusion. Teens seek to figure out who they are as individuals. They are concerned about how others see them and they begin to decide what they want to do in life.

Erikson's theory did not stop with adolescence. He believed that development occurs throughout a person's life. People are always changing and developing. Even elderly adults must face conflicts as they try to assess their lives.

Kohlberg's Theory of Moral Development

Should you steal medicine from a pharmacy if you really need it but do not have the money to pay for it? What if it is a matter of life and death? Lawrence Kohlberg asked a similar question to children, teens and adults as part of his work to better understand how people decide what is right and wrong. His research led him to identify three different levels of moral development. He believed that, beginning in childhood, everyone follows that same progression, although not all individuals attain the highest level. Each level involves different ways of thinking and solving moral problems.

He called the first level *preconventional morality*. Decisions about what is right or wrong depend on whether you will be punished or rewarded for your behavior. For example, very young children believe that stealing is wrong because they may be caught and punished. Moral decisions are viewed from a personal perspective.

The second level of moral development is *conventional morality*. Some older children, many teens, and some adults are in this stage. There is an understanding that society depends on people to observe basic rules of behavior. Moral decisions are motivated by society's laws and rules and how a person who disobeys might be perceived. People may set their own personal interests aside for the good of society as a whole.

Kohlberg's last level is *postconventional morality*. Some teens and most adults make moral decisions based on principles such as justice and individual conscience. They believe that there are universal moral laws related to human rights that are most important to follow. Decisions are motivated by integrity rather than personal interest or punishment.

Kohlberg believed that instead of being taught about specific *virtues*—commendable moral qualities or traits such as kindness and honesty, children and teens should move to the next level of moral development with the help of adults. He felt students should work together with teachers to agree on school rules and policies.

Since Kohlberg observed men and boys to develop his theory, some researchers believed his findings did not include the way women and girls make moral decisions. Carol Gilligan was one of these researchers. She believed that the idea of justice was typical of males, but less typical of females. She believed many women used the idea of caring for others as a motivating factor in making moral decisions.

Which Theory Is Correct?

Although there are many different, yet sometimes conflicting ways to explain human development, each is valid to some extent. Some theories may be more credible than other theories. Sometimes the conflict between two theories leads to more valid insights. As a teacher, you can benefit from understanding several approaches to development and applying them to the classroom (Figure 6.11).

Throughout your teaching career, more theories will emerge as knowledge about human development grows. This makes teaching and learning exciting! For example, in recent years scientists have been debating whether the specific characteristics or traits of people, such as mathematical problem-solving abilities, are inborn or learned. Gaining greater understanding of the way humans learn would help teachers develop teaching strategies that are more effective.

Figure 6.11 By understanding different developmental theories, teachers can apply them to their own classroom situations.

Chapter 6 Review and Assess

Summary

- The study of human development provides insight to how people change from birth to old age, including progression in physical growth, intellectual or cognitive abilities, and social and emotional development.

- Knowing the general principles of development is helpful in understanding how people change throughout life.

- In trying to understand the precise nature of human development, researchers observe, experiment, and study people, forming theories based on their findings.

- Developmental theories try to explain and predict behavior. These range from the basic debate over the impact of heredity versus environment to theories seeking to explain learning, personality, and moral development.

- Theories are not facts, but they help increase understanding of human development. This is especially beneficial for teachers whose work is to assist their students in developing as human beings, not just to teach them information.

Review and Study

1. Contrast growth and development.
2. Name the four major areas in which people develop over time. Give an example of each.
3. What are four principles of human development?
4. What is a developmental theory?
5. Summarize Skinner's concept of operant conditioning.
6. What is the basic premise of Bandura's social cognitive theory?
7. According to Piaget's cognitive theory, why do young children think differently than teens?
8. What is constructivism?
9. How does Vygotsky's sociocultural theory differ from Piaget's theory?
10. Summarize Kolb's theory on experiential learning.
11. Describe Erikson's psychosocial theory.
12. Contrast Kohlberg's level of preconventional morality with postconventional morality.

Vocabulary Activity

13. Work with a partner to write the definitions of the *Content* and *Academic* terms on page 128 based on your current understanding after reading the chapter. Then pair up with another pair to discuss your definitions and any discrepancies. Finally, discuss the definitions with the class, asking your instructor for any necessary correction or clarification.

Critical Thinking

14. **Draw conclusions.** If development were not an orderly process, draw conclusions about how education would be different. Use the text and other reliable resources to cite evidence for your conclusions.

15. **Identify evidence.** Choose two members of a family who are biologically related. Make a list of at least five characteristics that they share. List at least five characteristics that they *do not* share. Which of these shared or individually distinct traits do you think are due to heredity? Which are learned characteristics, or due to environment? Give reasons for your answers.

16. **Make predictions.** Predict how believing that only heredity determines intelligence might influence the way a teacher relates to students. How might the student-teacher relationship differ if the teacher believed that only environmental factors determined intelligence? Cite text evidence and other sources to support your predictions. Share your predictions with the class.

17. **Make inferences.** Imagine the following scene: *Six-year-old Mateo, his dad, and his baby sister are visiting the local park and swimming pool. Mateo's dad is pushing the baby's stroller. Mateo begins exploring, moving farther and farther away. His dad calls out, "Mateo, come back here right now. Mateo, I mean it! Come here. Mateo, listen to me." Mateo keeps his distance and slowly moves farther away. He does not acknowledge his dad's instructions. His dad begins again, "Mateo, come here. I need to be able to see you. You have to stay with me." Mateo continues to explore.*

    How would a behaviorist view this situation? How might a social cognitive theorist, such as Bandura, interpret Mateo's behavior? Discuss your inferences in small groups. Cite text evidence to support your inferences.

Core Skills

18. **Research and writing.** Use Internet resources to locate an example of the four principles of development explained in the chapter. Note each on a sheet of paper for reference. Then use a school-approved web-based application to post your examples for each principle to the class discussion board. Do all of the examples accurately represent each principle? Why or why not? Post your responses.

19. **Observing and writing.** Observe someone you know, your age or younger, and identify the stage of Piaget's cognitive theory the person is in according to his or her age. Then give three to five specific examples of that person's cognitive development at that stage.

20. **Research, writing, and speaking.** Choose one or more of the following developmental theories:

    - Behaviorist (Pavlov or Skinner)
    - Bandura's Social Cognitive Theory
    - Piaget's Cognitive Theory
    - Bruner's Constructivist Theory
    - Vygotsky's Sociocultural Theory
    - Kolb's Experiential Learning Theory
    - Erikson's Psychosocial Theory
    - Kohlberg's Theory of Moral Development

    Use presentation software to create an informative, visual narrative that explains the influence of one or more of these theories on teaching practices. Cite the text and other reliable academic resources to support the evidence as you give your report.

21. **Technology application.** Locate an online video that effectively demonstrates one of the theories described in this chapter. Share the video in class. Discuss key points of evidence that support your chosen theory.

22. **CTE College and career readiness practice.** A debate involves the discussion of a topic or question by considering opposing arguments. Expressing your thoughts well is important to an effective debate. In two teams—A and B, debate the topic of *heredity versus environment* as it relates to influences on human development and learning. Team A will present text factors and those from other reliable sources that support *heredity*. Team B will present text factors and those from other reliable sources that support *environment*. Your teacher will serve as moderator. What conclusions can you draw about heredity versus environment from the debate?

College and Career Portfolio

Your e-portfolio may contain documents that you create. You may also include scanned images of lesson activities, awards, and certificates you receive. Because others will review your e-portfolio, you need to decide which file formats to use to save electronic documents. Several options (such as Microsoft Word and Excel) are available; however, the easiest way may be to scan and save your documents as PDF (portable document format) files. Others can easily view your documents with Adobe Reader software and some other programs. Complete the following as you learn to create an effective e-portfolio:

- Research and read Internet articles to learn more about using PDF documents. Download a free program, such as Adobe Reader, that opens these files.

- Practice saving a Microsoft Word document as a PDF file. Note: Use the *Save As* command and refer to the *Help* link if necessary.

- Create a list of the formats you will use for storing electronic files.

Chapter 7
Middle Childhood: Growth and Development

Content Terms

developmental delay
visual-motor coordination
hand-eye coordination
conservation
self-concept
seriation
classification
transitivity
executive strategies

Academic Terms

dexterity
proficient

Objectives

After studying this chapter, you will be able to

- **explain** the importance of readiness for learning for children entering kindergarten.
- **analyze** the growth pattern of children during middle childhood.
- **analyze** the physical and cognitive skills required to master a task.
- **compare** children's thinking skills at various ages to Piaget's stages of development.
- **develop** a list of the social skills children must learn.
- **summarize** how the development of self-concept during this period is related to Erikson's psychosocial theory.
- **identify** the change in moral development that occurs about the end of this period.

Reading Prep

Write all of the chapter terms on a sheet of paper. Highlight the words that you do not know. Before you begin reading, look up the highlighted words in the glossary and write the definitions next to the terms.

At the Companion Website you can

- **Practice** terms with e-flash cards and interactive games
- **Assess** what you learn by completing self-assessment quizzes
- **Expand** knowledge with interactive activities

Companion
G-W Learning

www.g-wlearning.com/teaching/

Study on the go

Use a mobile device to practice terms and review with self-assessment quizzes.

Mobile
G-W Learning

www.m.g-wlearning.com/0094/

Case Study

As a class, read the case study and discuss the questions that follow. After reading the chapter, revisit the discussion questions. Have your answers changed? If so, explain how.

It is recess and the sun is shining! Stefanie and Latisha can hardly keep from running as their class walks in a line to the playground. The two girls have been friends since kindergarten. Both athletic and social, together they have been the leaders among their peers. They usually decide recess activities and other girls quickly follow; however, things seem to be changing in the fourth grade. Latisha is spending more time with another girl, Thanh, as they now play on the same soccer team together. They are even joining the boys in their soccer games on the field. Stefanie tries to join in but the boys will not pass her the ball and she is left standing on the sidelines. She really does not like the boys. Stephanie tries to join the other girls from their class but their friendship "clubs" are already formed and she thinks that they are not willing to include new members. Stefanie goes home that night and cries to her mother. She tells her that everyone, including her teacher, is mean.

Let's Discuss

- Are the feelings that Stefanie is articulating normal or typical? Why or why not?
- How might you explain Stefanie's feelings about friendships?
- How might you explain Stefanie's assessment of other people's actions?
- How might you explain Stefanie's feelings about gendered friendships?

The first years of school are crucial for children. The degree to which children feel comfortable and successful impacts their achievement in school for the years ahead. Not every child has the background knowledge, high intelligence, and social skills for that to happen automatically. Teachers can make the difference. They set the tone in their own classroom. They evaluate each child's abilities and monitor progress, providing extra support and encouragement as needed. All of this takes knowledge and skill. Most essential is a thorough understanding of how children develop.

As you recall from a previous chapter, development follows predictable patterns. Researchers know much about children's typical physical, cognitive, and social-emotional development at each age.

Figure 7.1 summarizes the developmental stages described by Erikson and Piaget. In this chapter, you will learn more about the development of children ages five to 12. This spans the years from children starting school to the beginning of adolescence.

It is also important to remember that information about development is based on averages. Each child's development actually unfolds in an individual way, and slight variations are normal. Significant deviation in any area of developmental needs, however, requires professional evaluation. Some children show a **developmental delay**, a noticeable lag in a particular aspect of development. It is important to identify and treat developmental delays as early as possible before the gap widens. Children who fall behind at this stage can often catch up fairly quickly, depending on the severity of the issue and if their problems are addressed. Children whose development is significantly above average in any area may also need evaluation and support. Teachers who see classrooms of children the same age every year are in a unique position to evaluate their development.

Remember that development is a logical, step-by-step process. Even if you eventually teach children who are younger or older than this age group, understanding how development progresses through adolescence is essential.

Figure 7.1	Erikson's and Piaget's Developmental Stages	
Stage/Age	**Erikson's Psychosocial Theory**	**Piaget's Cognitive Theory**
Infancy (birth to 1 year)	Trust versus mistrust	Sensorimotor
Toddler (1 to 3 years)	Autonomy versus shame and doubt	Preoperational
Early childhood (3 to 6 years)	Initiative versus guilt	
Middle childhood (6 to 12 years)	Industry versus inferiority	Concrete operational
Adolescence (13 to 18 years or older)	Ego identity versus ego diffusion	Formal operational
Young adulthood (18 to 40 years or older)	Intimacy versus isolation	
Middle adulthood (40 to 65 years)	Generativity versus self-absorption	
Older adulthood (65 years and older)	Integrity versus despair	

Beginning School

Most children start their formal schooling at age five as kindergarteners (Figure 7.2). Each state sets age requirements for children starting school, usually identifying a date by which a child must turn five in order to enroll in kindergarten. Consequently, children within a single grade may be up to 12 months apart in age. This may make little difference for older children, but gains in maturity and skill levels during a single year can be significant in kindergarten and first grade. Teachers may notice great differences between some of the youngest and oldest students in their classrooms.

As scientists have learned more about how children's brains develop, educators have applied those findings. Researchers have discovered that about half of a child's critical brain development takes place before a child enters kindergarten. The importance of the early years of life on influencing a child's intellectual abilities is clear. This information has led to efforts to educate parents, children's first teachers, about ways to stimulate brain development from birth. It has also spotlighted the importance of making sure preschools and child care centers have high-quality programs that foster learning.

Initiatives such as these help children enter kindergarten prepared to learn. The first years of formal school are also crucial to brain development and to school success. Most schools offer readiness assessments for children or issue guidelines to parents regarding kindergarten readiness (Figure 7-3). These help parents and educators make certain children come to kindergarten with the skills they need for learning.

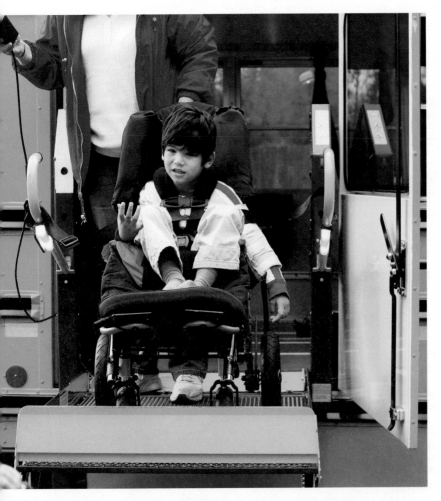

Figure 7.2   Regardless of challenges, most kindergarteners are eager to begin school.

Figure 7.3	Kindergarten Readiness Skills

Gross-Motor Skills

- Throws a ball overhand
- Jumps forward
- Skips
- Walks on tiptoe
- Rides a tricycle

Fine-Motor Skills

- Holds a crayon or marker correctly
- Cuts with scissors
- Copies a square and triangle
- Completes a puzzle with 10 to 12 pieces

Self-Help Skills

- Dresses self without help
- Eats independently
- Uses the bathroom without help

Cognitive Skills

- Knows own full name
- Speaks in complete sentences of five to six words
- Counts to 10
- Knows most colors and some letters
- Understands basic concepts such as in/out, front/back, on/off
- Can tell a simple story
- Sorts items by size, shape, and color
- Engages in make-believe play

Social-Emotional Skills

- Plays with a small group of children
- Expresses feelings
- Developing self-control
- Understands right and wrong
- Follows directions and rules
- Can work independently for a short time
- Adapts to changes

To maximize the opportunities uncovered by brain research, more children today are attending full-day kindergarten programs. In the past, most programs met for half a day or on alternate days. Educators are still studying the effects of full-day schedules. It appears that children in these programs develop learning skills that provide a smoother transition into first grade and beyond. Results also suggest long-term learning gains. Educational researchers will continue to evaluate children from both types of programs to determine how to best support young learners.

Children Ages Five to Seven

You only have to walk into a classroom of young children to be convinced about each child's individuality. Every student has a distinct personality and unique combination of interests, abilities, and experiences. Some children cannot sit still, while others are quiet. Some children are comfortable with change, while others are fearful of new experiences.

As a group, five- to seven-year-olds are talkative, imaginative, and are great at exploration. They focus on the present rather than the future. They show their feelings through laughs, smiles, and tears. Adult approval is important to them, and they are eager to learn. Children at this stage can be sensitive to the needs and feelings of others. In their friendships, they can be cooperative yet competitive.

Physical Growth and Development

Compared to the fast pace of growth from birth through age four, height and weight slows somewhat during the period from ages five to seven. On average, children grow two to three inches and gain four to five pounds per year. Heredity primarily influences height. Weight is also dependent on nutrition and adequate exercise. During this time, children's bodies look longer and leaner. Boys and girls are similar in size.

The toothless smile of a first or second grader is one of the happiest smiles you will find (Figure 7.4). Over a period of several years, each baby tooth falls out and a larger permanent one replaces it. As the child's jaw grows to its adult size, additional permanent teeth grow in place.

Gross-Motor Skills

Children at this stage are generally eager to conquer new physical skills. Development of their gross-motor skills is better than their fine-motor skills. Successfully swinging across the bars at recess, throwing a ball, or making a swing fly as high as it will go makes them feel grown-up and independent.

Five- to seven-year-olds are full of energy. Not only can children jump, skip, and hop, but they can also run fast, dodge objects, and change directions. They can jump over objects, climb trees, and roller skate. These activities build muscle strength and continue to improve balance and coordination.

Figure 7.4   As physical development continues, first and second graders experience the loss of baby teeth, which are replaced by permanent teeth.

Unfortunately, children this age, lacking the judgment that comes with maturity and experience, also tend to be more fearless. Accidents can happen when they go beyond their abilities.

At this stage, children's visual-motor coordination improves. **Visual-motor coordination** involves matching body movements to coordinate with what the child sees. Improvement allows children to learn to jump rope and to catch a small ball.

Fine-Motor Skills

As children practice fine-motor skill activities, their hand-eye coordination and dexterity improve. **Hand-eye coordination** consists of the ability to move the hands precisely in response to what the eyes see. It is a specific type of visual-motor coordination. **Dexterity** is the skillful use of the hands and fingers.

Many fine-motor skills require and build the ability to make precise movements. This is important in accomplishing new tasks, such as writing. Writing combines cognitive development with physical development. For example, printing the letter "D" requires recognizing its shape and understanding it consists of a straight vertical line with a connected curved line to its right. Then a child must be able to reproduce these lines with a pencil or crayon. Only after much practice does the process become automatic. Even then, some children continue to reverse similar letters, such as lowercase "b" and "d."

Consistent improvement in fine-motor skills is evident in many ways. Children can draw recognizable objects that become increasingly detailed. They begin writing individual letters in kindergarten and move to writing sentences in second grade. Children also master cutting with scissors, coloring, and building elaborate structures with blocks. Fine-motor skills help them become more **proficient** (able to move forward in accomplishment) with using handheld electronic games.

Self-care skills also depend on fine-motor development (Figure 7.5). Children this age can dress independently, buttoning and zipping clothes and learning to tie their shoes. They handle forks and spoons skillfully and learn to cut most foods with a knife. Some difficult tasks may require the help of an adult.

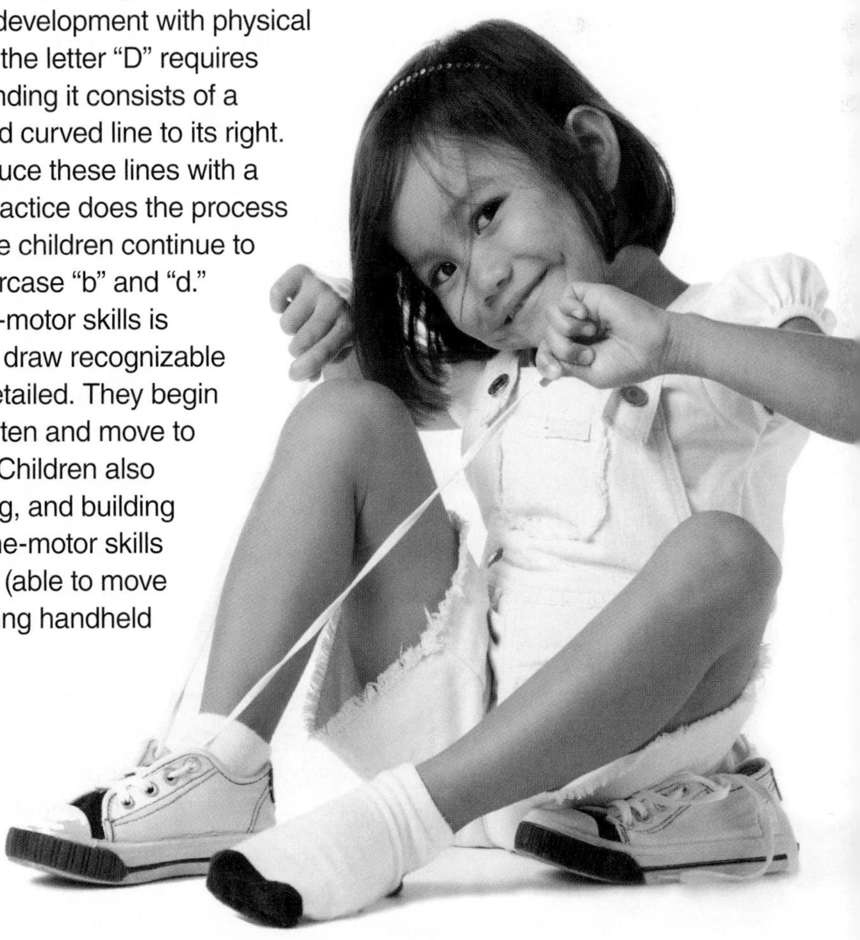

Figure 7.5   Learning to tie shoes is just one self-help skill of many that young children develop.

Cognitive Development

By the time children enter elementary school, their brains are almost at full adult size. Brain pathways become stronger. The frontal lobe part of the brain grows significantly, making it easier for children to complete increasingly difficult cognitive tasks.

Children at this stage are eager to learn. They are excited about starting school, and they want to do well. Curiosity and a desire for independence drives them. They simply want to understand the world and learn new skills. Succeeding at learning increases their feelings of competence. They believe that they can accomplish what they try to do.

Five- to seven-year-olds have limited attention spans. In school, this means lessons must be fairly concise. Children at this stage learn best through experience, rather than listening to explanations. For example, numbers are more real for kindergarteners when they count actual objects or pictures of them.

Professional Tip

Creating an Effective Environment

Professional teachers know the impact of starting and creating a positive environment. They are always on time for work, even early. They smile and greet students and coworkers, knowing that a positive attitude can impact others. For children, having a teacher who exudes warmth and positivity can impact the way they view themselves throughout life. Truly professional teachers will prepare ahead of time and give themselves time to reflect, so as to mentally be ready for the day ahead. A professional teacher understands the need to start the day well, every day.

Dig Deeper

Observe how those in service jobs such as a grocer, postal worker, barista, or medical professional with whom you interact today impact your own attitude. How can a teacher "be real" or authentic but still promote a positive attitude each and every day?

Thinking Skills

Between five and seven years of age, children become more logical thinkers. This paves the way for improvements in problem solving, planning, and decision making.

Jean Piaget's experiments highlight these changes in thinking. According to Piaget, five-year-olds are unable to solve logic problems involving conservation. **Conservation** refers to the fact that something can remain the same (its properties are conserved), even if the way it looks changes. Children at this stage are only able to focus on how things *appear*. For example, a five-year-old believes that a tall, narrow bottle of milk contains more milk than a short, wide bottle, even when observing the teacher pour the same amount of milk into each. The greater height of the milk in the taller bottle makes it appear as if there is more milk. At about age seven, most children begin to consider multiple aspects of the bottle when solving the same problem. They may take both height and width into account. This is one of the signals of improved thinking skills that indicate a shift in Piaget's concrete operational stage.

Understanding a sequence of steps is the basis for the ability to plan. At the beginning of this stage, most children can follow simple two-step directions. This builds to the understanding of multistep directions by the end of second grade. A first-grade teacher may instruct his students to "put your pencil down and place your paper on my desk." At the end of second grade, a teacher might add "and line up at the door" to that instruction. Children begin to base plans of their own on simple sequences.

Many five- to seven-year-olds love to tell jokes to anyone who will listen (Figure 7.6). As their cognitive skills become more sophisticated, they are able to mix words and logic. Humor has various aspects. It can be a positive form of self-expression, or can aid cognitive development. Sometimes, children also use humor as a coping mechanism, especially when they are uncomfortable. For example, when a classmate receives a reprimand for misbehavior, the child's classmates may laugh as a way of distancing themselves from the situation.

Although logical thinking improves during this stage, imagination is still vivid. Children use their creativity and imagination in their drawings and the stories that they create. Sometimes, they still confuse fantasy and reality. They may believe that objects, such as a stuffed animal, have feelings.

Figure 7.6   Children ages five to seven express their understanding of humor with anyone who will participate, including their parents.

The use of imagination plays another important role for children. It allows them to express their anxieties and conflicts. For example, acting out roles using action figures or dolls can help a child dramatize situations that are causing feelings, such as fear, sadness, or jealousy.

Language and Reading

Language is composed of symbols that communicate meaning. In earlier years, children make tremendous strides in verbal communication. It continues at this stage as they build language skills and learn to read and write.

Although reading should begin with being read to before starting school, formal reading instruction begins with the identification of alphabet letters, followed by the recognition of the sounds they make. Children learn letter combinations, and then they begin to read whole words. Whole words are combined into sentences and paragraphs. Before long, children are reading books.

Although some children learn to read before entering school, most begin the process during kindergarten and first grade. First and second graders typically make great strides in their reading ability. By the time they reach the end of their second grade year, many children are competent readers enjoying books with chapters.

It is important that children who have difficulty with reading at this stage receive extra help. Sometimes, additional one-on-one instruction by the classroom teacher or a reading specialist is enough to help the child catch up with the class. Sometimes, testing is needed to determine the specific cause of the problem and identify appropriate intervention strategies. Reading skills are central to future school success so problems cannot be ignored.

Social-Emotional Development

Erik Erikson described the task at this stage as *industry versus inferiority*. This is the need to develop feelings of competence by learning and mastering new skills. As they can do more for themselves, children grow in self-confidence. They like to feel grown up and often boast about their abilities. If often compared negatively to other children, however, their feelings of inferiority can surface. Parents and teachers play a vital role in providing the encouragement children need.

Peer Relationships

As children move into the world of school, peers play a more important role in their lives. They have "best" friends, but their choice of friends may change often. Sharing secrets, sticking up for each other, choosing partners, and playing together become prominent elements of their friendships (Figure 7.7). New social skills enable them to form closer one-on-one and group relationships. Although boys and girls comfortably play together in preschool, girls usually play with girls and boys usually play with boys in early elementary school.

Figure 7.7   A secret shared with a best friend helps children form relationships.

Family Relationships

What are family relationships like at this stage? In general, children want to please others, especially their parents and other adults. They respond well to established expectations and family rules. Tattling on others is a common way to attract adult attention. Given clear instructions, they are also very capable of completing simple household tasks (Figure 7.8).

Relationships with siblings vary from helpfulness to arguments, depending on their mood. Boys tend to have more physical fights than girls do.

Self-Concept

Self-concept is a person's own assessment or view of himself or herself. The basis of self-concept is an evaluation of personal abilities, successes, failures, and comments from other people. Childhood is a critical time for developing self-concept. Those who see themselves

Figure 7.8   Young children are capable of helping with family tasks and are eager to please their parents or guardians.

in a positive way see themselves as capable, worthwhile people and are likely to act in ways that enhance their abilities. Those who develop a negative self-concept often adopt self-defeating behaviors. Once a person's self-concept is established, it can change, but that is a difficult task to achieve.

Erikson's description of the conflict at the stage of industry versus inferiority links to self-concept. Children have a drive to learn new skills and become more independent. When adults help them succeed, their sense of competence gives them the self-confidence to keep meeting new challenges and mastering additional skills. They develop the positive self-concept they need to move forward and believe in their abilities.

Moral Development

Moral development most closely relates to social-emotional development, although cognitive skills are also a factor. It focuses on decisions about right and wrong as well as how society expects people to interact.

Five- to seven-year-olds can tell the difference between right and wrong. As you recall from studying Kohlberg's theory, children often base their judgments about right and wrong behavior on potential rewards and punishments rather than on universal moral truths or family values. They start to care more about doing the "right" things. For example, six-year-olds may decide not to steal candy from a store because they fear being caught. Because of their increased cognitive skills, they are also capable of making up stories to avoid punishment.

An understanding of rules and abiding by them is one aspect of moral development. Children at this stage are able to wait for their turn when playing in a group or on a team. They know how to share toys and often come up with rules for doing so. They do best when activities are based on cooperation, rather than competition. When competition is fierce, children may express anger and jealousy in physical ways. This is a sign that they are not emotionally ready to compete.

Children Ages Eight and Nine

Children who are ages eight and nine are usually in second through fourth grades. During this time, the newness of starting school is over and the preteen years have not yet begun. Children at this stage have increased skills, greater knowledge and better judgment, resulting in increased independence. Eight-year-olds tend to be more easygoing than children at the age of nine.

Physical Growth and Development

Physical growth among eight- and nine-year-olds shows more individual variation than at younger ages. The primary reason for this is the wide range of ages at which puberty begins. A few children show distinct signs as early as age eight or nine. For others, it may not happen until well into their teen years. Most children at this stage continue to experience steady growth. Girls tend to have slightly larger gains than boys.

- ***Gross-motor skills.*** Children's strength increases during this period, allowing improvement in gross-motor skills. Better body control also helps children become more graceful. This makes it a good age for physical activities such as sports, dance, and gymnastics. Physical activities such as these help children build stamina and confidence.

- ***Fine-motor skills.*** Hand-eye coordination also continues to improve. Children become better at activities that rely on this skill. They can shoot basketballs with more accuracy and learn to play musical instruments (Figure 7.9). They also enjoy electronic games requiring hand-eye coordination and quick reflexes.

Figure 7.9   Hand-eye coordination is important in learning to play a musical instrument.

Cognitive Development

Children in third and fourth grade face new challenges at school. Their learning becomes more complex. Although most are still eager learners, teachers note that more students have a downturn in interest and enthusiasm. If they fall behind in their studies, they have a more difficult time catching up later, since the pace of learning continues to increase.

Thinking Skills

Improvements in key thinking skills help students cope with greater demands in the classroom. They are able to focus their attention for longer periods of time. Memory improves. This is important for a variety of tasks including remembering math facts, doing well on spelling tests, and retaining content from one lesson to the next.

Eight- and nine-year-olds are in Piaget's *concrete operational period* (ages 7-11). They continue to learn best through experience with actual objects. Piaget's experiments, however, showed that children between the ages of 7 and 11 are learning to think in more complex ways. They are learning to solve problems mentally. Piaget noted development of the following important skills during this period:

- **Seriation** is the ability to place objects in order by a characteristic, such as smallest to largest.

- **Classification** is the ability to sort items by one or more characteristics they have in common. Children at this stage are able to identify objects with two or more characteristics, such as separating out all of the small green balls from a group of balls of mixed colors and sizes.

- Conservation (discussed earlier in this chapter) is the ability to understand that a simple change in the shape of an object does not change its amount. (Water poured into a container of a different shape is still the same amount; a ball of clay that is flattened retains the same amount of clay.)

- **Transitivity** is the ability to understand that relationships between two objects can extend to a third object. For instance, if Ashley is taller than Justin, and Justin is taller than Thomas, then Ashley is taller than Thomas.

Language and Reading

At this stage of development, children's improved thinking skills help boost their reading and writing abilities. In kindergarten through second grade, the emphasis is on learning to read. For third- and fourth-graders, mastery of basic reading skills allows them to focus on understanding and thinking about what they read.

Children should be able to recognize most words by sight. This allows them to concentrate on meaning. Their ability to identify main points, summarize, and make predictions continues to improve. They learn new ways to figure out unfamiliar words by using context clues and meanings of prefixes and suffixes. Reading skills help improve writing, and writing improves reading. Reading well depends on practice. Children who are encouraged to read for pleasure are more likely to be good readers. Any student who still has difficulty reading needs extra help to catch up.

Social-Emotional Development

Eight- to nine-year-olds mature rapidly in additional ways. They are often eager, friendly, and responsible. They can also be irritable, critical, and careless. Their improving cognitive skills allow them to complete more complex tasks, such as organizing their clothes. Having responsibilities at home and school gives them a sense of accomplishment (Figure 7.10).

Although praise and encouragement continue to be important, children in this stage begin to be sensitive. Children do not want others to talk down to criticize them. They are beginning to appreciate reasonable explanations, since they are becoming more rational thinkers.

Peer Relationships

Socially, eight- and nine-year-olds like to be part of a group. They want to have friends. Children at this age may have a best friend. They look for someone who will share in activities and who will give them acceptance and loyalty. It is at this time in their development that children belong to several groups, such as scouts and a sports team.

Figure 7.10   Children who learn to care for a pet develop responsibility.

Experiences such as these offer children opportunities to develop social skills. Children begin to show empathy and caring at a level that was not possible before. They can also show a lack of compassion and may hurt others, intentionally or unintentionally. Some children may experience exclusion from groups, which may result in bullying problems. At this stage, adults can help children learn important skills by identifying other people's viewpoints, talking through possible courses of action, and offering ideas for resolving conflicts. They can also help children learn how to better understand and express their own feelings.

Family Relationships

Children begin to focus outside their families for ideas and activities. This has an impact on family relationships. They still look up to their parents or guardians, but they are more likely to argue or ignore instructions. Children do not like others to tell them what to do and are very sensitive to criticism. They are often at odds with their siblings, particularly those who are close to them in age. Children at this stage are in need of consistent rules and limits.

Self-Concept

At this stage, children desperately want to feel a sense of belonging and that they are competent. This primarily depends on gaining skills, especially at school, and on acceptance by others. At the same time, they are full of doubts; not trying may be a way to cope with fear of failure. Dressing just like everyone else is an attempt to ensure acceptance. Criticizing others may be a way to look better in comparison. Competition is exciting, but it brings with it the possibility of not measuring up. No wonder emotions can be close to the surface.

Moral Development

Eight- and nine-year-olds generally remain in Kohlberg's *preconventional* level of moral development. They may follow rules selectively, depending on whether they see a benefit in doing so. They sometimes like to make deals, essentially saying, "I will behave if you give me something in return." They do not yet see rules as changeable, so they may not always follow them. At the same time, children this age are concerned about fairness. They complain about rules that seem unfair to themselves or others.

Children Ages 10 to 12

As children move into the next stage, even more changes are in store, usually including the move from elementary to middle school. Children in this age span are in fifth, sixth, and seventh grade. They are often tagged as *preadolescents* or *preteens*. As these terms suggest, they have an interesting and challenging blend of childlike and teen characteristics.

Physical Growth and Development

Individual variation in size and maturity becomes apparent at this stage (Figure 7.11). Some children experience a characteristic growth spurt leading up to puberty. Others maintain the looks and size of children. Most show some early signs of puberty, such as increased sweat production and odor.

Growth can be very uneven. A child's hands or feet may grow to about adult size before the rest of the body catches up. Girls tend to develop ahead of boys and some tower over most of their male classmates.

Figure 7.11   Children between the ages of 10 and 12 can vary considerably in size and maturity.

Depending on the timing of these physical changes, this can be a time of uncertainty or a time of growing self-confidence.

- *Gross-motor skills.* Muscle strength and reaction time continue to improve. Most children enjoy active play, and organized sports are popular. Often, it takes trying out a number of activities to find those that match a child's personal interests and natural abilities. Activities that require complex skills are now within reach. Children delight in flashy moves, such as skateboard stunts. It can, however, take time after a growth spurt to regain coordination.

- *Fine-motor skills.* Children make similar gains in fine-motor skills. At this stage, children write and draw with more skill. They are able to complete complicated projects, such as designing a clay relief map, paper collage, or clay sculpture. Electronic games require and improve dexterity.

Cognitive Development

In school, 10- to 12-year-olds face new challenges. The move to middle school means adapting to multiple teachers, more independent learning, and additional homework. Teaching also relies more heavily on verbal explanation. That increases the importance of listening skills and note taking. At this stage, students like to discuss topics and are better able to work in groups.

Thinking Skills

Children between the ages of 10 and 12 become capable of much more complex thought. They master sequencing and ordering, which are skills needed for math. They move past simple memorization to more complex skills such as memorization of state capitals. Their short-term memory grows, and experiences make longer lasting impressions.

One of the most significant changes in the way older children think is the development of executive strategies. **Executive strategies** are skills used to solve problems. These skills include assessing problems, setting goals, and developing a plan to meet goals. They also involve implementing and evaluating solutions.

The ability to use executive strategies opens up a world of possibilities for classroom learning projects. Students enjoy using various methods and materials to solve creative problems. Without guidance and encouragement, some older children struggle with the completion of projects. For example, they may finish homework but never turn it in.

Language and Reading

When children begin school, they know over 2000 words. For the next couple of years, they will learn about 1000 new words per year.

By fifth or sixth grade, they are learning about 20 new words a day and know about 40,000 words.

Preteens use more complex sentences in speech and writing. They can understand grammar and the rules of writing. Most assignments involve writing to gain practice for later grades. They know words have multiple meanings. This is just one of the techniques they employ in jokes and riddles.

At this stage, students are often proficient readers. Many spend hours of free time reading for pleasure. Books of fantasy and adventure are popular.

Reading competence is important for learning now and in the years ahead. Some older children may continue to struggle with reading. With assistance, older children who are now experiencing delays can still become proficient readers.

Social-Emotional Development

The ages of 10, 11, and 12 can be a period of calm or a stormy one. Most older children move back and forth as they struggle to deal with new feelings, problems, and expectations. Preteens see themselves becoming independent. They can be eager to please or have a bad attitude, both in the same day. Because adult relationships are important to them, they can develop strong bonds with their teachers, coaches, or club leaders.

Peer Relationships

The importance of peers continues to grow (Figure 7.12). Children at this stage need to feel accepted by others, as friends and as part of groups. A best friend not only provides companionship, but also someone who can be counted on for support and understanding. Group activities give a sense of belonging.

Figure 7.12 Communicating with peers is an important part of the social-emotional development of 10- to 12-year-olds.

Most 10-year-olds do not interact much with the opposite gender. By the time they reach age 12, however, that may change. Classroom romances and crushes become more common.

Students this age highly value the opinions of peers. Fitting in becomes very important, and life is difficult for those who do not. Lack of acceptance may result on anything from level of physical maturity to poor social skills to lack of the "right" clothes. This makes preteens very vulnerable to peer pressure, and peers can be very critical of others.

At the same time, children at this stage are able to understand the positions or opinions of others. They can be caring, empathetic, and nurturing. This makes them better friends. They also respond enthusiastically to projects that help others, such as food drives for the hungry.

Family Relationships

While children from 10 to 12 generally respect their parents, parent-child relationships are starting to change. At times, preteens defy parental authority by talking back, ignoring what parents say, or doing things they know that their parents would not approve. At home, as at school, they shift back and forth between cooperation and difficult behavior.

The role of parents is very important at this stage. Even though preteens are more capable, they need their parents' time, understanding, and wisdom. It is also important to keep strong lines of communication open as they move toward adolescence. Teachers also provide a source of adult feedback for many.

Sibling relationships can be pleasant or challenging. Preteens tend to be bossy with younger siblings and annoying to older siblings. At around 12 years of age, moodiness increases, and can cause strain in sibling relationships.

Self-Concept

By the end of this stage, boys and girls tend to see themselves as capable of functioning quite well on their own. They fail to see their own limitations. They often define themselves in terms of their appearance, their material possessions, and their involvement in activities.

In the meantime, preteens deal with many worries, including school failures, family problems, and possibly the loss of a loved one. They may worry about world events and natural disasters. Socially, these students may demonstrate fear through argumentative, aggressive, or apprehensive behaviors. Preteens often confide in friends, rather than parents, even though the quality of the advice they receive may be questionable (Figure 7.13).

The terror of rejection is strong. Preteens often become very self-conscious, particularly toward the end of this period. They feel as if everyone notices even the smallest of differences. Riding in the family's older car, a new haircut, wearing clothing of less than the latest fad, or an overly enthusiastic greeting from a parent can all cause a child to feel embarrassment.

Figure 7.13   Preteens often confide in their friends about worries.

Moral Development

Questions about right and wrong become more of an issue at this stage. A number of influences are at work.

Some children are still in Kohlberg's *preconventional* stage of morality. They still base decisions on the possibility of reward or punishment. For instance, cheating on a test may result in the reward of a higher grade or punishment of a failing grade. Others have moved to Kohlberg's *conventional* stage of morality. They tend to make moral decisions based on the desire to have others perceive them as "good" or "bad." Some preteens base their decisions on rules or laws. School rules forbid cheating. "Good" students do not cheat. Unfortunately, some children at this stage have accepted a label of "bad." They base their behavior on this label.

At the same time, preadolescents often begin to question some of their parents' values. This, if combined with negative peer pressure, can lead to experimentation with alcohol, drugs, smoking, or sexual behavior. For a few, crimes such as shoplifting and burglary, may seem like exciting challenges.

For parents and teachers, this stage can be challenging. Preadolescents want and need guidance, but they do not always accept it. Since they are so sensitive to criticism, it can be hard to offer suggestions. Preteens need to learn to make and live with their own decisions, but they often tackle ones that they are unequipped to handle alone. They need more independence, but too much or lack of supervision, can lead them into serious trouble. The emphasis needs to be on helping children choose good friends, adopt strong values, and develop the social skills to withstand negative peer pressure.

Perspectives on Teaching

Li Shao is a Chinese-American kindergarten teacher. Today had been a heart-warming day in her kindergarten classroom. A new student joined the class who speaks very little English. The other students welcomed her with open arms, communicating in a way only kindergarteners can without words. As Li Shao pondered the day, her thoughts went back to her kindergarten experience.

Li Shao's Thoughts...

Today, I am a kindergarten teacher, but I can still remember being a kindergarten student. Because of my circumstances, starting school left a lasting impression.

My parents came to America from China as young adults. They spoke only Chinese in our home when I was young. They socialized with other Chinese people, so when I started kindergarten, I neither spoke nor understood English.

Of course, school was bewildering at first. I can remember standing back and watching the other children, trying to figure out what they were saying. Fortunately, children pick up new languages easily. My parents told me I began to learn English words and phrases rather quickly. Each day when I came home, I would play school with my younger brother and sister, teaching them what I had learned.

I was fortunate to have a wonderful teacher. She spent extra time helping me with the language, but she did much more than that. She made me feel special instead of different. She incorporated learning about China into many lessons. She even invited my mother to come and share some of our Chinese customs and foods with my kindergarten class. I never forgot that experience or my kindergarten teacher.

Today, many schools have special classes for students who do not speak English. My own experience taught me that a creative and caring teacher can make a real difference in students' lives. I try to remember that every day with my own students. Each child needs acceptance and recognition. Acceptance and recognition do not just help them socially and emotionally. When children feel secure, they learn more, as well.

Analyze It!

After reading *Perspectives on Teaching*, analyze Li Shao's comment about caring teachers. "My own experience taught me that a creative and caring teacher can make a real difference in students' lives." Discuss points of evidence in the narrative that supports this statement. To extend this activity, interview a student who moved from another country and who did not speak English at first. How is this student's experience similar to or different from Li Shao's?

Chapter 7 Review and Assess

Summary

- Most children begin formal school with kindergarten at about age five.

- From ages five to seven, children grow at a steady pace. They are enthusiastic learners, which helps them develop physical, social-emotional, and cognitive skills.

- Children, ages eight and nine, are settled into elementary school and may show less enthusiasm. They continue to gain more control over small muscles and fine-motor skills. There is more emphasis on friends.

- Children ages 10 to 12 have both traits of childhood and adolescence.

- Some 10- to 12-year-olds are entering puberty whereas others are squarely in childhood.

- Preteens are capable of much more complex thought, and highly value the opinions of peers. Fitting in becomes very important.

Review and Study

1. What is a developmental delay? Why is it important to respond promptly when one is suspected?

2. Why is stimulating brain development critical prior to kindergarten?

3. Name three examples of fine-motor skills that require hand-eye coordination and dexterity.

4. How does a child's ability to understand a logic problem that involves conservation change between age fives and seven?

5. Why is childhood a critical time for development of positive self-concept?

6. How does children's sensitivity to negative comparisons relate to Erikson's explanation of the task for this stage of industry versus inferiority?

7. Contrast seriation, classification, and transitivity. Give an example of each.

8. How do family relationships begin changing for eight- and nine-year-old children?

9. What are executive strategies? Give an example showing how children ages 10 to 12 use executive strategies to write a report.

10. What shift in moral development occurs for some preteens?

Vocabulary Activity

11. Write each of the *Content* and *Academic* terms on page 152 on a sheet of paper. For each term, quickly write a word you think relates to each of the terms. In small groups, exchange papers. Have each person in the group explain a term on the list. Take turns until all terms have been explained.

Critical Thinking

12. **Formulate explanations.** Much emphasis is placed on making sure children enter kindergarten with the skills they need to learn. Choose eight kindergarten-readiness skills from *Figure 7.3*. As a kindergarten teacher, formulate explanations you would give to parents regarding why each of these skills is important.

13. **Analyze outcomes.** Electronic games have become very popular with young children and preteens. Use the text and other reliable resources to analyze the possible positive or negative outcomes of frequent game use on each of the following: physical fitness, motor skill development, cognitive development, and social skills. Cite the sources supporting your analysis.

14. **Identify evidence.** Use text to give an example of positive peer pressure and of negative peer pressure that a 10- to 12-year-old might experience. Research reliable resources to identify evidence of ways teachers can help reinforce positive peer pressure. Discuss your findings in class.

Core Skills

15. **Research and writing.** Use the text and Internet resources to research how peers, teacher behavior and attitudes, and student experiences, interests, aptitudes, family, and culture influence development of self-concept and academic performance. Write a paper summarizing your findings.

16. **Observing children.** Observation is a great technique for learning about children and teaching. Find a place to observe parents and children interacting such as at the library, a playground, or your own home (obtain permission to observe). Take notes on what you see, looking for a verbal exchange between a parent and child, preferably about the child's behavior. Record what the parent said and the child's verbal and nonverbal responses. Also note the circumstances of the observation (date, time, place, and situation) and the child's approximate age. Use your notes to write a factual account of your observation. Then, write your comments. For example, comment on the effectiveness of the adult response and describe it as positive, negative, productive, or counterproductive. Ask for your teacher's feedback. Make any appropriate revisions, and add the observation to your portfolio.

17. **Technology application.** Use the Internet to research various free and low-cost quality "apps" to help reinforce children's learning of such skills as writing letters and numbers, tying shoes, and other skills that foster brain development. If possible, demonstrate how one of these apps functions for the class.

18. **Research and speaking.** Develop a demonstration, for example, to teach a five-year-old how to tie shoes. Begin by identifying the steps involved. Then figure out what you would say and do to demonstrate each step. Pair up with a classmate, and take turns being the "teacher" and "child." Combine the best from each of your plans to present to the class.

19. **Speaking, listening, and writing.** Speak with a children's librarian or media specialist about choosing appropriate books for children ages five to seven, eight to nine, and 10 to 12. Read at least two books for each age group. Then start building a digital reference log (that you can add to continually) that includes the following information for each book:

- Book title, author, publisher, and date of publication

- Summary and your evaluation about the story, language, length, and difficulty

- Summary of what you learned about the development of reading skills by reading books for different ages

20. **Create a math learning tool.** Create a board game (using simple materials such as a file folder and construction paper) or a digital learning game with a school-approved program or application to help children ages seven to 11 build the skills of *seriation* and *classification*. Demonstrate your game for the class. Discuss the criteria that makes this game beneficial for children.

21. **Speaking, listening, and writing.** Collaborate in groups to develop a list of the specific social skills a child needs to

develop to get along well with peers for the following age groups: five to seven, eight to nine, and 10 to 12. Identify strategies a teacher might use to help promote two of these skills for each age group. Discuss your groups' suggestions with the class. Which strategies does the class think will work better than others? Why?

22. **Technology application.** Use a school-approved web-based application to create a growth and development digital-photo collage of someone you (with the person's permission) know from age five to about age 18. What factors may have affected the visible growth and development changes? What invisible changes do you assume? Post your digital collage to the class web page. Do your classmates agree or disagree with your assumptions? Why or why not?

23. **CTE College and career readiness practice.** Suppose a group of preteens in your school is displaying strong terror of rejection and poor self-concepts. Your department head has asked your teaching team to come up with ways to reduce this terror of rejection and encourage development of positive self-concepts. Your first effort to creatively solve the problem is to ask questions. Create a mind map like the following to dig deeper into this problem. Then share your team's thinking with your department head (your teacher).

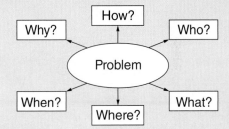

College and Career Portfolio

Community service is an important quality for potential teaching candidates. Serving the community shows you are a well-rounded person who is socially aware. Create a list of nonprofit organizations in your community that may relate to children and teaching. Choose a place or project that interests you and volunteer to serve. As part of your community service, begin a list of your community-service activities. Remember, this is an ongoing project. Plan to update your list when you have new activities to add. Use the following guidelines to formulate your list:

- List the service projects or volunteer activities in which you take part. Name the organization or leader, the dates of service, and the activities you performed. If you received an award or certificate, mention it here.

- Give the document an appropriate name, using the naming system you created earlier. Place the file in your e-portfolio.

- Put a print copy of the list in the container for your print portfolio.

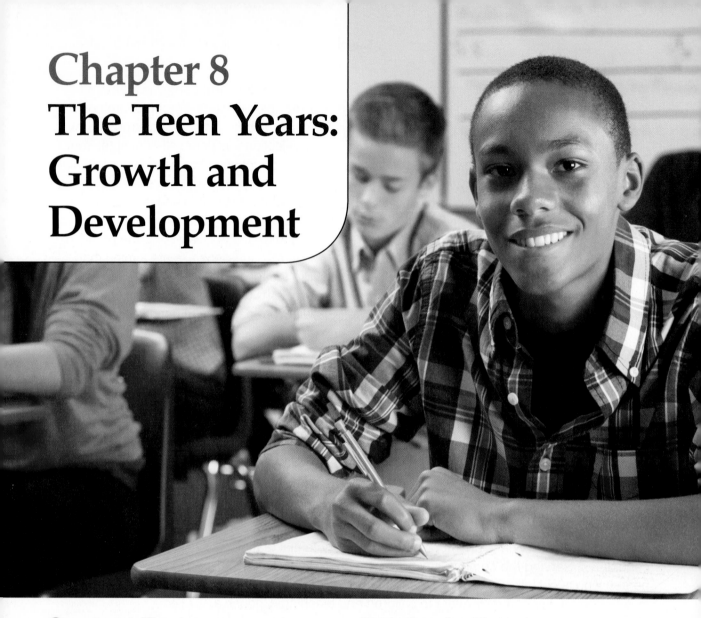

Chapter 8
The Teen Years: Growth and Development

Content Terms

puberty
growth spurts
asynchrony
egocentrism
metacognition
gray matter
amygdala
prefrontal cortex
neural connections
autonomy

Academic Terms

multitasking
resilience
hypocrisy
invincibility

Objectives

After studying this chapter, you will be able to

- **compare** the rate of growth and development during adolescence to previous periods of development.

- **analyze** the cognitive skills commonly required of teens in school.

- **summarize** the social-emotional skills teens need to develop for adult success and devise strategies for teaching one such skill.

- **identify** the impact of various influences that impact moral development and personal values of teens.

Reading Prep

Before you read the chapter, examine all of the photos and read all of the photo captions. What do you do you know about the material covered in this chapter just from evaluating the photos and reading the captions?

At the Companion Website you can

- **Practice** terms with e-flash cards and interactive games
- **Assess** what you learn by completing self-assessment quizzes
- **Expand** knowledge with interactive activities

www.g-wlearning.com/teaching/

Study on the go

Use a mobile device to practice terms and review with self-assessment quizzes.

www.m.g-wlearning.com/0094/

Case Study

As a class, read the case study and discuss the questions that follow. After you finish studying the chapter, discuss the case study and questions again. How have your responses changed based on what you learned?

It is already warm on this early September morning as Alex waits at the bus stop. Today is the second day of seventh grade for Alex. Yesterday, he was feeling excited and confident about moving up to the junior high school campus. His older brother Brandon loved junior high but he moved up to high school yesterday.

Alex was looking forward to having seven different classes and classrooms rather than just the one he had in elementary school. He will turn thirteen next month, finally becoming an official teenager. But his first day had not gone as well as planned. It seemed that everyone had grown so much over the summer and he had not. Having seven classes was already overwhelming and he didn't know where to begin when his father asked him "do you have any homework?" His best friends, Thomas and Lindsey, had completely different schedules and things seemed socially awkward with Lindsey.

Let's Discuss

- Are the feelings that Alex is articulating normal or typical?
- How might you explain Alex's feelings about his physical size?
- How might you explain Alex's feelings about his organizational skills?
- How might you explain Alex's feelings about his social relationships?

Few birthdays are as anticipated as the 13th birthday. Officially becoming a teen seems to open the door to the promise of independent adulthood. In fact, the road is longer and bumpier than it seems at the time.

Teens, ages 13 through 18—the focus of this chapter—typically begin adolescence in middle school or junior high. Overall, this is a time of tremendous growth and development. During this period, physical, cognitive, social-emotional, and moral development are significantly interrelated. Seemingly ordinary situations and events may be influenced by what is happening in all of these areas. The reverse is also true. Where teens are in their development, influences how they deal with situations and events.

When learning about development, it is important to remember that it is a process that occurs over time. Individuals move through development at their own pace (Figure 8.1). In some cases, they move forward, and then they seem to regress a bit before again making any strides. Although teens of a particular age or stage may typically have certain characteristics, not all do. That does not mean that those who do not match averages are not normal. There is just a great deal of variation to what experts consider is normal for teens.

You may recognize yourself or people you know in some of the information about adolescent development. Understanding development is relevant because each stage of development influences the abilities of teens and their interactions. This, in turn, affects teaching and learning. As you learn more, also keep in mind how various aspects of development impact how teachers teach and how learners learn.

Physical Growth and Development

The rate of physical growth and development from ages 13 through 18 is second only to infancy. This development links to **puberty**, the physical transformation from a child to an adult capable of reproduction.

Figure 8.1   Remember that there is great variation among individual teens as they move through development.

This process begins when the *pituitary gland*, located at the base of the brain, signals the *endocrine system* to release specific *hormones*. Teens usually welcome this growth as a signal of maturity; however, it also brings challenging adjustments.

Perspectives on Teaching

Tim Jeffers watched students stream into the building for freshman orientation with a mixture of interest, amusement, and empathy. He had been asked to give a welcoming speech as a representative of the faculty.

Tim's Thoughts...

They are all sizes and shapes. Some of my new students are arriving in groups, chatting animatedly, but sticking close together. Others are coming alone, seeming to know no one and trying to be invisible. I've noticed their conversations range from bragging to answering questions with only a nod. It's apparent that most of my incoming students are very self-conscious.

It doesn't seem that long ago that I was part of a group like this, although I might well have been overlooked. My middle school graduation picture still makes me wince! I was the shortest boy in class. Most of my peers didn't make smart remarks probably because I was funny, athletic, and a good student.

At this age, I loved baseball and hoped to play on the high school team. It seemed like a reasonable hope. My older brother matured early, almost needing to shave in eighth grade. I imagined myself as a power hitter on the freshman baseball team. When the time came, however, my hopes were shattered! I was *too* small to even have a chance of making the team.

I actually didn't start growing until my sophomore year. It seemed like it took forever for my parents to complain that they couldn't keep me in clothes. I grew four inches a year as a sophomore, junior, and senior, plus another three inches in college. Now, at six feet four, I tower over my older brother. I wish that instead of making a formal speech today, I could whisper in the ear of every undersize freshman, "Don't give up. Your time will come!"

Analyze It!

After reading *Perspectives on Teaching*, analyze Tim's final statement about what he wishes he could tell every undersized freshman, "Don't give up. Your time will come." Cite text evidence that shows how statements such as this help encourage positive self-concept. Discuss your points of evidence in class.

Understanding Adolescent Growth and Development

Growth spurts, or rapid increases in height and weight, mark the growth that occurs during *adolescence*. Adolescents can grow as much as three to four inches in a year. Significant weight gains increase both muscle mass and fat tissue.

Growth does not always occur in an orderly way. Growth usually begins with the feet and hands, followed by legs and arms. The arms and legs often grow at different rates. A young teen, for example, may have long legs and short arms, or the reverse. This is called **asynchrony**—the lack of simultaneous occurrence. In early adolescence, teens often look and feel uncoordinated because of rapid changes in their body proportions.

In addition to changes in size, hormone shifts trigger sexual development. Much of this takes place internally, but there are a variety of external signs, as well. For example, breast development in females begins by about ages 12 to 13 (some as early as 10 or 11). Many girls also begin their periods, although it is not unusual to begin later. Because menstrual cycles are just beginning, they may be unpredictable. On average, boys do not experience a growth spurt until around the age of 14. One characteristic sign of development is when a male's voice begins to change, often called "cracking."

Growth continues even after teens reach sexual maturity. Females may gain an inch or two of height in a year. Males, with their later growth pattern, have larger gains in height and still experience significant weight gains. Their physical growth continues until about age 21. Males' shoulders broaden. They build more muscle mass. During these years, the heart doubles in size and lung capacity greatly increases, giving both females and males greater strength and endurance.

Coping with Physical Changes

The timing of puberty is highly individual. A number of factors influence puberty including heredity, environment, and gender. Girls, as a group, mature before boys. That variability, as well as coping with the process itself, can cause real anxiety. Those who develop early must deal with being out of sync with their classmates. Sometimes adults perceive them as older and have unrealistic expectations. Those who develop late feel left behind. They often fear something is wrong with them and feel conspicuous. At some point in the process, most teens wonder if they are normal.

Young teens are dealing with changing bodies and unfamiliar feelings. In fact, during this period, teens seem to see themselves as the main character on the stage of life. They believe that everyone is watching them. This is called the *imaginary audience*. Their own self-consciousness leads them to assume that everyone is paying attention to them.

Since they think that everyone is watching, young teens often excessively focus on how they appear to others. Are they dressed right? Are they saying the right things? With their strong desire to fit in, they are painfully self-conscious. They hate comparisons with others or feelings of embarrassment. A term for this self-focus is **egocentrism**.

At this age, body image is a major concern. Many young teens worry excessively about their size and shape, (Figure 8.2). Media images feed this concern. Models and stars, whose images often have electronic enhancements, rarely represent achievable reality. For girls, seeing overly thin models at a time when they are sensitive about normal weight gains often leads to dieting. Dieting due to a negative body image can lead to unhealthy habits. Since an increasing number of teens are significantly overweight, many may resort to unsafe and ineffective dieting methods. Their diets already tend to be deficient in calcium needed for bone growth and iron. For both females and males, there is an increased risk of developing serious eating disorders. This increases the probability of related health problems, in addition to negative body image. In addition, some, particularly male athletes, use dangerous anabolic steroids to gain strength and body mass. These, too, can cause permanent physical damage.

By early high school, fewer teens focus on development, but most have much concern about their personal appearance and attractiveness. They spend a great deal of time on grooming, exercising, experimenting with new hairstyles, and choosing clothes.

Older teens may continue to be uncomfortable with how well their body meets perceived cultural expectations. Dieting continues to be an issue. As in earlier stages, good food choices and exercise are positive steps teens can take to improve their body image and health.

Figure 8.2   Concern about body image is common in adolescence. Good food choices and appropriate exercise can help teens improve their health and body images.

Cognitive Development

During adolescence, significant changes occur in brain development. You only need to consider the differences in knowledge and thoughts of a sixth grader and a student in college to get an idea of the progress made during the teen years.

Developing Abstract Thinking

In Piaget's theory of cognitive development, young teens stand at the edge of a stage change. They have been in the *concrete operational stage*. Their thoughts have mainly been limited to those things that are concrete—those that they can experience with the senses. Teens begin to move into Piaget's *formal operational stage*. This means that they gradually become able to think in more abstract terms.

Abstract thinking is a powerful tool. It includes a variety of skills including the following abilities to:

- grasp abstract concepts such as honor and freedom
- think about the future
- consider multiple solutions to problems and the potential consequences of each
- figure out why things are the way they are
- understand complex math problems (Figure 8.3)
- think critically about a person's own thinking processes, or **metacognition**

It is important to remember that younger teens are just beginning to develop abstract thinking skills. Most of the time, they still use concrete thinking. Teachers can use various types of activities to help teens learn and practice abstract thinking.

As they move into high school, most teens become more skilled at complex thinking skills. They are systematic, rational problem solvers. They can identify and analyze multiple options. They enjoy trying new ideas and possibilities.

Figure 8.3 Understanding and completing complex math problems is an example of abstract thinking.

By the time teens reach older adolescence, they are better able to solve problems. They can plan, organize, and schedule their own time. They become better decision makers.

Understanding the Adolescent Brain

The brain of an adolescent is both physically and functionally different from the brain of a child or an adult. By the early years of adolescence, the brain is full sized and larger than a child's brain. **Gray matter**, or the cells that actually make one think, have reached their peak. What changes are the connections between nerve cells. New pathways develop throughout adolescence and early adulthood. As this is happening, parts of the brain develop at different speeds.

The **amygdala**, which is the part of the brain responsible for emotional reactions such as anger, develops early. The prefrontal cortex develops later. The **prefrontal cortex** regulates emotions and impulse control. This part of the brain is still changing and maturing into early adulthood.

Because the amygdala develops more quickly than the prefrontal cortex, adolescents' brains function differently from those of adults. The actions of adolescents are guided more by emotions when making decisions or solving problems. They are more likely to act on impulse without thinking about possible consequences of their actions. They can easily become overly emotional. They are also more likely to engage in risky, dangerous behaviors.

The ability to precisely document brain activity is a relatively new research tool. It has yielded findings that have significantly altered scientists' understanding of the brain. One outcome has been evidence that the teen years are a window of opportunity for boosting lifetime cognitive ability. **Neural connections**, the links between brain cells, can be strengthened through activities that repeatedly stimulate the brain. For example, when teens engage in the thinking that challenging classes require, playing a musical instrument, or participating in a sport, they are strengthening the brain's ability to function swiftly and effectively. Taking advantage of opportunities to increase the brain's functioning during adolescence can have long-term benefits, (Figure 8.4). On the flip side, inactivity wastes this opportunity. Activities such as alcohol use at an age while the brain is still developing can permanently injure the brain.

Figure 8.4 When teens engage in complex activities, they strengthen the neural connections in the brain.

Adults have long observed the unpredictable emotions and behaviors of young teens. Some days they act like kids, while other days they act more like adults. In the past, these swings in behavior were primarily blamed on hormonal changes. Today, scientists believe that brain development also plays a significant role in this as well. They also seem to think it plays a role in language learning.

Researchers have also found that development continues in some parts of the brain into early adulthood. (Learning, of course, continues throughout life.) Regulation of emotions and impulse control are two areas not fully developed in early adolescence. Younger teens are often thought of as immature, and adults often say, "Act your age," when in fact, their behavior matches their abilities.

Meeting School Challenges

Young teens in their final years of middle school or junior high are usually curious and anxious to use their new intellectual abilities. They continue to learn best through activities, especially those linked to real life. They like opportunities to work with others.

Beginning high school brings significant new intellectual challenges. Most teens understand that doing well in high school is important to future career options and success. The pace of learning is rapid, and students are expected to be more independent learners. Classes require more complex thinking, including participation in class discussions. Teens can plan and carry out tasks and projects. They are able to research topics and summarize their findings.

By the last years of high school, classes increasingly require abstract thinking. Teens often juggle many things at once, including school, work, outside activities, and friends.

Many students' academic performance actually declines during adolescence. Some declines are due to the many distractions and concerns in other aspects of their lives as possible reasons. Researchers are also evaluating the impact of **multitasking**, or trying to do many things at the same time. Most teens would say they can listen to music, text, check their online profiles, and write an essay for tomorrow's class at the same time (Figure 8.5). The evidence, however, shows that lack of focus is bound to make writing that essay take longer and lower its quality.

Figure 8.5 According to research, multitasking can have a negative impact on adolescent academic performance.

Setting Goals for the Future

In the early teen years, students know they must eventually choose a career path, but their ideas often change. In fact, most know about a fairly limited number of career areas. Learning more about options and opportunities, along with assessing their strengths and interests, can help them begin to sort out career possibilities.

Students in the early years of high school begin to think seriously about career goals, or at least the short-term future. They often hear from parents and teachers about the importance of doing well in high school classes. As teens mature, their improved thinking skills make them better able to understand the long-term effects of their decisions. At the same time, teens this age think in ways that can distort and inflate their opinions of themselves and their own importance. They may believe that they are on their way to becoming a film star, a major league baseball player, or a recording artist. This is called a *personal fable*. Until this phase passes, teens may not be realistic in their career plans.

For older teens, the question of what they will do after high school is much more immediate. Is college a goal? Is occupational training a good idea? Will they seek employment? Teachers, school counselors, employers, parents, and other adults play an important role in helping teens navigate the decisions they are making during this stage, but ultimately the goals must be the teens' own. The possibilities and importance of these decisions can seem overwhelming.

Social-Emotional Development

As you might expect, major physical changes, combined with brain development, play out in relationships and emotions. Teens are defining who they are as independent individuals. The importance and characteristics of various relationships also undergo changes. The movement toward greater independence increases the importance of relationships with peers and often puts strains on parent-teen relationships. At the end of this period, older teens are more secure in their personal identity and becoming more independent and self-reliant. They can better analyze their own social interactions and those of others.

Redefining Self

As abstract thinking skills develop, young teens begin to question who they are. They work to establish a personal identity, independent of their parents. This is a natural step in the move toward adulthood. Erickson called this quest for identity the most important task of adolescence.

Part of this new identity requires seeing oneself as a male or female. Teens get very conflicting messages about sexual identity and what it means. Media messages are everywhere and are often at odds with those from parents, religion, and a teen's cultural heritage. The issues go beyond how males and females should present themselves. They also include what roles, expectations, rights, and responsibilities link to gender. Sexual identity is usually established by the end of the teen years.

All this happens at a time when young teens are extremely self-conscious (Figure 8.6). They base their feelings of worth on their popularity and how they think their peers perceive them. Adults can help young teens develop a positive self-concept

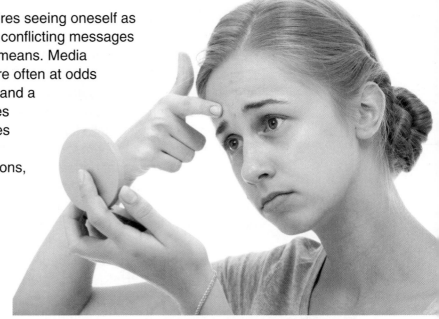

Figure 8.6   Teens can be very self-conscious about their physical appearance and how others perceive them.

based on teens' unique qualities. They can provide positive feedback and emphasize teens' strengths. They can help them learn alternative ways to analyze what is happening in their lives. They can also encourage teens to take part in activities that provide satisfaction and success.

By early high school, teens try out different roles and integrate opinions of others in formulating their sense of self. These years are the prime time for experimentation with likes and dislikes, values and beliefs, educational and occupational goals, and role expectations.

Older teens have more self-assurance. They have fewer self-doubts. They have a better understanding of who they are and what roles they play. Teens do not completely achieve a sense of self-identity, however, in adolescence. Most people continue to redefine themselves well into early adulthood.

Moving Toward Independence

In addition to brain development and maturity, the hormones that drive the body's push toward physical maturity also set in motion the drive for **autonomy**—independence that includes personal responsibility and decision making. Teens must become individuals, and less dependent on their families. They must develop a personal identity with their own beliefs and goals. Their increasing cognitive abilities help them with this process.

In addition to seeking peer approval, young teens begin to look to adults outside the family for acceptance and advice. They need role models. Teachers often fill these needs, but it is essential that teens realize the importance of those roles. Teachers have opportunities to help students over the rough spots and point them in the right direction, but this comes with real responsibilities, as well. Teachers are responsible for modeling adult coping skills for teens. Teachers should be supportive and provide information about resources and how to access them.

Establishing independence and autonomy from others, especially family, is an important part of establishing identity. Early in high school, teens tend to have the most conflicts with parents and other adult authority figures. They spend less time at home. They are also less likely than younger or older teens to confide in their parents. Breaking rules and accepted standards are often statements of independence that can sometimes have irreparable consequences. Therefore, teens still need parents to clearly explain their own values and the reasons for having them.

During high school, teens still need rules and limits that are applied consistently. Those limits, however, should gradually loosen as teens show that they are ready for additional independence. They can do so by proving that they are reliable and trustworthy. The freedom to make decisions helps them become better decision makers. Teens will make mistakes, but need to learn from them.

Older teens often have better decision-making skills. They take pride in their increased ability to be responsible. Although very capable, many older teens are still inconsistent about getting things done.

Gaining independence is just beginning in the late teen years. At this time, teens are building the many skills necessary to become self-sufficient adults. Older teens typically feel like they have reached the stage of full maturity. As a result, they expect others to treat them as adults, especially in day-to-day decisions. As they move into the wider world after high school and face new, complex issues, that confidence often lessens.

Professional Tip

Keeping Relationships Professional

Working with teens can be tricky. The closer you are in age to your students, the more effort it takes to maintain a warm, professional—but not too personal—relationship with them. So what is the difference? Like friends, teachers need to treat their students with respect. Relationships with students can be joyful: full of humor, adventure, and fun. Personal safety, however, must always come first. As professionals, teachers always focus on their desired learning outcomes. They must also take care to not personalize issues with students. Teachers should never publicly humiliate or belittle students, and should leave their own families, religious views, and personal circumstances out of the student-teacher relationship.

Dig Deeper

Think about teachers from whom you have learned the most. In what ways did these teachers act as mentors or facilitators of learning rather than friends or buddies?

Refining Relationships

During adolescence, the relationships teens have with others changes significantly. For children, parental and family relationships provide a stable base for life. With teens' emerging abilities to think critically, and the corresponding push toward independence, the importance of various types of relationships changes. Peer relationships, including those with the opposite sex, take on much more importance. Relationships with authority figures, especially parents, often become more strained.

Peer Relationships

The shift in peer relationships begins during early adolescence. Having friends gives a sense of belonging (Figure 8.7). Peer relationships can help emotional development, too. Teens bounce ideas off of one another in ways they would hesitate to do with family members.

For younger teens, popularity is very important. These teens typically measure popularity by the number of friends they have, making the opinions of peers especially important. Making a mistake in class, tripping, or even having a blemish can feel like a major disaster.

Figure 8.7 Strong peer relationships give teens a sense of belonging and can also benefit emotional development.

On a more serious level, the desire for acceptance often overrides the need to follow rules, meet parental or teacher expectations, or live up to personal values. For example, an otherwise caring teen may go along with a group's hurtful decision to exclude certain people. Teens tend to blame such lapses on the group, rather than taking personal responsibility.

For young teens, having friendships with popular classmates can seem important. Other friendships usually form because of some similar interest. This may be a common taste in music or clothes, or a specific sport or other activity. Teens begin to have various types of friends, ranging from casual to close. Friendships at this stage still change with some frequency. It takes time and experience to develop mature relationship skills.

Early in high school, peers are still a strong influence on teens. They tend to follow friends' tastes, and fads are quite common. Although teens may ask their parents or other adults for advice about values, education, and long-term plans, they may not necessarily follow the advice.

Older teens are able to develop friendships with peers that are close and more long lasting. They begin to place less value on appearance when choosing friends and more value on personality, character, and common interests. They often are loyal and care deeply about their friends.

Extracurricular activities provide opportunities for teens of all ages to meet new people and develop social skills. They make new friends, both male and female. Such activities can enhance a sense of social acceptance and may also provide leadership opportunities.

The wide availability of electronic communication is changing the way people interact. Figure 8.8 poses some questions about the impact of these devices on personal relationships.

Figure 8.8   Relationships in the Digital Age
Teens today live in a world where personal communication is almost instantaneous and always available. With the touch of a few buttons, they can communicate with someone around the world as easily as with the person in the next seat. The possibilities seem to expand all the time. This revolution is changing the nature of relationships. Consider the following:
• When people text rather than talk, how does it change the way they communicate? • How does being constantly available to others impact relationships? Other aspects of life? • What are the positives and negatives of social networking sites? • How likely are people to do or say things electronically that they would not say in person? • How are people without easy access to such technology impacted? • What restrictions, if any, does your school place on electronic devices? If you were an administrator, how would you change the rules and why? • Do you know individuals who have been harmed by misuse of this technology? How?

Romantic Relationships

When the teen years begin, teens are at various stages of puberty and social development. That translates into different levels of interest in the opposite sex. For many young teens, shyness, awkwardness, and fear of rejection are obstacles. Others may show few concerns.

Among young teens, socializing in groups is common. Males still primarily cluster with males and females with females, even in mixed-group activities. There is some pairing off, influenced by differences in physical development and what they see in the media. Teens who are 15 and 16 are more comfortable in mixed gender groups than they were in early adolescence. Group dating is common, although some choose to form couple relationships. It is not unusual for girls to date older boys. Older teens still enjoy group social activities, but some are in dating relationships. Some teens become sexually active. Most, realizing the risks involved or conflicts with their personal values, decide to delay sexual relationships (Figure 8.9).

Figure 8.9   Couple relationships begin to develop during the teen years.

In their eagerness for acceptance and love, some teens stay in relationships that are hurtful. They may be the recipients of put-downs, demeaning remarks, controlling behavior, or even violence. Such teens may feel love for the abuser, become convinced that they deserve such treatment, or are afraid to break off the relationship. Such situations are actually emotionally or physically abusive. The abuser may not mean to cause hurt but may lack the skills needed for an appropriate relationship. No one, especially a teen, should stay in such a relationship. Providing love is not enough to bring about change. In addition, accepting such a situation sets the teen up to accept other abusive relationships.

Family Relationships

The teen years are difficult for parents, as well as for teens. With children, parents employ a variety of methods to ensure their safety. They enforce rules, oversee play, teach appropriate behavior, and supervise their actions. In order for teens to learn the skills they need to become independent adults, parents must gradually give them more freedom and less supervision. In doing so, they know their teens will make some poor choices, and poor choices can cause teens harm, even serious harm. It is the nature of teens to constantly push for more independence. They complain about restrictions. It is parents' responsibility to set guidelines that strike a balance between the need for safety and the need for developing independence.

At the same time, the increasing influence of peers, combined with the ability to think more critically, can lead teens to question or reject the views and values of their family. During adolescence, teens must identify their own values and formulate their own ideas. In the end, the values and ideas often look much like those of their parents. Questioning is part of the process. In the meantime, parents are concerned about the choices their children will make.

Dealing with Emotional Challenges

People often describe adolescence as an emotional rollercoaster. Some teens experience a wilder ride than others. It can be a confusing and difficult time, and teens often experience a great deal of anxiety. Causes can range from size or looks to falling behind at school or problems with relationships. Family difficulties, whether they are normal parent-teen conflicts or more serious issues, bring added stress.

Methods of coping vary. Having a good friend, teen or adult, to listen can be helpful. Sports and activities can be good outlets for stress. Some teens keep diaries or journals. Another positive way of coping is developing *resilience*—the ability to bounce back after a defeat or setback.

Others adopt coping behaviors that are self-defeating. Alcohol and other drugs, reckless driving, and sex may seem like escapes, but they only make problems worse. Some teens lash out in violence or seek a substitute family in a gang. Sudden weight loss, not sleeping, a steep decline in grades, prolonged sadness, uncontrolled anger, or lack of interest in life can all be signs that someone needs help. Notifying a counselor or other person in authority can help turn someone's life around (Figure 8.10). It is better to be wrong in thinking a problem exists than to fail to reach out for help.

Figure 8.10   Talking with a counselor or other person in authority can help teens effectively cope with the emotional challenges of adolescence.

Moral Development

Moral development undergoes major changes during the teen years. As cognitive and social-emotional development occurs, teens' beliefs about right and wrong and what is fair and right continue to evolve.

As younger teens move from concrete to more abstract thinking, they begin to think in all-or-nothing terms. This type of thinking may affect moral reasoning. For example, when taking a political view, moral thinking tends to take on a strong stance with no room for variances or exceptions. The concepts of justice and equality become intriguing.

Young teens are just beginning to make moral decisions based on universal principles. Kohlberg termed this *postconventional morality*. Teens may begin to believe that it is wrong to cheat or steal because it is morally wrong. Previously, they may have based that decision on whether or not they were likely to be caught, perceived in a certain way, or breaking rules. This transformation, however, is far from complete. Most young adolescents still struggle about whether to report a friend for breaking a rule or law, such as cheating on a test or shoplifting.

Teens have a tendency to see moral decisions in all-or-nothing terms. For example, it is typical for middle teens to label inconsistencies they see in adults as *hypocrisy* (acting in contradiction to a person's stated beliefs or values). Older teens are able to see that many situations do require consideration. They are often idealistic and concerned about their personal impact on the world. They can embrace moral issues with conviction.

Establishing Personal Values

One of the most important tasks of adolescence is development of personal values and a related code of conduct. During childhood, parents must help their children learn positive values and appropriate behavior. Children respond, but they do so mainly to get approval and praise from their parents and other adults. During adolescence, teens must decide for themselves the type of people they will be. This involves evaluating, choosing, and committing to specific values and ideals.

This is not a quick or easy process. It also takes place at a time when so much else is going on in teens' lives.

Establishing values begins with questioning existing ones. Teens' increasing ability to analyze and reason causes them to reexamine their parents' and society's beliefs, rules, and laws. This can be a difficult period for parents. Teens sometimes seem to ignore all that they have been taught about right and wrong. They want and need to understand the reasons behind their parents' beliefs, but teens tend to push them away as a result of their arguments.

To teens, everything often seems contradictory. Media portray a "think of yourself first" lifestyle as personally rewarding. At the same time, teens are developing more empathy and find real satisfaction in helping others, such as through service projects (Figure 8.11).

Ultimately, teens must consider what kind of adult they want to be. What are their personal goals? Many look to role models, people who have the characteristics they would like to show. Even role models change with more maturity. For a 13-year-old, it may be the latest star. For a 17-year-old, it is more likely to be someone with true character.

Figure 8.11 Developing empathy and helping others is a sign of maturity in adolescents.

Understanding Risk-Taking Behaviors

In early and middle adolescence, teens simply do not believe anything bad will happen to them, regardless of what they do. They think addiction to smoking or drugs only happens to others—not themselves. This is a feeling of *invincibility*, which means feeling incapable of being defeated or having anything bad happen. This also links to the personal fable that makes them believe they will be rich and famous.

With more independence and outside influences, including media, there are many opportunities for teens to take risks. Teens complain about parents who check up on them. It is without this supervision that problems are more likely to arise. Many such problems can have serious, long-term consequences.

Many 15- and 16-year-olds are likely to engage in high-risk behaviors. Many teens at this age get a driver's license and have access to a vehicle (Figure 8.12). The combination of lack of driving experience, speeding, and feelings of invincibility can lead to highly dangerous situations. Too often, alcohol and peer pressure are added to the mix. Accidents are the leading cause of death among teens, and most involve vehicles. Another common scenario is participating in unprotected sex while believing that pregnancy or infection will not occur.

Figure 8.12   Teens who avoid high-risk behaviors are often responsible drivers.

High-risk behaviors are more common in later adolescence than ever before. Unlike younger teens, older teens begin to feel more vulnerable and realize that they are mortal. Older teens usually are very informed about the risks of substance abuse. Likewise, they know the risks of unprotected sex include unplanned pregnancy, HIV-AIDS, and other sexually transmitted infections. They have the ability to make informed choices. Why, then, is participation in high-risk behaviors so high? Partly, the increase comes from added independence. Partly, it comes from a greater ease in availability. Older teens want control over more aspects of their lives, and sometimes engaging in high-risk behaviors gives them a sense of control and independence from society.

Scientists think that brain development may play a role in risk-taking behavior. Even though most brain development is complete by the end of the teen years, some parts of the brain are still developing into adulthood.

These include those areas that regulate judgment, self-control, and emotions. This may mean that teens are not as capable of making as good decisions as they think they are.

Researchers have identified other characteristics associated with teens that are more likely to engage in high-risk behaviors. Those with low self-esteem and those who struggle in school fall into that category. Negative peer influence is a risk factor. Also, teens from families with less parent-teen communication and lack of parental supervision are more likely to take risks.

Engaging in high-risk behaviors can have life-altering consequences. Teen pregnancy, a serious car crash due to drinking, drug dependency, and HIV do happen to teens. It takes more than luck to avoid becoming a statistic.

Teens need to set clear goals for their future. They know what types of behavior carry high risks and must think through the pros and cons of each in terms of their personal goals and values. Deciding their personal limits before situations actually arise can help them make appropriate decisions when they are under pressure. Many find that preparing an answer for why they choose not to take part in such behaviors helps them deal more easily with difficult situations (Figure 8.13). Such decision making, planning, and follow through show real maturity in action.

Figure 8.13 As teens set goals for the future, deciding on personal limits regarding high-risk behaviors helps them make appropriate choices when under pressure.

Chapter 8 Review and Assess

Summary

- The growth and development associated with puberty significantly change the size, shape, and functioning of a teen's body.
- Teens enter the stage that Piaget termed as *formal operational.*
- Significant physical and functional changes in the brain allow abstract thinking.
- Engaging in challenging activities strengthens the brain's ability to function swiftly and effectively.
- As teens develop socially and emotionally, they must redefine who they are as individuals, develop the skills they will need as independent adults, and form new relationships.
- As teens push toward independence, the importance of various types of relationships changes, with peer relationships taking on more importance.
- Learning positive ways to cope with the emotional challenges of adolescence helps teens develop resilience.
- During adolescence, teens decide which values they will adopt as their own—a process that can cause conflicts with the family.
- Adolescence is a time when some teens engage in risk-taking behaviors, some of which have potentially serious consequences.
- Setting clear goals and thinking through personal limits before serious situations arise, can help teens make responsible, appropriate decisions under pressure.

Review and Study

1. How does the rate of growth during adolescence compare with that during childhood? during infancy?
2. How does the individual timing of early and late puberty impact teens?
3. Name three abilities of abstract thinking.
4. Contrast younger teens with older teens in regard to abstract thinking abilities. How can teachers encourage abstract thinking?
5. What is metacognition?
6. What are the functions of the amygdala and prefrontal cortex of the brain? How do they impact adolescent brain functioning?
7. As young teens begin defining who they are, name three ways adults help them develop a positive self-concept.
8. What aspect of development helps teens in the process of autonomy?
9. How do parent responsibilities change as they help teens move toward independence?
10. What is resilience? Give an example of a way teens can develop resilience when dealing with emotional challenges.
11. What is postconventional morality? Give an example of a decision that a teen might make showing use of postconventional morality.
12. According to scientists, what role may brain development play in risk-taking behavior?

Vocabulary Activity

13. For each of the *Content* and *Academic* terms at the beginning of the chapter, sketch a cartoon bubble to express the meaning of each term as it relates to the chapter. Share your cartoons in small groups. Do your classmates understand the meanings of terms from your sketches? Why or why not?

Critical Thinking

14. **Draw conclusions.** Based on what you have learned about stages of adolescent development (young teens to late teens), draw conclusions about which are most likely to bend to peer pressure and why. Post your conclusions to the school-approved class discussion board. Do classmates agree or disagree with your conclusions? Why?

15. **Analyze evidence.** Use the text and other reliable academic sources to analyze evidence regarding the impact of *multitasking* on teens and academic performance. What conclusions can you draw from the research? Write a summary of your findings.

16. **Make inferences.** What messages do teens receive most from the media about what is considered "normal" behavior and appearance? Make inferences about which messages seem to have the greatest impact on teens. Discuss what actions teachers can take to counteract such media images.

17. **Identify cause and effect.** The author states, "In their eagerness for acceptance and love, some teens stay in relationships that are hurtful." Use the text and other reliable resources to identify and examine the causes and effects of hurtful, abusive relationships on teens. What are the short-term and long-term effects of such relationships? What should teachers do if they find out any of their students is in such a relationship?

Core Skills

18. **Research, writing, and speaking.** Use the text and reliable online resources to create a visual digital report on the physical, cognitive, social, and emotional developmental milestones of adolescents. Create an informative narrative to accompany the visuals.

19. **Research and create.** Research educational websites to review a variety of activities that can help teens take advantage of the window of opportunity to strengthen neural connections and boost lifetime cognitive ability. Then create a learning activity teens could use to strengthen brain functions. Share your activity with the class.

20. **Research and writing.** Use the text and other educational resources to research the influence of the following on the relationship between self-concept and academic performance: peers; teacher attitudes and behaviors; and student experiences, interests, skills, family, and culture. Write a summary to share with the class.

21. **Writing and speaking.** Use a textbook from one of your classes to find examples of 10 questions or activities that require abstract thinking. Write each question or activity on a note card. Work in teams to sort the cards according to the specific abstract-thinking skills required. Which skills occurred most often? Discuss how such questions and activities generate more learning than other types.

22. **Create an activity.** Identify a social skill teens need to develop or improve to function effectively in the adult world. Develop an activity that helps teens learn the skill. Write a plan for the activity, identifying the skill, what students will learn, and specific information on how you would present the activity. Present your plan and activity to the class. Discuss class reactions in regard to the effectiveness of the activity in learning the skill. What improvements could you make?

23. **Research, writing, and speaking.** School counselors provide a variety of services to students. Use online and print resources to locate: the requirements to become a school counselor in your state; the main responsibilities of a counselor at the middle school, junior high, or high school levels; and the employment outlook for school counselors. Write a report to share with the class. To extend this activity, consider job-shadowing a counselor, interviewing a school counselor, or listening to a presentation by a counselor. Give a brief oral report of your experience to the class.

24. **Technology application.** Use a social media site to keep track of the status updates of at least 10 young teen friends. At the same time, keep track of the updates of a similar group of older teen friends. How are the updates similar and different? How might typical teen cognitive and social development play a role in differences noted?

25. **CTE College and career readiness practice.** Employers value employees that can set and achieve reasonable, attainable goals. School districts are no exception. Here are a few things you should know about goals. They should be specific and positive, measureable, and have a target deadline. Think about your potential career as a teacher and how it relates to you as an employee. In writing, set a goal for teaching one concept discussed in this chapter, determine how you will measure achievement of the goal, and identify a deadline for meeting it.

College and Career Portfolio

When interviewing for a teaching job, an employer may ask you about your travels or experiences with people from other cultures. Many schools serve students from a variety of ethnic and cultural backgrounds. Teachers that speak more than one language and have traveled or studied in other countries can be valuable assets in the classroom. These teachers may better understand diverse students' needs and wants. Do the following to document your experiences:

- Identify travel or other educational experiences that helped you learn about another culture, such as a foreign language you studied.

- Write a paragraph that describes the experience, explaining what you learned and how it might help you be a better teacher in the classroom.

- Save the document in your e-portfolio. Put a printed copy in the container for your print portfolio.

Unit 4
The Teacher

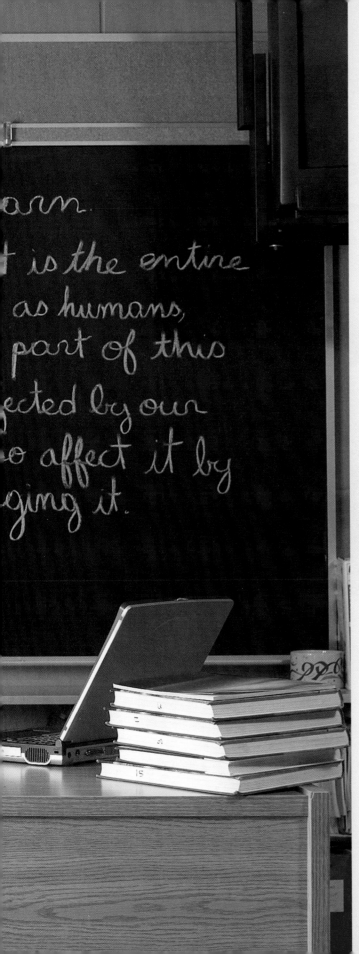

Event Prep
Role-Play or Interview

Some competitive events for Career and Technical Student Organizations (CTSOs) require entrants to complete a role-play or interview. Participants will receive information about a situation or topic and time to practice the event. A judge or panel of judges will review the presentations or conduct the interviews.

To prepare for the role-play or interview event, complete the following activities.

1. Read and analyze the guidelines your organization provides for this event.

2. Visit the organization's website and look for role-play and interview events from previous years. Many organizations post these events for students to use in practicing for future competitions. (Note: Many organizations post online videos of top performers in their competitive events.) In addition, locate the evaluation criteria or rubric for this event. Such information helps you determine what the judges will look for in your presentation.

3. Practice speaking in front of a mirror. Are you comfortable speaking without directly reading your notes? Do your eye contact, facial expressions, and gestures convey the same message as your words?

4. Ask a friend to practice your role-play or interview with you as your instructor takes the role of competition judge. Give special attention to your posture and how you present yourself. Concentrate on your tone of voice—it should be pleasant and loud enough to hear without shouting. Make eye contact with the listener to engage the person's attention.

5. After making the presentation, ask for constructive feedback from your instructor. Implement any necessary changes and keep practicing.

Chapter 9
Teaching Diverse Learners

Content Terms

learning diversity
learning styles
visual learners
auditory learners
kinesthetic-tactile learners
differentiated instruction
multiple intelligences
exceptional learners
special needs
Individualized Education Program (IEP)
accommodations
mainstreaming
inclusion
special education
limited English proficiency (LEP)
English language learners (ELL)

Academic Terms

motivation
ethnicity
arduous
stereotype

Objectives

After studying this chapter, you will be able to

- **analyze** personal learning styles and multiple intelligences.

- **identify** methods schools can use to help gifted and talented learners and students with special needs reach their potential.

- **develop** classroom strategies that embrace cultural diversity and ensure an atmosphere of respect for all students.

- **identify** the challenges English language learners face and how classroom teachers can help.

Reading Prep

Before you read the chapter, interview someone in the teaching workforce who has significant experience in working with diverse learners. Ask the person why it is important to know about the chapter topic and how this topic affects the classroom. Take notes during the interview. As you read the chapter, highlight the items from your notes that are discussed in the chapter.

At the Companion Website you can

- **Practice** terms with e-flash cards and interactive games
- **Assess** what you learn by completing self-assessment quizzes
- **Expand** knowledge with interactive activities

Companion
G-W Learning

www.g-wlearning.com/teaching/

Study on the go

Use a mobile device to practice terms and review with self-assessment quizzes.

Mobile
G-W Learning

www.m.g-wlearning.com/0094/

Case Study

Read the following case study and discuss the questions that follow. Then, after reading the chapter, reread the case study and review the questions. How have your answers changed?

Brynn is perplexed. She is not making the progress she had hoped to make with her fifth graders. It is a diverse class with many different learning styles represented. One student in particular is not responding to her active and collaborative teaching strategies. The student, Jenna, is extremely shy. She barely speaks in front of others. Several of her students are loud and boisterous and have difficulty staying focused on tasks. When these students lose focus, they tend to get into mischief and distract the other students in their groups. When this happens, Jenna shrinks back even further into herself. Another student, Lazaro, is so focused on the assigned group project guidelines that he is oblivious to his fellow group mates. He needs to be encouraged to let others join in his problem solving. Mostly, he just wants to use his ideas and is more interested in completing the task than collaborating with others.

Let's Discuss

- Do you know someone who is shy like Jenna? What strategies have you observed that work for this student?

- How might Brynn better utilize classroom management techniques to help her boisterous students stay focused?

- How could Brynn help Lazaro become more interested in collaborating with classmates?

Imagine that you and your family just moved to a new country that has a culture very different from your own. When you start school, you do not speak the language or understand much about the culture. It is difficult not knowing what teachers expect of students. The teaching style is quite different from that in the United States. The daily struggle to understand and learn creates constant stress.

For a variety of reasons, many students do not feel like they fit into schools in the United States. Sometimes, it is because the way that they learn best does not fit well with the way that schools teach. Other students have physical, social, emotional, or mental challenges that make learning difficult. Highly intelligent students may feel bored or unchallenged.

Others may find that language barriers or differences in ethnicity or cultural customs set them apart.

Every student comes to the classroom with a unique combination of experiences, expectations, and abilities. This presents challenges for both learners and teachers. Too often, feeling that they do not fit into the expected mold hinders student learning. **Learning diversity** (differences in learning based on abilities, interests, or experiences), however, is also what gives schools their richness. If everyone were alike, little learning would take place. The variety of backgrounds, knowledge, skills, and perspectives encourages learning.

It is up to schools and teachers to help every student feel comfortable, accepted, and valued. Teachers who are sensitive to the differences in how students learn best provide varied learning experiences (Figure 9.1). Schools have the responsibility to create a climate where acceptance and appreciation of differences are encouraged.

Figure 9.1   Varied learning experiences encourage success among diverse learners.

Learning Styles and Multiple Intelligences

Educators and researchers are continually analyzing the complex factors that affect learning and achievement. There is an ongoing desire and push to improve education.

One of the biggest concerns today is how to help *all* students learn effectively, not just most students. There is better recognition that each student is an individual. While the majority of students function in regular classes, many fail to reach their real potential. When teachers better understand the differences in how students learn, they can more effectively teach in ways that maximize learning and achievement for more students. Information about learning styles and multiple intelligences are two helpful guides to gaining insight into such differences.

Understanding Learning Styles

Imagine that you just got a new game. How would you choose to learn how to play? Would you read the directions? Perhaps you would ask a friend to explain the rules of the game. Maybe you would learn best by jumping in and playing, and learning the rules as you go.

People learn in different ways. **Learning styles** are the methods individuals prefer and find most effective to absorb and process information. Some people are **visual learners** who learn best by seeing. **Auditory learners** learn most easily by hearing or listening to information. Those who learn best by performing hands-on or physical activities are **kinesthetic-tactile learners**. Most people learn in all three ways, but one style is often dominant.

Learning styles is an important concept for teachers. When they realize that the ways students learn most effectively varies, they can plan their lessons to incorporate different modes of learning. Knowing how each student learns best allows teachers to help individual students. Also, when teachers know their own preferred learning style, they can make certain they do not emphasize only that style in teaching or favor students with a similar style. There is no one right way to learn. See Figure 9.2 for the characteristics of people with each of three learning styles, along with which learning strategies typically work best for them.

Visual Learners

Visual learners learn best when they can see the information to be learned. When presented with a spoken math problem, a visual learner often responds by saying, "Wait a minute, let me write it down." Seeing the problem on paper is a key to comprehending and processing it.

Figure 9.2	Learning Styles		
Learning Styles	**Visual**	**Auditory**	**Kinesthetic-Tactile**
Characteristics	• Prefers written and visual materials • Remembers details of how things look • Takes detailed notes • Often distracted by movement • Doodles • Prefers written directions	• Prefers to listen to information • Sounds and songs stimulate memory • Takes incomplete notes • Often distracted by sounds or talking • Prefers oral directions	• Prefers to learn by doing • Remembers how things were done • May not take notes • Often distracted by movement • Finds it difficult to sit still • Prefers directions with examples
Learning Strategies	• Reading • Photos, diagrams, charts • PowerPoint® presentations • Films, television • Flash cards	• Lectures, explanations • Discussions • Listening to recordings • Films, television • Reading aloud • Repeating information	• Demonstrations • Hands-on activities • Models • Projects • Field trips • Dramatizing • Labs, experiments • Singing, clapping • Games

Imagine that you are learning about the main battles of the Civil War. As a visual learner, you could learn the material visually in several ways. You might read about the battles (seeing written words) and take notes. You might draw a time line to be able to visualize the sequence of the battles. You could view pictures, watch a movie about the battles, or see someone act them out. When studying, you could highlight the main points in your notes, assigning a different color to each battle. Each of these techniques could help you visualize the information and help you recall it during assessment.

Auditory Learners

Can you sit in a class and without taking notes or looking at the board or computer, learn by simply listening? Do you find it easy to remember spoken directions? Auditory learners learn best when they hear information. Although lecturing is generally considered the least effective teaching method, auditory learners get the most from lectures.

Auditory learners often say, "Can you explain that to me?" They find information presented orally easiest to understand and remember.

To learn about Civil War battles, as an auditory learner, you would prefer to listen to a teacher explain when and where important battles occurred. Discussing the significance of each battle further reinforces learning.

You might study by reciting the battle sequence out loud. During a test, mentally pretending to tell someone about the battles might help you as an auditory learner formulate answers.

Many auditory learners can easily recognize song tunes and rhythms. Young children who are auditory learners often find it easy to repeat lines from a movie or a television show. Young auditory learners are often praised for their ability to remember what they have been told to do.

Figure 9.3   Hands-on activities provide kinesthetic-tactile learners a mode in which they learn best.

Kinesthetic-Tactile Learners

You have just purchased an item that requires assembly. If you open the box and attempt to put the item together without instructions (the trial-and-error method), you are probably a kinesthetic-tactile learner. (*Kinesthetic* refers to using bodily movement. *Tactile* refers to touch.) Kinesthetic-tactile learners learn best by doing or through hands-on activity (Figure 9.3). They often say, "Let me play around with it for awhile."

A kinesthetic-tactile learner may find it hard to sit still during a lecture. A student may take many breaks when reading a textbook chapter. To learn the sequence of Civil War battles, as a kinesthetic-tactile learner, you might physically place numbers on a map showing, in sequence, where the key battles occurred. Another technique would be to use an object to represent each battle and place them in order by date. Briefly dramatizing the battles could also serve as a memory aid. Studying with others, particularly other students with a similar learning style, might be helpful. During a test, you might visualize the memory of placing the numbers on the map or objects in order.

Young children are especially open to kinesthetic-tactile learning. Babies explore their world through touch. Dancing to the rhythm of a song can help a child learn the alphabet. A special clap may help a young child remember to quiet down. Similar to older kinesthetic-tactile learners, physical actions reinforce the learning for younger children.

Determining Learning Styles

A multitude of tests, quizzes, and assessments exist for determining learning style. The quickest and often the most meaningful way to determine if a student favors visual, auditory, or kinesthetic styles of learning is through simple observation. Watch to see how a student naturally expresses himself or herself to the world. Does the student use words, laughing, or singing? Are artistic gestures and facial expressions typical? Does the student express himself or herself through dancing, performance, hugs, kisses, or other body gestures? Sometimes socialization influences learning styles; however, if self-expression repeatedly falls into one camp—auditory, visual, or kinesthetic—that may be a clue to the learning style.

Interests can also be an indicator. Observe activities, tasks, hobbies, or academic subjects that naturally attract learners. Observe how they solve problems. Which do they rely on most for taking in information—visual, auditory, or kinesthetic senses?

In addition to the three basic styles of learning, many theorists propose additional styles or *learning preferences*. Some of these can be difficult to measure or observe. In addition to observation, there are many *learning-style inventories*—assessments that help determine learning style—available online. Your school counselor can also provide insight. Teaching specialists who have training in working with students who have special needs, including exceptional or gifted students, are good resources for information on learning styles.

When meeting the different learning styles and needs of students, teachers often employ **differentiated instruction**, or different modes of instruction to match a student's preferred mode of learning, disability, or background.

Understanding Multiple Intelligences

The term *intelligence* typically refers to learning ability. In the 1980s, Howard Gardner, a professor of cognition and education from Harvard University, published his theory of **multiple intelligences**. His research and observations led him to the idea that individuals have a broad range of types of intelligence, each to a different degree.

Gardner identified a variety of types of intelligences (Figure 9.4). The list is still evolving. Gardner believes that each person possesses all of these types, but to different degrees.

Figure 9.4	Gardner's Multiple Intelligences		
Type of Intelligence	**Strengths**	**Student Characteristics**	**Preferred Learning Activities**
Logical-mathematical	Good with logical problems and math	Performs well in math and science, abstract thinking, classifying	Strategy games, experiments, math problems, logic exercises, problem solving
Visual-spatial	Good at visualizing	Has artistic skills, imagination, can think in three dimensions	Drawing, picturing, making models, seeing patterns, visual puzzles
Bodily-kinesthetic	Good with movement, hands-on activities	Coordinated, athletic, may like art, crafts, or building	Drama, dance, crafts, experiments
Linguistic	Good with words	Has good written or oral communication skills and large vocabulary, learns languages easily	Reading, storytelling, writing, note taking, summarizing, word puzzles
Musical	Good with rhythm and sound patterns	Understands rhythm, tone, sings or hums to self, emotionally sensitive	Music, auditory activities, those requiring emotional sensitivity
Intrapersonal	Good analyzer of self, own strengths and weaknesses	Reflective, goal-oriented, instinctive, makes good personal decisions	Journaling, reflection exercises, self-paced work, personal projects
Interpersonal	Good with communication	Communicates well, leadership, sensitive to others, understands others, resolves conflicts	Group activities, discussions, group projects
Naturalistic	In tune with and analyzes environment	Observes, classifies, visualizes	Collections, observations, journaling, creating charts
Existentialist	Good at asking philosophical questions	Learns best through seeing the "big picture" of human existence	Interactive communication tools, such as e-mail, teleconferencing

Schools typically focus on just a few of these types of intelligences in core subjects such as English language arts and math. For instance, students with strong *linguistic* skills have a good command of words and may have excellent writing skills. If students have strong *logical-mathematical* intelligence, they may get high grades in math; however, students may not directly receive grades on strong interpersonal skills or dramatic abilities (bodily-kinesthetic).

Gardner's work has prompted many schools and teachers to take a broader view of intelligence. When using activities that draw on more types of intelligence, teachers find that students learn more, all areas of intelligence improve, and there is a reduction in behavior problems.

Tapping Individual Learning Strengths

As you read about learning styles and multiple intelligences, you may notice similarities. Although they look at different aspects of learning, teachers can use many of the same techniques to incorporate both into their teaching. Experienced teachers who have made such changes have reported increased enthusiasm for teaching and significant gains in both attitude and learning among their students. Specific benefits include the following:

Understanding student potential. When teachers begin to evaluate students' potential on more than whether they score well on written tests or contribute to class discussions, a change often occurs in their own attitudes. They look for other strengths, particularly in underperforming students, and begin to devise ways to use these strengths to improve learning. This, in itself, can improve students' attitudes toward learning. Feeling that a teacher has confidence in their abilities, makes students want to try harder. When activities take into account diverse learning styles and intelligences, students are more likely to connect to the material.

Using varied teaching techniques. Good teachers know that they cannot teach a concept in just one way, and that different topics lend themselves to different teaching methods. Incorporating learning styles and multiple intelligences simply builds on this knowledge. Teachers can consciously expand their choices to include more learning styles and intelligences. Here are some examples.

A third grade teacher who is introducing the concept of the free enterprise system could assign students to read the related chapter in their social studies textbook and fill out a worksheet. Both of these activities match the strengths of visual learners and those with linguistic intelligence—often the same students.

An alternative would be to introduce the concept by asking questions to generate students' interests and determine their knowledge of the topic. "Does anyone have a savings account?" "How is that different from putting money in your piggy bank?" "What happens when everyone wants a popular video game, and it is in short supply?" Questions such as these can set the stage for learning. The teacher might still have the students read the textbook, but perhaps read as a class, discussing points and filling in a worksheet together as they read.

Students could also work in groups to develop a plan to sell an item other students might want to buy, deciding such things as what to sell and how much they would charge. They could develop an advertising skit, a song, or a rap. The second plan draws on a wider range of student strengths and learning styles.

Allowing more student choice. Sometimes, teachers can allow students to choose how to explore a topic in more depth (Figure 9.5). The teacher may give a limited number of options or allow students to suggest their own alternatives (that meet certain criteria and have approval of the teacher). For example, a health lesson on the importance of exercise for people of all ages would lend itself to this approach.

Students could work individually or in groups. Possible projects might include developing brochures, a digital video of exercises for older adults, an interview with a health professional, a radio ad promoting exercise, posters, charts with possible weight-loss calculations, media presentations, and a game incorporating physical activity, a personal exercise journal, or a design for a fitness trail.

Figure 9.5   Giving students a choice in how they learn course topics can produce amazing results when students draw on their own strengths.

When students work on projects of their choice, they often produce amazing results because they can draw on their strengths. At the same time, the whole class learns more when individuals and groups share the range of projects they have developed.

Helping individual learners. Teachers can help students better understand their specific strengths and how to use them effectively. For example, a teacher can help a student understand that learning styles vary and discover which style is personally dominant. The next step would be assisting the student in finding learning, studying, and test-taking techniques that match his or her personal strengths.

Helping all learners. The foundation of both learning styles and multiple intelligences is the premise that everyone uses all styles and possesses all intelligences to some extent. By improving the areas that are not natural strengths, learning becomes easier and more complete. When teachers incorporate many techniques, students gain practice and skills in more of these areas. Those with a predominately kinesthetic-tactile learning style can learn to take better notes (Figure 9.6). With practice, a person with high *intra*personal intelligence who is not outgoing can gain *inter*personal intelligence and function more effectively in groups.

One key aspect that many teachers miss is incorporating tips and techniques for gaining such skills into regular lessons. For example, a teacher might suggest three good ways to study for an upcoming test, each appropriate for a different learning style. Teachers at every level can help students better understand how their textbooks are structured and how to use them effectively. If students are to make a display or poster, briefly reviewing the aspects to consider helps more students succeed. Often, teachers take for granted that students have learned and have remembered how to successfully tackle a wide range of tasks. Simple reminders, explanations, examples, checklists, and organizational aids help students fill in the gaps and become more effective learners.

Figure 9.6   Learning becomes easier and more complete when students focus on using and improving areas that are not their natural strengths.

Exceptional Learners

For most students, the regular classroom with a caring and competent teacher can provide sufficient opportunities to learn well. **Exceptional learners** are students that require special educational modifications and, perhaps, other services that align to their abilities and potential. There are two main groups of exceptional learners—gifted and talented students and learners with special needs.

Gifted and Talented Learners

Do you know someone who can solve complex problems quickly? Perhaps you know a young child with exceptional language skills or a classmate who always gets top scores on tests. You may have a friend who is a natural leader or a talented artist. Gifted or talented students have abilities that are significantly greater than those of other students their age and have exceptional potential. *Gifted* most often refers to those who excel academically. *Talented* refers to those who have outstanding skills in other areas, such as music, art, theater, dance, or leadership (Figure 9.7). The terms are often used together and sometimes interchangeably.

Figure 9.7 Talented students are exceptional learners who often have outstanding skills in areas such as music.

Although a typical description of gifted students is usually "smart," there is no one definition or test to determine who qualifies. Some students seem to have high intelligence that helps them do well in most subjects. Others excel in one or two areas, such as math or writing. Some students who make high grades may not have exceptional intelligence but succeed mostly because of **motivation** (personal incentive or drive to succeed), good organizational skills, and hard work. In general, gifted students are those who are at the very top of a school's population or who have scores in a specific range on an indicator (standardized) test.

Howard Gardner's multiple intelligence theory has been influential in increasing the recognition of students who have talents or intelligences in other areas. A student who plays in a youth symphony may have exceptional talent. A teen that can turn a pile of miscellaneous parts into a helpful invention would seem to deserve as much credit as someone who excels at physics. Many school districts now find ways to support both gifted and talented students.

Within society and education, however, people have different views about schools' responsibilities toward gifted and talented students. Some believe that since these students usually excel with little special training or support, there is no need for special programs or efforts. Others feel that it is important to help gifted and talented students reach their highest potential so that they can better help society in the future.

The wide variation in the types of gifts and talents raises other issues. Schools and teachers face many challenges in determining the best ways to help students with so many different exceptional potentials and abilities. Some strategies include the following:

- **Providing in-class enrichment**. Students remain in regular classes but their teachers tailor some learning opportunities and projects to their special interests and abilities.

- **Using self-paced learning**. Students learn at their own rate. *Self-paced learning* allows students to spend the amount of time they personally need to master concepts. Students who are more advanced can move on to more difficult concepts as soon as they are ready. Students progress at individual rates, rather than as a class.

- **Skipping a grade**. Gifted students sometimes skip one grade and move on to the next. This approach is less common today than in the past. Students, particularly younger ones, often lack the social and emotional skills to handle this successfully. They may also miss out on concepts taught at a particular grade.

Figure 9.8 Some academically gifted students go to magnet schools that emphasize a particular curriculum area such as science.

- ***Attending special schools***. Some larger school districts have schools for academically gifted students. Some also offer magnet schools. A *magnet school* is a type of public school that emphasizes a particular subject or curriculum area, such as science (Figure 9.8), or promotes an area of talent, such as the arts. High-achieving students from throughout the district may enroll.

- ***Providing pull-out programs***. Students attend regular classes for part of the day. During other periods, they participate in *pull-out programs*. In such programs, students leave regular classes to participate in educational sessions geared toward specific needs. Gifted pull-out programs can provide advanced learning and opportunities to work and socialize with other gifted students.

- ***Participating in extracurricular programs***. Most schools offer opportunities outside of the regular school day for students to pursue interests. Sports, clubs, special-interest classes, and similar options all give students possibilities for improving knowledge and skills in areas of interest.

- ***Taking advanced classes***. Community colleges in many states offer high school students the opportunity to take college courses while still in high school. Some colleges and universities allow gifted students to enter early.

Although some teachers specialize in teaching gifted and talented students, regular classroom teachers usually have gifted and talented students in their classes, too. Students with high academic ability in one or more subjects often need enrichment to the curriculum and assignments to keep them learning and interested.

Technology allows use of such techniques such as self-paced learning within the classroom. Teachers can give gifted students assignments with more rigorous requirements. Sometimes students join the class in a higher grade for a particular subject.

Grouping gifted or talented students for some projects and activities may be appropriate. Students with talents in other areas can be encouraged to use them to complete projects and activities. Depending on the student and the situation, classroom teachers have many options.

Learners with Special Needs

Special needs include a broad range of physical, mental, social, and behavioral challenges that affect learning. Students with special needs may include those who have speech, vision, and hearing disabilities, as well as those who have intellectual and learning disabilities. The effects of these conditions can range from minimal to severe.

As you recall, Congress passed the *Education for All Handicapped Children Act in 1975*. This required public schools to provide students with a free appropriate public education in the least restrictive environment possible (Figure 9.9). The law was renamed the *Individuals with Disabilities Education Act (IDEA)* in the 1990s.

Part of the *IDEA* requires that public schools create an **Individualized Education Program (IEP)** for each student who meets specific requirements. The IEP is developed by a team that includes the child's parent or guardian; one or more regular classroom teachers; a special education teacher; and a school counselor, psychologist, or administrator.

Figure 9.9   Learners who have special needs may include students with physical challenges.

An individualized education program is a written plan for providing a student with the most appropriate opportunity for learning. It describes the student's level of performance and how the child's disability affects academic performance. Academic goals and objectives are set. The plan describes specific **accommodations** or modifications to the environment, learning strategies, or materials that are made to help students with particular special needs succeed in the classroom (Figure 9.10). (For example, a student who is blind might need Braille copies of textbooks.) The IEP specifies services needed for the student to succeed in the classroom. The goal of an IEP is to provide the least restrictive, most effective learning environment for the student.

Depending on the individual student, schools may use various educational placements or a combination of them. These include the following:

- *Mainstreaming*. With **mainstreaming**, schools place students in one or more regular classes based on their expected ability to keep up with the standard curriculum. They may have extra learning aids, but they receive no treatment as special students. For example, a student who has a hearing disability may have an interpreter in class but is still responsible for all regular class assignments. Mainstreaming works for many students who have special needs.

Figure 9.10	Meeting the Needs of Special Populations		
Special Need	**Characteristic Indicators**	**Diagnostic Tests**	**Instructional Strategies or Accommodation**
Intellectual Disability	• Difficult or lack of understanding new concepts • Slowness or struggle in processing data • Organizational challenges • Below average intellectual functioning • Difficulty keeping up	• Prenatal screening Later, a team approach including: • Home and classroom observation • Medical exam • Mental health exam • Genetic and neurological testing • Intelligence or cognitive testing • Adaptive behavior assessment • Family history	• Physical, speech, and occupational therapy • Special education classes • Psychological counseling • Inclusive classroom environment that includes differential teaching methods • Mentoring
Developmental Disability	• Cognitive, social, emotional, or physical delays for age • Lowered maturity level for age • Inappropriate behaviors for age	A team approach including: • Home and classroom observation • Medical exam • Mental health exam • Intelligence or cognitive testing • Adaptive behavior assessment	• Physical, speech, and occupational therapy • Special education classes • Psychological counseling • Inclusive classroom environment that includes differential teaching methods • Mentoring
Emotional/ Behavioral Disability	• Inappropriate expressions for age • Overwhelming anxiety, fear, nervousness • Inappropriate expression of anger • Learning challenges not caused by other disabilities • Overwhelming sadness and depression • Bullying or victimization • Irrational obsessions	A team approach including: • Home and classroom observation • Medical exam • Mental health exam	• Special or alternative education classes • Psychological counseling
Autism Spectrum Disorder	• Difficulty expressing emotion • Difficulty making friends • Compulsive interest in one subject area • Lack of eye contact • Honesty to a fault or without regard or understanding of social norms • Appears distant or remote • High intellectual functioning	A team approach including: • Home and classroom observation • Medical exam • Mental health exam	• Special education classes • Psychological counseling • Inclusive classroom environment that includes differential teaching methods • Mentoring • Adhere to strict schedules • Utilize and offer interpersonal communication tools

(continued)

Figure 9.10	Meeting the Needs of Special Populations *(continued)*		
Special Need	**Characteristic Indicators**	**Diagnostic Tests**	**Instructional Strategies or Accommodation**
Communication Disorder	• Difficulty expressing ideas, thoughts • Inappropriate or incorrect use of words • Frustration over others' lack of understanding their message • Misunderstanding or inappropriate use of facial gestures or nonverbal cues	A team approach including: • Home and classroom observation • Medical exam • Mental health exam	• Physical, speech, and occupational therapy • Special education classes • Psychological counseling • Inclusive classroom environment that includes differential teaching methods • Offer printed instruction to reinforce verbal instructions
Hearing Loss or Deafness	• Diminished or loss of hearing • Unresponsive to loud noises or voices • Lack of startle reflex • Inappropriate or incorrect use of words • Incorrect pronunciation of words	• Observation • Hearing test • Medical exam	• Utilize visual images to relay messages • Integrate sign language • Use subtitles on audio visual presentations • Use signage in classroom • Offer printed instruction to complement verbal instructions
Low Vision or Blindness	• Diminished or loss of hearing • Unresponsive to visual cues • Squinting • Inability or low level reading • Illiteracy	• Observation • Vision test • Medical exam	• Seat in well-lit areas of classroom • Offer additional or more focused light source • Offer nonvisual means of communication such as tactile or auditory methods • Arrange classroom for easier physical movement
Attention Deficit Hyperactivity Disorder (ADHD)	• Moves quickly from one activity to the next • Forgetful • Difficulty following directions • Impulsive • Overreacts to situations and feelings • Difficulty sitting still	A team approach including: • Home and classroom observation • Medical exam • Mental health exam • Behavioral rating scale • Conners' Continuous Performance Test (CPT-3)	• Adhere to strict schedules • Utilize and offer organizational tools • Praise appropriate behavior • Vary instruction modes • Build in physical "breaks" • Utilize kinesthetic methods of teaching

- *Inclusion*. Sometimes students with special needs attend regular classes, even if they are not able to keep up academically with class requirements. With **inclusion**, the only requirement is that the student will benefit from the class. For example, a student with Down syndrome might be placed in a regular classroom, even if unable to keep up academically, to gain social interaction skills. A student included on this basis would complete modified assignments. Special education teachers serve as resources for classroom teachers when students are placed for inclusion.

- *Special education classes*. Students who have special needs may spend part or all of their day in classes with other students who have similar disabilities. **Special education** provides adapted programs, extra staff, and specialized equipment or learning environments or materials to help students with special needs to learn. Special education teachers receive training in methods to adapt and individualize learning for many different special needs. Students who have severe disabilities often spend the whole day in special education classrooms to best meet their learning needs.

Cultural Diversity

Part of this nation's strength comes from the fact that people with different backgrounds, languages, races, and religions have come together to form one society. The United States is a country of immigrants. From the first colonists to those who have come recently,

Figure 9.11 Culturally diverse learning environments help stimulate learning.

individuals and groups from many countries have added vitality and energy, as well as skills and knowledge, to their new country. Schools reflect the diversity of the United States (Figure 9.11).

Many people identify with a specific ethnic group based on their heritage. *Ethnicity* refers to a particular racial, national, or cultural group including that group's customs, beliefs, values, and often language and religion. Racial diversity is just one component of diversity. Some people identify with a racial group. Others identify with their country of origin or that of their ancestors. Many people simply see themselves as Americans.

Diversity Enriches Learning

It is natural to gravitate toward people with whom you have things in common. Listening to different ideas and opinions, learning to understand others, and trying new experiences, however, all stimulate thought and learning. This happens when you are part of a diverse learning environment.

To schools that see diversity primarily as a source of conflict, it presents an *arduous* (hard to accomplish or achieve) challenge. Such schools may view diversity as something that requires extra effort and resources. To those who embrace diversity, it can offer a competitive edge. Diversity is an integral part of the school's vision, mission, values, and student learning. Together, this unified climate delivers a rich learning environment.

School administrators set the overall tone for a school regarding diversity. Teachers who model acceptance, develop policies of tolerance, and incorporate interest in culture into learning create a positive atmosphere for learning. Classrooms where students receive respect and treatment as individuals enhance learning. In such an atmosphere, students develop the skills they need to succeed in the adult world.

Employers rely on employees who can collaborate with one another, using their individual strengths and experiences as positive forces. *Stereotypes*—preconceived generalizations about certain groups of people—and prejudice have no place in schools or the workplace.

Diversity Requires Sensitivity

A student's culture, background, and experiences affect his or her learning. All of these factors create a context in which a learner grows and develops, and they have an important impact on learning.

Teaching requires sensitivity to each student's personal situation. For example, some cultures discourage competition. Learning about students' cultures may come from meeting with parents, listening to the students'

personal stories, and studying cultural traditions (Figure 9.12). As with other students, teachers must take family structures and financial situations into account. For instance, students from families with lower incomes may not be able to participate in activities that require extra fees. Likewise, not all students have two parents. Instead of making Mother's Day cards, a sensitive teacher might introduce a class project of making thank you cards as a way of thanking someone who has been helpful.

Figure 9.12 Talking with parents and students helps teachers develop sensitivity to culture, background, and experiences that affect student learning. Learning about students as individuals helps maximize learning for all students.

Language Diversity

Language links to culture, but students from other cultures and countries who are not proficient in the English language face additional challenges in school. Students with **limited English proficiency (LEP)** have difficulty communicating effectively in English because English is not their native or primary language. A term often synonymous with LEP is **English language learners (ELL).** These students must learn English while also mastering the content of their regular classes.

The process of learning English is not an easy one. It involves developing reading and writing skills, as well as verbal communication. In addition to general vocabulary, every subject area has its own specialized terms. Understanding also depends on learning about popular culture, such as holidays and traditions, television and movies, music, magazines, and fashion.

Variables in English Language Programs

There is debate about how to best help students whose native language is not English. States and school districts have tried a variety of approaches. On one end of the spectrum, *bilingual* programs teach all classes in two languages, English and students' native languages. On the other end, students spend the school day in regular classes taught in English and receive some additional help outside of class. Sometimes students attend regular classes part of the day and a pull-out *English as a Second Language*

(ESL) program for other periods. ESL programs concentrate on teaching English language skills.

Many variables are involved in decisions about how to structure programs. Some school districts have a large percentage of English Language Learners (ELL). One language may be dominant, or students may speak dozens of different languages. Other districts have few students who are not proficient in English.

Helping English Language Learners

Classroom teachers who have students with limited English proficiency must be innovative in finding ways to help them. Younger children pick up the oral skills of a new language more quickly than older students. Older students also must deal with more difficult school subjects and a faster pace of learning.

Many techniques for these situations mirror those of good teaching in general. For example, when teachers use several methods to teach concepts, the English language learner has multiple possibilities for understanding.

The basis for other techniques is common sense. Speaking clearly, printing assignments on the board, summarizing, demonstrating, and giving step-by-step directions can all be helpful. Students often benefit from working in pairs and groups. Teachers may provide study guides emphasizing key points and vocabulary. Working collaboratively with experts in the school, such as an ESL teacher, to alter instruction is often helpful.

Professional Tip

Developing Cultural Sensitivity

Skilled teachers are sensitive to student diversity, treating each student with respect and sensitivity. Sometimes it is easy to identify diversity. Other times, diversity may not be so easily noticed. Examples may include learning differences, religion, or other cultural differences. Sensitivity to differences, both visible and invisible, is an essential competency for educators. Ethical dilemmas that arise in diverse student populations often reach resolution when the teacher is aware of the numerous ethical challenges that can arise. This should include self-evaluation to explore personal beliefs and potential prejudices held toward others along with continuing diversity education.

Dig Deeper

Check with your school to see if an *Ethical Code of Conduct* document exists for the school community. How does the document address diversity?

The Challenge of Teaching Diverse Learners

Perhaps, after reading this chapter, the idea of meeting the needs of so many different types of learners seems a bit overwhelming (Figure 9.13). There is no doubt that teaching is a challenging profession, but that is part of its appeal. Putting forth your best efforts to help all students succeed is worthwhile and can be immensely satisfying.

Meeting the needs of individuals does not require separate teaching plans for every student. It starts with the belief in each student's potential. It means learning about students as individuals, their knowledge, abilities, strengths, challenges, interests, and learning styles. Effective teachers plan their teaching to target a wide range of students. Classes of students often include individuals with special needs, gifted students, and English language learners, in addition to other types of diversity.

As with learning styles, many teachers use differentiated instruction to maximize learning for all students. With *differentiated instruction*, a teacher often provides options for learning a topic or skill. Either the teacher or the students may choose options that fit the students' needs or learning styles. For example, if students are to learn about the metamorphosis of caterpillars into butterflies, the options might include reading about it, performing an experiment, using a computer simulation, or creating a model of the process. For each option, the teacher provides guidelines for learning and identifies how that learning will be evaluated.

Teachers who use differentiated instruction often divide students into groups, but not always the same groups. For example, for one lesson, a teacher might divide students according to how much they already know about the topic. For another, English language learners might work together, supported with important vocabulary translated into the first language. Sometimes the teacher might have learning activities suited to different learning styles. You will learn more about differentiated instruction later in the text.

Learning more now about the spectrum of students who may one day sit in your classroom gives you a head start. You can pay attention to how your current teachers deal with learning diversity. As you study to become a teacher, choose projects, activities, and experiences that will prepare you well for this aspect of teaching. Commit to being a creative and caring teacher.

Figure 9.13   When putting forth their best efforts in meeting the needs of diverse learners, teachers help students achieve success.

Chapter 9 Review and Assess

Summary

- Learning styles influence the variety of ways students learn most easily.

- By understanding learning styles and multiple intelligences, teachers can help students learn more effectively.

- Students who are considered gifted and talented and those with special needs are called exceptional learners.

- Gifted students usually excel in one or two academic areas, not necessarily all areas. Talented students excel in other areas, such as fine arts.

- Students with special needs may have any of a variety of problems that impact learning, ranging from physical, mental, emotional, and social disabilities to speech, vision, hearing, and learning disorders.

- Cultural factors, backgrounds, and experiences also impact student learning.

- When schools view diversity as a positive force, it can enhance learning and prepare students to work effectively in a diverse society.

- English language learners face additional learning challenges. Teachers can use a variety of methods, as well, to help these students.

- Effective teaching requires identifying the characteristics of individual learners and devising ways to meet their needs.

Review and Study

1. What does the term *learning diversity* mean?

2. Name the learning style that links to the following ways a young child might learn the alphabet: (A) Singing the "ABC" song; (B) Placing magnetic alphabet shapes on a refrigerator door and identifying them; (C) Creating letter shapes with the fingers.

3. What are two ways a teacher can identify a student's learning style?

4. Which two multiple intelligence areas are most closely linked to success in core school subjects?

5. How could analyzing an underperforming student's strengths using the multiple intelligence theory help a teacher improve the student's learning?

6. List five strategies schools and teachers might use to help gifted and talented students meet their potentials and abilities.

7. Who makes up the team that develops an Individualized Education Program (IEP) for a student?

8. What is the difference between mainstreaming and inclusion?

9. How does a school environment that embraces diversity prepare students for success in the workplace?

10. Why does teaching require sensitivity to each student's personal situation?

11. List three common-sense strategies classroom teachers can use to help English language learners.

12. Why do some teachers use differentiated instruction? Give an example of differentiated instruction.

Vocabulary Activity

13. Working in teams, locate a small image online that visually describes or explains each of the *Content* and *Academic* terms on page 204. Print each image. To create flash cards, write each term on a note card and paste the image that describes or explains the term on the opposite side. Use the cards with your team members to reinforce the chapter vocabulary.

Critical Thinking

14. **Analyze evidence.** What would you consider your primary and secondary learning styles? Which do you think are your top four intelligences? Analyze evidence that supports your rationale for these selections. How are your preferred learning styles and top areas of intelligence related? How has having these particular traits affected your school experiences? Write a summary about your analysis.

15. **Draw conclusions.** Why do you think that schools have historically put more emphasis on academic giftedness over talents in other areas? Draw conclusions about some specific ways that schools could be more supportive of talented students.

16. **Compare and contrast.** Compare and contrast the experience of learning a foreign language as a school subject with learning English for the first time as a new student in school in the United States. Presume your classmates and you are a group of young teachers. What strategies might you use to help students succeed in the classroom? Discuss your ideas in class.

Core Skills

17. **Observation and writing.** Arrange to observe a group of young children at play at a local elementary school. During your observation, look for indicators of the preferred style of learning for at least two children. Following your observation, write a report and cite the specific examples that support your conclusions.

18. **Research and writing.** To learn more about students who have special needs, choose one or more of the following to complete:

    • interview a special education teacher or a parent of a student with special needs

    • observe a class for students with special needs and look for ways the teacher interacts with students, identifying specific techniques that enhance learning

    • conduct online research about a specific special need and strategies teachers can use to enhance learning success

    Write a brief proposal with specifics of your research project for your teacher's approval. Include a paragraph on whether your choice draws on specific types of intelligence that are your strengths or will help you improve skills in other areas of intelligence. Write your research report and discuss the details in class.

19. **Research, speaking, and listening.** Collaborate in teams to create a list of responsibilities for each of the following groups in making diversity a positive aspect of education: parents, community members, administrators, teachers, and students. Cite the text and other reliable resources as evidence supporting your list of responsibilities. Post your list to the school-approved class blog or discussion board for classmate comments.

20. **Speaking, listening, and writing.** In teams, develop a list of five key classroom rules you would use to foster respect for all learners in the classroom. Identify the grade levels for which these rules would be appropriate. Pair up with another team and discuss your lists of rules. Do the teams agree or disagree? With the class, discuss when it might be appropriate to involve students in decision making about classroom rules? What are the pros and cons of this approach?

21. **Speaking and listening.** Interview an exchange student or someone who immigrated to the United States. Develop questions to ask that relate to the experience of dealing with differences in language, customs, and schools. Share the results of your interview with the class. How were the results of your classmates' interviews similar or different from your own? How will the results of the interview impact your approach to teaching English language learners?

22. **Technology application.** Choose an individual learning strength or special need described in this chapter. Complete an online search for books that are available that might give more insight into teachers working with children with this learning strength or special need. Choose one book to read. Write a summary identifying the key concepts identified in the book. Post your report to the class blog or website for your classmate to review.

23. **CTE College and career readiness practice.** Read the definition of *integrity* in Webster's Collegiate Dictionary. How does this definition compare to your understanding of integrity? Write a short essay about the meaning of integrity in your life. How do actions, attitudes, and beliefs impact integrity? How do you act with integrity in the decisions you make and how you interact with others? How will your integrity impact your career as a teacher? What happens when people fail to act with integrity?

College and Career Portfolio

Your portfolio should contain samples of your work that show your skills and talents. Now is the time to start collecting items. Examine past school and work assignments, especially those completed for this class. Perhaps select a research paper, letter, digital slide show, or other work that demonstrates your writing talents. Look for projects that showcase your critical-thinking and problem-solving abilities. Have you completed a long or complicated project such as a teaching lesson or service project? Write a description of the project and tell how you managed its various parts to complete it on time. Include samples of the project in your portfolio.

- Save the documents that showcase your skills and talents in your e-portfolio, placing the documents in the appropriate subfolders.

- Place the hard copies of the same items in the container for your print portfolio.

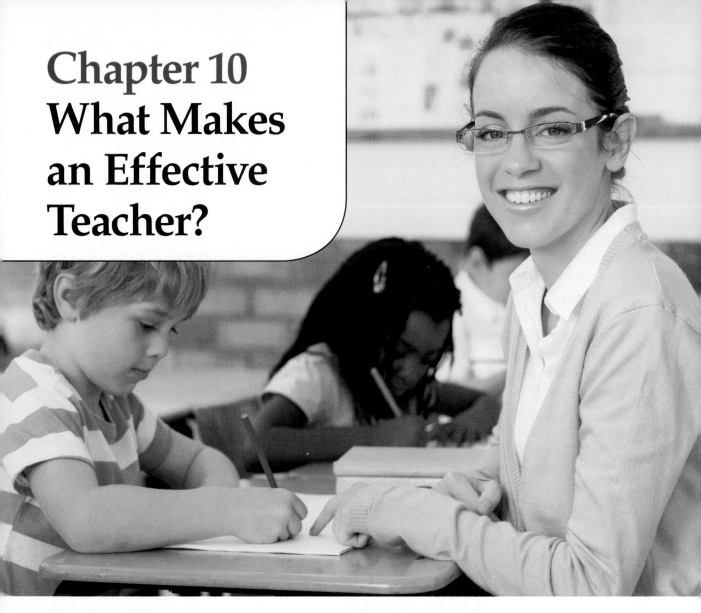

Chapter 10
What Makes an Effective Teacher?

Content Terms

facilitator
direct learning
teachable moment
assessment
mission statement
lifelong learner
professional development
mixed message
active listening
assertive communicator
aggressive communicator
passive communicator
mediator
mediation

Academic Terms

abdominal thrust
ethics
collaboration
optimism
proactive
organizational culture
intangible
chain of command

Objectives

After studying this chapter, you will be able to

- **describe** the major roles that teachers perform.

- **summarize** teachers' professional qualities that are needed for teaching success.

- **explain** how to work effectively within a school, including developing an understanding of a school's organizational culture.

- **summarize** the importance of subject-matter knowledge and effective teaching skills for teachers and how they can stay up-to-date.

- **demonstrate** your ability to communicate effectively verbally, nonverbally, and through clear, professional, written communication.

- **acquire** skills in constructive conflict management.

Reading Prep

As you read the chapter, record any questions that come to mind. Indicate where the answer to each question can be found: within the text, by asking your teachers, in another book, on the Internet, or by reflecting on your own knowledge and experiences. Pursue the answers to your questions.

At the Companion Website you can

- **Practice** terms with e-flash cards and interactive games
- **Assess** what you learn by completing self-assessment quizzes
- **Expand** knowledge with interactive activities

Companion
G-W Learning

www.g-wlearning.com/teaching/

Study on the go

Use a mobile device to practice terms and review with self-assessment quizzes.

Mobile
G-W Learning

www.m.g-wlearning.com/0094/

Case Study

As a class, read the case study and discuss the questions that follow.

I first met Ms. Rodriguez in middle school when she was my creative writing teacher. I learned more from her than anyone else in all of my years of school—not only what she taught me about writing styles, but about life and the vibrancy of the world all around us. She was the type of person who loved life and lived it to the fullest extent. Ms. Rodriguez always had good constructive ideas for her classes and she gave more individual attention to her students than any other teacher I knew. When a student had a problem, it was her problem, too. We adored her!

One day Ms. Rodriguez gave us the assignment to compose a poem. I have never been good at writing poetry so I went to our school library and pulled out the oldest book of poems I could find. It was a book by Carl Sandburg. I copied the poem verbatim and handed it in. When Ms. Rodriguez returned my poem, she had written "this poem reminds me of a poem of Carl Sandburg's; what a coincidence." She knew full well that I had plagiarized. I didn't receive credit. She never shamed me publically,

only reprimanded me privately. But more importantly, I learned something important that day that changed me. That is the kind of teacher I hope to be someday.

Let's Discuss

- In what ways did Ms. Rodriguez exemplify the characteristics of an effective teacher?

- In what other ways might you surmise she would encourage student learning in creative writing?

You, like every person thinking of becoming a teacher, want to be a great one. Perhaps your inspiration was a wonderful teacher who made a real difference in your life.

If you put a group of highly effective teachers together in a room, their obvious differences might surprise you. They would, for example, vary in personality. By looking deeper, however, you would find they have much in common. They are comfortable in the numerous roles that teachers play. They display important characteristics of professionalism. They understand how to work effectively within their school. Everyone respects their knowledge and teaching skill. They are effective communicators and are able to deal effectively with conflicts that arise.

This chapter will help you learn more about what it takes to become that great teacher. Although you will explore many of the topics here, you will learn more about them in greater detail in other chapters. As you read, think about how you can start now developing the attitudes, skills, and knowledge you will need to have a positive impact on students' lives.

Teaching Roles

If you were asked what teachers do, how would you answer? In the most simplistic terms, they teach. How that plays out on a daily basis varies infinitely.

Teachers have many roles. These change quickly, sometimes minute by minute. Although the roles may change, all focus on helping students learn. The following five key roles deserve a more in-depth look:

- information provider
- facilitator
- planner
- learning evaluator
- role model

Teachers Provide Information

Students know that teachers are great sources of information, and providing information is an essential teaching role. Competent teachers know the content of the subjects they teach well. A middle school math teacher may not have the depth of math knowledge that a math professor at a university may have, but that makes sense. A teacher's knowledge base should be appropriate in scope and depth for the level taught. Today, the problem is that there is often an overload of available information. Knowing their subject matter well helps teachers evaluate information. It allows them to choose what is most accurate and relevant to present to their students (Figure 10.1).

Figure 10.1 Teachers who know their subject matter are a great source of information for their students and engage students in learning.

Parents and students expect teachers to provide appropriate, current information. If you are learning the **abdominal thrust** (Heimlich maneuver, or an action to dispel an object from a choking victim's throat) for choking victims, you want to be confident that your teacher knows the technique and guidelines, and correctly demonstrates the procedure. At the very least, providing inaccurate information is a waste of everyone's time. In cases such as this, it can be the difference between life and death.

At the same time, considering teachers only as information providers would not be accurate. Information is readily available, especially with today's technology. If you want to know more about English grammar, you can easily read a grammar book or find a tutorial online. Most people, however, learn better when teachers present the best information at the right level in a variety of interesting ways. Interaction, feedback, review, and practice are also keys to learning. That is where some of teachers' other roles come into play.

Teachers Facilitate Learning

Teachers play the role of **facilitator,** meaning they create situations that help students learn by actively involving students in learning, rather than just presenting information. They do this in a variety of ways. Teachers plan what to teach and figure out how to best present the material. They lead discussions. They ask questions. They suggest alternative ideas. Teachers devise and guide student activities, and help students to work together. Simply put, teachers guide students' learning.

Leading by facilitating is not the same as *directing learning*. Teachers who use **direct learning** tell students what to learn and provide all the structure for the learning to take place. Facilitators guide, rather than direct. Both methods are appropriate in certain situations. For example, having students follow set directions carefully is appropriate in a science experiment that involves chemicals that could be dangerous if combined incorrectly.

When teachers act as facilitators, they require that students do the work of learning. For example, when students ask questions, the teacher helps and encourages them to find the answers for themselves. Not every student is comfortable with the open-ended nature of facilitative learning. Some prefer knowing exactly what they are supposed to learn and the steps needed to understand.

One benefit of facilitated learning is that it can unleash students' creativity and self-motivation (Figure 10.2). They often feel more pride and ownership in their learning. Students who are motivated and engaged in the learning process are also less likely to exhibit problem behaviors.

Facilitation is a learned skill. Teachers who facilitate well know the difference between "getting the job done right" (the teacher's way) and making sure that students are learning. As a new teacher, you will develop this skill with practice.

Figure 10.2   When teachers serve as facilitators, students take an active part in their learning.

Teachers Plan for Learning

In planning for instruction, teachers determine what information students will learn, how to present it, and what the outcomes should be. They plan ways to assess whether or not learning took place. Teachers utilize resources to adapt lessons for different types of learners. They devise ways to make learning challenging, fun, inspiring, and effective.

Although teachers put a great deal of time into planning, they know that plans will not always work out. Emergencies arise and unexpected events happen. Sometimes unforeseen teaching opportunities (**teachable moments**) come along in the course of a lesson, and teachers decide to take advantage of them. Experienced teachers learn to adapt to the unexpected. Changes in plans can enhance learning and teach students flexibility.

Teachers Evaluate Learning

Another important role of teachers is to evaluate students' learning and progress. Sometimes this process results in a grade. Other times it does not.

When teachers assign grades to students' work, they are evaluating how much or how well the students have learned. (Actually, learning itself cannot be accurately measured. Teachers look at how well students can demonstrate what they have learned.) Grades are usually a letter (**A**, **B**, **C**, **D**, or **F**) or a number. Letter grades have standard meanings: an **A** is excellent, a **B** is above-average, a **C** is average, a **D** is below-average, and an **F** means failing. Report cards typically show letter grades, sometimes with a plus or minus sign.

Students need to understand their teachers' grading policies. With older students, grades are often a point of conflict. Having clear, consistent policies help minimize disputes. With younger children, understanding what "counts" helps them know what kinds of effort a teacher expects so they can benefit most from learning. For example, Anthony, a bright but shy third-grader, rarely raised his hand to answer a question. Once he found out participation counted toward his grade, he was more willing to volunteer. The class benefited from his contributions, and he gradually became more outgoing.

Assessment is a related, but somewhat different, type of evaluation. It involves determining how much a student or class has learned or is currently learning. When teachers assess student performance, they are simply reporting on achievement. There is no judgment or consideration of quality, as there is in grading. For example, if the lesson is on the impact of good nutrition on the growth of a baby chick, the teacher may use discussion to assess students' understanding. If the discussion shows students have not understood main points, the teacher might review or add an activity before moving on to another topic.

Both types of evaluation—grading and assessment—involve monitoring student progress. They vary primarily in purpose.

Teachers Are Role Models

Schools are one of the first, and most important, places where behavior and future educational success are shaped. Teachers are important role models for their students (Figure 10.3).

Figure 10.3 Many students look to their teachers as positive role models, helping shape students' educational success.

Serving as a role model comes with a great deal of responsibility. Teachers' behavior can have either a positive or negative effect on students' behavior and future success. The best teachers live in ways that demonstrate the values, attitudes, and behaviors that go with the roles of learner, professional, and citizen.

Whether they are at school or in the community, teachers must show honesty, respect, and responsibility. Effective teachers do not simply talk about examples, they *act* as examples. They live out the expectations they have for their students by coming to class well prepared, showing competence, commitment, and integrity. They model how to handle disagreements. They set high standards for themselves, as well as others.

Developing Professional Qualities

Qualities related to professionalism are critical to teaching success. The term *professional* is used frequently to indicate a high degree of skill, competence, and **ethics** (conduct based on moral principles). Your reputation as a professional is important to being successful as a teacher. This section identifies some of the important skills, habits, and attitudes that professional teachers exhibit.

Be Dependable

In the workplace, employers highly value dependability. For teachers, it is doubly important. Each school day, students rely on their teachers to be there on time and to be prepared to teach. People who are dependable are reliable and loyal, and others know they can count on them to do what they say. Think about what would happen if a coach does not show up for a game or a teacher is three days late turning in grades. One employee's lack of dependability can have far-reaching consequences.

Professional Tip

Work-Life Balance

Exploring a career is the perfect time to consider how you can balance all of the remarkable parts of your life and understand the dynamics of issues surrounding work-life balance. You understand that as individuals, there will be competing interests, responsibilities, and needs. There will also be competing opportunities. Likewise, there will be people who will tell you how to balance your work-life. Ultimately, however, only you can figure out how to pack it all into one lifetime journey. It is a challenge that must be revisited again and again as your life and work change. As you begin discovering the teaching profession, take some time to observe how teachers attempt to balance competing demands both inside the classroom and as far as you can surmise, in their personal lives.

Dig Deeper

Seek an opportunity to interview a teacher about how he or she balances work-life, health and exercise, intellectual stimulation, spiritual sustenance, and personal or family demands. Then, reflect on your own life and identify ways that you can intentionally strive for work-life balance.

Be Responsible

Imagine that you are a kindergarten teacher. You are gathering up your things to leave school on a Friday afternoon when you receive a call from the mother of one of your students. She is obviously upset. She tells you that her daughter may not be in school on Monday because the family has just been evicted from their home. She does not know if or where they will be able to find a place to stay (Figure 10.4).

It would be easy to say that you are sorry and ask the mother to notify the school office on Monday. Instead, you alert the school counselor to the issue and she is able to secure a place for the family at a shelter. You assure the mother that you will be especially sensitive to her daughter's needs as she adjusts to an abrupt lifestyle change.

Because you took the time to follow through, you will be a bit late for dinner with friends. Taking the time to aid this family is worth the minor inconvenience. You feel a responsibility for your students that goes beyond the classroom.

Being responsible means showing a commitment to your obligations, relationships, and actions. It means not blaming someone else when things do not go exactly as planned. When working on a team, you commit to doing your best, which may result in personal satisfaction. Facing difficult challenges helps you earn respect from others and a reputation for accomplishment and trustworthiness.

Figure 10.4 Responsible teachers are sensitive to the needs of their students and parents, showing commitment to their obligations and relationships.

Responsibility means carrying a task through to the end, whether or not the process is easy. You commit to being the person who has the ultimate responsibility to get the job done. Those who handle responsibility well usually receive requests to take on more. They find that facing difficult challenges can bring real satisfaction.

Be Committed to Students

As you read in the previous chapter, effective teachers come to the classroom believing that all students can learn, though how they learn best may differ. Through careful observation, teachers can better understand each student's abilities, skills, interests, strengths, and relationships. In addition to helping students gain specific content knowledge, teachers also help foster self-esteem and motivation to learn. This requires a real commitment to each individual.

Show Respect

Showing respect involves showing regard for others' dignity, ideas, and expectations. As a student, you show a teacher respect by being courteous and meeting his or her course requirements or standards. Teachers treat students with respect when they show regard for each individual's needs, feelings, and potential.

For teachers, showing respect within their school or other workplace is a key skill. They expect respect from their students. At the same time, they need to show respect for their students and for everyone on staff.

Many new teachers fail to understand and acknowledge their place in the workplace organization. Even the most casual, unstructured schools have organizational structures, although they may be difficult to identify. You owe respect to those above you, but a professional treats everyone well. Too often, the roles and importance of *support staff*, all the nonteaching personnel from bus drivers to food-service personnel and counselors, are underestimated. You show respect through your attitude, how you communicate, and the courtesy you show others.

Be a Team Player

In survey after survey, employers list effective interpersonal skills as the primary characteristic they look for in potential employees. People with good interpersonal skills get along well with others in the workplace and are good team players.

Almost all jobs require **collaboration**—working cooperatively with others. Because teams accomplish so much work, it is essential to be a team player. With effective teams, members encourage one another and utilize the skills

Figure 10.5 Sharing technology skills with other staff members is an example of being a team player.

and talents of individual members (Figure 10.5). They focus on group success, rather than on taking individual credit. Ineffective teams are usually due to a poorly defined task or, more likely, a lack of teamwork.

Teachers not only work with students, they also work with fellow teachers, staff, administrators, and school board members. Effective teachers work in collaboration with other school personnel on everything from curriculum to developing school policies.

See the Big Picture

"Seeing the big picture" means looking past the small details and focusing on the larger purpose. Some people get so overwhelmed in their own tasks or day-to-day problems that they lose sight of the real goals. For example, if a teacher solely focuses on getting through a lesson, he or she may overlook the special learning needs of individual children.

Seeing the big picture does not mean overlooking the details of a job. In fact, many jobs require a high level of attention to details. The larger purpose or goal, however, should always be at the forefront of the teacher's mind.

Develop a Positive Attitude

Why do some people love their work and others do not? Two factors are usually involved. People who love their work have a positive attitude, and they get satisfaction from what they do.

Having a positive attitude means having the *optimism* (the inclination to see favorable outcomes) and energy to positively relate to others and to complete a job. It is the desire to make something happen.

Keeping a positive attitude has many benefits. When you see the potential good in situations, you energize those around you by your enthusiasm. Conversely, constantly complaining drags you and others down. While individuals often have a tendency toward optimism or negativity, each person can make a conscious choice to try to keep a positive attitude.

What if you find yourself in a difficult work situation? Being *proactive*— or anticipating the need to find solutions to future problems, needs, or changes—will help improve your attitude. Take a step back to note what you like most about your job. Do you feel excitement about helping students learn? Focus on the positive strides your students are making, rather than on an administrator who is not as supportive as you would like. If you are dealing with students whose behaviors are interfering with the learning of others, network with colleagues for a new approach to managing difficult behavior. Can you restructure the environment to minimize the negative behaviors? What is within your power to make your job more personally rewarding?

Think about the benefits of establishing these habits—thinking positively and improving difficult situations—now (Figure 10.6)! They will help you through rough spots in school, work, and life. Most of all, you will enjoy life more and have a positive impact on others. You cannot control life, but you can control your reactions to it.

Figure 10.6 Teachers who proactively find ways to deal with challenges have a positive impact on students.

Working Effectively Within a School

You have landed your first teaching job. You are off to the back-to-school picnic for teachers, wearing shorts and flip-flops. When you arrive, all of the other teachers are dressed in coordinated sportswear, mainly khaki pants, and pressed shirts. Is it all in your mind or is everyone a little guarded in conversations with you? Did you miss a memo about what to wear, or do you not understand the organizational culture?

Perspectives on Teaching

Anna stepped onto the subway for the long ride home. It was a brisk, autumn day and Anna was looking forward to relaxing and reflecting on the day during the ride. It had been a day of familiar routines, dealing with the unexpected, and quickly adapting her teaching plans.

Anna's Thoughts...

Today was another crazy day! There were no boring days teaching fourth grade. Let's see…today's lessons included reading, long division, spelling, state history, and folk dancing. I had students work in groups for reading. Some struggled with long division, others with spelling. A few didn't want to dance with a partner. Other students were excited about everything. These were my planned topics, but the day, like most, didn't go entirely according to plan.

On top of everything else, there was a long fire drill today with everyone standing outside in the brisk wind. After lunch, two boys came close to trading punches. A normally shy girl told a funny joke that made the whole class laugh. The twins brought a picture of their new baby sister. Another student cried when he missed the bus. One boy remembered his homework for the first time in a week. Another gave me a big smile when he passed his spelling test—those smiles just make my days seem brighter.

I managed to smooth over the disputes, give feedback as students asked questions, and share emotions with those who were struggling. Tomorrow will bring a new set of challenges and rewards—and I will love every minute!

Analyze It!

As you read through Anna's day, what roles and professional qualities did you identify as necessary for an effective teacher? Cite evidence from Anna's narrative that supports these roles and qualities.

What is ***organizational culture***? It is the "personality" of an organization based on the assumptions, values, standards, behaviors, and actions of people, as well as the tangible signs of an organization. For teachers, the organization is the school. Some signs of organizational culture are easy to recognize. They include the things you can see or observe, such as the *look* of the space, the way people dress, and which accomplishments receive recognition. Others are ***intangible***, or abstract and less concrete. These include people's assumptions, values, and the reasons behind their behaviors and actions.

How can you figure out the culture of a school? A good place to start is with the school policies and procedures and the structure of the school or school district. Many schools and school districts have a manual for new teachers. This may include a **mission statement**—the official version of an organization's purpose and goals, along with policies and procedures. Official websites may give information about the ***chain of command,*** or the official organizational structure that tells who reports to whom. For example, department heads may report to the principal who reports directly to the superintendent. What responsibilities do those in various positions have? Understanding the chain of command and how it works in your school is important.

In many workplaces, you are expected to discuss problems and issues with your immediate supervisor, rather than go directly to people above that person. Look for how the school values and uses people, facilities, space, and other resources, such as technology. Do the school's stated goals match what you observe?

The next step in understanding organizational culture is to ask questions. Fellow teachers are usually willing to share information. Pay attention to conversations and how people negotiate issues. How do things get done? Who has the most influence? (Remember that the official chain of command does not always reflect what is really happening.) Understanding and assessing the organizational culture can mean the difference between success and failure in the workplace.

Subject Knowledge and Teaching Skills

Teachers must have a thorough understanding of the subjects that they teach. For instance, a Spanish teacher must know Spanish through speech and written text. A kindergarten teacher must understand the developmental abilities of five- and six-year-olds.

The best teachers have a broad understanding of their subject matter. They understand how it is organized, how it has changed over time, and how it may change in the future. They know how their subject matter relates to other subjects such as reading, math, and writing. Teachers also need to understand how their subject matter relates to careers students might later pursue.

New discoveries and information changes are ongoing, so teachers must be **lifelong learners,** people who commit to staying up to date in their knowledge and skills (Figure 10.7). Some of this requires reading and study. Effective teachers also take advantage of opportunities for professional development. **Professional development** involves taking part in professional organizations, attending seminars and conferences, pursuing an advanced degree, or other activities meant to improve professional knowledge and skills.

It is not enough for teachers to just know their subject matter. They must also know how to teach it. A driver's education teacher must be able to demonstrate and quickly communicate accident-avoidance techniques.

Teachers must be skilled at many teaching techniques and know which work best with particular topics and students. One class may have great discussions and learn effectively from them. Another may have few people who volunteer ideas. In every class, individual students have unique combinations of learning abilities and styles. An effective teacher adapts teaching techniques accordingly.

Figure 10.7 Effective teachers stay up to date by seeking opportunities for professional development and being lifelong learners.

Teachers must utilize many different creative teaching methods to capture their students' interest. Not all students learn in the same ways, so variety helps enhance learning. Choosing the best technique for particular material and adapting it skillfully is the sign of a good teacher.

Communicating Effectively

At the core of virtually every aspect of teaching is *communication* (Figure 10.8). Teachers determine what content to communicate and decide how best to convey it. The act of teaching depends on effectively communicating with students. Teachers, administrators, school boards, and community members all must exchange ideas. Parents, too, are part of the communication loop. This process can work well, but communication is complex, and there are many ways it can break down.

People communicate continually, even when they are not aware they are doing so. Your best friend ignored you at lunch. Did you offend her, or is she worried about her mom's health again? Every word you speak, and every gesture, action, and facial expression sends a message that the receiver interprets. The person who transmits a message or messages is the *sender*. The *receiver* in communication is the person who accepts a message from another. Normally, communication involves being both a sender and receiver.

For effective communication, the words the sender speaks and nonverbal messages must match. The nonverbal messages may come from a person's posture, tone of voice, facial expressions, eye contact (or lack of it), and many other things. A discrepancy between verbal and nonverbal messages results in a **mixed message**. Mixed messages confuse receivers. A teacher who laughs while scolding a child for breaking a rule is sending a mixed message.

While there are many components of effective communication, this chapter will explore two key components. First, communication must occur in the context of positive relationships. Second, each form of communication—verbal, nonverbal, written, and electronic—depends on specific, but related, skills.

Figure 10.8 Communication between teachers and students is vital in order for learning to take place.

Creating Positive Relationships

Good communication begins with positive relationships. Negative relationships create barriers that impede effective communication. For example, suppose you are angry with your brother. He asks you to swap chores with him, and you snap back that he is just trying to get out of work. His message was about a trade of jobs, but all you hear is that he wants you to mow the lawn so he doesn't have to do it. Because of your feelings, you put a negative spin on a neutral message from him.

Several factors go into building positive relationships. These include the following:

- *Take ownership in the relationship*. This means taking responsibility for your own feelings and behaviors, rather than blaming others. For example, if you are feeling sad, acknowledge "I feel sad," rather than thinking "You make me sad." Your feelings are your own. Events may influence your feelings, but another person does not cause them.

  Understanding this difference will help you to realize that although you can influence others, you cannot control their feelings. For example, you can encourage young children to act appropriately in the classroom, but you cannot force them to want to behave. Rewards, encouragement, or punishments may influence a child toward a particular behavioral goal, but the motivation must come from the child.

- *Be an active listener*. **Active listening** involves asking questions and restating ideas to discover the true message of the sender. By giving verbal feedback, you tell the sender that you are listening and understanding the message.

  Review the conversation between a teacher and student in Figure 10.9. Each time the student makes a statement, the teacher demonstrates that he or she is listening by asking another clarifying question. By the end, it is clear that the student is feeling left out and friendless. From actively listening to the student, the teacher can then help solve the problem.

Figure 10.9   Example of Active Listening
Chaney: I don't want to go to recess.
Mr. Griggs: Are you unhappy when you go to recess?
Chaney: Yeah. People are not very nice.
Mr. Griggs: What do they do that isn't nice?
Chaney: No one includes me.
Mr. Griggs: You feel left out of games?
Chaney: Yes. I wish I had more friends.

Listening requires that you focus on the other person. It helps you to stay in the present moment and increases the exchange of clear communication.

- *Use assertive communication*. **Assertive communicators** freely express their thoughts, ideas, and feelings respectfully and allow others to do the same. **Aggressive communicators** aim to hurt or put down other people and show disrespect. A third group, **passive communicators**, are unwilling to say what they feel, think, or desire, wanting to avoid all conflict.

Improving Communication Skills

Effective teachers rely on exceptional communication skills. They are able to communicate clearly through speech and writing. Their nonverbal messages are consistent with what they say. They also use electronic communication to their advantage.

Speaking

Even though effective teachers are good listeners and involve students in activities, the many aspects of teaching involve a great deal of talking. Unlike casual conversation, teachers must speak with thought and purpose.

In the classroom, time is a limited commodity. Teachers must be conscious of using it effectively. Lesson plans help them figure out how to achieve as much learning as possible within a class period. Experienced teachers do not need to write out exactly what they will say, but they do identify the points students are to learn and key questions to discuss. This allows them to achieve their goals while staying flexible enough to improvise based on what actually happens during the lesson.

Effective speaking requires tailoring what you say to your particular audience. What are their needs and interests? What motivates them? What will keep their attention and interest? Think about how what you say will affect your listeners. Simplicity and clarity are important. Choose words that your audience understands. When using unfamiliar words in a lesson, briefly explain their meaning. As you speak, check your audience for signs of understanding and interest. It is important to tailor your message and how you present it to the specific audience.

As representatives of their school and role models for their students, teachers must remember they are almost never "off duty." A conversation with a friend while waiting to check out at the supermarket may be overheard and repeated. As professionals, teachers understand that it is never appropriate to speak badly about coworkers or students.

Similarly, teachers have an ethical responsibility not to reveal personal information about students or confidential work-related information to anyone else, except as part of their job (Figure 10.10).

The old saying "Think before you speak" is a wise one. Words are powerful, and once they are spoken, they can never be taken back. It only takes a few seconds to think about what you will say before you speak. No one will notice the slight pause. Making it a habit to do so can save you and others much embarrassment, hurt feelings, and perhaps your job.

Writing

In these days of dashing off text messages, formal writing may seem too time-consuming. Important information, however, particularly in business and education, is still conveyed in writing. It is essential that teachers are able to write well.

Most of the guidelines for effective speaking also apply to good writing. A few additional points important to remember include

- ***Avoid trying to impress people with complicated words and long sentences***. Sometimes people think that complex writing full of difficult or trendy terms will make them seem more intelligent. Actually, this type of writing frustrates readers and may make them feel like the writer is trying to put them down.

Figure 10.10 Teachers are almost never "off duty" and have an ethical responsibility never to reveal information about students or confidential work-related information.

It is best to convey your message clearly and concisely. Consider your tone. Remember that your purpose is to communicate your message.

- **Organize your writing effectively**. Make sure your main points are clearly stated. Check to see whether you move logically from one topic to another. If what you have written is long, use headings to divide sections, and provide a brief summary.

- **Check your grammar and language**. Never rely on your computer's spelling- and grammar-checking features. They often miss problems or suggest incorrect solutions. Learn the rules of good grammar, keep a grammar reference at hand, and proofread what you have written (preferably more than once) before you send anything in writing. Always use formal, Standard English, not slang or texting abbreviations. Poor grammar and writing keeps many people from getting or advancing in jobs. If you are unsure of your writing skills, have someone else proofread your work and learn from your mistakes.

- **Realize that anything you write may be permanent**. Once you deliver a printed document, you have no control over where it goes. Think carefully about what you put in writing, and make sure it represents you and the school professionally (Figure 10.11).

Nonverbal Communication

While words can be powerful, so are other aspects of communication. Your facial expressions, body posture and movements, your tone of voice, and appearance are all forms of nonverbal communication. They can reinforce your words, take away their power, or confuse your listener. Even when you are not speaking, your body is speaking.

You can improve the effectiveness of your communication by becoming more aware of your nonverbal cues. For example, you can make sure you are dressed appropriately for situations. Make an effort to speak calmly, even when you are upset. Pay attention to the messages your body is sending.

Figure 10.11 Make sure that what you write always represents you and your school in a professional manner.

Nonverbal cues account for a major part of miscommunication and often cause stress in relationships. For example, a teacher's facial expression may communicate anger, even when the words do not. A smile may mask a message of seriousness.

Electronic Communication

While e-mailing and text messaging may seem like private forms of conversation, they illustrate some of the special problems that can come with electronic communication. Because it can seem so spontaneous, it is easy to quickly translate your thoughts and feelings into words and hit the Send button. The problem is that once you have sent them, you have no control over what happens to them. A message can be forwarded to others without your permission. Information posted on the Internet, such as on a personal web page, may stay there indefinitely.

Jacob found that out when he applied to be a camp counselor after his sophomore year in college. He was studying to be a teacher and thought the job would give him great experience working with middle school students. Unfortunately, the camp staff checked to see if applicants had personal web pages. Jacob's included obscene language and pictures of him at a drinking party. He had posted these after high school graduation, and he had forgotten they were still on the site. He did not get the job.

Electronic communication has enormous benefits for teachers. It allows them to stay in touch with students and parents. It can be a great link to other teachers. It comes, however, with additional potential pitfalls. See Figure 10.12 suggestions for effectively using e-mail, the most common form of electronic communication.

Figure 10.12	Tips for Effective E-Mail

- Before you send a message, think what might happen if someone forwarded it without your knowledge or permission. Remember that your identity as the sender goes with your message.
- When you start using e-mail for any professional purpose (such as job applications or work-related correspondence), make sure you have an e-mail address that sounds professional.
- E-mails should have a descriptive subject line.
- Briefly summarize any necessary background information.
- Remember that all communication with teachers, potential employers, and the public should use formal Standard English—no abbreviations.
- For professional messages, include your name, title, and contact information.
- Proofread your message carefully before sending it.
- Never say anything in an electronic message that you would not say in the same way directly to the recipient.
- Avoid large attachments.
- If you are replying to an e-mail, never "Reply to All" unless you really mean to do so. Your unflattering comment could go to those you don't intend.
- In most work situations, your employer can monitor your e-mails and computer use. Inappropriate use can be grounds for dismissal.

Resolving Conflicts

Conflict is inevitable in any active relationship. People simply have different ideas, beliefs, and priorities. When they communicate, it is easy for these differences to surface.

People react to conflict in different ways. Some people view all disagreements as negative and try to avoid them. Others find conflict positive and enriching. Be aware of your own feelings about conflict, and remember that others' feelings may be different.

Certain situations increase the likelihood of conflict. It is common in close relationships. This is especially true when one person is comfortable communicating (especially communicating feelings) and the other is not. Conflict is common when people are under stress. They often say things they regret later.

Teachers routinely encounter situations where disagreements or miscommunication leads to conflict. They can help those involved deal more effectively with their differences.

Constructive Conflict Resolution

When two (or more) people work through a conflict in a constructive way, the result is greater understanding and relationship growth. When people do not handle conflict well, conflict can lead to continued conflict. One effective approach is *constructive conflict management*.

Constructive conflict management is a step-by-step method of coming to a solution. Think of conflict as a process that moves from decision making to problem solving to crisis resolution. The following are the steps in the process:

- ***Step 1: Clarify the issue***. The process begins with identifying the problem. Remember that when two people are in conflict, they often identify the problem differently. Each person must honestly and clearly state the problem from his or her perspective. Each person must also listen carefully to the other person.

- ***Step 2: Find out what each person wants***. Each person in the conflict must identify and express what he or she wants or needs in order to resolve the situation.

- ***Step 3: Identify various alternatives***. The next step is to identify various ways the conflict might be resolved. In constructive conflict resolution, both parties are open to suggestions. They are willing to brainstorm creative solutions. They try to focus on finding a solution, not just on meeting their own needs.

- **Step 4: Decide how to negotiate**. Decide on a resolution strategy. Will the areas of conflict be discussed with the hope one person will change his or her mind? Will each person give up part of what is wanted? Will they toss a coin? The people involved need to agree on how to proceed.

- **Step 5: Choose the best alternative**. There is rarely a solution that makes everyone happy. It is usually a matter of agreeing on which alternative both can accept. Sometimes a compromise just isn't possible, and the two sides simply agree to disagree.

- **Step 6: Solidify the agreement**. The parties must accept the choice they have made and agree to implement it.

- **Step 7: Review and renegotiate**. What happens when an agreement does not solve the problem? Perhaps one person does not follow through or accept the agreement. In that case, the decision requires review and compliance requested. As a last resort, renegotiating the conflict may be in order.

Mediation

Of course, solving disagreements is not always easy. Often, the people involved are so emotional or convinced they are right that they will not negotiate. That is when a third party who is neutral—a **mediator**—can often help the process. Through **mediation,** the mediator tries to help those in the dispute reach a peaceful agreement.

Teachers frequently act as mediators, especially with students (Figure 10.13). For example, two young children argue over whose turn it is to play with a toy. Their teacher may help them figure out a way to take turns. Older students may disagree over perceived personal rights.

When acting as mediators, teachers play the role of an objective third-party (not directly involved). They help each participant move through the process of reaching a settlement or agreement.

Figure 10.13 Sometimes teachers serve as mediators when students are experiencing a conflict.

Chapter 10 Review and Assess

Summary

- Teachers play a variety of roles, but all relate to helping students learn.
- Effective teaching depends on developing key personal habits and attitudes that link to supporting students, school, and community.
- Establishing a good personal reputation is critical to teaching success.
- Understanding how a school works helps a teacher effectively function within it.
- Teachers who learn and adapt to the organizational culture of their school are more successful and productive.
- To teach well, teachers need not only a thorough background in their subject area, but also the skills to motivate students to learn.
- Teaching techniques must fit the concepts the teacher is presenting and the characteristics of the students.
- Excellent communication skills are essential for teachers, beginning with positive relationships to minimize barriers to communication.
- Teachers must maintain professionalism in their speaking, writing, nonverbal communication, and electronic communication skills.
- Conflict is inevitable in any active relationship, yet positive resolution helps strengthen relationships.
- Constructive conflict management is a useful tool in actively pursuing a solution to a conflict.
- Teachers often act as mediators when conflict arises between students.

Review and Study

1. List the five main roles performed by teachers. Explain which you think is most important and why.
2. How do grades and assessment differ?
3. Name three of the personal and professional qualities needed for teaching success. For each, briefly describe a teaching-related situation that requires this quality.
4. What is organizational culture? Name a tangible and intangible sign of organizational culture.
5. List two ways a new teacher can learn about the organizational structure.
6. How can teachers stay up to date with the information in their subject areas?
7. What are two reasons teachers should use a variety of teaching techniques?
8. What is a mixed message? Give an example.
9. What is active listening?
10. Contrast assertive and aggressive communication.
11. Name the steps to conflict resolution.
12. What role does a mediator play in resolving a conflict?

Vocabulary Activity

13. With a partner, create a T-chart. Write each of the *Content* and *Academic* terms on page 230 in the left column. In the right column, write a *synonym* (a word that has the same or similar meaning) for each term. Discuss your synonyms with the class.

Critical Thinking

14. **Analyze evidence.** Identify a lesson in one of your classes in which the teacher acted as a facilitator. Using the text as your guide, analyze the planning the teacher did to prepare this lesson. What evidence made this lesson a facilitated lesson? How might this lesson have been taught in a directive way? By which method do you think students learn more effectively? Discuss factors that influence learning.

15. **Analyze behavior.** What actions or behaviors do teachers display that show they are positive role models, leading others by example? Without using names, describe two ways they led others by their example.

16. **Draw conclusions.** Think of a teacher you have had who showed strong subject-matter knowledge and exceptional teaching skills. Draw conclusions about the impact this teacher had on you and other students. How did this teacher's skills impact learning? Discuss in class.

17. **Analyze evidence.** Based on text criteria, analyze your spoken and written communication skills. Which are stronger? On what evidence did you base your conclusions? Cite some specific ways you could improve your skills in the other area.

Core Skills

18. **Research and writing.** Students interested in teaching often visit classrooms to observe, assist teachers, or present lessons. Research a list of guidelines about appropriate dress for such situations. Create a digital poster using school-approved software and include pictures of two outfits that serve as good choices. How is dress related to respect? How is it a form of nonverbal communication? Discuss your poster with the class.

19. **Reading and writing.** Read your school's student handbook and website. Write a description about the school's organizational culture. Compare your description to your observations about the school organizational structure. Note any ways in which the official version varies from your observations and perceptions.

20. **Speaking and listening.** To demonstrate your skills with *active listening*, with a partner, create a role-play in which the teacher intervenes for one of the following situations: two first graders fighting on the playground; a middle school student showing frustration over a math assignment; a high school student distraught over a relationship. Write and present your role-play scenario to the class utilizing effective active-listening skills. Have the class assess the effectiveness of your communication.

21. **Writing.** Suppose you are the teacher of a middle school student who has not been turning in class assignments and is failing your class. Write a letter or e-mail message to the student's parents outlining the situation. Request a conference with the parents to discuss possible solutions. Be sure to utilize the guidelines for writing professional correspondence in the chapter.

22. **Writing.** Write an article for a parent newsletter about an event in your school. This can be an interesting class or school activity, volunteer opportunity, or other topic of interest. In writing your article, keep parents' needs and interests in mind. Communicate information clearly and concisely. Proofread your work. Make sure that the tone is positive, enthusiastic, and constructive.

23. **Writing, speaking, and technology application.** In teams, create a digital video demonstrating effective conflict management skills. Choose a conflict that is common among students in your school or in another school. Your video should show all involved in the conflict (including a classroom teacher) working through the steps of effective conflict management. Share your videos in class and discuss the effectiveness of the conflict resolution.

24. **Technology application.** Create a simple survey about effective teachers that your friends and family can answer. You might want to ask: Who was/is your favorite teacher? Why? What professional qualities did this teacher exhibit?

From which of your teachers have you learned the most? Why? Compile your answers on a spreadsheet such as Excel® and create a report.

25. **CTE College and career readiness practice.** Presume you are a high school teacher. You have a reputation among students for strong interpersonal skills—your abilities to listen, speak, and empathize with reason. A student comes to you with a problem she is having at home. What questions do you ask? How do you show empathy? What questions show you are listening? How can you help the student make the connections she needs to solve her problem?

College and Career Portfolio

Colleges and employers review candidates for various positions. For example, important skills for many jobs include the ability to communicate effectively, get along with coworkers, solve problems, and resolve conflicts. Another name for these types of skills is *soft skills*. Making an effort to learn more about and develop soft skills will be important in your teaching career. Complete the following to learn more:

- Do Internet research and read articles about soft skills and their value to a teaching career. Write a summary of the articles you read and cite how the articles support the text information.

- Refine your assignments and save completed Items 17, 20, 21, 22, and 23 in your e-portfolio. If appropriate, place a printed copy in the container for your print portfolio.

Chapter 11
Planning for Instruction

Content Terms

educational standards
curriculum development
course plan
instructional units
lesson plans
instructional objectives
Bloom's taxonomy
learning activities
assessment
transitions
guided practice
independent practice

Academic Terms

controversy
formulaic
viable

Objectives

After studying this chapter, you will be able to

- **analyze** the types of information included in the educational standards for a state.

- **compare** curricula for the same course or level from two different sources.

- **identify** initiatives that influence educational standards and curriculum development.

- **explain** the relationship between instructional units and course plans.

- **summarize** the key parts of a lesson plan.

- **write** an educational objective that includes all necessary components.

- **create** a lesson plan on a chosen topic.

Reading Prep

Review the chapter headings and use them to create an outline for taking notes during reading and class discussion. Under each heading, list any term highlighted in yellow or bold italic. Write two questions that you expect the chapter to answer.

At the Companion Website you can

- **Practice** terms with e-flash cards and interactive games

- **Assess** what you learn by completing self-assessment quizzes

- **Expand** knowledge with interactive activities

www.g-wlearning.com/teaching/

Study on the go

Use a mobile device to practice terms and review with self-assessment quizzes.

www.m.g-wlearning.com/0094/

Case Study

As a class, read the case study and discuss the questions that follow. Then, after reading the chapter, go back and review your answers to the questions. How would your answers change?

Aaron dreams of living in the city but has always been the kid with the long bus ride out to his family's farm. When he was in junior high, he was embarrassed because he knew more about farming than he did about current movies, coffee shops, and other trendy places to hang out. Even the city bus did not go out as far as he lived, and he wished that he could hang out after school with friends like his classmates did.

When the bus line finally extended to his farm, his world expanded. Now in his senior year of high school, Aaron has a job in the food court at the mall and is job shadowing an eighth grade biology teacher, Ms. Frank. The funny thing is, he is now beginning to appreciate his family life on the farm. Why? His life seemed so much easier and was less chaotic. There was less pressure to conform…and he knows a lot about plant biology. In fact, so much so that Ms. Frank has asked him to come up with some ideas for teaching her class unit on water transportation in plants. Her desired learning outcome is for students to be able to label and identify the process plants use to take in water. She asked Aaron to come up some with ideas.

Let's Discuss

- Make a list of possible learning activities Aaron could use to meet this learning outcome goal. Be creative and include "hands-on learning" as much as possible.

- If the plant-life teaching unit was expanded to a whole semester, what other topics and activities might be included?

- What unique life experiences have you had that you could share with others?

Who determines what teachers teach? The answer is much more complicated than it would seem. Teachers make many day-to-day decisions about what they teach, but there are many influences on those decisions. They do not simply decide what they would like to teach.

The quality of education is of great importance to every child's future, but also to the nation as a whole. Society, parents, and employers, as well as teachers, all have a stake in making the educational system work. That does not mean that they all agree about how best to do so.

As at every other time in history, the educational system works better for some students than others. Currently, there is more emphasis on trying to make certain that all students learn well. The debate about how to improve education impacts how individual teachers function in the classroom, both directly and indirectly.

This chapter focuses on how teaching decisions are made and what influences those decisions. The process works somewhat like a funnel with the classroom at the bottom. Decisions about what will be taught and how it will be taught become more detailed and specific the closer they get to the classroom.

Standards: What Should Students Know?

Many people believe that choices about what should be taught in schools should begin with decisions about the desired end product. **Educational standards**, sometimes called *instructional goals*, are statements about what students are expected to know and be able to do at certain points in their education. Advocates of educational standards say that when you first decide what outcomes you want, you can plan what to teach to reach those goals (Figure 11.1).

Various groups have created standards. As you read in Chapter 1, *national standards* have been developed by teacher organizations for different subject areas in conjunction with state departments of education. Many states have also written standards for the schools within their states. These *state standards* often draw on the national standards but differ in some ways. Some local school districts have also developed their own standards.

Standards link to the movement for accountability in education. Published standards tell the public what students will be able to do when they complete this particular part of their education. Administrators and teachers must make certain that students meet these goals at acceptable levels.

Figure 11.1   Teachers plan lessons to meet educational standards or instructional goals.

Standards tend to be fairly general statements. For example, one of the national standards for language arts for grades K-12 reads:

"Students adjust their use of spoken, written, and visual language (e.g., conventions, style, vocabulary) to communicate effectively with a variety of audiences and for different purposes."

As the example shows, standards do not include details about how students will learn the topic or how schools and teachers will prove attainment of the standard. More of those details emerge at the next step—curriculum.

Curriculum: What Will Be Taught?

As you know, *curriculum* can refer to the courses taught in a school and what is to be taught in each course. (The plural of curriculum is *curricula*.) It is this second definition that most directly impacts what teachers teach.

While curriculum links to national, state, and sometimes local standards, the expectations are much more specific about the content that teachers must teach. You may be surprised to learn that decisions about what is included and not included in curriculum can be the subject of intense debate. One current area of argument is whether science courses should teach both evolution and creationism (sometimes called *intelligent design*). Issues such as this exist in other subject areas, too.

Determining what to teach in each course and at each level is **curriculum development**. States, local school districts, and individual schools may all develop curriculum.

The curriculum-development process generally involves a team, including administrators, teachers, and others (Figure 11.2). For example, if a school district is currently writing curriculum for a culinary program, representatives from industry may help the writing team determine the specific skills essential for entry into that field. National and state standards typically influence

Figure 11.2 This curriculum development team is made up of teachers, a parent, and an administrator.

curriculum written at the local or school level, called *school-based curriculum*, but there is also room for local input. One reason for the influence of state standards is that most states test students at various grade levels to determine their mastery of the content designated in the standards by that grade.

Initiatives Influencing Curriculum Development

Several national initiatives inform curriculum development and teaching today. These include the *Common Core State Standards (CCSS)*; *Science, Technology, Engineering, and Math (STEM)*; *Next Generation Science Standards (NGSS)*; and the *Race to the Top* initiative.

Common Core State Standards (CCSS)

The *Common Core State Standards (CCSS)*—a movement toward more comprehensive standards in K-12 (Kindergarten through grade 12) education—began and was supported by several presidential administrations, state governors, and corporate leaders with the goal of improving graduation criteria. The standards, written by groups of educators and others invested in improving education across the board, sought to increase graduation requirements, improve assessment of student learning, and reinforce accountability of teachers. The standards were eventually adopted by a majority of the states in the late 2000s. Some states, such as Texas, Oklahoma, Virginia, Alaska, and Indiana, have not adopted the CCSS.

The CCSS focus on math and English language arts competencies. Math competencies evolve from number recognition in the early years to algebra, geometry, and statistics and probability in high school. English language arts competencies include writing, reading, speaking and listening, language, and media literacy standards throughout the K-12 grades (Figure 11.3).

Figure 11.3 Effective reading and writing skills are essential for all students.

The CCSS have not been without **controversy** (discussion marked by opposing views), even after their adoption in many states. Supporters believe strongly in the importance of meeting standards that demonstrate competence, especially in math and reading. Opponents' concerns about the CCSS include the following: lack of adequate testing of the methods for evaluating whether the standards have been met; and insufficient evidence showing these standards will achieve the desired outcomes. In addition, many opponents of CCSS feel decisions about educational standards should be made at the local and state levels without federal involvement.

Other opponents include teachers who believe that the standards are too rigid and do not allow for flexibility in meeting the needs of individual students, classes, or schools. Even though the CCSS are controversial, there is general agreement that educational reform is necessary to prepare graduates to compete in the job market.

Science, Technology, Engineering, and Math (STEM)

You may have heard the term *STEM* in your school or in the news. A little known acronym before the 2000s, wide use of STEM is now common. *STEM* stands for *Science, Technology, Engineering, and Math* concepts and content as integrated into curriculum. It is not just for courses that naturally integrate these topics such as geometry or physics. Educators include STEM concepts and content in seemingly unrelated courses such as occupational education.

Why the renewed emphasis on STEM? By the end of the twentieth century, students in the U.S. educational system were falling behind in math and science. On a global scale, they were ill-prepared to enter the growing engineering and high technology industries. The U.S. government decided to do something about this, initiating funding programs to stimulate creativity and support for math and science learning.

In reality, STEM concepts are common in most lines of work or professions. Often, high-paying and high-growth jobs are in the STEM fields, and many believe that the success of the U.S. economy depends on effectively preparing youth for these jobs (Figure 11.4). Subsequent legislation encourages programs that inspire females to gain knowledge and skills in STEM.

Next Generation Science Standards (NGSS)

Educational standards must keep up with the growing body of knowledge in the fields of science, technology, engineering, and math. Major scientific advances over the decades made updates in national and state science education standards a necessity.

The *Next Generation Science Standards (NGSS)*, issued in 2012, are a recent example of educators and practicing scientists working together

Figure 11.4 Developing knowledge and skills in science, technology, engineering, and math (STEM) help move students on the path to high-paying, high-growth careers.

to create a framework or guideline for what students need to know in the areas of science and technology. It is not just about what students need to know, however, but also how they should be able to think critically, analyze, and solve problems.

Using the NGSS, individual states can set their own science, technology, engineering, and math standards. The NGSS are not in competition with the Common Core State Standards or the National Science Standards but instead refine and deepen them. Likewise, because science is a quantitative field, the Common Core State Standards in math align with the NGSS.

Race to the Top

The intention of the *Race to the Top* initiative was to motivate individual states and school districts around the U.S. to significantly raise standards and better prepare children and youth for college and careers.

The initiative includes

- higher learning standards

- better data collection about learning outcomes

- support for teacher-effectiveness training

- strategies for helping struggling school districts succeed in educating children

School districts competed for the initiative grants and hundreds of millions of dollars were awarded toward these efforts. With a goal of transformative change for the betterment of schools, *Race to the Top* continues to impact U.S. education.

Figure 11.5 Curriculum organizes content in a logical way and helps determine the topics and skills most important to teach.

Organizing Curriculum

While the format and content of curriculum varies considerably, it generally determines which topics and skills are most important to teach and how much emphasis each receives. The curriculum organizes the content in a logical way. For example, because students must be able to multiply in order to divide, they learn multiplication before division. When a subject is taught at more than one level, the curriculum identifies what to teach in the introductory course and the advanced course.

The role of organizing what teachers will teach in which class and at what level is a key element in making education an orderly, step-by-step process. Imagine that you are a fourth grade teacher in a large school. Your new class of students came from several different third grade classrooms. The third grade teachers decided independently what they would teach during the previous year. Consequently, it would be difficult for you to know where to begin. In math, for example, some students learned their multiplication tables last year, but others did not. Should you spend a month teaching them again, divide the class up, or try some other strategy? A curriculum sets a plan outlining which main concepts and skills will be taught in each grade or course, regardless of the teacher (Figure 11.5).

Curriculum goes beyond a list of topics to teach. It includes important skills and attitudes, as well. The curriculum integrates many key skills, such as problem solving, into different parts at all levels. Students learn a skill over time and are able to apply it in various circumstances. Curricula also identify suggested teaching methods and ways to determine whether learning has occurred.

Course Planning: How Will Learning Be Organized?

As a teacher, even though your state or school district has a recommended curriculum, you still need to translate those guidelines into a plan that will work for you, your class, and your circumstances. A **course plan** is a detailed outline of what a particular teacher will teach throughout a course or year based on curriculum but adapted to the characteristics of the teacher, students, and teaching circumstances.

A course plan typically includes a series of instructional units. Your course plan must incorporate any required content and skills to enable students to meet educational standards. You still must choose and organize, however, what you will teach during the course or year. This plan provides a road map for your day-to-day teaching.

Putting together such a plan requires consideration of many influences and variables. Some of these include the following:

- *Class and school schedules*. How often does the class meet and for how long? This will tell you how much time you have for instruction during the entire course or semester, once you have subtracted holidays, assemblies, or teacher professional development days.

- *Characteristics of your students*. If you have taught the grade and class before, you will have had experience with similar groups. If not, you can make reasonable assumptions about them based on what you know about typical child development. For example, first graders have a fairly short attention span and new learning requires frequent review. Test scores can be helpful. Previous evaluations may show a particular class, as a group, is behind grade level in reading. Whatever information you can gather can help you plan your course more effectively.

- *Instructional units*. Teachers organize what they will teach in a logical order. They group similar topics together into **instructional units**, and then place these units on the schedule in an order that makes sense. A child development instructor might teach units on prenatal development, infants, toddlers, preschoolers, and school-age children, in that order.

Figure 11.6   With instructional units, teachers can group topics together in an order that makes sense. On what theme do you think this kindergarten teacher is focusing her lessons?

A kindergarten teacher might plan a unit around a particular theme, such as life on a farm, and identify specific related activities to teach math, reading, science, and other skills (Figure 11.6).

Teachers often take into consideration the sequence of topics in the textbook they are using in planning the order of content in their course. For each unit, the teacher identifies the specific information and skills to be learned, often in outline form.

- **Opportunities for learning**. Teachers try to take advantage of special opportunities and incorporate those into their teaching. For example, a social studies or government teacher might plan to teach about elections while local, state, or national elections are in process. A physical education teacher may choose to highlight the Olympic Games. This requires scheduling certain learning topics from the curriculum at that time.

  Other factors also impact where a teacher places certain topics on the course plan. If teaching in a cold climate, a physical education teacher typically schedules most outdoor activities to be taught during warmer weather.

- **Teacher characteristics**. Every teacher has different strengths, interests, and a personal teaching style. The teacher's course plan reflects these characteristics.

Having a course plan helps a teacher make certain that every concept or requirement has a place on the schedule. Once everything is on the list, the next step is deciding how much time to allot to various topics or sections of the plan. Without such designations, it is easy to spend more time on topics near the beginning of the semester or course and then have to rush through or skip topics at the end of the semester when time runs short.

Even with a plan and good intentions, teachers always make adjustments as they move through the course. A teacher may have to spend an extra day on an essential topic or an unscheduled assembly may wipe out a class period. Having a course plan helps a teacher make minor adjustments and still stay on track.

Lesson Plans: How Will Learning Take Place?

As a teacher, once you establish a course plan, you must make specific decisions about how you will teach each part of it. Together, the individual lessons build the knowledge, skills, and attitudes designated for the course and allow students to meet the standards that have been set.

Lesson plans—sometimes called *instructional plans* or *teaching plans*—are detailed outlines of topics to teach, how to teach them, why they are necessary to teach and learn, and how to evaluate learning. Teachers develop lesson plans for individual topics or groups of related topics. One lesson plan may include concepts or topics to teach in a single lesson or over a number of days.

Lesson plans serve a number of important purposes, which is why most schools require that teachers prepare them. First, they document what is being taught and how that aligns with curriculum guidelines and standards. In addition, the process of developing a lesson plan helps teachers think through what and how they will teach. They come to class better prepared. Lesson plans also allow a substitute teacher to step in and continue the learning process.

Elements of a Lesson Plan

Professional Tip

Back-Up Plans for Lessons

Professional teachers plan thoroughly for every lesson and class unit. They know what will happen in class each day and have a learning outcome in mind. They are committed to their plan, ensuring to the best of their ability that everything is covered while at the same time, responding to the individual needs of students. But then the unexpected happens: a fire drill…an online movie that will not "buffer"…a guest speaker who is delayed. What to do now? Professional teachers always have a back-up plan to deal with unexpected occurrences. Experienced teachers know that some of the best learning happens when plans change; however, this does not just happen by chance. A professional teacher remains in charge, guiding his or her students toward appropriate responses to the change in plans.

Dig Deeper

Over the next week, take a mental note of unexpected changes you observe in a classroom or in another professional setting. How did the teacher handle the changes? What did you learn from this experience? How could you apply this information in your own classroom?

Lesson plans vary in format from place to place and person to person. Some schools have a standard format that all teachers must use. In other cases, teachers find a format that works best for them and use it for their personal plans.

The sample lesson plan in Figure 11.7 includes various elements that help teachers carefully plan their teaching. Although this type of thorough format is helpful for all teachers, it is especially worthwhile for newer teachers. Experienced teachers may use a shortened version.

Figure 11.7	**Sample Lesson Plan**
Lesson Plan Title:	Topography: The Ups and Downs of States
Topic:	Map skills: Identify shape, topography, location of U.S. state
Standard(s) Addressed:	Understand how to use maps and other geographic representations, tools, and technologies to acquire, process, and report information from a spatial perspective. *(State Social Studies Standard 8B)*
Students/Participants:	Fifth grade social studies
Specific Objectives:	*Students will* • use outline and topographic maps to create a 3-D topographic map of a state • indicate the correct locations of at least four key water features and three major cities
Time Period:	Two consecutive class periods
Introduction:	Students will draw slips of paper to determine their assigned state. **Ask:** *What does your state look like?* Using play dough, give students 3 minutes to make the shape of their assigned state without a reference map. Expect interesting interpretations. **Transition:** *Let's look at some maps and see what your state really looks like.* **Supplies:** paper slips with state names, play dough, hand wipes
Step-by-Step Procedures:	1. Give each student an outline map of his or her assigned state. Students will duplicate the shape of their state using salt dough on a cardboard base. (**Supplies per student:** handout with state outline, cardboard, salt dough, dowel for rolling, plastic knife for cutting) 2. Provide each student with a color topographic map of his or her state. Briefly review previous lesson on topographic maps. Using additional salt dough, students will construct a 3-D map of the topography of their state on the outline base (using coils or slabs of dough). Note that during the next class period, students will paint their dough maps to show elevation changes and the location of major waterways and cities. (**Supplies per student:** topographic maps of students' state, additional salt dough) 3. Provide a place for the dough maps to dry overnight. 4. During the next class period, students will paint maps, using colors to indicate elevation changes. Using classroom or textbook maps, they will use a marker to identify the locations of four major water features (rivers, lakes, coastlines) and three main cities. (**Supplies per student:** topographic map from last class, textbook, watercolor set and brush, cup of water, fine marker, hand wipes)
Guided/Independent Practice:	Teacher will interact with students as they work, asking them to explain what they are doing. Explanations will verbally reinforce their visual and kinesthetic learning. Teacher will provide feedback.

Figure 11.7	**Sample Lesson Plan** *(continued)*
Summary:	Students will form groups based on the location of their state (divisions from textbook: Pacific Northwest, West, Plains, South, Central, Southeast, and Northeast). In groups, students will present their map, briefly describing the topography (flat, mountainous, etc.) and identifying their state's major water features and cities. Group members will use textbook maps to verify, and students will correct their maps as needed. Students will note the location of their states within their region.
Assessment:	Students will present their completed map to the whole class, identifying the state, four major water features, and the names and locations of three major cities. They will give a verbal description of the topography of the state.
Materials and Equipment:	• Folded paper strips with names of states to be used (one per student) • Container for drawing state names • Play dough • Hand wipes • Outline maps of students' states • Corrugated cardboard bases for topographic maps • Salt dough clay (*See Notes*) • Pieces of wooden dowel for rolling (or clay rollers borrowed from art department) • Plastic knives • Topographic maps (color) for students' states • Watercolor sets with brushes • Plastic cups, half-filled with water on tray • Pitchers with water • Paper towels or newspaper • Fine-point markers, black • Textbooks for maps
Adaptations for Students Who Have Special Needs:	One student with color-deficiency syndrome: label watercolor paints
Notes:	• For smaller classes, use states from a limited number of geographic regions. • Eliminate states with extreme topographical variation. Maps take too long to construct. • Recipe for salt dough in "Materials" file. Each batch sufficient for five students. Make one extra batch.

The three most basic parts of a lesson plan are the instructional objectives, the learning activities, and the assessment. Most of the other elements flow from these decisions.

Instructional Objectives

Each lesson plan includes one or more instructional objectives. **Instructional objectives,** or *learning outcomes*, are clear statements of what students will achieve as a result of a lesson that they exhibit in an observable way. By starting with the end—or learning outcomes—in mind, the teacher identifies the purpose of the lesson. The teacher then develops the lesson to allow students to meet the objective. As such, objectives provide a focus for teaching.

How does a teacher determine and write instructional objectives? What kinds of thinking skills do different learning tasks require? Several theories exist that guide teachers through the rigorous process of developing instructional objectives.

Theories About Instructional Objectives

For over half a century, teachers and teacher-trainers have used **Bloom's Taxonomy,** a theory for establishing educational objectives as a basis for understanding and teaching various levels of thought. Developed by Benjamin Bloom in the mid-1950s, Bloom's theory is divided into three domains of learning: cognitive, affective, and psychomotor domains. Each domain consists of categories that are organized from simple to complex, knowledge-based thinking to deeper critical thinking.

The *cognitive domain* focuses on intellectual ways of knowing. In this domain, objectives might include such verbs as identify, define, classify, differentiate, conclude, and justify. These objectives show what students know, understand, and comprehend. Figure 11.8 illustrates the categories and their use in Bloom's cognitive domain.

The *affective domain* centers on behaviors, feelings, attitudes, or emotional ways of knowing. Objectives in this domain might include such verbs as debate, rate, defend, or discuss.

The *psychomotor domain* focuses on what students will be able to do and concerns their motor skills. In the psychomotor domain, objectives might include such verbs as throw, trace, assemble, operate, or rearrange.

Dr. Robert J. Marzano proposed his *New Taxonomy of Educational Objectives* that he claimed filled in the gaps or deficiencies of Bloom's widely used model. Marzano's model fell in line with the new standards-based instruction more popular in recent years. His model of thinking skills incorporates a wider range of factors that affect how learners think. It also provides a more research-based theory to help teachers create effective learning goals and outcomes. Marzano's theory proposes three systems, including the Self-System, Metacognitive System, and the Cognitive System.

Figure 11.8   Applying Bloom's Taxonomy
Level 1—KNOWLEDGE: *Acquiring and recalling information*
Sample associated verbs: define, describe, list, label, match, memorize, name, recognize, tell **Sample question:** Who were the main characters in the story? **Sample objective:** Students will match at least 20 of 25 words with their correct definitions.
Level 2—COMPREHENSION: *Understanding and making use of information*
Sample associated verbs: describe, discuss, explain, outline, predict, summarize, translate **Sample question:** Describe the main characters in the story. **Sample objective:** Students will identify at least four statements that support the author's point of view.
Level 3—APPLICATION: *Using information learned in a new situation*
Sample associated verbs: apply, build, complete, demonstrate, develop, examine, illustrate, plan, show, solve, use **Sample question:** How would the rule apply if the angle were 90° instead of 45°? **Sample objective:** Students will use the guidelines to write a business letter requesting an interview that contains all key elements.
Level 4—ANALYSIS: *Examining the parts of a whole and their relationships*
Sample associated verbs: analyze, classify, compare, contrast, categorize, distinguish among, examine, investigate, separate, test **Sample question:** Which two of the three musical selections are in the same key? **Sample objective:** Students will analyze a photo of a room, correctly identifying an example of effective or ineffective use of each principle of design.
Level 5—SYNTHESIS: *Using parts in a new way to create something*
Sample associated verbs: adapt, combine, construct, create, design, develop, imagine, improve, invent, organize, plan, produce **Sample question:** How would you adapt the exercise guidelines to fit your personal situation? **Sample objective:** Students will develop a sketch and description of a new product that would be helpful for someone with limited hand strength.
Level 6—EVALUATION: *Assessing or judging value based on information*
Sample associated verbs: assess, choose, criticize, debate, decide, defend, evaluate, judge, prioritize, rank, rate, select **Sample question:** What choice would you have made if you were in Churchill's place, and what is your reasoning? **Sample objective:** Students will develop a rating scale to evaluate the posters submitted for the "Stamp Out Litter!" campaign.

The *Self-System* begins with the student deciding whether or not to participate in the learning activity or task at hand. The *Metacognitive System* sets goals or desired learning outcomes. This system also keeps track of how well students are reaching the goals.

The *Cognitive System* processes all the necessary information including the necessary content students need for learning. Marzano proposed that educational objectives must be considered in each of these areas for students to effectively learn.

Another educational theorist, Norman Webb, was concerned about meeting standards and maintaining rigor in the classroom. He focused on creating rich educational environments that encouraged high-level thinking. In Webb's *Depth of Knowledge* levels, he proposed four levels of learning that become more complex at each level: Recall and Reproduction, Skills and Concepts, Strategic Thinking, and Extended Thinking.

The first level, *Recall and Reproduction,* includes simple recall of information or simple **formulaic** (an expression of facts, rules, or procedures in mathematical symbols) procedures. The second level, *Skills and Concepts,* involves student decision making such as comparing, organizing, or summarizing. The third level, *Strategic Thinking,* requires more complex tasks and often includes abstract thinking. Problem solving is a good example of level three thinking. Finally, the fourth level, *Extended Thinking,* requires even more complicated reasoning. Analyzing data and drawing conclusions after comparing multiple sources of information are examples of this high-level thinking.

Sometimes teachers desire a simple-to-measure outcome such as accuracy and speed in math computation or spelling. At other times, a desired outcome is centered on skill performance such as using scissors correctly or performing knife skills correctly in a culinary course. On other occasions, outcomes involve identifying key information or reciting dates. Many times, however, learning outcomes are centered on more complex learning skills that are not as easy to measure. This is especially true when it involves higher-order thinking such as analyzing, synthesizing, or making judgment calls.

Writing Instructional Objectives

Instructional objectives translate educational standards into specific smaller segments. Together, these form the stepping-stones toward meeting the goals of a standard.

Instructional objectives are often called *performance objectives* because they focus on what students will do to demonstrate learning. A well-written objective includes these characteristics:

- **Specifies observable behavior**. The verb in the statement tells how the student will show learning in a way that the teacher can see. "Sort *into categories*" is observable. "Understand *similarities*" is not. When objectives are observable, teachers can judge whether or not they are met by viewing student behaviors. Figure 11.9 lists some common verbs used in instructional objectives that lead to observable evidence of learning.

Figure 11.9	Examples of Verbs for Observable Objectives			
add	create	identify	plan	select
analyze	debate	judge	predict	sort
apply	define	label	prepare	spell
calculate	demonstrate	list	present	suggest
categorize	describe	make	produce	summarize
combine	design	match	rank	throw
compare	draw	measure	rate	translate
complete	estimate	operate	revise	weigh
compute	evaluate	organize	rewrite	write
construct	explain			

- **Identifies an action or product**. Students must do or produce something concrete to indicate learning. A kindergartener might "assemble *a 20-piece puzzle*." A high school student studying personal finance might "create a *list of all personal expenses*."

- **Describes any conditions**. An objective usually tells under what circumstances the student will demonstrate learning. Phrases such as "*working independently,*" "*without a calculator,*" and "*within a 10-minute period,*" are examples of such conditions.

- **Indicates acceptable level of performance**. The objective should specify what determines successful performance. Students might be required to "identify *three reasons,*" "complete *30 problems with 80 percent accuracy,*" "score *at least 7 of 10 points,*" or "rewrite *the sentence with no errors.*"

Identify the four characteristics of a well-written objective in the following examples.

"*Students will be able to serve the tennis ball within bounds in 6 of 10 attempts.*"

"*Students will identify in writing four characteristics of each of the three major types of government: autocracy, oligarchy, and democracy.*"

Learning Activities

Learning activities are the second major component of a lesson plan. These are the learning experiences that help students learn the content and achieve the outcome of the instructional objectives.

Possible types of activities range from discussions, labs, hands-on activities, debates, problem solving, and field trips to computer exercises, simulations, and experiments. Other titles for learning activities are *instructional methods* or *learning experiences*.

There are many teaching options for every topic and objective. How do teachers choose? This is where teachers' knowledge of their students, experience, and creativity come into play. Activities must match the abilities and interests of the students in the class. For example, high school students are better able to bring new ideas to a class discussion than first graders. An elementary teacher may want to alternate quiet activities with ones that are more physically active throughout the day. Chapter 12 discusses the pros, cons, and best uses of various types of activities in more detail.

Available resources can impact teachers' decisions about learning activities. For example, a teacher might decide a field trip to a museum would best teach a concept; however, if no travel funds are available, a virtual museum tour on the Internet is a **viable** (reasonably successful) substitute (Figure 11.10).

Figure 11.10   Field trips are just one of many activities teachers use to engage students in learning.

Assessment Strategies

Assessment strategies must link directly back to those identified in the instructional objectives. **Assessment** refers to *how* the teacher evaluates whether the learning specified in the objectives has taken place. In some concrete way, teachers must be able to observe that students have learned the important content of the lesson. Chapter 14 describes many different assessment techniques and their uses. Developing and implementing effective assessments takes time, creativity, and energy; however, the ability to truly evaluate students' learning makes the effort worthwhile.

Other Lesson Plan Elements

Once you have decided on the activity or activities that will make up the lesson, you can complete several related portions of the lesson plan. These include the following:

- *Title*. Give your plan a clear, but descriptive, title.
- *Topic*. Identify what concept or skill you will teach in the lesson.
- *Standards*. List the educational standards (state or local) that the lesson plan helps achieve.
- *Students/participants*. Identify the grade level and subject area.
- *Time period*. Specify how long the lesson plan will take to complete, such as one or two class periods.
- *Introduction*. Finding a good way to introduce a lesson is important to its success. An effective introduction must meet three goals: capture students' attention and interest, convey your expectations during the lesson, and link what students will be learning to what they already know.
- *Step-by-step procedures*. Thinking through the sequence of what will take place during the lesson and identifying the specific steps helps the actual lesson go smoothly. This process allows you to visualize how things will happen and identify potential problems that may arise. You can note questions you will ask and plan **transitions**—smooth ways to move from one part of the lesson to the next. This section acts as your guide as you present the lesson.
- *Guided/independent practice*. A good lesson includes opportunities for students to practice what they have learned. **Guided practice** is an activity designed to reinforce and apply learning that includes feedback from other students or the teacher (Figure 11.11). For example, students might work in small groups to complete math problems related to the lesson.

Figure 11.11   During guided practice, the classroom teacher or other students provide feedback that helps students apply and reinforce learning.

At other times, **independent practice** can be a personal activity outside of class that students complete on their own, such as a homework assignment that helps students apply and reinforce recent learning.

- *Summary*. A good summary not only reviews what was learned, but helps students apply it. Verbal summaries of a lesson are just one option. Students can summarize by performing a skill they have learned. They can apply knowledge to a different situation or solve a problem using information from the lesson. They can create something that tells someone else about what they learned.

- *Materials and equipment*. When you prepare a complete list of everything needed to complete the lesson plan, it is easier to assemble everything when you are ready to teach.

- *Adaptations for students who have special needs*. Depending on the nature of the lesson, it may be necessary to modify some activities so that students who have special learning needs can successfully complete them.

- **Notes**. Use this space for additional information, reminders, and ideas for improving the plan.

Thinking through all of the elements of a lesson plan and putting them in writing helps teachers effectively prepare for teaching the lesson. They know what they need and how they will proceed. By keeping the instructional objectives in mind, teachers can make any necessary adaptations during the actual lesson, concentrating on the essence of what students need to learn.

Finding Ideas and Inspiration

How can you come up with interesting ideas for lesson plans? As you learn more about teaching, you will begin to see learning opportunities in many aspects of life. Good teachers jot down notes about teaching ideas and accumulate materials that they could use to enliven future lessons.

Teachers also freely share ideas with one another (Figure 11.12). This may happen formally with a mentor or informally, teacher to teacher.

Figure 11.12 Teachers often collaborate to share ideas of lesson plans.

Professional conferences typically include sessions where teachers present ideas that work well for them. Teaching magazines and many websites can also be excellent sources of ideas. The teaching materials that accompany textbooks suggest many different ways teachers can supplement, expand, and apply text topics.

Many schools use teams to develop teaching plans. Groups of teachers collaborate to design lessons for effective instructional units. Working in teams encourages creative thinking and provides opportunities for teachers to share individual areas of expertise. It can also be invigorating as one person's idea inspires another person's idea. While each teacher may still personalize the plans somewhat, team planning allows teachers to share preparation tasks and resources.

If you are interested in becoming a teacher, it is not too early to start keeping track of ideas you might use or adapt in your own classroom. You might use a combination of electronic and paper files to organize your materials.

Making Lesson Plans Come Alive

A lesson plan may look good on paper, but how do you make it work in the classroom? The way you present a lesson to students has an impact on how well your students learn.

The introduction is the first key element. By capturing students' interest and attention, you begin the process of engaging them in learning. There are endless possibilities. You might ask a question, show a video clip, tell a story, or have students perform a task. In addition, let students know what to expect in terms of what they will learn and, perhaps, how you want them to work. Finally, linking the learning to prior knowledge or experiences helps enhance their understanding.

Your choice of activities will also affect the success of your lesson. You may have experienced a class in which the teacher depended heavily on worksheets instead of more variety and active learning. Worksheets can be useful at times, but a steady diet of them is not very motivating. Students need variety. Engaging activities usually involve manipulating information either physically or mentally.

Incorporating an unexpected element into an important lesson can make it memorable. Imagine the following: A history teacher comes to class dressed as Thomas Jefferson. A first grade teacher incorporates a colorful parachute into a physical exercise activity. A science teacher displays a covered tray of objects related to the lesson as students enter the classroom and then removes the cover. All are out of the ordinary and can help generate interest and boost learning.

Remember, too, that a class is a collection of individuals, each with different learning styles, abilities, and interests. Include opportunities for visual, auditory, and kinesthetic learners in presenting your activities. The more senses you activate, the more likely learning will occur.

Lesson plans often appear linear on paper, simply moving from one point to the next. In reality, effective teachers often take a few steps forward, then a step back, and then take a step forward again when teaching new concepts. They allow time to encourage students, provide feedback, and check on students' progress. They take breaks from new learning by reviewing and reinforcing what students have learned.

How you present activities is as important as which activities you choose. A teacher's excitement is contagious. Be enthusiastic about learning and the opportunities you have planned. Your enthusiasm can help even reluctant students become engaged in activities (Figure 11.13).

While you are learning teaching skills, it is easy to become flustered when a lesson does not go as planned. Practicing your presentation and learning activities can help give you confidence. Effective preparation and having a step-by-step procedure in your lesson plan can keep you on track.

Figure 11.13 An enthusiastic teacher is likely to actively engage students in planned activities.

If you have thought through potential problems in the planning process, you will have solutions in mind. If something unexpected occurs, experienced teachers' best advice is to stay calm. Often, students are not even aware something is not working out as planned. Even if they are, showing that you, like all good teachers, can be flexible and adaptable will keep the lesson moving forward. Keep a sense of humor. Not everything can be planned for. Good teachers simply keep their goals in mind and adjust their plans.

Evaluating the Lesson

At the end of a day of teaching—even those days that are somewhat hectic—teachers know it is well worth the time to reflect on the day's lessons. They make notes about what worked well and how they might modify their lesson plan to make it better (Figure 11.14). Notes made while the experience is still fresh can be invaluable later. Teachers often reuse lesson plans that they have found to be successful. Effective teachers, however, continually make improvements and try new ideas.

Figure 11.14 Taking time to reflect on lessons and making notes for improvements and new ideas to try is characteristic of an effective teacher.

Chapter 11 Review and Assess

Summary

- Standards, statements of what students should know and be able to do at certain educational levels, can be very influential.

- Curriculum development is the process of deciding, more specifically, what topics and skills should be taught and what attitudes should be developed in different subjects and grade levels.

- Standards often influence curricula, including those from several national initiatives.

- Teachers translate the curriculum into a course plan showing the organization of what needs to be taught, including a sequence of instructional units.

- Lesson plans record teachers' decisions about how they will teach specific topics to produce desired learning.

- Writing effective instructional objectives is key to successful lesson planning.

- Several theories exist that guide teachers in writing effective objectives, including *Bloom's, Marzano's,* and *Webb's* theories.

- Lesson plan formats vary, but all generally include objectives, learning activities, and assessment.

- Careful planning and enthusiastic presentation of lessons help boost learning.

- Sharing and collecting teaching ideas and inspirational ideas help teachers personalize and enliven lessons.

- Effective presentation of lessons is key to capturing student interest and engaging them in the learning process.

- Taking time to evaluate how well lessons work can help teachers identify improvements for future lessons.

Review and Study

1. What are educational standards and what do they link to?

2. Why do many people believe that setting educational standards should be the first step in deciding what is taught in schools?

3. What are four national initiatives that influence curriculum development in many states?

4. Why is it important for curricula to determine what to teach at each grade level?

5. If there is a set curriculum, why does a teacher need a course plan?

6. What are instructional units?

7. Name the three most important parts of a lesson plan.

8. What are three theories that influence the development of instructional objectives?

9. List the four key parts of an instructional objective. Write an objective that includes all four.

10. What is the purpose of learning activities?

11. Contrast guided practice with independent practice.

12. How do teachers evaluate a lesson?

Vocabulary Activity

13. Read the text passages that contain the *Content* and *Academic* terms on page 256. Then write the definitions of each term in your own words. Double-check your definitions by rereading the text and using the text glossary.

Critical Thinking

14. **Make predictions.** Predict who might have been involved in developing a new state curriculum for this course for students who are interested in the teaching profession. What standards or initiatives might be most influential? Why? Cite text and other reliable resources to support your predictions.

15. **Analyze evidence.** Use the text and other authoritative print or Internet resources to gather relevant information regarding national initiatives that influence curriculum development (for instance, the *CCSS*, *STEM*, *NGSS*, and *Race to the Top*). Analyze factors regarding development of these initiatives, their intended influence on education, and any pros and cons about the initiatives. Cite specific evidence to support your findings.

16. **Draw conclusions.** Examine two curriculum documents for the same subject area and level. Choose a topic common to both curricula and compare what is to be taught. How are the recommendations for teaching this topic similar and different? Draw conclusions about how the two curricula match up in terms of format, detail level, and types of information included (for instance, objectives or activity suggestions). Which version do you think would be more helpful to a teacher?

17. **Infer assumptions.** Think of a memorable lesson you experienced as a student. What was the topic of the lesson? Make assumptions about how the teacher prepared the lesson. What theories about instructional objectives may have influenced the lesson? What student factors did the teacher consider? What sources of inspiration helped make the lesson memorable? Share your assumptions in class.

18. **Evaluate outcomes.** Describe an incident in a class when a lesson did not go as planned and evaluate the outcomes. What happened to upset plans? How did the teacher handle the situation? What was the result? What might have been done to improve the outcome? Write a summary (avoid using names).

Core Skills

19. **Research, reading, and writing.** Use online resources to investigate national and state curriculum standards for an area of your choice. Write a report explaining how these standards guide teaching to impact student learning. Post your findings to the class website or online discussion board to compare and contrast findings with your classmates.

20. **Research and writing.** Use text and Internet resources to further research the work of Benjamin Bloom (*the original and the New Bloom's Taxonomy*), Robert Marzano, and Norman Webb. Create a digital chart comparing details about the levels of thinking among these theories. Which theory do you think is most useful to teachers? Cite evidence to support your response.

21. **Research, writing, and speaking.** Work in teams to collaboratively analyze course content requirements for several subject areas and grade levels in your state. Compare examples of educational objectives and performance outcomes for each. How do they provide teachers with the necessary content expectations to teach effectively? Have each team member choose a standard to rewrite for clarity and measurability according to chapter guidelines. Use presentation software to prepare your team report for the class.

Discuss the rewritten standards for clarity and measurability.

22. **Listening and writing.** Obtain permission to observe an elementary or middle school classroom teacher introducing and teaching a lesson. Using the lesson plan format provided by your teacher, note as many parts of the teacher's plan as possible based on what you have observed.

23. **Technology application.** Online ideas and resources abound for teachers. Choose a topic you are passionate about such as children's rights or water sanitation. Choose an age group that you might teach. Search for teaching plans or instructional methods that could be used to teach about this topic. For example, the United Nations Children's Fund and UNICEF often have teaching unit ideas.

24. **CTE College and career readiness practice.** Ability to apply your academic and technical skills is important for teachers. Using chapter and online resources, create a lesson plan (using your teacher-provided template) on a topic and for an age group of your choice. Prepare all elements and activities to execute the lesson, and then present your lesson to the class. Evaluate the effectiveness of your lesson in follow-up discussion with the class. What improvements could you make to the lesson?

College and Career Portfolio

Employers and colleges review candidates for various positions and abilities that focus on *hard skills,* or skills that help you produce an observable result. For example, do you have ability to use a variety of software programs, computers, and other digital media important to carrying out effective teaching lessons? If not, begin now to learn those hard skills that can benefit you as an effective teacher.

- Use the Internet to locate articles about hard skills, especially those that benefit teachers and help them succeed.

- Make a list of hard skills you possess that you think are important to a job in teaching. Choose two of these skills. Write a paragraph about each that describes your abilities. Give examples that illustrate your skills.

- Save a copy in your e-portfolio and in your print portfolio container. In addition, save copies of your work for Items 20, 21, and 24 for future reference.

Chapter 12
Instructional Methods

Content Terms

instructional method
critical thinking
open-ended questions
wait time
pacing
closure
teacher-centered method
learner-centered method
panel discussion
simulation
skit

role-playing
case study
reflective response
productive lab
experimental lab
cooperative learning
individual accountability
collaborative learning
differentiated instructional
    method

Academic Terms

repertoire
moderator
consensus
empower

Objectives

After studying this chapter, you will be able to

- **summarize** the role of all teachers in the development of critical-thinking skills.

- **develop** critical-thinking questions appropriate for instruction based on upper levels of Bloom's Taxonomy.

- **identify** the characteristics and uses of specific types of instructional strategies.

- **analyze** a lesson, identifying the teaching strategies and use of questioning, examples, and closure.

- **summarize** teachers' primary considerations when deciding which teaching strategies to use.

Reading Prep

Take two-column notes as you read the chapter. Fold a piece of notebook paper in half lengthwise. In the left column, write the main ideas. In the right column, write subtopics and detailed information. After reading the chapter, use the notes as a study guide. Fold the paper in half so you only see the main ideas. Quiz yourself on the details and subtopics.

At the Companion Website you can

- **Practice** terms with e-flash cards and interactive games

- **Assess** what you learn by completing self-assessment quizzes

- **Expand** knowledge with interactive activities

www.g-wlearning.com/teaching/

Study on the go

Use a mobile device to practice terms and review with self-assessment quizzes.

www.m.g-wlearning.com/0094/

Case Study

Read the case study and complete the activity that follows. After reading the chapter, review your chosen instructional activities for these topics. Would your selections remain the same? Why or why not?

What perfect timing! Not only is it a U.S. Presidential Election year, but it is also an election year for your city mayor. For a history teacher focusing on U.S. government and civics, the timing could not be better. You will be teaching a unit covering political parties, the practice of democracy, the electoral process, politics and the media, political special interests, and the Bill of Rights. Your desire is to explore each of these topics with your students and for them to be able to accurately articulate how each operates in society.

Let's Discuss

Brainstorm at least one instructional activity that could be used for each of the topics within this unit. Think broadly and include as many different types of instructional activities as possible. Discuss with the class why you selected specific activities for certain topics.

Teachers face a similar dilemma all the time. They know what they want students to learn. Next, they must decide how best to achieve it.

Chapter 11 explored the process that determines what to teach. The end result, a lesson plan, is an individual teacher's strategy for teaching a particular topic. Learning activities form the heart of lesson plans. Teachers can create successful learning activities because of their knowledge of and experience with various instructional methods. **Instructional methods**, often called *instructional strategies* or *teaching strategies*, are the basic techniques used to promote learning. Teachers know the uses of these methods—such as discussions, skits, and demonstrations—and choose the best one for a particular learning objective, topic, and class situation. They then use that method as the basis for developing a specific learning activity (Figure 12.1).

This chapter looks at the characteristics of a variety of common instructional methods. There are certainly other strategies that you may want to add to your instructional **repertoire,** your list of skills, activities, and methods or strategies for teaching. You will often combine several methods for one lesson. You have the perspective of experiencing these strategies as a student. Now, you will see how teachers view and utilize them.

Figure 12.1   Teachers choose instructional methods best suited to their topics, learning objectives, and class situations.

Before you read the descriptions of these specific teaching strategies, however, the chapter explores some essentials for success with any instructional method. Teachers build students' development of critical-thinking skills at every level and in all subjects. There are also some skills directly related to effective teaching that you should add to your tool kit. These skills are keys to making instructional methods work in the classroom. The end of the chapter includes some guidelines for choosing the most appropriate instructional method for a particular situation. Together, these topics will give you a better understanding of considerations involved in teaching decisions.

Engaging Learners in Critical Thinking

Too often, people think about education in terms of the amount of information learned. Knowledge is certainly important; however, in this age of swiftly changing information, well-developed thinking skills are even more essential. They prepare learners to deal with new situations and challenges far into the future.

What kinds of thinking skills do different tasks require? As you learned in Chapter 11, Benjamin Bloom considered that question when developing *Bloom's Taxonomy*. Many teachers still use his taxonomy as a basis for understanding and teaching various levels of thought. (*Because this original version is so well-known and widely used, switching to the dramatically different Revised Bloom's Taxonomy is moving very slowly. You will likely encounter use of the revised taxonomy in future college courses.*)

As you know, Bloom's has six levels of thinking. The lower levels—Knowledge, Comprehension, and Application—are the most basic. The upper levels—*Analysis, Synthesis,* and *Evaluation*—are more difficult to learn but very important. Together, the complex combinations of skills in the three upper levels require *higher-order thinking skills*, or **critical thinking**. Critical thinking allows people to gather information, evaluate its quality, and use it effectively. Figure 12.2 identifies some verbs to use that indicate critical thinking or higher-order thinking skills.

Building students' abilities to use progressively more complex thinking skills is a major goal of education. Younger children are not able to see problems with a perspective other than their own, a skill necessary for critical thinking. They can, however, learn to think about different possibilities when presented with a problem. Young children also have a sense of curiosity, an important part of learning to think critically. They can ask questions and learn to ask better ones. Teachers can use these abilities to begin to lay the framework for critical thinking in the elementary grades.

The ability to think abstractly comes in later childhood and adolescence. Students gradually develop the ability to take charge of their own thinking and learning. They learn to ask probing questions and

Figure 12.2	Verbs for Higher-Order Thinking	
Analysis	**Synthesis**	**Evaluation**
Analyze	Assemble	Conclude
Compare	Categorize	Critique
Contrast	Compose	Deduce
Diagram	Create	Defend
Differentiate	Design	Discriminate
Distinguish	Devise	Evaluate
Illustrate	Explore	Formulate
Outline	Hypothesize	Interpret
Parse	Infer	Judge
Predict	Integrate	Justify
Question	Organize	Plan
Recognize	Rearrange	Predict
Select	Summarize	Revise

find new solutions. Students begin to rely on reason, not just emotion, in analyzing points of view. They can develop criteria and standards for evaluating their own thinking. As they enter adolescence, students can learn to examine problems closely and reject information that is incorrect, irrelevant, or biased. Skills such as these evolve through activities that incorporate critical-thinking skills.

In Chapter 11, you learned about the importance of setting clear learning goals that identify how students will demonstrate their learning. This is especially important in developing objectives that promote critical-thinking skills. Note that the whole objective, not just the verb, must reflect a particular level.

Because of their students' abilities, elementary teachers primarily use objectives at the lower end of the thinking scale as students build their knowledge base. As students move to middle and high school, the proportion of objectives shifts to those in the higher levels. High school teachers must include more objectives and learning activities that focus on analysis, synthesis, and evaluation levels to help students refine important critical-thinking skills necessary for success in college, career, and life.

Key Instructional Skills

No matter which activities you devise to meet your learning objectives, there are basic teaching skills you will utilize constantly. Several directly relate to developing and presenting learning activities. These include developing effective questions and examples to stimulate learning (Figure 12.3). Teachers also must know how to judge timing within a lesson and help students reflect on their learning at the end of a lesson.

Teacher education students learn these skills and practice them in various situations. It is in student teaching and their first years as teachers, however, that they truly understand their importance. That is why even experienced teachers continue to look for ways to enhance these key teaching skills.

Figure 12.3 Effective questions engage students and help stimulate learning.

Questioning

There is no skill more basic to teaching than the ability to use questions effectively. They are a key part of almost every learning activity. Teachers use questions for many purposes. They can generate interest, stimulate learning, check for comprehension, encourage participation, develop thinking skills, and evaluate learning.

Throughout your years as a student, you have answered thousands of questions, both oral and written. As a teacher, it will be your responsibility to decide when questions are appropriate, how to ask them, and how best to respond to students' answers. Begin now to pay more attention to the ways your teachers utilize questioning. As you practice developing questions of your own, keep these guidelines in mind:

- *Plan questions along with the lesson*. Preplanning questions allows time to make sure they match your learning objectives and the wording is clear. They provide a structure for the lesson. As the lesson progresses, you can add or modify questions, but having the original plan helps keep the lesson on track.

- *Ask questions of varying difficulty*. Look again at *Figure 11.8* to review Bloom's Taxonomy. Focus on the sample questions. Questions at different levels serve specific purposes. For example, simpler questions can check for understanding and comprehension. Just be sure to include questions from all levels appropriate for the abilities of the students.

- *Include open-ended questions*. Using **open-ended questions**, ones that require more than a few words as an answer, generally encourages higher-level thinking.

Encouraging Participation

What if you ask questions and no one answers? You have probably experienced a class where there was little student participation. There are ways to minimize this possibility.

Activities that include oral discussions depend on student participation. Most importantly, learners should feel comfortable participating (Figure 12.4). Teachers must create an atmosphere where respecting everyone is a value. That means that neither the teacher nor other students tease or put down anyone for a wrong answer or a different opinion.

Questions asked should be appropriate for students' level of knowledge and experience. Otherwise few will be willing to venture an answer.

Questions must generate interest. That means that they should be applicable to learners and varied in type. Questions can encourage students to classify, rank, or sort things. Others might focus on opinions

Figure 12.4 When students feel comfortable and respected in a classroom, they are more likely to participate in the learning process.

or attitudes. Some questions direct learners to one right answer. Other questions help students explore an appropriate answer for a specific circumstance.

Students need time to think before responding. Providing **wait time**, or a brief period of silence between asking a question and calling on a student, allows all students to mentally process the question and formulate their replies. Although it may feel awkward at first, this brief period of silence encourages participation and more and better answers.

Varying methods of asking for responses keeps students thinking. Sometimes a teacher might randomly call on students for a response. Other times, the same teacher might call on those who volunteer. With encouragement, students who are more hesitant to speak may be more willing to participate. It is important, however, to remember and respect the fact that various cultures have different traditions regarding asking and answering questions.

Responding to Students' Answers

How should you respond to students' answers to your spoken questions? That depends on the answer and the situation. If an answer is inaccurate, an effective response helps lead students to the right answer. Saying, "No, that's wrong!" discourages further participation. Instead, a teacher may say, "Let's look at this again," or "Let me state the question in a different way." Some answers are partially correct. A teacher should acknowledge what is accurate first. For example, "Yes, using a virus protection program is one way of protecting personal information, but using an alias may not be appropriate. Who can suggest other steps to take?"

In responding to answers, teachers can help students process learning by posing follow-up questions to the class. Teachers usually develop these on the spot, which can lead to deeper understanding.

Responding to Students' Questions

Not all questions are teacher initiated. In an interactive learning environment, students feel free to ask questions (Figure 12.5). These deserve a thoughtful and respectful response. If the question furthers the discussion, the teacher can provide an answer or counter with another question.

Figure 12.5 Responding to student questions in a thoughtful and respectful manner keeps students engaged in an interactive learning environment.

What happens if you are teaching and a student asks a question you cannot answer? It is fine to acknowledge that you do not have an answer. You can say that you will find one and get back to the student or class. You could also ask if anyone else has an answer or help the student figure out how to find an answer.

Many times questions are slightly off topic. In that case, it is best to give a brief answer to avoid distracting other learners from the lesson. A question may be interesting, but definitely off track. A good way to respond would be to say, "That is an interesting question but not what we are discussing right now. If you stay after class, we can talk about it."

Sometimes students' questions are inappropriate in their timing or are personal in nature, but still require a reply. For example, a kindergartener may ask about your personal life in the middle of a lesson. Helping the student understand when a question is appropriate is an important part of education.

Using Examples

Sometimes when a teacher presents new information, it is difficult to grasp the concept. Often, however, when the teacher offers a concrete example, everything falls into place. Examples help bring information to life for learners.

The use of examples increases understanding and retention of subject matter. Examples can show how theory applies to the real world. Other times, as in math, they help make sense of a process. When learning is complex, using multiple examples can improve understanding for more students.

As a teacher, planning effective examples as you develop lessons is important. When choosing examples, start with simple and progress to more complex. Be sure the examples are relevant to what you are teaching. Ask students to provide examples to check their level of learning.

Try to include different formats to match varied learning styles. A diagram, photo, or demonstration might serve as a visual example. Include verbal examples in oral explanations. Sometimes examples can involve student movement to help kinesthetic learners. For example, a teacher might have students physically show the formation of chemical compounds. Using sodium chloride as an example, one student might act as the electron in a sodium atom and others the electrons in a chlorine atom. The sodium electron joins the chlorine electrons, moving the atoms together as a sodium chloride ion.

Pacing

Pacing refers to the rate at which a teacher moves through the components of a lesson or the lessons throughout the day. If the pace is too slow, students become bored. If it is too fast, they cannot keep up and fail to learn all that they should.

The ability to pace a lesson appropriately is a learned skill. When you understand the various points to consider with pacing, it is easier to learn how (Figure 12.6).

- ***Know your natural style***. During your preparation to become a teacher, you will have many opportunities to develop and present activities. In most instances, a teacher or your peers will provide feedback and suggestions. This helps you find out whether your natural pace of presentation tends to be fast, slow, or on-target. If necessary, you can consciously adjust your style to better meet learners' needs.

- ***Look for signs of understanding***. Students learn at different rates. Teachers watch students' reactions and use questions and activities to gauge when most students understand a lesson. Remember that the age of students and complexity of the information will affect pacing.

Figure 12.6   When a teacher paces a lesson appropriately, students are more likely to remain actively engaged in learning.

- *Alternate types of activities*. Using a variety of types of activities helps keep students involved, attentive, and learning. Particularly for younger students, balance quiet individual work with activities that involve movement and talking. Even older students need a change of pace during the class period.

- *Plan for smooth transitions*. As you learned in Chapter 11, transitions are methods teachers use to move students from one activity to the next. Unless well planned, too much time can be lost changing activities. Inappropriate behaviors can occur. Effective teachers often alert students to finish up their work in preparation for a new activity. They set clear guidelines for transitions, including behavioral expectations.

Learning appropriate pacing in teaching takes practice. It requires a balance between having a lesson drag and having it speed along too quickly. Proper pacing requires knowledge of learners, both as a group and as individuals. Sometimes teachers must pace a lesson at different speeds for different students. As the school year progresses, an effective teacher knows the class well enough to achieve a "natural" pace.

Achieving Closure

While participating in activities, students engage in the process. At the end of an activity, it is essential to help students reflect on what they have learned, its purpose, and meaning. This process, or *closure*, is more than a quick summary. **Closure** is a process that helps students draw conclusions based on what they have learned. It helps them apply learning and lends a sense of achievement.

A teacher can handle closure in many ways. It is generally part of the *Summary* section in a lesson plan. For learning to be effective, students need to relate new knowledge to past knowledge and to future knowledge. In the end, students should be able to answer the question, "What did I learn and what does it mean to me today?"

Basic Teaching Strategies

Common instructional methods or teaching strategies form the foundation of most specific learning activities that teachers plan in their lessons. There are dozens of strategies teachers can use. This section discusses the pros, cons, and uses of some that teachers use frequently.

Educators sometimes classify these strategies as either teacher-centered or learner-centered. In **teacher-centered methods**, the teacher's role is to present the information that students are to learn and to direct their learning process. Students then practice what they have learned. For example, with

Figure 12.7 With group projects, students help direct their learning and achievement.

lectures, the teacher provides information, and students learn by listening. They may discuss the information in small groups after the lecture. **Learner-centered methods** are different. In these approaches, the teacher acts as a facilitator, or guide, for learning. Students more actively engage in directing and achieving their own learning. Group projects are an example of learner-centered instructional activities (Figure 12.7).

There is no one perfect instructional method or activity. Teachers use multiple factors in deciding which to use. They also vary their methods to keep students interested and engaged in learning.

Lectures

In its most basic form, a lecture consists of a teacher presenting information orally and students learning through listening. Although the use of lecture is frequent, especially in upper grades, it has drawbacks. Most students are stronger visual learners than auditory learners, so they find it more difficult to learn simply by listening. In addition, the lecture method puts students in the role of passive listeners. A lecture supplemented with visual aids would also reach a visual learner.

Still, lectures have benefits. They can be useful with any content and are particularly suited for presenting factual information. They are a good way to present information to large groups of older students.

How can you improve the effectiveness of lectures? Keeping the lecture period short helps improve lecture effectiveness. Adding visual elements can increase interest and improve understanding. For example, some teachers use digital presentations along with their lectures. There are also ways to make lectures less passive. For example, you might insert a question-and-answer period within or after the lecture. Some teachers facilitate note taking by providing partial outlines for students to complete or written questions for students to answer during a lecture.

Teachers who lecture must be especially effective presenters. This starts with preparing well-organized material. Main points must be clear and presented in a logical order. Examples help clarify information, especially ones that link new material to what students already know. Conveying enthusiasm is important, and teachers need to make eye contact with students around the room, not just read from notes. This also helps detect signs of restlessness, boredom, or misunderstanding. Asking a question, clarifying a point, or using another technique as a change of pace can help maintain student interest.

Reading

Your teacher has likely assigned you to read from this textbook. While not particularly creative, reading is one of the basic ways of learning a wealth of information. In addition to textbooks, students might read periodicals, Internet articles, and other researched material. You will continue to learn by reading. This is one reason why there is so much emphasis on literacy skills.

Discussions

Discussions may be teacher- or learner-centered, depending on the role the teacher plays. They help students explore options and ideas and develop key communication skills (Figure 12.8).

Figure 12.8 Teachers often play a key role in class discussions. What skills do students develop by participating in discussions?

A discussion begins with a stimulating question or problem based on a learning objective. It must be one without a simple answer. Discussions encourage and provide practice in thinking skills, especially critical-thinking skills. In participating in a discussion, students draw on their own knowledge and experiences. A series of questions guides the discussion toward the learning objective. At the end, a student or teacher summarizes or draws conclusions.

Participating effectively in discussions is a learned skill. Teachers must set the ground rules. Even young children can learn to take turns, be polite, and respect others' opinions. Teachers can encourage quieter students to participate and talkative students to listen. Seating arrangements in which students face each other promote discussion.

Discussions can take different forms. In a teacher-led discussion, the teacher keeps the discussion on task, moving forward with a logical progression of ideas. In small-group discussions, each group takes on this responsibility, so these are appropriate for older children and teens.

Groups often must report their conclusions to the class. In **panel discussions**, a group of people present and discuss a topic. The teacher acts as a *moderator* (leader) by introducing the panel, summarizing the main points, and relaying students' questions to panel members. Panelists may be outside experts or students who have prepared for their roles. In a debate, participants try to persuade others to their opposing points of view. Sometimes the teacher divides the students into two groups and they must argue for or against an issue.

Demonstrations

A demonstration is the best way to teach a process. Students see how to complete each step, helping visual and kinesthetic learners. At the same time, the accompanying verbal explanation helps auditory learners. This technique is particularly helpful when a process is complex, procedures are difficult to explain, or visual cues are important. For example, a teacher might show how to balance a checkbook, the steps in making a mask out of paper and plaster, or how to perform various knife skills in a culinary class.

Demonstrations are usually teacher-centered, putting students in a passive learning role. There are ways, however, to make them more interactive (Figure 12.9).

Figure 12.9 When students participate in a demonstration, they take on an interactive role in learning.

The teacher can have students make predictions about what will happen or ask a student to perform a step or two of the procedure. For a science experiment, students might fill out a lab sheet as the demonstration progresses. Asking questions throughout the demonstration involves students. In other situations, such as a demonstration of how to use a computer program, students might perform the process at the same time as the teacher demonstrates it. Adding activity and involvement generates interest and aids learning.

A demonstration requires careful preparation, especially if the process involves a complicated explanation. What is the sequence of steps? How can they best be shown and clearly explained? Are there any safety precautions to observe and emphasize? What equipment and materials must be gathered and ready to use? How can the room be arranged to make sure all students will have a clear view of the demonstration? What questions and examples will help students understand the process?

Sometimes teachers reverse roles and have students prepare and present demonstrations. This may be a learning activity with students researching the topic they will demonstrate. The teacher can use this role reversal as a way of checking students' mastery of a process.

Guest Speakers

Guest speakers can bring outside expertise into the classroom and generate interest. For example, for young children, having a firefighter talk about fire safety and show firefighting gear can be an exciting and memorable way to learn the topic.

Before inviting a speaker, be sure you understand your school's policy regarding outside guests. Having a guest speaker in the classroom may require administrative approval and, in some cases, a background check. These policies help ensure students' safety.

When using a guest speaker, it is essential to make sure the experience is a positive one for all involved. When inviting the speaker, be clear about the topic, the objectives, and the time frame. Agree on the format the speaker will use and identify any special arrangements, such as equipment needed. You might have students prepare questions for the speaker ahead of time. When you, as a teacher, have a community member in your classroom, you and your students represent your school. If students are attentive and polite, the speaker will leave with a positive impression. Be sure to follow up with a personal note or notes from students thanking the speaker for sharing his or her time and knowledge.

Figure 12.10 In sciences classes, simulations help bring concepts to life.

Simulations

Simulations are useful to put students in situations that feel real, even though they are not—eliminating any harmful risks. Simulations give students opportunities to experience certain aspects of a situation as if they are in them, including making decisions and solving problems.

Simulations come in many forms. High school students may hold a mock trial. A group of fourth-graders might spend a morning as students at a pioneer school, learning as children did then. Computer-based simulations are very common today. For example, instead of providing real frogs for dissection, frogs can be virtually dissected using computers (Figure 12.10).

While simulations are most common in social studies and science, they can be useful in other areas that require student involvement. Simulations work well when students are learning new skills or exploring feelings and attitudes. Skits, role-playing, and case studies are variations of simulations.

Skits

Skits are learner-centered simulations that involve students in acting out stories. They are mini-plays based on scripts written by the teacher or students. Students play the various parts.

Skits actively involve students in learning. Performing a skit involves auditory, kinesthetic, and visual learning. Students speak, listen, perform, and watch the skit. Adding costumes and props helps make situations more real, increasing student involvement. Interacting with the content provides more understanding than simply reading or watching media.

Skits are adaptable to different ages, subject areas, and educational objectives. For example, a first grade teacher might develop a simple skit to help young students learn addition and subtraction. After arranging chairs to represent seats in a bus, the teacher could use a simple story line about people getting on and off the imaginary bus to help students practice the concepts of addition and subtraction. Older children might write and perform skits about the *Revolutionary War*. The process of writing requires review of prior learning and additional research. What additional skills would students build through editing the script, gathering props and costumes, and practicing and presenting the skit?

Role-Playing

Although similar to a skit, **role-playing** is also a learner-centered simulation that involves students in acting out a role but *without* a script. The teacher clearly describes a situation that includes an issue or problem. Students act out the role of the people in the situation, basing their actions and conversations on how the person they represent would likely react. Playing their roles, students work through the situation or solve the problem. After the role-play ends, students discuss what happened. They explore why the various characters acted as they did and how the people playing the parts felt in those roles. The teacher helps summarize how the experience relates to the instructional objective.

Teachers can use role-playing situations for a variety of purposes. It can help students understand feelings and behavior. For example, it could be useful as young children learn about the danger of interacting with strangers. The teacher might create a simulated situation in which a child can role-play an interaction with a stranger, without risks. Role-plays can provide practice (Figure 12.11). In a French class, students could take various roles, simulating buying tickets and boarding a train in France while using the French vocabulary terms they have just learned. Teachers can also use role-playing to check and strengthen students' understanding of information. For example, a teacher might have students represent the positions of various nations on a topic of disagreement. Follow-up discussions could focus both on understanding points of view and reactions to conflict.

Case Studies

Case studies involve groups of students working together to analyze a situation, or "case." A **case study** is a description of a realistic problematic situation

Figure 12.11 Role-playing helps students work through situations or solve problems.

that requires a solution. Case studies allow teachers to direct learning by using a case that focuses on the exact issues that meet the learning objective. For example, in a lesson on ethics, a business teacher might present students with a case in which a supervisor directs an employee to do something contrary to company policies. Case studies

- allow students to apply new knowledge and skills for solving complex, real-life issues

- provide opportunities for students to work in small groups or teams to consider the case and come up with possible solutions

- engage students in listening to individual groups present and explain their proposed solutions and their reasoning behind these solutions

- provide students with opportunities to practice debating the merits of different options

- help students learn to form a *consensus*—a general agreement that requires analysis and negotiation to reach a solution on which the majority agree

Teachers can use case studies to actively involve students in dealing with real issues. The cases must be well written. Sometimes teachers start with a current news story, and add or subtract information to make it fit the learning situation. They clearly outline what students are to accomplish in their groups, set time limits, and move from group to group listening and helping students move forward. They use the large-group discussion at the end to help students identify the issues and principles involved. As with other learner-centered methods, the teacher starts with a clear plan. As the lesson plays out, however, the teacher decides how best to guide students toward the desired learning goal.

Reflective Responses

When teachers use **reflective responses**, students think deeply about an issue or something they have learned. When using reflective responses, they ask students to think about thinking (cognition). For example, a teacher may ask students to take out a piece of paper and write about what they have just learned in their own words. A teacher can also use reflective responses at the beginning of a lesson to capture a learner's attention. In this way, reflective responses can give a teacher a sense of where the students are in their learning. They can then build on what students already know. Reflective responses offer students the opportunity to be thoughtful and insightful and can be either written or spoken.

Labs

Labs offer students the opportunity to work with materials, ideas, people, or processes to solve a given problem. For example, kindergartners may plant seeds to experiment with the effects of sunlight and water—or the lack of them—on growth. Middle school students may experiment with the effects of discrimination through a controlled environment that takes away privileges of some members.

Basically, there are two types of labs used by teachers. A **productive lab** focuses on producing an end product. For example, a middle school student may produce a children's book written in elementary Spanish. A third grader may produce a replica of the solar system. A high school student in a culinary program may produce three kinds of appetizers.

Another type of lab, the **experimental lab**, uses a formal process to research a problem. This type of lab is common in scientific experiments (Figure 12.12). The teacher gives students a problem and they must find an answer through experimentation. Because they are experimenting, specific results are not always a guarantee. The question, "What will happen if…" motivates learners in experimental labs.

Figure 12.12 Safety is an important consideration when conducting labs.

Labs require careful planning. Teachers act as planners and organizers, as well as managers, during the lab activity. Clear instructions are essential. It takes practice to accurately estimate the amount of time students will need to complete a lab activity. In experimental labs, safety may be a concern. Students, equipment, and facilities must be considered and rules established. Although labs can be expensive in terms of time, materials, and resources, they can provide excellent opportunities for learning.

Student Presentations

Student presentations are common in all grades. They give learners the opportunity to share what they have learned. Depending on the assignment, presentations may be oral, visual, or use both formats. Presentations help students build communication skills (Figure 12.13).

Figure 12.13 When making presentations, students must think about the best way to engage their classmates and communicate information.

Learners must think about how to best relay the information they are attempting to communicate to their audience. This helps them achieve a higher level of understanding. Sometimes teachers use group presentations. These add practice with cooperation and organizational skills.

Games

Remember the sense of accomplishment you felt when mastering a new game? Games can be fun and challenging. They can be useful to reinforce learning, build skills, and provoke thought. These attributes make games effective instructional activities to meet many learning objectives.

Paper-and-pencil games include hidden-clue puzzles, word searches, crossword puzzles, or other word games. Word games give students a chance to practice spelling and other language skills. Students can complete them independently or work together in groups.

Card games are effective for reviewing factual information. They may have a basis on traditional games such as *Go Fish* or *Memory.* Rules can be simple or complex and may change once students learn the game. Students often create their own rules for card games as they become more familiar.

Students typically play board games in small groups. Sometimes teachers adapt well-known board games to meet their learning objectives. Commercial board games designed to teach various topics are available, and teachers often share ideas for making their own. Games that use dice or play money can be effective ways to practice simple math skills.

Active games offer opportunities for students to be physically involved in learning. Active games appeal to young children who learn through play and movement and to kinesthetic learners. Such games also offer a change of pace in learning.

Many educational games are available for the computer and other forms of digital media (Figure 12.14). They can be used with individual students and

Figure 12.14 Games can help meet and reinforce learning objectives.

can help meet specific learning needs. With some games, the student competes against the clock, trying to complete a game within a given time period. Computer games often have more than one level, allowing students to progress to more difficult knowledge or skills.

When used appropriately, games can generate enthusiasm and increase learning. In choosing or constructing games, it is important to evaluate the type of learning involved, student appeal, initial cost or effort, and whether the time involved produces sufficient learning.

Cooperative Learning

Cooperative learning is a form of small-group learning in which students work together to achieve a common goal. The group is responsible for making sure all members participate, contribute, and learn. With effective use, cooperative learning is a highly effective learning technique.

Cooperative learning takes many different formats and is adaptable to most subject areas and age groups. The specific assignment requires careful planning. The teacher divides students into groups, usually of two to six students with diverse characteristics. The structure of the learning task encourages students to work together and to be responsible for each other's learning. At the same time, the teacher builds in **individual accountability**, or a way to assess each student's participation and learning. Group members share ideas and propose solutions. The group must resolve differences and work together to complete the assignment. The teacher acts as a facilitator, monitoring the groups to keep them on track, but not offering solutions.

Cooperative learning offers many advantages. The ability to work together in a group is an important life skill. Opportunities to work together build students' willingness to contribute, listen to and respect others' opinions, help one another, and negotiate differences. Self-esteem and responsibility improve, as well. Most students enjoy learning more when working with their peers.

Professional Tip

Collaboration

In the classroom, effective teachers execute a plan keeping in mind the specific subject matter learning and their students' longer-term success in their specific subject or learning area. In doing so, most teachers rely a lot on others for ideas. Professional teachers are collaborative. They cooperate with other teachers who work with similar students and with teachers in grades before and after. It may not always be evident on the surface, but they are team players. They work as a team with other teachers, aides, specialists, and administrators.

Dig Deeper

Take notice of the number of professionals that contribute to your own education. Inquire about how they find time to collaborate with one another. How do they facilitate communication? Discuss your findings with the class.

Collaborative Learning Teams

Working in a team is a skill students must develop just like writing and critical thinking. The terms *cooperative learning* and *collaborative learning* are often used interchangeably but they are significantly different. What is the difference?

In cooperative learning, a teacher may switch between lecturing and group discussion. Cooperative learning teams may also perform a task or solve a problem but their work is usually not complex or interdependent. They may instead end up divvying up the work and then combining their answers. They do not need to work on it together to get the job done.

In **collaborative learning**, assignments involve a task or problem students must solve using their complementary and interdependent skills, experiences, or opinions. The team members have clearly defined and recognized differentiated roles. The task is designed so that they must come together to coordinate the outcomes of their responsibilities (Figure 12.15).

Figure 12.15 Collaborative learning requires students to work interdependently to solve a problem or achieve a goal.

One person may be the leader or facilitator, another, the recorder, and others in roles such as brainstormer or mediator. Similar to cooperative learning teams, collaborative teams utilize the social benefits of group work. Collaborative teams, however, place greater emphasis on completing the task at hand *together* as a group rather than as individuals working together. The results tend to be more dynamic and in-depth with less emphasis on teacher-led activity and more emphasis on group-directed activity.

In collaborative teams, students gain additional critical-thinking skills, teamwork and communication skills, social skills, empathy and sensitivity, and more insight into a topic. Teamwork in classes can often be part of career preparation as team projects serve as a bridge between school and the work that students may encounter in the workforce. Indeed, surveys of hiring managers regularly note the importance of past teamwork experience and interpersonal skills when hiring recent college graduates. Collaborative teams consistently outperform individuals acting alone in the completion of complex tasks.

There are two overriding goals for collaborative learning teams: to function together and to complete their work. After establishing goals, the next step in effective teaching is to set specific, measurable learning outcomes. The learning outcomes are the written hopes that the teacher has for each student individually and for every team as a whole. They are what the instructor anticipates the students or team can know or realistically do by the end of the experience.

By definition, in collaborative learning groups, the teacher steps out of the authoritative role and **empowers**, or gives authority to, students to complete the task set before them. Together, the group completes a task.

The task is often open-ended, complex, and needing more definition. This requires that the task at hand must have shared meaning and that the end product must require collective participation or voice. This complexity adds to the richness of the assigned task or assignment. It also adds to the complexity of planning learning outcomes. This does not mean that there cannot be instructor planned and measurable learning objectives. It does mean that the specific outcomes may not be what the teacher intended or expected when designing the learning outcomes. The instructor, like the collaborative learning team, needs to be flexible and adaptable to a changing environment.

Perspectives on Teaching

Aneka is finishing her first week of student teaching in Mr. Sanchez's third grade classroom. It has been a great experience so far. She has been primarily observing the class, getting to know the students, and working with individuals who need extra help. She is impressed with Mr. Sanchez's ability to focus the students' abundant energy into excitement toward learning.

Aneka's Thoughts...

Right now, ideas are swirling through my brain. I met with Mr. Sanchez after school to go over the teaching plan for the next two weeks. In science, the students will be starting a new unit on weather. They will learn about seasons, clouds, forms of precipitation, tornadoes and hurricanes, and weather forecasting. Mr. Sanchez asked me to develop and teach a lesson to introduce the weather unit. He challenged me to get the students enthused about the study of weather so they will be motivated to master the stated learning/performance objectives. I am truly excited about my first solo lesson with the class!

Since that discussion, possibilities keep popping into my head. Because this is an introductory lesson, I have much more flexibility in choosing a topic. This almost makes it more difficult! My brainstorming list so far includes having students...

- think about a particular weather-related memory. How did the weather make them feel? Was it exciting, scary, or relaxing?

They could draw a picture of their weather memory and describe it to the class.

- use thermometers to measure the temperature of different places and substances (cold water, warm water, dirt, near a window) and record their readings. As a class, they could record their readings on a giant chart and discuss them.

- create a giant wall mural picturing different types of weather.

I have more ideas but none seem quite right—although several have potential. I want this lesson to be great! Maybe the activity planning chart from Ms. Neeley's teaching methods class last semester will help me test my ideas. Coming up with ideas is only one part of the process. I know I need to meet the objective, match the students' needs with the topic, and make sure the activity is practical. Not all of my ideas pass these tests—but this process has helped me with planning in the past and, hopefully, it will again! This is *real* and it needs to be *right*!

Analyze It!

After reading *Perspectives on Teaching*, analyze the process Aneka used to develop ideas for an introductory lesson for a unit on weather. What additional "tests" might Aneka use to determine whether her ideas are workable for this introductory lesson?

Differentiated Instructional Methods

All students do not learn in the same way or at the same pace. In Chapter 9, this was described as *differentiated learning*. In response, teachers may use **differentiated instructional methods** to meet the different learning styles and needs of their students. That is, they use different techniques of instruction to match a student's preferred mode of learning, disability, or background.

Does differentiated instruction mean that teachers must prepare a different lesson for each individual student? The answer is *yes* and *no*. Teachers who utilize differentiated instruction do tailor their lessons to individual students but they do not teach different content or a different subject to each student. Instead, they assess where each student is at and adapt their pace or mode of instruction to each learner. It can be as simple as individually pacing the speed of the instruction or as complex as designing different methods for each learning style. Sometimes teachers form student groups that share common learning styles.

Differentiated instructional methods require teachers to be flexible and adaptable, and to know their students well. They must be diligent in assessing and responding to their students' needs. Lastly, they must give students choices and ownership in their own learning for differentiated instruction to be effective. Figure 12.16 offers examples of differentiated instruction for a number of student characteristics.

Choosing Appropriate Teaching Strategies

Where do you start in choosing an appropriate teaching approach? Once again, it begins with your learning objectives. Your learning activities must lead students toward meeting the objectives. With this factor in mind, see how various teaching strategies fit your situation. Then develop your activity based on the teaching strategy that is the best match. Be sure to consider the following:

- *Student characteristics*. A strategy must match the ages and developmental abilities of your students. For example, you would not choose a lecture format for first graders. If this is a whole-class activity, make certain it is a strategy in which all students can participate. Keep variety in mind along with students' preferred learning styles.

- *Subject matter*. The subject you are teaching and topic of the lesson play a large part in narrowing your choice of appropriate strategies. Some subjects require teaching methods that involve much content repetition. Perhaps students must learn other facts.

Figure 12.16	Differentiated Classroom Instruction by Learner Characteristics
Student Characteristic	**Example of Differentiated Instruction**
Culture	In a social studies class, the teacher does not assume that every student has the same cultural understanding of U.S. history. He or she starts first with each student researching the life events of a grandparent, including such things as political conflict, economic turns, and social changes. Stories are shared and used as a starting point for understanding modern history.
Educational background	In a middle school math classroom, the teacher has students work through problems at their own pace. When mastery is achieved, students then proceed to the next unit.
Ethnicity	A teacher conscientiously presents instructional materials that are representative of a multitude of ethnicities and racial heritage. The environment provides readiness for learning when there is multiethnic representation.
Gender	A kindergarten teacher structures her classroom to meet the physical and relationship needs of both boys and girls by providing inviting, carpeted reading areas with pillows; open spaces for tumbling and climbing; and an area to create art. On cold winter days when outside temperatures dip, she holds recess inside and allows the children to choose their preferred activity. The teacher asks students to form social pairs or small groups.
Language	For a writing assignment, a high school teacher modifies the grading rubric to reflect writing improvement rather than a single standard.
Preferred learning style	An elementary school teacher reads a story to his class. Visual learners are asked to create a visual display of the story using art materials. Auditory learners are asked to give an oral synopsis of the story utilizing music as a background. Kinesthetic learners are asked to perform the book story in dance or skit format.
Religion	A high school teacher checks the calendar dates of representative religious holidays celebrated by religiously diverse students before setting exam or major assignment due dates.
Socio-economic status (SES)	A high school teacher of lifespan development asks her students to create a visual portrayal of a family member's physical development by collecting family photographs from infancy through adolescence. This year, she has several economically disadvantaged students in her classroom including one who is currently living in a homeless shelter. Another lost everything to a house fire this past year. The teacher alters the assignment so that students can choose to collect photographs of celebrities or public figures whose images can readily be found online using school computers and printers.

Other subject areas require more creativity and exploration. Sometimes you may need to reinforce other skills while teaching the subject content. For example, students may need to develop interpersonal skills along with content skills.

- *Teaching situation*. The strategy you choose must work from a practical standpoint. Time, materials and equipment availability, space, and any additional cost are all considerations. If taking the class on a field trip to a symphony performance an hour away is not an option, how else could you meet your learning objective?

All of these options and considerations may seem overwhelming. In fact, having options is a great part of teaching! It allows you to pair your creativity with your learning objectives to develop unique activities for your students. When you spend time with a group of students, as you will as a teacher, you become attuned to their needs and preferences. You quickly develop an instinct for what will work well and what will not. (Of course, there are always surprises, too!) In the meantime, as you gain experience, you can use a checklist like the following to help you make appropriate choices (Figure 12.17).

Figure 12.17	Checklist for Choosing a Teaching Strategy
✓	Meets objective(s)
✓	Is age and developmentally appropriate
✓	Meets varying learning style needs
✓	Includes all students in learning process
✓	Engages students' interest
✓	Respects cultural differences
✓	Is appropriate for the subject matter and topic
✓	Allows for active involvement in learning
✓	Promotes thinking skills
✓	Allows appropriate reinforcement of content
✓	Allows for completion within available time
✓	Works in available space
✓	Uses available resources/materials
✓	Matches teacher's experience and skills

Chapter 12 Review and Assess

Summary

- Teachers use instructional methods, also called teaching strategies or instructional strategies, to meet their objectives.

- Because students need to learn the complex skills required for critical thinking, teachers at every level and in every subject area must provide opportunities to practice these skills.

- Effective questions and examples are essential to most teaching strategies.

- An atmosphere of comfort and respect helps encourage students to participate and answer questions.

- Examples that appeal to all learning styles help bring life to learning.

- Appropriate use of pacing and closure helps maximize learning.

- There are many basic teaching strategies. Some are more teacher-centered, while others are learner-centered.

- Teaching strategies, and activities based on them, must lead students to meeting the lesson's objectives.

- Strategies that require involvement actively engage students in the learning process.

- In addition to matching the topic with an appropriate strategy, when planning lessons teachers must consider the specific characteristics of their students and other aspects of the teaching situation.

- As teachers spend more time with students, they become more attuned to needs and preferences, developing an instinct for methods that will work well and those that will not.

Review and Study

1. What are instructional methods?

2. Explain why well-developed thinking skills are even more essential than knowledge.

3. What is critical thinking?

4. Give an example of an open-ended question, and identify the level of thinking it requires based on Bloom's Taxonomy.

5. What is wait time? What is the reasoning behind its use?

6. Name one way using examples benefits students.

7. What are four points to consider when learning how to pace a lesson?

8. Contrast teacher-centered methods and learner-centered instructional methods.

9. How are skits and role-plays similar and different?

10. What are three ways case studies help students work together to solve a problem?

11. What is the difference between productive and experimental labs?

12. What is the starting point for choosing a teaching approach? What factors should you assess when choosing appropriate teaching strategies?

Vocabulary Activity

13. On a separate sheet of paper, list words that relate to each of the *Content* and *Academic* terms on page 284. Then work with a partner to explain how these words are related.

Critical Thinking

14. **Analyze roles.** Analyze the teacher's role in helping students develop complex thinking skills from the early grades through high school. Use the text and other reliable authoritative resources to cite evidence supporting your analysis.

15. **Draw conclusions.** Some students purposely ask off-track questions to disrupt the flow of lessons. Draw conclusions about how teachers can handle these situations most effectively. Cite the text and other reliable resources to support your conclusions. Post your responses to a school-approved class discussion board. How do your conclusions vary from your classmates'?

16. **Analyze variables.** Analyze the characteristics of the various teaching strategies described in this chapter and identify three that might pose particular pacing problems for teachers. What variables influence pacing for these strategies? Discuss your analysis with the class.

17. **Outline examples.** If you were teaching a second grade class about cause and effect, outline an appropriate example that you might use to clarify the concept.

18. **Analyze criteria.** Why is individual accountability a concern with cooperative and collaborative learning activities? Analyze criteria for two ways to accomplish accountability. Cite the text and other reliable resources as evidence to support your criteria.

Core Skills

19. **Writing.** Choose a topic that you are studying in one of your classes. Write one original critical-thinking question,

based on your topic, for each of the upper levels of Bloom's Taxonomy—*Analysis*, *Synthesis*, and *Evaluation*.

20. **Speaking and listening.** In small groups, discuss why closure is important to learning and achievement. Identify three ways a teacher might handle closure. Discuss your ideas with the class.

21. **Writing.** Based on your experiences with taking part in discussions, develop a list of guidelines to use as a teacher to ensure students feel comfortable participating. Are your guidelines for elementary, middle, or high school students? Cite text or other reliable resources that support your guidelines.

22. **Research, writing, and presentation.** Choose three or more of the following basic teaching strategies and develop a lesson using each. Use the text and other reliable resources to learn more about implementing various strategies. Identify your target student audience, the subject matter or topic, and any special situations that impact teaching. Write your objective(s) for each and use questioning to check for comprehension and encourage participation. Utilize a differentiated instructional method with each strategy. Determine a method for closure. Then present your lessons and strategies to your classmates, requesting their feedback on your execution.

- Lecture
- Discussion
- Demonstration
- Simulation
- Skit or role-play
- Case study
- Lab
- Game
- Cooperative learning
- Collaborative learning

23. **Technology application.** Compare traditional and electronic games for effectiveness in teaching math skills. Locate a traditional game that teaches math concepts—such as counting or addition—and play it with a young child. Think about which math concept was taught. Next, play an electronic game that is intended to teach a similar math concept. Were both methods equally effective in teaching math skills? Why or why not? Which do you recommend and in what circumstances?

24. **Observation and writing.** Arrange a classroom visit to observe a teacher conducting a collaborative learning activity. Write a report on your experience from an instructional viewpoint. What is the topic and level of the lesson? Describe how the teacher facilitated the experience and used questioning and examples to encourage student participation and responsibility for learning. How did the teacher maintain individual accountability and achieve closure?

25. **CTE College and career readiness practice.** Review the lesson plan you created for Item 24 in Chapter 11. Based on what you have learned in this chapter, analyze the adequacy of your lesson in choice of teaching strategies, use of questioning and examples, and closure. Where your choices adequate in meeting learning objectives and providing for learner achievement? Then develop an alternative or additional learning activity using a different teaching strategy. Write a rationale for your new choice. Formulate at least eight questions to use as part of the activity, applying various appropriate levels of thinking.

College and Career Portfolio

Employers and educators are interested in people who impress them as being professional and serious about a position. Involvement in academic clubs or professional organizations can help you make a good impression, and offer learning opportunities to help with your studies or career. While you are in school, you might belong to such groups as National Honor Society, Future Educators of America, or Family, Career and Community Leaders of America. When employed, you may belong to a national educator's organization. Update your online information to reflect your membership in clubs and organizations. Make sure information about you on the Internet does not detract from your professional image. Remove any information you have posted on social networking sites, blogs, wikis, or other sites that does not give a favorable impression of you.

- Identify clubs or organizations you can join to help you learn and build a professional image. Give the name and brief description of each.

- Save the file in your e-portfolio or a print copy in your traditional portfolio.

Chapter 13
Technology for Instruction

Content Terms

instructional technology
distance education
online learning
virtual school
interactive whiteboard
model
acceptable use policy
WebQuest

Academic Terms

accredited
real time
plagiarism
copyright
Teach Act of 2002
multimedia

Objectives

After studying this chapter, you will be able to

- **summarize** the current status of technology use in education.

- **identify** ways that technology makes learning more accessible.

- **describe** technology tools that assist teachers with planning, teaching, communicating, and managing information.

- **summarize** ways teachers use technology to enhance learning opportunities.

- **evaluate** online websites for teaching and learning.

- **create** a lesson plan, integrating technology into the plan's learning objectives and activities.

Reading Prep

Arrange a study session to read the chapter with a classmate. After you read each section independently, stop and tell each other what you think the main points are in the section. Continue with each section until you finish the chapter.

At the Companion Website you can

- **Practice** terms with e-flash cards and interactive games

- **Assess** what you learn by completing self-assessment quizzes

- **Expand** knowledge with interactive activities

www.g-wlearning.com/teaching/

Study on the go

Use a mobile device to practice terms and review with self-assessment quizzes.

www.m.g-wlearning.com/0094/

Case Study

As a class, read the case study and discuss the questions that follow. After you finish studying the chapter, discuss the case study and questions again. How have your responses changed based on what you learned?

"You are young, and your ideas are fresh and current," exclaimed Ms. Nguyen, David's lead teacher in his new job-shadowing experience at the middle school. "In fact, that is exactly how I am hoping I can use you for this semester." Ms. Nguyen taught English literature at the middle school. Along with the district mandated books, she liked to supplement her students' literature experiences with references to what was currently trending related to popular literature, fashion, movies, music, and celebrities. She was counting on David to keep both her and her students up-to-date with what was trending so that they could relate these trends to the classic literature they would be reading.

Let's Discuss

- Which social media do you suggest that David use to keep current?
- Follow a social media of your choice and report on a few current trends from the past week.
- How might Ms. Nguyen relate one of these trends to help her students' relate to a past historical period?

In the last decades, technology has changed virtually all aspects of society and continues to do so. Education is no exception. While computers were originally developed for use by business and government, their application to other areas, including education, quickly became apparent. Other related forms of technology soon followed.

The term **instructional technology** was coined to describe the application of technology to enhance teaching, learning, and assessment. Everything from computers in the classroom to the use of multimedia for educational presentations is a form of instructional technology.

Teaching and Learning in the Digital Age

Today, you will find technology of various types in use at every level of education (Figure 13.1). For example, kindergarteners play simple computer games that help build reading skills. Elementary students create data bar graphs comparing the daily high and low temperatures of their city with others across the country by entering the information in a spreadsheet program. Middle school students studying the Louisiana Purchase read excerpts from the journals of Lewis and Clark and view artifacts from the journey through the Smithsonian Institution's website. A high school sociology class has a live discussion with a similar class in Canada via the Internet using a web link.

In each of these cases, the teacher created the activity to help students reach course learning objectives. Developing knowledge and skills for using technology in everyday life and work is a useful by-product, but it is normally not the main goal. Choose technology as a tool only when it is effective for the situation.

As technology continues to evolve, new classroom applications will emerge. As part of your teacher education, you will learn how to select, evaluate, and use technology appropriately in the classroom. You will also have opportunities to see how it can help with many of the other tasks teachers perform. The *International Society for Technology in Education (ISTE)* has developed a set of educational technology standards for teachers.

Figure 13.1   From learning games to complex design projects, instructional technology is used at all levels of education.

These standards help teacher education programs make certain that new teachers feel prepared to use instructional technology. They identify specific skills teachers need in order to incorporate technology into their teaching and model appropriate use of technology for work and professional growth.

Assessing Current Practice

Technology offers countless options for enhancing learning, inspiring teachers, and speeding routine tasks. At the same time, there are vast differences in its use in schools. In some schools, each student has a laptop, digital tablet, or similar device to use at school and take home to complete assignments. Other schools do not yet have an Internet connection. Most schools fall in the broad spectrum between these extremes.

Why is there such wide variation? The primary reason is cost. Computers and other technology are expensive, especially when multiplied by the number of teachers and students in a school district who would like to use them. Add on related expenses such as software, Internet access, and technical support. In addition, equipment and software need frequent updates or replacement.

As you learned in Chapter 5, school funding methods vary from state to state. In many states, some school districts have much less to spend per pupil than in other districts. One way this shows up is that less wealthy districts tend to have significantly fewer technology resources. Federal and state government programs, grants, even local fund-raising efforts have helped some schools, but real inequities still exist.

Even in schools where technology is available, its use varies from teacher to teacher. This may be due to differences in technology skills, teaching style, or even subject area. As a group, younger teachers are more likely to embrace technology. Most grew up using a computer and acquired new skills gradually along the way. Some teachers find new technology intimidating and do not want to base lessons on something that may or may not work when they need it. Other teachers use more traditional techniques very effectively. Technology is also more applicable and important to some subject areas and grade levels than to others.

Adapting to the Situation

What happens if you believe in integrating technology in teaching, become prepared to do so, and end up in a school with little available technology? You can use what is available as effectively as possible. If you have one computer in your classroom, design activities that allow students to use it individually or in small groups (Figure 13.2). If there are computers available in the library or a computer lab, make use of them.

Figure 13.2 Creating small group activities that students can do with one classroom computer is just one way of using limited technology to the best advantage.

If you have a computer at home, use it for research and planning. You may have other personal technology, such as a digital camera or digital tablet that you could use to enhance lesson material. Investigate the possibility of grants or community support to improve the situation.

You might find yourself in a situation where the school has many technology resources, including ones new to you. You can ask the technology coordinator or another teacher to help you learn new skills. Look online for ideas about successful applications. Practice on your own. Then try using the technology in a small way. As your confidence increases, take advantage of professional development opportunities to expand your skills.

You may also be able to share your technology successes with other teachers. Think about ways that you could approach this so that teachers feel comfortable. You might form a study group, with teachers volunteering to show how to use equipment, software, or applications in various classes. If a teacher seems to need one-on-one support, ask the teacher to teach you something in return. Everyone has different knowledge and strengths. As part of a committed faculty, sharing these skills with one another is an asset. Most schools have a technology resource person that staff members can utilize for assistance and to build skills.

Technology: Making Learning More Accessible

While the American educational system is open to all, some students face real barriers to learning. Technology offers very practical ways to overcome some of these obstacles. Students and teachers no longer need to be physically in the same classroom in order for quality learning to take place. In addition, technology allows many students with disabilities or other learning challenges to participate more fully in their education.

Expanding Classroom Walls

Technology allows teachers to go beyond traditional classrooms to meet the needs of students. **Distance education**—a learning situation in which the teacher and student are not in the same location—is not a new concept. Technology, however, has made it much more widely available. In addition, there are now options that make the experience more similar to classroom learning (Figure 13.3).

Figure 13.3   Distance education can connect teachers and students around the world.

These arrangements use various technologies. Most commonly, lessons are available to students through the Internet as **online learning** or *virtual education*. Students complete assignments, participate in discussion boards, and may even take exams online.

Distance education first gained popularity at the college and university level. Students could take some, or even all, classes with few trips to campus. Now, online courses and even virtual schools are available for students at the secondary level and below. Students may take individual classes or perhaps complete all their graduation requirements via computer. Traditional schools may offer some online courses. **Virtual schools**—those that exist only online—are another option, but students need to make sure that they are accredited. An *accredited* school has passed a quality assessment and credits earned generally qualify for graduation at traditional schools.

With online courses, students submit their work to the teacher electronically. They usually interact with the teacher and other students on a regular basis. Sometimes classes take place in *real time*, meaning all students are online for class at the same time and function more like a traditional classroom. Most often, however, students complete lessons at times convenient to them but must meet assignment deadlines just as in a regular class.

One of the greatest advantages of distance learning is its accessibility. It can make educational opportunities available to those who cannot physically attend a regular course. It can give three high school seniors in a small rural high school access to an advanced physics class their school cannot provide. It gives options to a student unable to attend school because of a medical condition. It also appeals to students for whom school schedules are a problem. Distance learning makes learning more available by overcoming barriers to traditional classroom attendance.

This type of education is not right for all learners or teachers. Students need to have access to a computer and need basic computer skills. They must be motivated and self-disciplined to keep up with course assignments. One characteristic of high-quality classes is that teachers and students communicate frequently. In fact, some students who might be shy about expressing their ideas in a regular classroom are more willing to do so online. Teaching virtual classes requires technology skills, an emphasis on learning through projects, and a commitment to be available to students. Successful teachers also make use of the many technology tools to make learning as rich and interactive as possible.

Assistive Technology

Technology can assist students who have a range of disabilities and characteristics that affect the learning process. These include students who have some physical or learning disabilities and English Language Learners (ELL).

The ability to utilize a computer can open up learning opportunities for students who have a variety of disabilities. Some, however, may have difficulty using a normal keyboard. Keyboard modifications help many, but some use other devices such as trackballs, rollerballs, or joysticks which require less mobility to maneuver.

With great strides in improvements of voice recognition software, translating spoken words into writing on the computer screen is valuable for some. For students who have difficulty with speech, text-to-speech software can "read" words typed into the computer using a synthesized voice.

Students with low vision can use programs that magnify computer type on the monitor, while braille note-taking devices exist for those who have total loss of vision. Handheld magnifier technology can make books more readable. These and other uses of technology help many students function more easily in the classroom.

Technology can also aid students in coping with various types of learning disabilities (Figure 13.4). While the adaptations must be learner specific, these examples can help you see the possibilities. An increasing number of books, including many textbooks, are available in electronic format. Using computer or tablet functions, it is easy to alter the appearance of the text (words) in these books. Many students who find reading difficult do better when the words are larger, there is more space between the lines, and the text is very dark on a white background. Devices such as a spell-checking dictionary, grammar checker, or a speaking dictionary can help students with the details of writing and allow them to focus on self-expression. Calculators can improve math skills. Electronic organizers can help students remember due dates and tasks they must do.

Figure 13.4 Assistive technology can enhance learning for students who have a wide range of disabilities or learning challenges.

English Language Learners (ELL) can benefit from some of the same technology. In addition, computer programs that build English skills are sometimes useful in specifically helping students learn English. Classroom teachers often use technology in other ways to help students. Online picture dictionaries can help students with vocabulary. Some students use handheld translation devices. Video presentations and visual demonstrations aid ELL students' understanding.

Continual updates in technology undoubtedly bring additional options to the teaching and learning toolbox. Finding ways to boost learning can make a real difference in students' lives.

Technology: Providing Tools for Teachers

Technology offers tremendous tools for teachers. Most types of technology have multiple uses within education. That makes it worthwhile to learn how to use new types and explore additional applications for technology you already use. Existing technology can aid in planning, teaching, communicating, and managing tasks. It can also serve as a great source of inspiration for teaching.

Planning

Technology has brought real changes to the way teachers plan for learning. The Internet offers easy options for discussing and sharing ideas with other teachers and for finding information and resources for teaching. Many teachers find that using these technologies in producing lesson plans has many benefits.

The Internet gives teachers easy access to colleagues worldwide. There are countless websites and other forums for sharing ideas and concerns (Figure 13.5). For example, a science teacher might seek advice on how to adapt science labs for a student who has cerebral palsy and limited mobility. Other teachers can respond, sharing their experiences and advice. Online discussions can help teachers explore the pros, cons, and uses of new teaching trends.

Figure 13.5 Internet technology allows teachers to connect with colleagues to share ideas for teaching and learning.

Many teachers post activity ideas online that spark others' creativity. These range from brief descriptions to full lesson plans. While teachers must adapt these ideas to their own teaching situations, they can help stimulate creative new ways to help students learn.

The Internet is an unparalleled information and research tool. Teachers can easily search for information on any topic to expand their knowledge and enrich their lessons. Information from experts, government, business, and industry is available in an instant. In addition to regular Internet searches, it is helpful to check links from sites for teachers. These can lead to new sources of information on teaching topics that other teachers find to be useful. Information on the Internet, however, is *not* always correct. Teachers, as well as students, must be aware of the credibility of Internet sources.

Textbook publishers routinely make electronic teaching aids available to supplement students' textbooks. These typically include materials keyed to topics in the book that teachers can incorporate into lessons.

Technology can also help speed the process of creating written lesson plans. Many software programs exist that assist teachers in lesson plan development. Some school districts provide their own versions for teachers to use. Using electronic lesson plans makes it easier to store copies of plans and related resources for future reference and possible use. It also simplifies the task of meeting administrative requirements to turn in lesson plans. Additionally, teachers may share such plans—or parts of them—as well as assignments with students and parents to assist with makeup work for absent students or as home tutorials.

Professional Tip

Creativity in Teaching

Creativity is a mark of a professional teacher. New ideas are constantly being sought about how to connect subject content with student interests. Technology, especially the Internet, can provide some of the best resources for introducing, planning, instructional activities, and assessing learning. But how does a teacher draw a line between being inspired and outright stealing another person's ideas?

Dig Deeper

Do a search online for teaching ideas. How many require site registration? How many invite use? How many are copyrighted? Talk with your school librarian about the most ethical way to use electronically sourced ideas or images.

Teaching

Technology offers teachers exciting options for presenting information in diverse ways that can bring learning to life. It takes effort, imagination, and a willingness to learn new skills. Some options require more sophisticated technology than others, but even with limited equipment, teachers can add variety to lessons.

In this section, "teaching" refers to providing information and instruction to students. Another aspect of the teaching process, developing learning activities, is discussed later in this chapter. Assessment is the topic of the next chapter.

Because of differences in learning styles, teaching that integrates as many of the senses as possible helps to maximize learning (Figure 13.6). Technology provides additional ways to do so. It also provides teachers with resources to more easily provide differentiated instruction.

Most of the technology options discussed in this section can also be utilized in learning activities. Similarly, those highlighted in the activities section can be adapted for instruction.

Interactive Whiteboards

One of the most versatile types of teaching equipment is the **interactive whiteboard**, which connects to a computer and projector to allow the board to become an extended computer touch screen. Some interactive whiteboards can function like a traditional dry-erase board when the computer and projector are not in use. Teachers and students can access the computer functions at the board or the computer. An interactive whiteboard can significantly expand the usefulness of a single computer in a classroom.

Notes placed on the board can be captured and saved as electronic files. These might be e-mailed to an absent student, made available to a student who learns best through repetition, or stored as a record of the lesson.

Figure 13.6 Technology training offers teachers many options to maximize student learning.

Interactive whiteboards come with useful tools. A math teacher may use the graph paper background for students to plot points on a graph. Students can add those points with a special pen or even their fingers. An English teacher might project a paragraph and have students use highlighting tools to identify the thesis, supporting statements, and conclusion. Even routine tasks are more interesting with interactivity and whole-class participation.

Teachers can utilize the functions of the computer's software during presentations and activities, projecting them on the whiteboard (Figure 13.7). A lesson on earth science might include a live shot of lava flowing from a volcano in Hawaii projected on the board. If a student asks a question, the teacher could link to a relevant website, such as National Geographic, to find an answer or a relevant picture. Students can follow the teacher's search on the whiteboard screen. Its large surface makes it easy for the whole class to easily see all aspects of a teaching presentation or interactive class activity.

Figure 13.7   With the use of interactive whiteboards such as these SMART® Boards, learning becomes more interesting and relevant.

Sight, Motion, and Sound

Technology has revolutionized the visual aspects of teaching, helping information come alive for students. In the past, a teacher might go through magazines hoping to find a relevant picture to post on a bulletin board. Today, teachers can search the entire Internet and easily find visual images—photos, drawings, diagrams, video segments, and more—that can enhance lessons. The teacher can save these electronically and call them up instantly, ready to print or insert in a document or presentation.

Many sites contain excellent pictures, videos, television programs, or other materials that they allow teachers to use in class presentations. A 3-D animation segment might help students understand the process of division. A video clip from a Shakespearean play can help set the stage for studying it. A first-person account of life in the trenches during World War II might make the lesson's factual information come alive for most students. Searching out such resources is worth the effort.

Teacher-developed visuals can also be effective teaching tools. When teaching tennis skills, a physical education teacher might play a video of a student game, projecting it on an interactive whiteboard. The teacher could use the whiteboard tools to show how players could better position themselves for shots. The teacher might also use a second video to show students how their serves and strokes compare with ideal ones.

Audio files, although often overlooked, can also be useful teaching tools. When talking about the heart, a teacher might play audio files of the heartbeats of a healthy and an obstructed heart. Many free audio files are available. *Podcasts*—audio broadcasts available on the Internet—can also provide relevant material. They can be downloaded to a computer or digital audio player and played, or saved and played later. Teachers might prepare podcasts of key information for students who have learning disabilities or English language learners (ELL) students to use as study aids.

Simulated Experiences

It is not always possible to give students hands-on experiences, even when these experiences can improve understanding. Time, money, and lack of equipment may all be barriers. Technology offers opportunities to bring some of that realism to the classroom. Sometimes the virtual version is more accurate and clearly presented than if it occurred live in class.

Simulations can show how things happen. They may employ actual video, art, animation, or a combination. For example, a video clip might clearly show what happens when two different liquids combine and a new mixture forms. Math and science are typical areas for simulations, but they work in other subject areas as well. A foreign language teacher might take students down the aisles of an open-air market in Germany. These experiences are known as *virtual field trips*. (School administrators find them very cost-effective.) A child development or parenting teacher might send a baby simulator home with students to give them an idea what it is like to care for a newborn. Interactivity possibilities vary, but simulations can bring students' learning closer to the real world. You will learn about computer simulation games, which utilize similar technology, later in the chapter.

Virtual Field Trips

Many historic and cultural sites offer virtual educational tours, often with related activities. Teachers can show students eggs hatching into chicks, experience life in Colonial Williamsburg, or follow scientists as they work in Antarctica (Figure 13.8). Other virtual field trips may highlight more everyday places and activities. They vary in quality. Some have related student activities or allow students to ask questions.

When teachers consider virtual field trips, they need to choose carefully to fulfill course objectives. They need to view the experience and make sure it is worthwhile and that the technology will work smoothly. When teachers set appropriate related learning tasks for students as they take the "tour," students stay on task. A follow-up discussion or other activity is important to solidify learning.

Figure 13.8 Students can take a virtual field trip to a jungle halfway around the world from the safety of the classroom.

Communicating

Technology gives teachers options for enhancing communication. In fact, today's teachers have more avenues for connecting with students, parents, coworkers, administrators, and the public than at any time in history. Choosing an appropriate method and using good communication skills, discussed in Chapter 10, are keys to effectively sharing information and ideas.

As part of a school district or school website, teachers often have individual or class websites. These enhance communication with students, parents, and others.

Teachers often post homework assignments, links to helpful online resources, announcements, calendars, and other useful information. Some have blogs or discussion boards, and there is usually an e-mail link.

There are many communication options, including e-mail, text messaging, online posting, as well as phone calls. Each can be appropriate in certain circumstances to get the needed information to the right people. While such forms of technology can make communication more accessible, there are situations in which direct face-to-face contact is the best way to communicate.

Managing Information

Teaching involves keeping track of and using numerous types of factual information, or data, for future use. Computers are particularly suited to simplifying those tasks.

Keeping accurate grades is essential for teachers. Each time a teacher grades an assignment, he or she must record and save the information for future use. At the end of a grading period, teachers must calculate students' many individual grades to determine grades for report cards. Electronic gradebook programs, chosen by the teacher or school, can simplify this process greatly (Figure 13.9). Any files that include confidential information should be password protected.

Figure 13.9 Computers offer countless ways to help teachers manage classroom data and communicate with parents and colleagues, increasing their productivity.

Electronic spreadsheet programs, such as Excel™, allow information to be adapted for different uses. For example, a teacher might set up a basic spreadsheet with a list of students in a class. This could be made into an attendance log. It could also be adapted to keep track of each student's progress toward meeting specific class goals or any other need. Various types of reports could be generated, based on the data in a particular spreadsheet.

There are countless other ways that teachers can use technology to boost their productivity. For example, a teacher might send out a newsletter to parents weekly or monthly. After developing the newsletter template, the teacher can simply add new information monthly. If the teacher has an electronic contact list of parents and guardians, this could speed the process of sending the newsletter electronically or printing labels for mailing. Many school districts encourage teachers to have their own classroom websites. With frequent updates to the website, this tool will keep students and parents constantly informed.

Technology: Enhancing Learning Opportunities

This section explores many types of technology teachers use to strengthen learning activities. This discussion is certainly not complete. In fact, by the time you read this, new technology will be available, perhaps replacing some of these options. Teachers must stay current with technology and how to use it effectively in the classroom. When examining various uses of technology in learning, it is important to consider how teachers can plan and manage these successfully.

Planning Technology-Based Activities

The considerations teachers take into account in choosing and planning any activity also apply to those that incorporate technology. (You may want to review *Figure 12-9 Checklist for Choosing a Teaching Strategy* in the previous chapter.) Technology-based activities are not automatically better, more appropriate, or more interesting than those without the use of technology. It all depends on the situation, the activity, and the skill with which it is presented.

Activities that include technology require particularly careful planning. Classroom teachers who successfully use technology suggest that starting with easy applications and working toward more complicated uses helps lead to achievement. This will help you gain confidence as you learn about what works best, how long things take, and students' abilities.

Experienced teachers make certain that students know:

- ***The goals of the lesson***. Sometimes with technology, it is easy for students to get sidetracked.

- ***The procedures they are to follow***. Step-by-step directions can help students succeed. This is particularly important when new technology skills are involved.

- ***How much time they have***. For younger students and complex activities, consider setting time limits for various sections of the activity (Figure 13.10). Most activities that utilize technology require more time than those without. Timing is not always easy to predict, so be prepared to adapt as you go.

- ***What they are to achieve***. Each activity must produce something that shows that the desired learning has occurred.

- ***How they will be evaluated***. When students know how they will be rated or graded, they are more likely to achieve acceptable results. Having a **model**, a real example that shows the characteristics of excellence, helps students know what constitutes quality. Some teachers keep electronic files of exceptional student work from previous classes to use as models for future ones.

For group activities, each participant should have a specific role and be accountable for his or her contribution, as in cooperative learning. For complex activities, teachers often divide the class into groups and assign each group a different segment of the activity. This can allow better utilization of equipment and time. Each group then contributes its piece to the final product.

Assessing Students' Skills

Just as teachers vary in their technology skills, so do students. Even at the same grade level, classmates may have widely varying knowledge and skills related to computer and other technology use. This is usually due to differences in opportunities to use technology in and out of school. Some students also have more natural ability and interest than others.

Figure 13.10 Although activities that utilize digital technology can enhance student learning, they can require more time and instruction.

It is critical that teachers evaluate students' knowledge, as a group and as individuals. Depending on the level of the students, the teacher can accomplish this with simple activities, questionnaires, or a combination of the two.

Strategies for dealing with differences can take various approaches. Sometimes teachers explain and demonstrate the basics of the program or equipment students will use in an activity, and then they supply detailed instructions as a guide. They may divide students by level and provide more support for those just learning a program or technology device. Sometimes dividing students into pairs or small groups with mixed experience allows them to teach one another.

Dealing with Technology Problems

Just as they make back-up plans for technology problems as they present information, teachers must do the same for activities (Figure 13.11). They need to consider how they might cope if a problem arises with the technology planned for an activity. Technology glitches are inevitable. It pays to be prepared.

As you develop lesson plans, think about the possibilities. What if one group cannot access the Internet? What if three teams are all at a standstill because they cannot figure out how to make the program work?

Sometimes having back-up paper copies of important information can save the day. If a computer goes down, you might regroup students so that you have fewer groups with more members. Perhaps you could switch the order of activities and substitute tomorrow's lesson that is not technology dependent.

Learn as much as possible about how to solve common problems. You may also have students in class who have more expertise with certain types of equipment or software and can help out when difficulties arise.

Figure 13.11 Technology has many advantages in the classroom; however, teachers must be prepared with a back-up plan when problems arise.

(Sometimes teachers appoint such students as official "technology assistants.") For group projects, including a student familiar with the technology in each group can help keep everyone moving ahead. Also, consider the physical setup of the classroom. Are there enough outlets? Can the teacher "cruise" the room and see everyone's screen?

Guidelines for Student Use of Computers

For all of the learning opportunities that computers bring to the classroom, there are also potential problems and issues. As a student, you are probably already aware of many of these. As you begin to think like a teacher, you must shift your focus to how to minimize and deal with them. Often, these issues are equally applicable to other types of technology.

Safety and Security

The school and the individual teacher share responsibility for the safety and security of computers and their use. The school usually sets policies. Teachers are responsible for the equipment in their classrooms and its appropriate use.

- **Equipment**. Many schools distribute computers and related equipment among classrooms. Teachers need to make frequent checks to be certain all unsecured equipment is in place and report any problems immediately to their administrators.

- **Acceptable use.** Schools usually have specific policies in place regarding use of computers by students. Most schools consider computer use a privilege, not a right. Students are often required to sign a form stating that they know, understand, and will follow these rules (Figure 13.12).

Figure 13.12 Students must know, understand, and follow school policies regarding acceptable uses of school technology. Failing to follow the rules can have serious consequences.

This is sometimes called an **acceptable use policy** or presented to students as a "computer code of conduct." Those who violate the rules can be banned from using the computer temporarily or permanently or face other disciplinary action. Rules include topics such as not damaging equipment and only visiting websites related to classroom projects.

- *Internet safety*. Since the Internet is not censored, many sites contain material unsuitable for students. Schools attempt to shield students from these sites by installing filters or blocking software. Such protection attempts to screen out sites that may contain offensive material, however, they are not perfect. Unwanted sites may get through, and sites with legitimate educational use may be blocked.

  Computer screens should always face toward the classroom, and teachers must monitor students using computers. Student safety is a related issue. Students must never give out personal information, including their last names. Some schools do not permit students to access e-mail, chat rooms, and similar sites as a safety precaution.

Plagiarism and Copyright Issues

With seemingly endless information available on the Internet, it is understandable that students may be confused about how they can use that information. Not all adults know what they should about fair use.

From the time that students start using the Internet (and print resources) to gather information for projects or reports, teachers need to clearly explain the *rules* of research. The main issue is **plagiarism**, the use of someone else's original words or ideas without giving that person credit. Well-known facts, such as the date a state was founded or the categories of trees are common knowledge. They can be found in many resources and can be used freely. In contrast, copying paragraphs from various resources without acknowledgment and piecing them together with some original writing is plagiarism. Basing a paper analyzing the characters in *Huckleberry Finn* on someone else's analysis as if it is a writer's own is plagiarism. Turning in a paper that someone else wrote as your own goes beyond plagiarism. At the college level, plagiarism is often grounds for dismissal from school.

A paper can include other people's ideas and words if it is clear they are not the writer's own and if the original sources receive credit. For example, a paper on the first English colony at Roanoke Island might contain some brief descriptions from the writings of Thomas Harriot, one of the early colonists. The paper must acknowledge the source of descriptions. Teachers need to explain how to give credit (within the paper, in a source list, in a footnote), depending on what is appropriate for the students' level.

Books, movies, music, and much online material are copyrighted (Figure 13.13). This means that the work's ownership and the right to its use have protection by **copyright**—the body of exclusive rights granted by laws of the United States to copyright owners for protection of their work. The copyright symbol, ©, is generally part of the copyright notice along with the year of first publication and the name of the copyright owner. Materials with copyright protection can only be used in limited ways unless the copyright owner grants permission for use.

Teachers, as well as students, must follow copyright law. The **TEACH Act of 2002** allows some use of copyrighted material for educational purposes. Teachers must obtain permission from the copyright owner, however, to make copies of copyrighted material semester after semester to give to students. Many teaching materials available online, even if they are copyrighted, specifically say that teachers may copy and use them in their classroom. The *TEACH Act* does allow a teacher to make a copy of a copyrighted work and display it, such as in a teaching presentation or posted on a bulletin board. Many websites have more information on acceptable use of copyrighted material for teaching.

Figure 13.13 Before using or duplicating copyrighted material, be sure to follow copyright law.

Research Activities

Learning how to find, evaluate, and use information is certainly not a new educational goal. In today's digital environment, however, these skills have become much more important. One reason is that the rate at which new knowledge and information is being developed continues to increase. Students will need to keep learning throughout life at a pace far greater than their parents did, just to keep up with the demands of everyday life and work. Graduation cannot be the end of learning. A second reason is that the Internet and other technology have caused an explosion in the amount of information available to the average person. No longer must information be published in a newspaper, magazine, or book. Anyone can "publish" on the World Wide Web. The downside is that there are few controls on the accuracy of much of that information. It is up to the reader to determine what is true, accurate, and worthwhile. Schools must teach these skills.

Many learning activities incorporate some form of research. Teachers need to structure such activities so they are appropriate for the grade level and skills of students. Besides helping students use research to gain and use information on specific topics, such activities must also actively teach research skills using print and electronic sources.

This is a gradual process. For young students, a teacher might limit research to a single reputable site. For example, the White House website for education includes information on a variety of topics at different levels of difficulty. Students can learn about the presidents, the White House, the functions of various branches of government, or the latest government initiatives. They can learn online information-gathering skills within a limited secure environment (Figure 13.14).

Figure 13.14 Learning research skills is a gradual process for students which involves much guidance on the part of the classroom teacher.

For students at the next step, a teacher might review and select several websites for students to use for a research assignment. By saving these as bookmarks in a file copied to class computers, the teacher allows students more exploration under controlled conditions. There are also search tools designed specifically for students that bring up student-appropriate sites for topics.

WebQuests are a popular form of web-based learning. **WebQuests** are inquiry-based learning projects utilizing information from preselected websites. They emphasize higher-order thinking skills. WebQuests are usually group activities with each group member taking on a particular role or responsibility to complete the group task. For example, a WebQuest might have students identify the causes and a possible remedy for depletion of fish populations in an area, using provided web links. Individual teachers can develop WebQuests, but many are also available on the Internet.

Older students can learn the skills needed to search effectively on the Internet. This includes how to use "word" search requests and identify which sites are most likely to yield appropriate information.

The process of learning to evaluate sites can start early. Even young students can learn how to identify sites from government, educational institutions, and other fairly reliable places. As students develop research skills, they learn to check the reliability of information for the following:

- *Datedness.* Is the research current?
- *Source of authority.* Who is the author and what are his or her credentials, qualifications, and affiliations?
- *Bias and objectivity.* Does the research address several points of view or just one view? Is the research sponsored by a political entity or special interest group?
- *Publisher.* Is the publisher an educational, commercial, or trade publisher known for quality?
- *Quality.* Is the information in a logical sequence? Can you clearly identify key points? Do key points support the main idea?

Online research is not limited to information on websites. There are also online library sites. In addition, many local libraries allow members to search online to find out what books and other resources are available.

Figure 13.15 Learning how to analyze and use data is important to developing critical-thinking skills. Government websites, such as the National Oceanic and Atmospheric Administration, offer a wealth of information and rich data.

Data Collection and Analysis

Many math and science activities involve gathering facts and statistics, exploring their relationships, and drawing conclusions. Activities that analyze data, however, can be useful in many subject areas, from social studies and art to physical education and music. Technology makes it easier for students to practice data-related skills.

Younger children can collect data (measuring the heights of students in their class or finding the seating capacity of ballparks) and turn the information into simple computer graphs. Middle school students might find the fat and calorie content of burgers or fries at various fast-food chains and use spreadsheet software to calculate the differences and determine pounds gained if eaten daily for a year. High school students can participate in real science experiments along with teams of scientists using data available online. Students can develop a realistic budget for living life on their own. Many government websites, such as the National Aeronautics and Space Administration (NASA), the National Oceanic and Atmospheric Administration (NOAA) (Figure 13.15), the National Geological Survey, and the United States Department of Agriculture are rich sources of real data.

Spreadsheet software has other capabilities. It can be used to translate data into many kinds of graphs and charts, generate time lines, or even turn a spreadsheet into a poster-size print version.

Using Visuals and Sound

Activities that incorporate technology often take advantage of the visual and audio capabilities readily available today. These may be part of the material provided for student learning, or students may choose or make visual or audio materials to enhance the projects and products they produce. Students are accustomed to **multimedia** (a technique for combining several forms for media to express an idea) in so much of everyday life that they respond to it in learning, as well.

Visual capabilities range from the simple to the complex. Young students can learn to print pictures from free online sources and to copy them into documents. Middle school students might distill the content they have learned into an electronic slide-show presentation. This would involve writing the copy, choosing the backgrounds and size and style of type, and perhaps adding graphics. High school students might develop a multimedia public service announcement. Some common technologies, in addition to those mentioned in the teaching section, include:

- **Digital cameras**. With digital cameras, students can take photos, download them to a computer, and print them or use them in reports or electronic presentations.

- **Webcams.** Webcams are digital video cameras that capture footage that is saved online. Many webcam feeds are available on the Internet and may show everything from weather to ships in the harbor, animals at the zoo, or a falcon's nest with young birds hatching. These can be used for activities, or students can shoot their own footage. Using software, students can create visual projects. In doing so, they learn to plan, script, present, edit, and publish.

- **Graphics programs.** The capabilities of computer graphics programs vary. The most basic allow students to draw and paint. Most sophisticated and specialized programs allow animation, 3-D designs, web page development, graphic design and page layout, and presentation development. Some even have CAD (computer-aided design) capabilities.

- **Audio files.** In many cases, audio files, without accompanying video, can be an appropriate choice for learning activities. They require less equipment and skill to develop and play. Students might record their spelling words for practice, conduct interviews, develop radio commercials, or put together a presentation on orchestra instruments.

Figure 13.16 Electronic communication makes it possible for students and teachers to form global connections.

Communication Activities

As with other forms of technology, educators have found uses for electronic communication as learning tools. A teacher could arrange for students to have *keypals* (electronic pen pals) with a class in another city anywhere in the world using simple e-mail exchanges (Figure 13.16). For example, students studying Spanish could pair up with an English class in South America. Discussion boards or forums can allow students to discuss topics or post information (such as essays) and get feedback from others. Online conferencing allows communicating directly. Chat rooms are one example, but *VoIP* (voice over Internet protocol) allows direct audio (and video links with a webcam) through the computer instead of using a phone. This could be used for direct communication between classes in different places or collaboration between classes in distant schools on a single project. Communication technology options are applicable to all levels and subject areas.

Games and Simulations

As you learned in Chapter 12, games can provide diverse auditory, visual, and kinesthetic ways to learn. Computers have revolutionized the world of games. Simple games, such as crosswords and word searches, can be made with easy-to-use software. When students develop such games, it reinforces factual information or vocabulary. Many other learning games are available online. Some are interactive, and computers can serve as an electronic opponent.

Computer simulation games use the power of computers to offer a virtual representation of a situation. In a fantasy or real-world environment, students perform specific tasks involving problem solving and decision making and then justify their reasons for certain decisions. They give the user the opportunity to build a city, family, or even to be a zookeeper. Computer simulations imitate the stock market, a historical war battle, or pioneer life. They can help students develop strategic thinking and planning skills.

Other simulations mimic real-life experiences. They may replicate what it is like to fly an airplane or bat a baseball, for example. Science simulations offer experiences such as virtual dissection, virtual microscope experiences, or a trip through the human body. They can give the experience of being in an earthquake or various types of weather. Simulations allow alternatives to hands-on experiences.

Social Networking

People are surrounded by advancing technology and media. With constant use of digital technology, including smartphones, video and photo sharing, tweets, and social networking, users can instantly access information or to connect with others. Text and instant messaging lets friends, students, family, and teachers communicate with each other more frequently. These types of media are more personal and can directly affect student learning in both positive and negative ways (Figure 13.17).

Figure 13.17 Social networking can enhance educational opportunities among people who are geographically distant. What parameters should teachers set to help protect students from the negative influence of social networking?

Social networking sites are also prominent and can be highly influential in teaching and learning. This modern cultural trend can evoke positive and negative reactions. Social networking sites can be beneficial for keeping in contact with other students, teachers, subject experts, and friends and family that live far away. As an educational method, social networking can enhance and offer new opportunities between people who are geographically distant. Students can share stories and images to reduce the feeling of physical distance and to maintain a sense of involvement in learning activities.

Social networking sites can also affect self-identity. By developing a personal profile, users can shape and visually see who they are and who they might like to become. Profiles can also positively affirm identity and goals. Users can explore and share interests, while developing goals and ideas for the future.

Social networking sites can also negatively influence self-identity. They can be distractive in the learning environment as other users can readily access personal sites. With the display of so many pictures, online friends, and interests, users may feel that they are not living up to perceived standards. They may feel excluded from social activities. With instances of *cyberbullying*, social networking sites can create a negative effect on self-identity and may cause feelings of depression.

When using the Internet, it is important to remember that posting pictures and information can also have negative consequences. Once pictures and information are posted online, they are out of the control of the person who posted them (Figure 13.18). Another person can repost them without the original person's consent or knowledge. Individuals should avoid posting images or content that has the potential of causing professional or legal consequences or personal embarrassment for themselves or others. This is true for students and especially teachers.

Figure 13.18 Scrutinizing information carefully before posting it on the Internet helps teachers manage their online images. What can you do now to manage your personal information to enhance your professional image?

Chapter 13 Review and Assess

Summary

- Innovations in technology have changed how teaching and learning take place and will continue to do so in the future.
- A very real benefit of technology is its role in making education more available and accessible.
- Technology also helps improve learning opportunities for many students who have disabilities or other challenges that affect learning.
- Teachers can take advantage of technology for planning, teaching, communication, and information management.
- Well-planned technology-based activities can stimulate learning.
- Innovations in technology with interactive whiteboards; sight motion, and sound; simulations; and virtual field trips increase student opportunities for interactivity and enhance learning.
- A benefit of technology-based activities is that students learn important technology skills they will need for everyday life and work.
- Technology changes rapidly, requiring teachers to stay current with how to use it effectively in the classroom.
- Technology helps increase the frequency of communication for teachers, students, and parents.

Review and Study

1. What is the application goal of instructional technology? Give an example of technology currently used in education today.
2. Why do schools vary significantly in the amount of technology resources available for teachers and students?
3. What is distance education and what is its greatest advantage?
4. Why is it important to choose a class from an accredited school if you want to try online learning?
5. What is assistive technology? Give an example.
6. When using technology-based activities, what are five factors teachers must make sure students know?
7. What are the responsibilities to schools and teachers related to the safety and security of computers and their use?
8. What is plagiarism?
9. What is the meaning of copyright?
10. List two reasons why learning skills to find, evaluate, and use information is even more important in the digital environment.
11. What is a WebQuest? Give an example of a WebQuest you might use in the classroom.
12. Name a benefit and a drawback of social networking as a teaching tool.

Vocabulary Activity

13. With a partner, use the Internet to locate illustrations that depict the *Content* and *Academic* terms on page 316. Print the illustrations or use presentation software to show them to the class, describing how they depict the meaning of the terms.

Critical Thinking

14. **Analyze reasoning.** In the chapter, the author states, "Technology-based activities are not automatically better, more appropriate, or more interesting than those without the use of technology."

Use the text and other reliable resources to analyze the reasoning behind this statement. What relevant evidence can you find that supports this claim? Discuss your ideas and evidence with the class.

15. **Evaluate worth.** For a week, keep lists for each class noting how your teachers use technology for teaching and how they include it in learning activities. Evaluate your lists. From each list, choose the use that you think incorporated technology most effectively. Write a description evaluating the worth of the technology use. How was the technology used and why was it effective?

16. **Identify evidence.** The text cites that the *TEACH Act* allows teachers to use some copyrighted material for educational purposes. Use the text and other reliable resources to identify further evidence regarding the requirements of the TEACH Act for teachers and students. What specific uses does the TEACH Act *not* allow? Discuss your findings with the class.

17. **Analyze consequences.** The text states that social networking sites can be highly influential in teaching and learning; however, there can be many negative consequences. Why should you, as a potential teacher, be careful about the types of images and information you post on the Internet? Analyze the potential professional and legal consequences. How can you protect yourself from misuse of your personal information by others?

Core Skills

18. **Speaking.** Describe specific examples of how teachers might use the Internet in each of the following areas: *planning, teaching, communicating,* and *managing information.*

Discuss your descriptions in class or post them to the class discussion board for responses.

19. **Writing and speaking.** Based on the chapter and any personal experience, write a brief description of how you might use an interactive whiteboard to teach a lesson (any subject and grade level). To extend this activity, write a lesson plan and present an actual lesson for a subject and grade level of your choice using an interactive whiteboard.

20. **Demonstration.** Use a school-approved web-based application to create a learning game, simulation, or an *app* (application) for a learning activity. Then demonstrate your technology activity for the class, describing its functions and benefits as a learning tool. If possible, post your activity to the class website for your classmates to try. To extend this activity, create a digital simulation that would help prepare students for a real-world work assignment.

21. **Writing and technology application.** Develop a *technology code of conduct* or acceptable use policy for elementary, middle school, or high school students. Keep the language, rules, and length appropriate for the age group. Format your list as a poster for the class website or a form that students could sign.

22. **Research, evaluation, and writing.** Locate at least two websites that include helpful information for teachers regarding the use of technology in the classroom. In addition, find two or more sites with educational materials that students could use. Write a review of each site, including the URL (web address), sponsor or source of the site, types of information available, and an evaluation of its usefulness according to text guidelines for reliability.

Combine your information with that of your classmates in a single resource list for future reference.

23. **Technology application.** Conduct research about videos, apps, and computer games that are marketed toward early readers. Choose three to evaluate. How do these toys and games meet the educational needs of elementary school children? In what ways do they stimulate learning? Are they interactive? How do they promote a love of learning? Write a summary of your findings.

24. **Creating a lesson.** Experience education duties and responsibilities by creating a lesson for elementary or middle school students on a topic of your choice (or topic agreed on with your instructor). Integrate some form of technology described in this chapter into the plan's objectives and activities. Identify how you will inform students about your expectations of them for the technology activity as identified on page 346. How will you assess students' skills and ensure their safety and security? Discuss your plan with the class, making adjustments as needed.

25. **CTE College and career readiness practice.** Using the lesson plan you created for Item 24 in Chapter 11, identify one or more specific ways that you could alter the plan and utilize technology in teaching the content or in an activity within the lesson. Describe what technology would be used, how it would support the lesson objectives, benefits of its use, and whether you currently have the necessary technology skills or would need to learn them.

College and Career Portfolio

Your portfolio should not only showcase your academic accomplishments but also the technical skills you have developed such as your computer and technology skills. These skills are very important and potential employers will want to know about your skills with technology.

- Write a paper describing the technology skills you have acquired. Summarize your skills, level of competence, and any other information that showcases your skill level. Save the paper in your e-portfolio.

- Create a subfolder for each of your technology skills. Use a naming convention such as *Skill01_Simulations, Skill02_Learning Games*. Save well-developed examples of each skill in the appropriate folders. Save printed copies in the container for your print portfolio.

- Save lesson plans and activities you created for Items 19, 20, 21, 22, 24, and 25 in your portfolio.

Chapter 14
The Role of Assessment

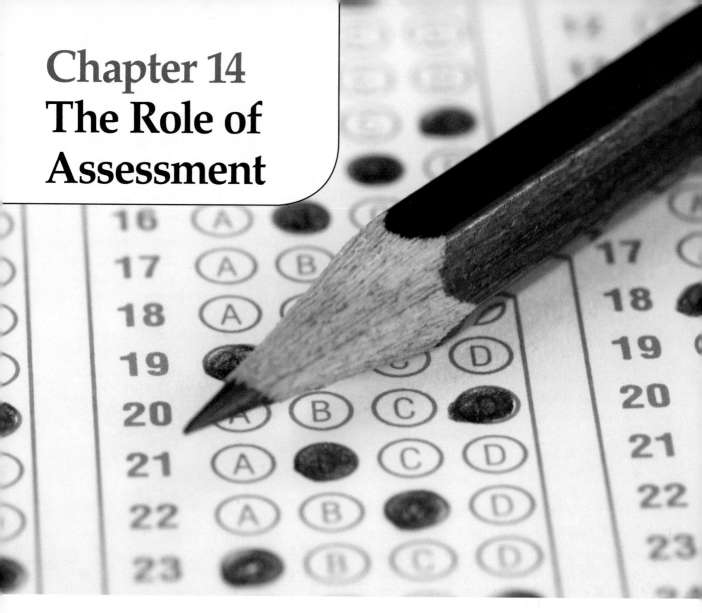

Content Terms

formative assessment
summative assessment
mentor teachers
alternative assessment
student portfolio
rubric
checklist
scorecard
self-evaluation
peer evaluation
course evaluation

Academic Terms

subjective grading
validity
reliability

Objectives

After studying this chapter, you will be able to

- **identify** the purpose of assessment.

- **distinguish** between the purposes of formative and summative assessments.

- **describe** types of information assessments can measure.

- **summarize** the use of tests in assessing learning, and write examples of appropriate and effective test questions.

- **describe** how alternative assessment strategies help demonstrate student learning, and create an evaluation tool for assessing learning.

- **summarize** how teachers choose appropriate assessment strategies.

- **analyze** the importance of grading and providing effective feedback to students.

- **develop** questions a teacher might use for course evaluation.

Reading Prep

Arrange a study session to read the chapter aloud with a classmate. Take turns reading each section. Stop at the end of each section to discuss what you think its main points are. Take notes of your study session to share with the class.

At the Companion Website you can

- **Practice** terms with e-flash cards and interactive games

- **Assess** what you learn by completing self-assessment quizzes

- **Expand** knowledge with interactive activities

www.g-wlearning.com/teaching/

Study on the go

Use a mobile device to practice terms and review with self-assessment quizzes.

www.m.g-wlearning.com/0094/

Case Study

As a class, read the case study and discuss the questions that follow. Then, after reading the chapter, go back and review your answers to the questions. How would your answers change?

What a crazy day it turned out to be! The day began with an unexpected dusting of snow, a school bus mechanical problem followed, a parent chaperone was a "no show," and the worst traffic in the city that she could remember occurred on the way back to school.

Stacey's class just returned from a field trip to the local historical society museum. Her seventh graders seemed to love it, especially since the museum had recently been renovated and the new displays were interactive and fun, focusing on the area's natural resources, native leaders, immigration patterns, manufacturing industry, and most recently, the expansion into the high technology industrial fields. The students were energetic and cooperative. But did they learn anything? As she reflected on the day, she wondered if all the effort was worth it. Did the field trip enhance their learning or was it just a distraction and busywork?

Let's Discuss

- How might Stacey assess the students' learning on this field trip?
- What did she need to know or do prior to going on the field trip to assess their learning?
- What might she have done after the field trip to assess their learning?

*A*ssessment, the methods teachers use to gain information about students' learning, is central to the educational process. The term may bring to mind tests and grades; however, there are other ways to assess learning. The information that teachers gain from assessments may be useful for determining grades, but it has other uses, as well.

Assessment completes the cycle of instruction. In Chapter 11, you learned that a lesson plan begins with formulating the objectives you expect students to achieve. In Chapters 12 and 13, you learned more about activities that guide learners toward achieving these objectives. This chapter focuses on ways to determine whether that learning results in accomplishing the objectives. You will also explore some of the other uses of assessments in improving learning and teaching.

The Purposes of Assessment

Assessment strategies are tools for evaluating and maximizing student learning. Through analyzing what students know, teachers, administrators, and others can make decisions about how to improve the education students receive. There are generally two types of assessment, *formative* and *summative*. They differ in their purposes and use.

Formative assessment is an ongoing part of instruction that provides feedback about students' learning as it occurs. It takes place *during* instruction. The results allow teachers to adjust their teaching during a lesson to help improve learning. Because the purpose of formative assessment is to make instructional decisions, teachers do not use such assessments as part of students' grades.

Teachers use many different methods to check on students' learning as they are teaching. For example, a teacher may give an ungraded quiz to help gauge how well students understand the roles of key nutrients in overall health. If the quiz shows students are meeting the learning objective, the teacher can move on to the next topic. For example, if students seem confused about water- and fat-soluble vitamins, the teacher may spend additional time clarifying that topic.

Informal assessment occurs when teachers ask questions in class and monitor how well students complete learning activities to assess understanding. In summary, they may ask students to identify the most confusing point in the subject's lesson. As you become a more seasoned teacher, you will be able to "read" your classes so you will know when learning is taking place. Do students raise their hands? Are students engaged in an activity?

Summative assessment is an evaluation of students' learning *after* instruction has taken place. It measures results, assessing whether students are meeting learning objectives. (These objectives may be ones identified by the teacher, a district or state curriculum, or some other source.) Summative assessments are often scored or graded and allow teachers to track students' progress over time. They are also useful in judging the success of educational programs.

Tests are the most common use for summative assessment (Figure 14.1).

Figure 14.1   A test grade can let both the student and teacher know whether learning objectives have been met.

These include chapter or unit tests, state tests, and other types of achievement tests. Summative assessments can take many other forms, as well.

Teachers use both formative and summative assessments to evaluate learning and teaching. As you read through this chapter, think about how you could use the assessment tools described for these assessment purposes.

What Can Be Measured?

What exactly can assessments measure? There are three main ways assessment can be useful in improving education. It can measure students' achievement of learning objectives and also their growth and progress over time. In addition, assessment can measure teaching effectiveness. Some forms of assessment give information on all three.

Measuring Student Achievement of Objectives

Assessment of learning occurs at various levels. Classroom teachers constantly monitor whether students are reaching the goals set out in their learning objectives. This happens during the lesson (formative assessment) and at the completion of a lesson (summative assessment). In addition, students, classes, and schools are periodically measured against district, state, or national standards. These assessments are often in the form of achievement tests.

In their classrooms, teachers usually use tests for some assessments. They also evaluate students' learning in other ways, such as through projects. District, state, and national tests are usually *standardized tests*. These are administered to large numbers of students and are scored in a consistent manner, most often by computer.

Measuring Learner Growth and Progress

Assessment of students' growth and progress occurs over time. For example, a teacher can document a child's expanding vocabulary and reading ability along with tracking changes in classroom behavior. Through assessment, educators can measure improvements in math computation skills, the ability to express ideas, or cooperative group behavior.

By tracking students' growth and progress, teachers can report it to learners and parents. Teachers can also monitor what topics and skills require review or reinforcement. Assessment gives feedback that can offer encouragement or highlight issues of concern. It can also provide necessary information for diagnosing learning difficulties or giftedness so that students can receive appropriate learning support, (Figure 14.2).

Measuring Teaching Effectiveness

Evaluation of student outcomes is only one component of assessing learning. Teachers are also part of the equation. Traditionally, teachers were evaluated in comparison to each other rather than their own effectiveness. Teachers were ranked and those who were considered effective were rewarded and those considered ineffective were not; some were even fired. The focus was on the teacher alone rather than on the system or school where they worked. As a result, sometimes good teachers were dismissed but the ineffective school systems remained.

Today, there is a much greater appreciation for the complexity of teacher evaluation. To only focus on evaluating students' learning tends to create classroom environments that only "teach toward the test" rather than the whole student. More focus now is on assessing teacher effectiveness *and* student learning progress together with an emphasis on improving both. Of course, hiring highly skilled teachers is a key factor.

Figure 14.2 Assessment provides feedback that helps teachers offer students encouragement and appropriate learning support.

With effective training and thorough knowledge of their subject matter, such teachers know how to teach and manage learning.

Teachers also need continuous support. This requires comprehensive teacher growth and development opportunities such as mentors, educational workshops, and supportive teams and administrators. Part of being a good teacher is continual self-improvement. In addition, schools use more formal methods to evaluate teachers and help them become more effective.

Personal assessment needs to be a part of everyday teaching, too. Low student scores on a quiz can cause a teacher to analyze why a lesson did not bring the desired results. Was the explanation unclear? Did the activity fail to teach the necessary skill? Did the students need more practice? Sensitivity to and awareness of learning helps teachers modify their teaching to maximize student achievement.

Sometimes teachers use other techniques to evaluate their teaching. They may make a video of a lesson for later review and analysis. They may ask another teacher for feedback and suggestions. They may network to learn about and try new teaching techniques.

Analyzing how well the students meet learning objectives is one way to measure teaching effectiveness. Many factors, however, influence individual students' learning. Even with excellent teaching, there are a variety of reasons students may not completely meet all learning objectives.

Schools have a responsibility to make certain their teachers are effective. Review and evaluation of teachers can be based on a number of factors. These may include observing the teacher in teaching situations, test scores of students on standardized tests, and parental feedback. Beginning teachers are often assigned **mentor teachers** who are experienced and skilled. Mentor teachers help new teachers assess and improve their skills, solve problems, and become comfortable in their new positions.

Using Tests to Assess Learning

Tests have long been the accepted way to check students' learning. While other methods have gained popularity, tests remain the most widely used assessment tools. Learning how and when to use them effectively is part of understanding a teacher's role.

Figure 14.3 Standardized tests are often scored by a computer.

Standardized Tests

Standardized tests assess students' learning (summative assessment), but they usually have other objectives as well. Thousands of students take the exact same test. Consequently, test scores can be used in a variety of ways. The results can show the achievement of individual students, schools, or even teachers (Figure 14.3).

The intention of *state* achievement tests is to assess the learning of students in an entire state. They may be given every year or at certain grade levels. The scores from these tests are carefully monitored and analyzed. States may hold underperforming schools accountable for raising test scores. Test scores sometimes link to the amount of funding schools receive.

School districts also utilize information from these tests. A district might note that its middle school science scores are below the state average. Administrators and teachers might work together to identify possible reasons and devise a strategy for improvement. If students' scores improve over time, it may indicate that the changes were successful.

Tests such as the SAT and ACT are standardized tests of students' knowledge. Students generally take them as part of the college admission process. Schools also evaluate how their students score on these tests. It provides feedback on how well their students compare with other students across the nation. Schools use high college-entrance test scores as evidence that their schools provide quality education.

Teacher-Developed Tests

As a student, you have taken hundreds of tests developed by your teachers. You may think of them primarily in terms of the grades you received. Teachers, however, develop tests to assess students' achievement of the lesson objectives they have set. For example, if your geometry teacher wants you to be able to calculate the area of a random shape on a grid, a test could measure your understanding and ability to perform this task. From the scores on the test, your teacher will not only know if you have met the learning objective, but also how well all of your classmates understood this concept. The results of teacher-made tests can also give teachers feedback on the effectiveness of their teaching.

Well-written tests can check students' knowledge and understanding, particularly of factual information. Teachers usually write their own tests, basing them on learning objectives, what they have taught, and knowledge of their students.

Teacher-developed tests are sometimes called "paper-and-pencil" tests because that is traditionally all students need to complete them. As schools utilize technology to a greater degree, students take more tests electronically, either in the classroom or as part of an online course. The questions may be the same as if written on paper, but the method of completion is different (Figure 14.4). Some online tests take advantage of available technology in the types of questions posed and their format.

Figure 14.4   Teacher-developed tests can also utilize online technology, offering students a different method of completing assessments.

Types of Test Questions

Traditional tests generally use a limited number of question types. These include the following:

- *True-false questions*. A true-false question requires students to distinguish whether a statement is true or false. Such questions usually test recall of information, but not higher-level thinking. A test should include about the same number of questions with true answers as false answers.

- *Multiple-choice questions*. Students must choose the best answer from among a list of alternatives. Multiple-choice questions are constructed so that there is an introductory statement or question (called the *stem*) followed by a series of possible alternatives. Experts advise avoiding use of "All of the above" or "None of the above" as alternatives or at least limiting their use. Multiple-choice questions can be written to test higher-level thinking.

- **Matching questions**. With matching questions, students must identify the relationship or association between two items. For example, on a test about the Civil War, questions may ask learners to match specific dates with occurrence of events. Another test may require students to match important terms with their meanings. When writing matching questions, give each column a descriptive title, such as "Terms" and "Definitions."

- **Fill-in-the-blank or short-answer questions**. With fill-in-the-blank questions, students must complete a sentence by inserting the correct word or words (usually no more than two). The sentences in such tests require careful construction so that there is one correct answer. Short-answer questions are similar. They pose a question that requires a very brief answer.

- **Identification questions**. Identification questions require the learner to label or locate the parts on a diagram or drawing. For example, a test in a biology class may require students to label the parts on a diagram of a cell. Similarly, students studying English grammar may need to label the verb, noun, and adjective in a sentence on a test.

- **Essay questions**. With essay questions, students must compose a more extended written answer to a question. Essay questions can measure not only knowledge, but also the ability to think clearly, organize information, and express one's thoughts. Essay questions can challenge learners to make connections, see relationships, and make comparisons. They often require higher-level thinking and are generally appropriate for older students.

  Teachers find essay questions easy to write, but they take time and effort to grade (Figure 14.5). When writing essay questions, teachers need to identify the ideas they expect students to include in the answers. This can serve as a model during the grading process.

Figure 14.5   Essay test questions require students to effectively demonstrate ability to think clearly, organize information, and express thoughts; however, they take more time and effort on the part of the teacher for grading.

Constructing Tests

A well-constructed test fairly evaluates students' learning, but not all tests meet this standard. Following these guidelines can help achieve that goal.

- **Write questions that match the levels of the objectives**. A true-false question can check for understanding, but not the ability to apply information. Use questions that evaluate whether students' learning matches that of the learning objectives.

- **Match the proportion of questions to the emphasis placed on various objectives**. Major objectives deserve more questions than those that are of lesser importance.

- **Limit the number of different types of questions to three or four**. Having too many types of questions is confusing and puts the emphasis on students' ability to follow test instructions, rather than on assessing content learning.

- **Group questions of the same type together**. Put all multiple-choice questions together, for example. Within each type, group questions about similar content together.

- **Be sure that questions do not give answers or clues to other questions**. This can easily happen when content is related. Each question should stand on its own.

- **Provide clear directions for each section of the test**. Even with familiar types of questions, specify in writing how students should indicate their answers. For example, writing out the words "True" or "False" avoids the problem of distinguishing between a handwritten "T" and "F" that may look similar.

- **Evaluate existing tests or questions carefully before use**. Teachers often save tests for possible reuse when they teach the same lesson or class again. In addition, many textbooks come with ready-to-use tests. In both cases, teachers must review such tests to make certain they reflect what has been taught and how it was taught, making modifications as needed. Sometimes individual questions may be suitable for use, but not the whole test.

- **Format the test for ease of use**. Make answer lines long enough for handwritten answers. Always begin a page with a new question, never starting a question on one page and finishing it on another. Avoid using negative statements. These can be confusing, evaluating understanding of the question rather than knowledge of the answer.

- **_Format the test for ease of grading_**. The way you arrange questions and spaces for answers on a page can make a difference in how difficult it is to grade students' papers. Teachers often find that placing the answer options, or lines for writing answers, to the left of the questions makes it easier to grade quickly and accurately. Number questions consecutively through all sections. (There will be only one question #1.) For older students, indicate the point value of each question. Include a line for the student's name on each page of the test in case pages become separated.

Be sure to proofread tests carefully. In addition to factual accuracy, correct grammar and spelling are essential. Make and double-check an answer key for the test to speed correction later.

Using Alternative Assessment Strategies

Giving a test is not the only way to assess student learning. Educators also use a variety of methods other than tests. Collectively, these are known as **alternative assessments** and range from written papers and multimedia presentations to real-life tasks and student portfolios (Figure 14.6).

Figure 14.6   Alternative assessment strategies offer students the opportunity to creatively show what they know and can do.

Sometimes the difference between tests and alternative assessment is explained by how they ask students to show what they have learned. With most tests, students *choose* an answer to show what they know. With an alternative assessment strategy, students *create* something that shows what they know.

Alternative assessments encourage teachers' creativity, as well as that of their students because these assessments can take so many forms. Teachers devise innovative assessments that allow students to demonstrate their knowledge and skills in ways linked to real life. For instance, an elementary teacher might have students demonstrate their math skills by measuring their classroom or playground. A middle school teacher might have students write and perform a play based on their study of a period in history. An automotive teacher might have students complete an oil change to verify mastery of that skill. A child care teacher might have students create games appropriate for preschoolers. Health students might choose appropriate media to develop an antismoking campaign. Reports, projects, posters, and presentations are all forms of alternative assessment. In each case, students demonstrate their learning.

The intention of some types of alternative assessment is to evaluate students' improvement over time, rather than achievement of a specific learning objective. As such, students may or may not receive a grade for them, depending on the purpose and situation.

Student portfolios are one type of alternative assessment that may be graded or not, depending on their purpose. A **student portfolio** is a collection of a student's work selected to show growth over time, highlight skills and achievements, or to show how well the student meets standards. The student is usually involved in selecting the material for the portfolio, often including reflections about his or her work and learning. Portfolios can provide important information about a student's attitude, level of development, and growth over a given period of time.

Giving Clear Directions

The ability to develop clear directions is a critical skill for teachers. They can affect the success of learning activities, impacting how well students learn. Similarly, clear directions in assessments make certain that students are able to show what they have learned (Figure 14.7). Confusing directions can actually prevent accurate assessment of learning.

Directions tell a person how to complete a task. You may have a natural ability to develop good instructions. Writing directions requires thinking in a logical, step-by-step way. If this does not come easily for you, take time to practice this essential skill.

Figure 14.7   Giving clear directions helps ensure students will be able to successfully demonstrate their knowledge and skills.

When creating directions for students, begin by identifying the goal or objective. What do you want your students to achieve? This will be the introduction to your directions. Then break the process of reaching that goal into steps. Be sure to place the steps in sequential order.

Use precise, descriptive language when giving written or spoken instructions. Directions need to be appropriate for the level of students. For all levels, sentences should not be overly complicated. Anticipate possible problems or misunderstandings and address them in the directions. Taking the time to think through directions is well worth the effort.

Evaluating Alternative Assessments

With traditional tests, it is the teacher who checks students' answers, determines their scores, and returns the tests to students. It is best for students to see which questions they answered incorrectly and learn from their mistakes. With alternative assessments, the teacher may play a similar role, but students are usually involved in the process.

Rubrics

Traditional tests typically contain questions that have specific correct answers. If you answer "True" to a question when the correct answer is "False," your answer is wrong. Evaluating and scoring many other types of assessments can be considerably more complicated. What is the difference between an excellent project, paper, or presentation and an average one? When students know specifically what "excellent" means, they can produce better work. To be fair, teachers need to judge every student's work by the same criteria.

In many situations, teachers use rubrics to solve these problems. A **rubric** is a scoring tool that lists the criteria for judging a particular type of work. A good rubric also describes levels of quality for each of the criteria. A rubric is often set up as a chart, with the *criteria* (characteristics that count for scoring) on the left, followed by columns that describe different levels of quality for each characteristic. (*Criteria* is the plural form of the term *criterion,* which is singular.) Quality ratings can be ranked using numbers and/or adjectives. Figure 14.8 is an example of a rubric for writing a letter of complaint.

A well-designed rubric provides clear grading criteria for both students and the teacher. In that sense, rubrics serve to communicate expectations and standards. They also help to communicate how student work did or did not meet expectations or standards.

When students receive grading rubrics before they begin their work, they can think critically about their work. They know what characteristics

Figure 14.8   Rubric for Letter of Complaint

Criteria	5–4 Points	3–2 Points	1–0 Points
Contact Information	Addressed to appropriate contact and sender's contact information is provided.	Contact information incomplete for receiver *or* sender.	Contact information for receiver *and* sender is incomplete or missing.
Purchase Information	Includes all required information (product, item #, date and place of purchase, attempts to resolve).	Missing one key piece of purchase information.	Missing more than one key piece of purchase information.
Problem	Problem clearly explained.	Problem explained but is somewhat unclear.	Problem inadequately explained.
Action Requested	Specific, reasonable action clearly requested.	Request for action is vague or time line is unrealistic.	No specific action requested or request is unreasonable.
Format	Utilizes business letter format, no grammar or spelling errors, neat, signed.	Missing one part of business letter *or* contains one or two errors.	Letter lacks more than one key part *or* more than two errors.

identify quality and can base their efforts on established criteria. As a result, students begin to accept more responsibility for their work and feel less like victims of **subjective grading** (grading on opinion rather than fact). Rubrics also help students know when they have met the learning objectives or if their work has met established criteria.

Many rubrics are available from teacher resources. It is not always possible, however, to find an appropriate existing rubric to use or modify. Rubrics are not difficult to create, but they do take time. The following are the steps for creating a rubric:

1. **Identify the criteria necessary for assessing performance.** Base the criteria on the intended outcomes of the learning objective. For example, the criteria for a book report might include descriptions of the main characters, setting, plot, and outcome, plus an appropriate format, grammar, and clarity of writing. Place the criteria down the left-hand column of the rubric.

2. **Determine the possible performance levels.** There should be a rating scale for performance. Levels can be described (such as *Excellent*, *Good*, *Poor*) and/or based on point ranges that directly correlate to a grade. List the performance levels at the top of the columns across the top row of the rubric.

3. **Write a description for each performance level and criterion.** These will fill in the blank squares on the rubric chart. Clearly describing the different levels of performance that match each criterion provides guidance for students. It usually works best to start with the highest level of performance achievement for each criterion. Next, describe the lowest level of quality. Fill in the middle levels based on your knowledge of common problems that students have in meeting the highest performance levels.

4. **Proofread.** As with traditional tests, it is important to proofread rubrics carefully before use.

After using a rubric, you can refine your descriptions of what constitutes each performance level based on students' actual work and any difficulties they had understanding the rubric.

Professional Tip

Guarding Against Bias

Can teachers be totally unbiased when grading or assessing student work? No, not entirely, because some subjectivity allows for the *human factor* rather than a more robotic or disengaged assessment of learning outcomes. All assessment activities have some inherent teacher bias that comes from personal experiences and subject knowledge. A mark of professionalism for teachers, however, is care in guarding against personal biases as much as possible. Cultural prejudices or favoritism—such as class, ethnic, or gender biases—are particularly damaging to the learning process and may create unfair assessment of students' learning.

Dig Deeper

Investigate the requirements for human relationships training for teacher certification in your state. What content does such training include? Discuss the ways human relationships training can help teachers to be attuned to any biases they may have and guard against such biases in assessing and working with students.

Figure 14.9   A checklist is a simple way to track a student's progress.

Checklists and Scorecards

A **checklist** is a simple list of items to note, check, or to remember when evaluating learning. It can be an instrument that consists of a list of qualities to check off or questions to answer with a *Yes* or *No* response. There may be a space for teacher notes and, if the assessment is to receive a score, a place to calculate the score. A kindergarten teacher might use a checklist to keep track of which letters a child knows and can print. While not used for a grade, the checklist can show the child's progress over time, (Figure 14.9).

Scorecards are somewhat different. Like a rubric, a **scorecard** lists the characteristics or factors to use when evaluating learning. Scorecards typically identify a maximum point value for each criterion but do not describe levels of quality. The automotive teacher evaluating students' ability to perform an oil change might use a scorecard. The teacher would identify the steps students are to complete and assign possible point values to each. The number of points would depend on the importance and complexity of each step. (Greeting the customer politely may be worth fewer possible points than draining the old oil completely without spillage.) While evaluating a student, the teacher would determine the number of points to award for each step, adding comments, as appropriate. The scorecard provides the student not only with a final score, but also information on which steps require additional practice.

Both checklists and scorecards are valuable for helping learners understand the criteria on which the teacher is evaluating their learning. They are, however, limited in describing quality or details.

Self-Evaluation and Peer Evaluation

Teachers are not the only people who can assess learning. An important goal of education is to teach students how to evaluate their own work and determine what improvements they need to make. As work situations in the adult world increasingly depend on group interaction and effort, the ability to evaluate peers has become more important. The abilities to give honest appraisals of others' efforts and to accept other people's assessment of one's own work are important job-related skills. Consequently, teachers often incorporate both **self-evaluation** (students' assessment of their own learning) and **peer evaluation** (students' assessment of each other's learning) into alternative assessments.

Although self-evaluation and peer evaluation are valuable assessment tools, they can be challenging for students. It helps if teachers introduce students to these methods, in simplified form, in the early grades. Using checklists, scorecards, and rubrics can help focus and structure students' analysis and feedback (Figure 14.10).

Teachers need to stress the importance of honesty. With peer evaluation, students need to learn how to phrase their comments in positive and helpful ways. Older students often worry that negative ratings or feedback of peers will affect their overall evaluations. Peer evaluations can be confidential, shared with peers personally, or serve as a general summary. Peer evaluation is a valuable tool for checking student understanding of a project.

Learning assessment does not always tie to grades. Teachers may need to have students practice using self-evaluations and peer evaluations until these tools become a natural and expected part of learning.

Choosing Assessment Strategies

There are a number of factors that play into selecting an assessment tool. *Validity* is an important characteristic which requires choosing an assessment that actually measures your learning objectives. *Reliability* is a characteristic of an assessment that measures the same over time—meaning the results will be similar with different learners and under different circumstances.

Figure 14.10   The use of rubrics, scorecards, or checklists can help students analyze and give feedback during peer evaluation.

The assessment tool you choose should be developmentally appropriate for the learners. Students should be able to understand and perform what you request of them. For example, an essay test is not an appropriate choice for a young child. The assessment should be at the appropriate difficulty level. It should measure the type of learning required for the developmental stage of the learner.

The assessment tool should not become the focal point, taking away from the learning process. For example, if a teacher focuses only on the test students are to take at the end of the learning unit, creativity and flexibility can be lost. Students may be less likely to internalize what is learned.

Time and other resources are always a reality for teachers. Teachers should consider what is available and how much time an assessment tool will require.

Figure 14.11 Effective teachers develop a fair and workable grading system.

Determining Grades and Providing Feedback

The learning process not only depends on acquiring new knowledge, but also on learning how to learn. Grades are one way teachers provide feedback to students about their learning, but they are not the only way. Direct feedback can play a major role in helping students improve their learning skills.

Grading Students

There are few aspects of education that cause as much anxiety, confusion, and concern as grades. This is true for teachers, as well as students and parents.

The main purpose of grading is to communicate students' performance and progress. There is often little consistency in the way students' grades are determined. Although some schools have written policies regarding grading, it is usually up to individual teachers to decide what counts toward grades and how they are calculated (Figure 14.11).

Keeping basic principles in mind can help teachers set up a fair and workable grading system. These include the following:

- Every teacher needs to establish a grading plan before classes begin and communicate the plan to students.

- Grades should reflect students' learning, not behavior, attendance, or other factors.

- Report card grades should be based on a variety of individual assignments, tests, and other work. Not every activity and assignment should be scored, especially those that are part of the learning process.

- While report card grades are often in letter form, record grades for student work as a number.

- When determining report card grades, the scores for some types of work may be weighted more than others. For example, the average of test scores might count for 50 percent of students' grades, while other types of work might count for smaller percentages.

Giving Effective Feedback

Providing students with personalized feedback about their learning is more effective at improving learning than assigning grades. The goal of feedback is to help individuals know what they are doing well and to provide specific areas for improvement if necessary.

Feedback can occur throughout the learning cycle. A teacher might emphasize particular parts of instructions for specific students. It might be verbal reinforcement during class activities or a written response to work completed.

From your own experience as a student, you know it feels great to get an "A" on a test or a "94" on a paper. This information only tells you that you did well overall. If you get a "C" on a paper, how do you know what you need to improve? Thoughtful comments, particularly written ones, can help you do better. Your teacher might write such comments as, "You raised an interesting point. Good thinking! Next time do more research to provide additional evidence to support your point of view." An elementary teacher might write on a student's test, "Jody, you often miss questions that you know the answers to because you don't understand the directions. Try reading the directions carefully before you begin and again as you check your work before turning it in. I think your grades will improve." In both these cases, the teacher provided the students with real guidance. Statements such as "Good job!" or "Try harder!" are too vague to be helpful.

Course Evaluation

Good teachers never stop learning. They want to be better teachers. They want to gain additional knowledge and find more effective ways to help students learn. As a teacher, you may sometimes leave the classroom thinking, "That really worked!" while other times thinking, "I need to use a different activity next time."

Earlier in the chapter, you learned that assessment can measure how well students meet objectives, their learning progress over time, and the effectiveness of teaching. All provide helpful information for **course evaluation**—making judgments about how well a course meets its goals and what improvements would make it better.

Course evaluation is important for several reasons. It helps teachers improve their teaching. They can identify what worked and what did not work in the classroom. They can evaluate their motivational methods, classroom management skills, effectiveness of the classroom arrangement, the schedule, or other factors that might improve teaching and learning. Change does not take place without taking time to reflect (Figure 14.12).

The basis for course evaluation may be a combination of the daily notes teachers often keep, feedback from others, and consideration of important questions about a course. Questions such as "Are most students meeting the learning objectives for the course?" and "Are students motivated and interested in learning?" can trigger insight.

Teachers may work individually on course evaluation, analyzing a unit of study or an entire course. Often, teachers teaching the same course will collaborate on course evaluation. Some schools have a formal process for doing so. Regardless of the form it takes, course evaluation can be a powerful tool for enhancing students' learning.

Figure 14.12 Taking time to reflect on how well a course meets its goals can lead to improvements in teaching and learning.

Chapter 14 Review and Assess

Summary

- The purpose of assessment is to evaluate learning and teaching.
- A teacher uses formative and summative assessment to assess student learning.
- Assessment can evaluate different aspects of learner achievement, growth, and progress, and effectiveness of teaching.
- Teachers use various strategies for assessment ranging from standardized tests to alternative forms of assessment, which allow for student creativity in demonstrating achievement of learning objectives.
- When using alternative assessments, teachers must provide students with clear directions and inform them about the evaluation procedure.
- Teachers consider various factors when choosing the type of assessment strategy to use, including learning objectives, the abilities of students, and the time available.
- Teachers must develop and then communicate their grading policies to students.
- Grades convey information about achievement, but giving feedback to students informs them about their learning strengths and identifies strategies for improvement to help them learn more effectively.
- Effective teachers evaluate their courses in order to make them better.

Review and Study

1. Contrast formative assessment and summative assessment and the purposes of each.
2. What are three ways assessment can be useful in improving education?
3. Why is there more emphasis today on assessing teacher effectiveness and student learning progress together?
4. Contrast the uses of standardized tests with teacher-developed tests.
5. List six types of test questions teachers can use to assess student learning.
6. Why is it important to match test items to the level of the learning objective they assess?
7. Name two examples of alternative assessments that allow students to demonstrate their knowledge and skills.
8. List the four steps for creating an effective rubric.
9. What is the difference between a checklist and a scorecard for evaluating learning?
10. What are two factors that play a role in selecting assessment strategies?
11. Why is providing personalized feedback to students about their learning more effective for improving learning than assigning grades?
12. Identify two reasons why course evaluation is important.

Vocabulary Activity

13. For each of the *Content* and *Academic* terms listed on page 348, identify a word or group of words describing a quality of the term—an *attribute*. Pair up with a classmate and discuss your list of attributes. Then, discuss your list of attributes with the whole class to increase understanding.

Critical Thinking

14. **Identify evidence.** Presume that you have just accepted your first teaching job. In your new school district, you will have a mentor teacher. Use the text and reliable Internet resources to gather more evidence about working with a mentor.

Then identify at least eight characteristics you hope your mentor teacher will have and write a summary explaining why each is important to you.

15. **Analyze criteria.** Think about three different standardized tests you have taken. Analyze intended purposes of the tests. What criteria appear to link to the intended purposes? What types of preparation, if any, occurred before the tests? What types of questions did the tests include? How was critical thinking addressed in each test? How difficult did you find each test? How were scores reported? Discuss your analysis with the class.

16. **Check reasoning.** The text states that course evaluation is important to improving teaching and learning. In teams, create at least eight questions (other than those in the text) that teachers might use for course evaluation. Check your reasoning by discussing how these questions will help teachers make effective judgments about course evaluation.

Core Skills

17. **Writing and speaking.** For three days, keep track of the types of assessment used in your classes. Make a list. Which were *formative* and which were *summative*? Which types of assessment helped you learn best? Discuss your responses in class.

18. **Writing, speaking, and listening.** Write a test for one of the chapters in this book. Write three examples of each of the six types of test questions described in this chapter. Follow the guidelines for a well-constructed test on page 358. With a classmate, evaluate each other's test against the guidelines. Which test items were most effective? On which type do you need to improve your skills?

19. **Writing and presenting.** Write clear, step-by-step directions for a learning activity. You may use an activity from a lesson plan you previously developed or another of your choice. Post your directions to the school-approved class website or discussion board for peer evaluation. As another option, do a live presentation of your directions for the class and have them follow the directions for the activity. Then conduct a peer evaluation of the directions. Make necessary changes and adjustments to your directions.

20. **Writing.** Design a *rubric* for a common type of alternative assessment, such as a written report, presentation, or group project, following the guidelines on page 363. Decide the approximate grade level that will use the rubric. Determine criteria that would be important and levels of performance. Then describe a quality at each level for every criterion. Review your rubric with your instructor and ask for specific feedback. Revise it as necessary.

21. **Writing.** Create a *checklist* of items to note, check, and/or remember for an alternative assessment or learning activity you created for a previous lesson plan. Then create a *scorecard* for the directions for the learning activity you wrote for Item 19, listing characteristics and point values to use when evaluating learning. Follow text guidelines on checklists and scorecards on pages 364. Review your checklist and scorecard with your instructor and ask for specific feedback. Revise the checklist and scorecard as necessary.

22. **Research, speaking, and listening.** Search the Internet to locate grading policy for an elementary or secondary school or school district in your state.

Print a copy. Write an analysis of the policy based on chapter guidelines. How detailed is the policy? Does it suggest using formative, as well as summative, assessment in determining grades? As a teacher, do you think you would find the policy helpful or limiting? Share your findings with the class. How do they compare to findings of your classmates?

23. **Technology application.** Design a survey that measures your classmates' participation in a group project. First decide what you want to measure. Participation could mean contributing ideas, taking on a task, or any number of items. Once you decide *what* you want to measure, decide *how* you will measure it. Will you use a rating scale? Yes and no answers? Will you evaluate the process or the final product? Decide whether it should be self-administered individually, administered by your teacher or other group members, or administered by and to all. How could you administer this survey electronically? After designing the survey in an electronic format, administer it to your select sample and record the results in an electronic spreadsheet format.

24. **CTE College and career readiness practice.** Use reliable Internet resources to further investigate different forms of assessment—standardized tests, teacher-developed tests, and alternative assessments. Read two or more articles and summarize your findings in writing. When evaluating the reliability of information:

- *Identify source credibility.* Who is the author or writer? Is the author or writer known for reliable fact-checking?

- *Verify details.* Can you verify the facts from other reliable sources and this text? Is the information current?

- *Identify bias.* Is the information presented from only one point of view? Avoid articles that lack objectivity.

College and Career Portfolio

You have likely used Internet resources while creating your portfolio. The Internet also provides ways to help you present and store materials for an e-portfolio. For instance, you could create a personal website to host the files or use the website of a company that specializes in e-portfolios. Some sites are free, and others charge a fee to help you develop and post your e-portfolio. Schools and other organizations may sponsor free sites. Some sites offer free basic accounts and charge for an account with more services such as tutorials, templates, and forms that make placing your materials in an e-portfolio easy. Be sure to read and understand the user agreement for any site in which you place your materials.

- Search the Internet using the term *free e-portfolio*. Review at least two websites to learn what portfolio tools and resources are offered free.

- Write a short summary for each site that includes the website name, the address, the sponsoring organization, and the tools or resources the site offers.

- Add examples of your work for Items, 18, 19, 20, and 21 to your portfolio.

Chapter 15
Classroom Management

Content Terms

classroom management
authoritarian style
permissive style
authoritative style
school policies
class rules
classroom procedures
nonverbal cues

Academic Terms

perseverance
insubordination

Objectives

After studying this chapter, you will be able to

- **analyze** the role of creating an organized classroom environment in effective classroom management.

- **summarize** ways to keep students involved in learning as part of classroom management.

- **develop** a behavior management plan for the classroom including establishing rules and procedures to enhance the learning environment, and to minimize behavior problems.

- **apply** appropriate behavior management strategies in response to common behavioral problems.

Reading Prep

Read the chapter title and tell a classmate what you have experienced or already know about the topic. Write a paragraph describing what you would like to learn about the topic. After reading the chapter, share two things you have learned with the same classmate.

At the Companion Website you can

- **Practice** terms with e-flash cards and interactive games
- **Assess** what you learn by completing self-assessment quizzes
- **Expand** knowledge with interactive activities

www.g-wlearning.com/teaching/

Study on the go

Use a mobile device to practice terms and review with self-assessment quizzes.

www.m.g-wlearning.com/0094/

Case Study

As a class, read the case study and discuss the questions that follow. After you finish studying the chapter, discuss the case study and questions again. How have your responses changed based on what you learned?

Mariko is a senior in college and is completing her student teaching at the local middle school. Much to her pleasure, she has been assigned to work under an art teacher. Mariko loves teaching art and mostly enjoys working under her lead teacher, Ms. Jones. The creativity and potential for self-expression found in exploring art mediums are important to Mariko. She loves working with students in the classroom as long she is not expected to discipline them. In fact, she believes that the school has too many rules. Today, when two students began using paints to mark each other with mock tattoos and then painting the clothing of unsuspecting classmates, Mariko ignored their behavior. Her lead teacher is insisting that Mariko actively participate in disciplining students' misbehavior.

Let's Discuss

- Why are classroom rules important?
- How can classroom rules be best communicated?
- Why should Mariko participate in classroom management?

Every class is really a group of individuals with different needs, desires, interests, and abilities. Some students concentrate intently on the learning activity. Others daydream. A few squirm and fidget. There are nonstop talkers and quiet reserved ones. There may be some students who show off, talk back, or tell exaggerated stories. Others only want to please you.

The goal of all teachers is to provide a classroom environment that promotes learning for all of these diverse students. To accomplish that, teachers need excellent management skills. **Classroom management** refers to the steps teachers take to organize their classroom for optimal learning, engage students in that learning, and minimize behaviors that disrupt it. New teachers find classroom management one of their greatest challenges.

Fortunately, there is helpful information available about classroom management, and you can learn these skills. Successful teachers develop the ability to observe, comprehend, and respond to quickly changing classroom behaviors. They know their students. As teachers become confident in their role as the classroom leader, classroom management becomes second nature. It also becomes more of an art rather than just a collection of skills. This chapter will give you a closer look at what is involved.

Creating the Classroom Environment

Even before the first student walks through the door, teachers set up their classroom environment. Similar to the set designed to stage a play, the arrangement and look of a classroom sets the atmosphere for learning. It can either support or undermine a teacher's attempts to maximize learning.

The environment where learning takes place does make a difference. As a teacher, you may find yourself teaching in a new state-of-the-art classroom or one that is 75 years old. Effective teachers find ways to make the best of what they have.

Once students arrive, a new challenge starts. Each new group of individual students must be brought together to form a class that feels and functions as a whole. Each of these elements contributes to making the classroom not just a functional learning environment, but an inspiring one.

Arranging the Space

Figuring out how to best arrange a classroom begins with the teacher's analysis of the ways in which he or she will use the space. A kindergarten teacher may need learning centers, such as those for blocks, art, and reading (Figure 15.1). Each center has equipment and materials for specific types of activities. An elementary classroom must be versatile to adapt to the variety of classes taught each day.

Figure 15.1   Kindergarten classrooms are often arranged according to learning centers with specific equipment.

A middle school or high school science classroom must accommodate learning new information, performing experiments, and secure storage of equipment and supplies. Regardless of specific use, some general guidelines for arranging space apply.

- *Ease of student use*. The arrangement of students' desks and other elements must be practical. Does it allow students to enter, exit, and move around the classroom easily and safely? Can everyone view the board and other areas critical for instruction? Is storage suitable for collecting students' work with minimum disruption? Signs and labels can help students find what they need within the classroom.

- *Ease of teaching*. Each teacher has a unique style of teaching. The organization of classroom space should accommodate this style. Depending on a teacher's preferences, student desks might be arranged in a circle, U-shape, groups of four, or traditional rows. One teacher may often use the computer for presentations, so its placement and students' ability to see the screen may be a critical factor. Another may have students work at the board on a daily basis, which requires space in front of it for ease of use. Some teachers use their desks as a work center, while others use it mainly for storage and place it out of the way. Such considerations shape decisions about classroom layout.

- *Ease of supervision*. The arrangement of a room can make it easier or more difficult for teachers to monitor students and critical areas. For example, some teachers prefer an arrangement that allows them to see every student's face during instruction to more easily gauge students' understanding. The ability to see what students are doing can minimize problem behaviors. Areas such as computer stations may need special supervision, so they should be placed accordingly.

Developing a Stimulating Learning Environment

You have experienced enough classrooms to know that some energize you for learning, while other environments are boring. The difference is teacher ingenuity and effort, along with an understanding of the impact that environment can make.

What makes a classroom inviting? That depends somewhat on the educational level. At all levels, the addition of objects and materials relating to the subject area can spark students' interest and prompt additional learning (Figure 15.2). A teacher might post a "Did you know...?" poster

Figure 15.2   Creating a stimulating learning environment with the addition of objects and materials helps capture student interest and enhance learning.

for each learning unit, giving students interesting related facts. Books and other reference materials are easily accessible. Elementary teachers often provide a reading corner with a soft chair, rug, or pillows where students can choose and read books. Displaying students' work adds interest. The paint colors in many classrooms are bland colors, so teachers try to add bright colors in other ways. They might put colored paper over a bulletin board or fabric over a table. Maps, pictures, and colorful charts can add color while reinforcing learning. The possibilities are endless. The goal is to have a rich environment that supports learning, not just a disorganized collection of things, which may be distracting.

Teachers periodically change elements to match the topics their students are studying. This generates new interest. Where do these items originate? Most teachers make the best possible use of what is available through their school. They may have a small budget for supplies, but this must cover all learning needs. Teachers often supplement school materials with things they find or buy on their own. They may repurpose pizza boxes to organize supplies, use bricks and boards to make additional shelves, or turn garage-sale finds into objects to organize classroom space. They rely on imagination and creativity to provide a better environment for their students.

Building a Sense of Community

How would you describe the ideal environment for learning? Perhaps you would like students to be relaxed, but focused on learning. They move from one activity to the next and quickly get started. They are able to work together effectively in groups, drawing on each other's strengths and respecting others' opinions. Students handle routine tasks automatically. Behavioral issues are minimal and dealt with quickly and fairly.

While no classroom is ideal all of the time, successful teachers find that building a positive atmosphere helps greatly. When students feel a sense of belonging within the class, they participate more, put forth greater effort, and are less likely to misbehave.

There is no single formula for developing a feeling of community, but most teachers focus on a number of key areas.

- ***Positive relationships***. Teachers set the tone by modeling acceptance of, and interest in, their students (Figure 15.3). It begins with learning students' names as quickly as possible. Getting to know students as individuals helps them feel they are valued. Most teachers balance authority with an attitude of friendliness.

Teachers also help students develop positive relationships. Depending on the grade level, teachers can use various techniques. In elementary school, this might include lessons on topics such as friendship. In middle or high school, a teacher might focus on teamwork skills or handling differences of opinion as part of group activities.

Figure 15.3 Getting to know students and engaging them in learning helps build a sense of community among class members.

- **Respect**. Respect is one of the most essential elements in classrooms that work. Teachers must not only expect respect from students but show them respect, as well. Disrespect among students is not something teachers should tolerate.

   Respect often begins with getting to know others, particularly those with whom students do not normally interact. Group activities and opportunities to share can help students learn about each other as individuals and break down barriers. Teachers may use various grouping strategies so that students have opportunities to work with all of their classmates. A sense of respect within the classroom is crucial to students' feeling that they can offer ideas and opinions without fear of ridicule or rejection.

- **Student involvement**. When teachers ask for students' feedback and ideas about classroom issues, students feel their opinions are important. It also helps them develop a sense of responsibility for the class. Student feedback can be valuable. Students may come up with workable solutions for class problems. They can identify which activities were most helpful and which were most enjoyable. They can share ideas on how to improve class routines. By asking and following through on useful suggestions, teachers build class bonds.

- **Class identity**. A sense of community depends on students seeing themselves as a group. It is much like the feeling of cohesiveness that members of a baseball or debate team develop. Such connections grow over time with the encouragement of a teacher. Classroom routines, traditions, and whole-class experiences help strengthen these bonds. One seventh grader, on seeing his third grade teacher, said, "I always remember that we started each day saying together, 'I *can* do my best. I *will* do my best. *We* will all succeed together.' It sounds kind of strange now, but in your class, we all worked hard and tried to help each other."

Professional Tip

Understanding Organizational Hierarchy

   Professionals treat their colleagues and supervisors with respect. Many new professionals make the mistake of not acknowledging their place in the workplace organization. Even the most casual and nonstructured organizations have hierarchies. They may just be more difficult to identify. Be sure you fully understand an organization's hierarchical structure when employment begins. Whether it is your students, another professional, a customer, or your boss, you will be the one who benefits in the long run by understanding the importance of deference, or showing respect. Even more importantly, show respect to your students. When you model respect to your students, gaining their respect will be much easier for you.

Analyze It!

   What is your definition of respect? How does your definition compare to the dictionary definition? To whom do you show respect in your daily life? How? Over a period of days, observe how the instructors and administrators in your school demonstrate respect to one another. Share your observations in class.

Keeping Students Involved in Learning

One of the biggest challenges for teachers is keeping everyone involved in the learning process (Figure 15.4). Whether a student is daydreaming, whispering, poking someone nearby, or texting during class, the result is the same. That student is not learning. Others are usually distracted, as well.

No teacher manages to have every student paying attention and on task every moment of every day. Students' lives outside the classroom come with them to school. You know, for example, that if you did not get enough sleep or argued with your best friend, it affects your concentration. Still, there is much that teachers can do to keep students' attention so they can learn effectively.

Presenting Engaging Lessons

Skillful teachers know that their efforts to make learning interesting pay off. Students learn and remember more. In addition, students involved in learning are less likely to engage in problem behaviors.

Making lessons relevant to students' lives increases their appeal. Math concepts become real when they link to their actual uses in business, industry, or everyday life. History can come alive when first-person accounts are included or students put themselves in a different time and place. In every subject area, there are many ways to add relevance and to engage students. Teachers know that a constantly quiet classroom is not necessarily an effective one.

In earlier chapters, you learned about the importance of using a variety of techniques for teaching and learning. This helps accommodate students' personal learning preferences and strengths.

Figure 15.4   When a lesson becomes relevant to students, they are more likely to participate in the class.

It also keeps learning fresh and interesting. Mixing lecture, demonstration, and discussion varies instruction. Using both individual and group activities and alternating desk work with activities that involve movement helps hold students' interest and keeps them alert. When students receive options for completing some assignments, they often learn more and show greater enthusiasm.

Managing Transitions

Effective teachers make a real effort to keep downtime to a minimum. Most problems occur during *transitions* when students are changing from one class or activity to another. Here are some examples of how experienced teachers handle transitions.

- *Greeting students*. When her middle school students are changing classes, you will find Mrs. Daniels in the hall by her door. She greets her students by name, asking questions of some and encouraging others (Figure 15.5). At the same time, she is on the alert for student conversations or body language that might be clues that certain students are having problems. Her presence in the hallway also helps keep overall behavior in check.

Figure 15.5 Greeting students as they enter the classroom, shows students the teacher is interested in them. It also gives the teacher a chance to observe behavior.

- **Class start-up assignment**. Mr. Menendez' high school math classes know that there will be a problem to solve on the board as soon as they get to class. The math problems usually involve challenging real-life situations. Students can work in small groups to solve the problem and there is friendly competition among them. Having the students engaged gives Mr. Menendez time to quickly take attendance and complete any other administrative tasks. It helps get the class off to a smooth start.

- **Students who finish early**. When Mrs. Chin began teaching third grade, she struggled with how to handle students who finished activities before their classmates. They often resorted to talking, disturbing those still at work. Now, she gives students two alternatives. Since she encourages reading for enjoyment, every student keeps a library book in his or her desk and can choose to read silently. Students may also go to a table in the back of the room and pick a puzzle or activity sheet from the table to complete at their seat. Students know that they must complete their work first, and they cannot disturb others.

- **Transition to small groups**. Mr. Poplau uses many different learning formats with his fifth grade class, even though his classroom space is limited. Often, this necessitates moving the furniture in the room to accommodate various learning activities. For group activities, he usually divides students into groups of four or five. Early in the semester, he showed students how he wanted desks and chairs placed for small group work and put tape on the floor to show proper placement. Now, if he says, "Let's move into groups," students automatically rearrange the furniture and find their groups. It has taken practice and **perseverance** (steadfast persistence in an undertaking), but now students try to better their previous time in getting everything in place. The payoff is less confusion, more time learning, and little disruptive behavior.

- **Lesson ends early**. Ms. Simpson has been teaching middle school health for six years. She knows it is not always possible to time lessons exactly. Occasionally, she and her students finish before the class period is over. She has developed techniques to help fill that time with learning. For most lessons, Ms. Simpson plans an extra optional activity to use in such situations. She also has a set of short activities on topics she would like to add to the curriculum. She keeps these in her desk for use when the opportunity arises. Students get a chance to tackle thought-provoking topics, and it eliminates a free time when unwanted behaviors can occur.

Noting Success

When a teacher commends a student for special effort, it reinforces that desired behavior. Most teachers praise top students. Not all go beyond that group, but doing so can yield real results. Students who feel they can be successful in school are less likely to have serious behavioral problems. Those who feel their efforts are unlikely to have positive results—that they fail to measure up—often eventually stop trying. If they are required to attend school anyway, being disruptive may seem like a reasonable alternative.

Teachers who take the attitude that all students can experience success can help break the cycle of failure. That does not mean giving good grades for inferior work. Helping students overcome a negative self-image and learning deficits requires a caring attitude, encouragement, and practical help in catching up (Figure 15.6). It takes long-term effort, often requiring outside resources. Changing attitudes can change lives.

Figure 15.6   When a teacher commends a student for successes, the student can develop a positive self-image which reinforces the desire to learn.

It is easy for busy teachers to simply respond to behavior problems in a sharp or harsh way. This may stop the behavior in the short term, but it creates a negative learning environment. Many teachers have found that changing their focus can significantly reduce behavioral problems over time. They try to notice and comment on achievement and good behavior more than bad. Perhaps a student who often plays the class clown puts real effort into a group activity. Another student who has trouble "remembering" to complete homework turns it in on time every day for a week. Giving positive feedback for real effort and following the rules helps encourage students to repeat such actions.

Managing Behavior

How well teachers manage behavior in their classroom has a direct impact on how much learning can take place. Even with a stimulating classroom environment and well-prepared and interesting lessons, behavioral problems inevitably occur. It is the teacher's role to keep them to a minimum and deal with them effectively when they do occur.

Understanding Teachers' Management Styles

Each teacher approaches classroom management somewhat differently. Personal beliefs, experiences, the unique group dynamics of the class, and the teacher's personality all impact classroom management. These differences are particularly evident in how teachers deal with student behavior. Educational researchers identify the three following general management styles:

- *Authoritarian style*. Teachers with an **authoritarian style** have regulations for everything and consequences for every infraction. It is a management style that seeks to control students' behavior through many rules, procedures, and consequences. Teachers who use this style try to control students' behavior by exerting power. Authoritarian management may result in lower student self-esteem and creativity and can provoke hostility.

- *Permissive style*. Teachers who have a **permissive style** may have some rules and expectations, but they rarely follow through with consequences when students fail to meet them. This is a management style that sets few expectations and rules for students and enforces them inconsistently. Basically, anything goes. Students often lack respect for permissive teachers.

- ***Authoritative style.*** Teachers who use an **authoritative style** have high expectations for students' behavior and clearly explain why some behaviors are acceptable and others are not. This management style seeks to shape students' behavior through setting high expectations, explanations, and consistent application of consequences (Figure 15.7). There are consequences for failure to meet expectations. Such teachers are firm, but friendly.

The *authoritative style* is the foundation for implementing many of the ideas in this chapter. Research shows this to be the most successful approach. Experienced teachers support the authoritative approach. The combination of high expectations, holding students accountable, and warm teacher-student relationships provides the best atmosphere for learning. Within that framework, individual teachers still must determine the most effective ways to implement this approach on a day-to-day basis in their own classrooms.

Figure 15.7   An *authoritative style* of teaching helps shape students' behavior by setting high expectations, using effective explanations, and consistently applying consequences for misbehavior.

Developing a Personal Behavior Management Plan

It is important for teachers to have a carefully considered plan for behavior management before classes begin. Some schools require them to submit a written version of the school plan. Even when this is not the case, effective teachers determine up front how they will manage and respond to behavioral issues. This helps them deal with problems in a consistent way and creates a classroom atmosphere that is conducive to learning.

Developing such a plan requires real thought. It begins with asking yourself some key questions. Some examples of key questions include the following:

- What realistic expectations for student behavior should you set?

- How will you reward students for appropriate behavior?

- What steps will you take when inappropriate behavior occurs?

Some of the answers to these questions form from your personal beliefs, while your knowledge of education and child development helps answer others. Some link to common sense.

Although the same general principles for student behavior may apply to all ages, your expectations for first graders would be different from those for sixth graders or high school juniors. It is important to hold older students to higher levels of behavior. They are capable of understanding the reasoning behind the need for standards of behavior.

Similarly, rewards for appropriate behavior may also vary by age. Verbal or written praise works with all ages. For example, a teacher might write a note to a student's parent or guardian complimenting good or improving behavior. Teachers of younger students, however, are more likely to use small prizes, such as stickers or stars, to reward students who show desired behaviors. Sometimes, in elementary or middle school, teachers use a point system, with points given for appropriate behavior. When used with a whole class, points can add up and be redeemed for class prizes such as an extra recess or a party. High school teachers are much less likely to use tangible rewards such as these.

Some authorities caution against using tangible rewards because it conditions students to expect them. Instead, praising specific behavior helps the students learn to reward or praise themselves. This helps the students develop self-discipline—an important goal of a good behavior management plan.

Both age and the severity of the problem generally guide the teacher's use of consequences for misbehavior. To a second grader, having a shorter recess period may be an appropriate consequence for some offenses (Figure 15.8). In general, the consequences should also relate to the inappropriate behavior. If a middle school student will not work to finish an assignment in class, a teacher might have the student stay after school to do so. If a student says something unkind about a classmate, the consequences may include apologizing and giving the classmate a compliment. Consequences should always be reasonable, respectful, and, ideally, related.

Figure 15.8 Consequences for misbehavior should relate to the inappropriate behavior. A student's age and the severity of the problem guide the teacher's use of consequences.

With younger students, teachers often devise a system to keep behavior in check. For example, some teachers use a green, yellow, and red card for each student. Each day, every student starts on green. The first time the student engages in misconduct, the teacher substitutes the yellow card for the green one. The second time, the red card is used, and the associated consequence is more severe. For example, the teacher may send a note to the child's parent. What works with one class or one child does not necessarily work with others.

In developing a personal behavior management plan, a teacher commits to its overall goals and methods—adjusting details as necessary. Every teacher learns by doing.

Establishing Classroom Rules and Procedures

There are several ways to identify appropriate student behavior. **School policies** (in some districts called *rules*, *regulations*, or *procedures*) set overall guidelines and generally address major issues such as attendance and dress code. These are the same for all students. **Class rules** are guidelines for student behavior specific to a class or teacher. They identify expected classroom behaviors and attitudes necessary for an appropriate atmosphere for learning. Teachers identify a set of general rules as part of their behavior management plan. **Classroom procedures** are more specific. They translate the class rules into concrete actions expected of students.

You have been on the receiving end of classroom rules for years, so developing them as a teacher may seem difficult. Educational experts and experienced teachers have some suggestions:

- ***Establish class rules during the first few days of class***. Knowing a teacher's expectations and limits can give students a sense of security. It also builds a positive classroom environment. Some teachers ask the students for input.

- ***Involve students in setting rules and procedures***. Being part of the process helps students take ownership of the rules. Students can suggest ideas. Through guiding the discussion, teachers can help students formulate statements that incorporate the teacher's own priorities. Even young students can take part.

- ***Keep the rule list short***. Many experts suggest about four to six rules. That is a short enough list for students to remember, but long enough to include key concepts (Figure 15.9).

- ***State rules and procedures in positive terms***. Instead of saying, "Never interrupt," you might say, "Only one person talks at a time." Stating things positively tells students what they should do.

- ***Define the terms***. If a procedure is to "Turn in homework on time," what does that mean? "All homework must be in the assigned box when the bell rings to be considered in on time," clarifies the procedure.

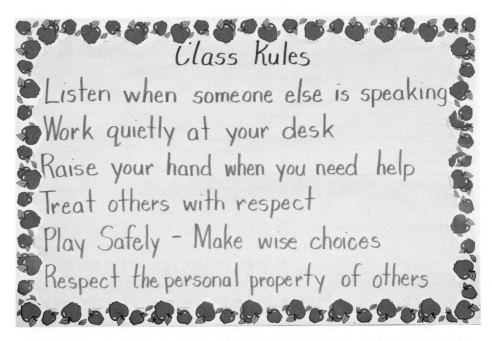

Figure 15.9 Keeping the list of class rules short helps ensure students remember and follow them.

- *Adjust rules and procedures if they are not working well*. A teacher may need to add or modify guidelines if the need arises. This is part of good management.

Minimizing Problem Behaviors

In addition to the measures discussed so far in this chapter, teachers use various techniques to avoid problems with behavior. They help students develop the skills needed to make good decisions that avoid unwanted behaviors. They identify common causes of problems and develop routines and procedures to help keep them at the lowest possible level.

Developing Personal Responsibility

The goals of education go beyond teaching students to read and write and compute. Schools are partners with parents in teaching students the skills they need to function effectively in society. Among these is developing the ability to make appropriate choices. When students take responsibility for their own behavior, they make choices based on an inner code of acceptable conduct. School and classroom rules are part of this effort. In other words, the goal of discipline is to help students develop self-discipline.

Young children behave primarily to gain adult approval. Even so, they need frequent reminders about what is acceptable and what is not. Over the years, brain development, experience, and explanations help students understand the reasoning behind expectations. They begin to think through the possible consequences of their actions for themselves and others. This helps them keep their behavior within acceptable bounds by choice. This ability to monitor personal behavior and accept the consequences of misbehavior can be fostered by the way teachers handle classroom management.

Utilizing Routines

Having class routines helps students know what to expect and how to behave accordingly. An elementary teacher can set up the order in which to teach particular classes. Each day might start with spelling, and students know to expect a particular type of spelling activity each day of the week. The teacher introduces new words on Monday, gives specific activities to occur Tuesday through Thursday, and students take their spelling test on Friday. Similarly, students in other grades and subjects know the routine for the beginning and ending of class. What are they to do when they come in? What is the procedure for collecting papers? Where are homework assignments posted?

Establishing and adhering to routines can reduce problem behaviors. In fact, students often remind those who are not following routines that they should do so.

Figure 15.10 Using assigned seating helps teachers quickly learn students' names and monitor behaviors.

Assigning Seats

Many teachers use assigned seating as a classroom management tool. In assigned seating, students do not choose their desks. Instead, teachers designate the seating arrangement (Figure 15.10). A seating chart will help substitutes as well as teacher aides in the classroom. Some teachers have "photo seating charts" to avoid any confusion.

Assigned seats have a number of benefits. With a seating chart, teachers learn students' names and behaviors more quickly. They may rearrange seating periodically to place students in the location where they learn best. A teacher may seat a student who is easily distracted away from the door and windows. Students prone to chatting with one another during class can be spaced farther apart. When seating students in groups, assigning different combinations helps them interact with new people.

Monitoring the Classroom

New teachers quickly understand the importance of keeping track of what is happening throughout the classroom, even when they are involved in an activity. Over the generations, students have described teachers who do this well as having "eyes in the back of their heads." In other words, they seem to see everything that is going on in the classroom. By scanning the classroom regularly, the teacher can stop minor misbehaviors quickly before they continue. Fewer people are distracted. When students believe that their teacher always knows what is going on, they think twice before misbehaving. Many teachers move around the room as they teach. This, too, is a deterrent to inappropriate behavior.

Using Nonverbal Cues

Teachers often use **nonverbal cues** to stop minor misbehavior. These include techniques such as eye contact, body language, gestures, and physical closeness. Sometimes, nonverbal cues are reminders to the whole class. For example, a teacher might momentarily dim the lights to get the attention of the class. The advantage of these methods is that they can occur without interrupting the flow of a lesson. They remind students to monitor their behavior.

Eye contact is a powerful way of communicating expectations. For example, if students are whispering when it is not appropriate, sometimes just a look from the teacher can stop the behavior (Figure 15.11). Adding gestures such as shaking the head or pointing to material on the board can add emphasis.

When a teacher moves closer to the misbehavior, it usually stops. For example, if the teacher moves close to

Figure 15.11   How can the classroom teacher use nonverbal cues when students are not paying attention during class?

the whispering students, it communicates to the students that the teacher is observing their behavior and that it is not acceptable.

In the past, teachers were taught to use touch to reinforce their message. A hand on a student's shoulder would get the student's attention. Today, teachers must be very careful about using touch, since it may be misinterpreted. Placing a hand on the shoulder may work with younger students to draw their attention back to the subject. In general, touch should not be used with older children or teens.

Handling Problem Behavior

Inappropriate behavior includes a wide spectrum. On one end, a second grader may be tapping a pencil on his desk and disturbing those around him. On the other, serious situations can sometimes erupt in classrooms. Fortunately, most problem behaviors are on the lower end of the scale. Regardless, the teacher is in charge and must make appropriate decisions about how best to handle situations.

A teacher's behavior management plan, along with school rules, district policies, and class rules and procedures, forms the basis for determining how to respond to problem behaviors. There are many possible approaches. Sometimes school procedures take precedence, but most often the teacher decides how to handle each situation.

Using Effective Strategies

Actually, how a teacher reacts when a behavior issue occurs is as important as the specific actions he or she takes. Whether they seem to be paying attention or not, students are keenly aware of how their teacher handles such situations. It affects their attitude toward the teacher and often shapes their own future behavior.

When teaching, it is essential to stay calm and project confidence. This sends the signal that you are in control and expect compliance. No matter what you are feeling on the inside, this is what must show on the outside.

It is easier to maintain this attitude when you see problem behavior such as a student having difficulty making an appropriate choice. The purpose of discipline is to help the student make a better choice in the future. Problems can be opportunities for learning better behavior.

Anger, humiliation, putdowns, and similar responses are inappropriate. They attack the student, not the behavior. They yield negative consequences, not positive. They also create a poor model for students on how to handle conflict. When a teacher goes up to a student to handle the problem behavior privately, rather than saying something in front of the whole class, the student's dignity is not as threatened, and compliance is more likely. Another reason for correcting a student in private is to keep the rest of the class from becoming the rallying section for the misbehaving student.

It is best to always use the least forceful method possible to deal with a problem (Figure 15.12). Keeping your response low-key and matter-of-fact can help prevent the situation from mushrooming. It also minimizes disruption to learning.

Figure 15.12 Talking privately with a student about misbehavior helps preserve the student's dignity, making compliance with class rules more likely.

Applying Rules Consistently

Consistency in dealing with inappropriate behavior is essential to good classroom management.

A teacher must respond in the same way each time when encountering a particular situation. That way, students know the teacher will follow through with consequences. They also know the teacher will apply consequences fairly, the same way for every student. Students gain respect for teachers who exhibit fairness. They are also more likely to accept consequences the teacher imposes if everyone receives the same treatment.

Some teachers, like some parents, threaten consequences when misbehavior occurs but rarely follow through. Others only enforce rules some of the time. In both cases, students are willing to take the chance that they will avoid any repercussions and continue to do what they please.

Dealing with Common Behavioral Problems

In a typical school day, most teachers deal with multiple behavioral problems. Most of these are fairly common and fall into the category of minor misbehavior. Forgotten homework, talking to classmates while the teacher or another student has the floor, failure to participate in a discussion or activity, and similar situations seem small individually. Left unchecked, these behaviors derail lessons and learning.

When teachers respond to such problems quickly and consistently, their impact on learning is kept to a minimum. Specific measures depend on a teacher's philosophy and practice, however, most use simple techniques that are usually effective (Figure 15.13). The goal is to draw the misbehaving student back into the learning process, not to embarrass him or her.

What are some of these methods? Often, the nonverbal cues, such as moving toward the student, are all that is needed. Asking the student a question related to the lesson is another useful technique.

Figure 15.13 Each teacher must develop his or her own philosophy and practice dealing with common classroom behavior problems.

For example, you might say, "Adrienne, what do you think the elephant should do?" By asking what she thinks, rather than asking for one right answer, the student does not need to feel embarrassed by providing a wrong answer. Sometimes, the teacher just inserts the student's name in the lesson, "As we learned yesterday, Seth, bears hibernate in the winter months," lets the student know the teacher is watching. A bit of humor may be all the teacher needs to make a point and regain attention. These sorts of interventions, if complied with, do not merit further disciplinary consequences.

A next step might be to simply state directly and clearly what the student should do, and then walk away. "Tomas, sit down in your seat and finish your math problem." This method has several advantages. It reinforces the expectation that the student will follow class rules or procedures. The student has the choice to obey, still saving face because, with the teacher gone, the focus is off the situation. If the student is just seeking attention, this does not feed that desire. (Saying, "Tomas, why are you not sitting down?" would do so.) In addition, there is no debate, so the situation is less likely to escalate to a higher level. Disruption of the class is limited.

If that does not stop the behavior, there is a pattern of repeated offenses, or the problem is more serious in nature, the teacher might simply say, "We will talk after class." Sometimes the teacher begins on a positive note, praising another aspect of the student's behavior that is appropriate. The discussion might include asking the student what happened and discussing the consequences and impact of the inappropriate behavior. If the teacher has set a specific consequence for such behavior, the student must accept this. Otherwise, the teacher and student might discuss how to appropriately make up for the misbehavior. In this case, the consequences should link as closely as possible to the offense. Keeping the focus on learning self-discipline, the teacher might ask, "How can I help you act appropriately the next time?" or "What can you do next time?"

When a situation is not completely clear, the teacher must gather additional information. For example, two students may blame each other for something that happens. The teacher might ask each to explain the situation. The real facts usually come out. It is always a good idea to restate expectations, especially honesty. The teacher often acts as a mediator, helping the students reach a settlement or an agreement (Figure 15.14).

Figure 15.14 When necessary, the classroom teacher may act as a mediator between students to help solve a problem and reach an agreement.

Dealing with Serious Behavioral Issues

From time to time, teachers may have to deal with behavioral problems that are serious in nature. These include situations such as attempts to undermine a teacher's authority, physical violence, bullying, serious threats, harassment, and issues such as drug and alcohol use. Common behavioral problems, if they continue for a long period and become worse, may also fall into this category.

One of the most difficult repetitive misbehaviors to handle is defiance or *insubordination* (disobedience to authority). Students who are defiant often show hostility, talk back, or refuse to do what their teacher asks them to do. Many teachers, particularly new teachers, find this behavior threatening, even frightening. It can easily become a power struggle between the teacher and the student. The best way to deal with defiance is to pause and react calmly. Reacting angrily tends to escalate the problem. Your actions should be quietly decisive. It is best to listen to the student before responding, and it is best to do this outside the classroom. A teacher should never respond with threats, but should treat the defiant behavior seriously.

Although teachers should feel confident in their ability to respond to disruptive or serious misbehavior, it is often appropriate to involve other school personnel. In a nonemergency situation, it is best to first analyze the problem behavior. Try to find out why students are misbehaving. This will help you find a solution. Sometimes finding a solution is best achieved when school resources are used. If not in a self-contained classroom, the student's other teachers may help to provide insight.

Keeping Records

As teachers deal with serious or repetitive behavior, it is important to keep accurate records. Each time a problem occurs, the teacher records the date and time, what happened, and any other useful information (Figure 15.15).

Figure 15.15 By keeping detailed records, a teacher can document patterns of misbehavior and devise ways to solve them.

This can be helpful in several ways including

- **Establishing the existence of a pattern of misconduct, and shows its frequency.** This can be helpful in communicating with students, parents, or administrators about the problem.

- **Helping the teacher remain objective about the situation or student.** Dealing with disruptive behavior can be mentally and emotionally wearing. By keeping records, the teacher can see what circumstances trigger emotional responses for both the teacher and the student.

- **Analyzing the problem and the effectiveness of the teacher's responses.** The teacher may better understand underlying causes. A colleague might suggest a different way of handling the problem.

- **Providing a basis for gauging improvement when new strategies or responses are put in place.** If the student's behavioral problems become less frequent or less severe, the notes will document the positive changes.

Involving Parents or Guardians

The need to involve parents or guardians in behavioral issues depends on the severity of the problem and the success (or lack of success) in dealing with them in the classroom. Most problems can, and should, be resolved directly with the student. Some teachers, especially in the elementary grades, do communicate with parents or guardians on a regular basis about their child's behavior.

When teachers establish regular communication with parents, contacting them about behavioral issues is easier. It is always best when the first contact is not a negative one. By cooperating, parents or guardians and teachers often can work together to help students get back on track.

Utilizing School Resources

As a teacher, you do not have to handle severe disruptive misbehavior alone. Schools have people and support systems to help you. Sometimes several teachers find they are having similar problems with the same student. They may coordinate efforts to improve the student's behavior. Administrators can reinforce with students the need to follow class rules and the consequences for not doing so.

In many schools, problems such as fights between students, drug or alcohol use, and safety issues violate school rules. The school administration deals with these behavior issues. The principal, dean, or other designated person will follow up according to school rules and/or district policies.

Perspectives on Teaching

Today was the first day that Jordan was to observe Mrs. Lee's second grade classroom. He was excited to be working with Mrs. Lee, the same teacher he had as a second grader. He had happy memories of the year spent with her and was looking forward to learning from her again. She was one of the reasons he was considering a career as a teacher.

Jordan's Thoughts...

When I walked into Mrs. Lee's classroom for the first time, the students became very quiet. They were aware that a stranger had entered the room and seemed curious to see how Mrs. Lee would respond. When she greeted me warmly, the students all settled in and watched and listened to our conversation. Mrs. Lee introduced me to her class, and told them that I would be acting as her assistant teacher and they should treat me as a teacher.

Before long, Mrs. Lee went into action. I tried to get a feel for the individual students' personalities and learn their names. The students were studying marine life and were getting ready for a trip to the local aquarium later that week. As Mrs. Lee led the students in a learning activity, I observed her walking among the students. When a couple of girls began whispering, Mrs. Lee move toward them and they quickly quieted down. When another student, Jimmy, started taking things off a classmate's desk, Mrs. Lee called him up front to help her set up a display of seashells. When Jimmy went back to his seat, he was no longer distracted by his classmate's things.

The class atmosphere was lively, and students had so much to say. I noticed that Mrs. Lee only called on students who raised their hands to speak and made positive comments about their contributions. When one student was handling a dry sea star, the point of the leg accidentally broke off. Mrs. Lee assured the student that it was an accident and then brainstormed with the class the proper way of handling a live sea star during the aquarium visit. The incident created a lively discussion.

When I left at the end of that first day, I was amazed at Mrs. Lee's skill in meeting the learning needs of all her students. Mrs. Lee knew what was going on around the classroom—even an unexpected incident became a valuable part of the lesson. I knew that I was learning from a master teacher.

Analyze It!

After reading *Perspectives on Teaching*, analyze Mrs. Lee's actions that support the best practices described in this chapter. Cite text evidence that supports these practices and discuss in class.

As a teacher, it is important to be familiar with school district policies so classroom rules and teacher practices are in alignment.

School counselors can be a valuable resource when emotional and social issues are involved. Sometimes a student is not misbehaving, but seems to be depressed or shows a marked change in attitude (Figure 15.16). A counselor may help directly or recommend the student receive outside counseling.

Effective teachers assume responsibility for classroom management issues. They try to solve most problems themselves before taking them to a school administrator or parent. Effective teachers, however, also know when to ask for help, rather than let a serious situation grow worse. That is in everyone's best interest. If a teacher even suspects that a student is contemplating suicide or that a student may be in an abusive situation, the teacher should not hesitate reporting these suppositions to the appropriate authorities. This is the law in most states.

Figure 15.16 School counselors serve as a valuable resource when students have emotional or social issues to resolve.

Chapter 15 Review and Assess

Summary

- Teachers want students to learn as much as possible. To accomplish this, they need effective classroom management skills.

- Classroom management involves creating an appropriate environment, keeping students involved in learning, and managing behavior.

- Teachers shape the classroom environment in a variety of ways to add interest, stimulate learning, and help students form bonds as a class.

- Students who are involved in a lesson learn more and misbehave less.

- Successful teachers work to present lessons that are challenging and interesting, and find ways to minimize misbehavior and smooth transitions from one class or subject to another.

- Acknowledging effort and appropriate behavior encourages students to maintain these behaviors and also helps minimize misbehavior.

- Teachers deal with behavioral issues on a daily basis.

- Up-front planning, clear rules and procedures, and consistent follow-through, helps keep problems to a minimum.

Review and Study

1. What is the goal of classroom management and how do teachers accomplish it?

2. How does creating a sense of community among class members help increase learning?

3. Name four factors important to building a sense of community.

4. List three ways experienced teachers handle transitions to minimize problems.

5. How might teachers with each of the three management styles react to a middle school student who breaks the rules or misbehaves?

6. What are three questions a teacher should ask of himself or herself when developing a behavior management plan?

7. Contrast class rules with classroom procedures. Give an example that shows their relationship.

8. What suggestions do educational experts and experienced teachers have for developing class rules?

9. How do students develop a sense of personal responsibility and how does it impact behavior?

10. Name three nonverbal cues a teacher might use to stop misbehavior. What is the advantage of these methods?

11. Why is consistency in dealing with inappropriate behavior so important to good classroom management?

12. Why is keeping accurate records helpful when dealing with serious behavioral issues?

Vocabulary Activity

13. Work with a partner to write the definitions of the *Content* and *Academic* terms on page 372 based on your current understanding after reading the chapter. Then pair up with another pair to discuss your definitions and any discrepancies. Finally, discuss the definitions with the class and ask your instructor for necessary corrections or clarification.

Critical Thinking

14. **Evaluate alternatives.** The text states that *ease of use, ease of teaching,* and *ease of supervision* are all guidelines for arranging classroom space that impact teaching and learning. In small groups, consider the following classroom settings: a fourth grade classroom, a middle school science class, and a high school English class. Evaluate possible arrangements for each class against the text guidelines and make a sketch of each. Share your group's ideas with the class, citing text evidence for your decisions.

15. **Draw conclusions.** Think of a class that you have taken in which students felt connected as a class. Draw conclusions about the following and discuss your responses in class: What was the grade level or subject area? What did the teacher do to foster this feeling? What was the impact on learning and classroom behavior?

16. **Analyze evidence.** Analyze the author's statement: "Teachers who take the attitude that all students can experience success can help break the cycle of failure." Cite text and other reliable resources that support this statement and share your evidence during class discussion. How can encouraging students' positive achievements influence their future efforts and behavior? Then write an essay describing how you can implement this attitude in your own teaching career.

17. **Generate a solution.** Generate a clear example of a direct statement a teacher might give to a fifth grader who is being disruptive, rather than participating in a small group geography assignment. Then discuss your solution with the class. Which solutions does the class agree are most likely to be effective?

18. **Make inferences.** As a new teacher, would you be more likely or less likely to ask for outside help with behavioral issues? Why?

Core Skills

19. **Observation and writing.** Make arrangements to observe in three classrooms: an elementary classroom, a middle school classroom, and a high school classroom. During your observations, focus on how the teachers used the following to promote effective learning:

- arrangement of space—ease of use, teaching, and supervision
- features that created a stimulating learning environment
- techniques for building community
- strategies for engaging lessons, managing transitions, and noting success
- strategies for management style, classroom rules, and minimizing behavior problems
- strategies for dealing with behavior issues

    Write a summary about what you learned from your observations and identify techniques you might implement in your own classroom.

20. **Research and speaking.** Use reliable Internet resources to investigate activities that help students learn about each other, build community, and encourage respect. Choose one activity and present it to the class. If possible, have the class complete the activity and discuss the effectiveness.

21. **Writing.** Suppose you are a second grade teacher. Create a plan for handling the transition from a science lesson to the lunch period for your class. Develop a routine that minimizes the transition time and behavioral problems that could occur during the transition.

22. **Writing.** Develop a set of class rules following text guidelines you think creates an atmosphere to enhance learning. Your list should include four to six general rules. Include a rationale for your choices. Post your list of rules to the class website or blog for feedback on effectiveness from your classmates and instructor.

23. **Demonstrate.** Create at least two nonverbal cues to communicate each of the following to first graders: "Quiet down," "Good job," "Sit still," "Line up," "Stop that behavior," and "You can do it!" With a partner, demonstrate your nonverbal cues to the class.

24. **Writing.** Create a chart for keeping records for documenting common and serious student behavior issues. Include at least two sample entries in the chart you develop. Discuss your chart with your instructor and ask for critical feedback.

25. **Technology application.** Search online for at least three area school districts within one state. Locate the "student responsibilities and expectations" document for a school from each district. What do they have in common? What differs? What might be the reason for these differences? Compare states with your classmates to determine how much geography and culture play a part.

26. **CTE College and career readiness practice.** Identify your desired teaching situation (grade and subject area) and your personal management style. Using the text and other reliable resources as a guide, write a summary of your personal behavior management plan for establishing classroom rules, minimizing behavior problems, and handling problems that do arise.

College and Career Portfolio

An important part of any portfolio is a list of references. A reference is a person who knows your skills, talents, or personal traits and is willing to recommend you. References can be an instructor, a teaching-site supervisor, or someone with whom you provided community service. Someone from your personal life—such as a youth group leader—can also be a reference. Because those who view your portfolio may not see relatives as objective, do not list them. When applying for a teaching position, consider which references can best recommend you for the position. Always get permission from people before using their names as references.

- Ask several people with whom you have worked or volunteered if they are willing to serve as references for you. If so, ask for their contact information.

- Create a list of names and contact information for your references. Save the document in the appropriate subfolder in your e-portfolio and a print copy in your portfolio container.

- Save your best work from Items 20, 21, 22, 24, and 26 in your portfolio.

Chapter 16
The Next Steps to Becoming a Teacher

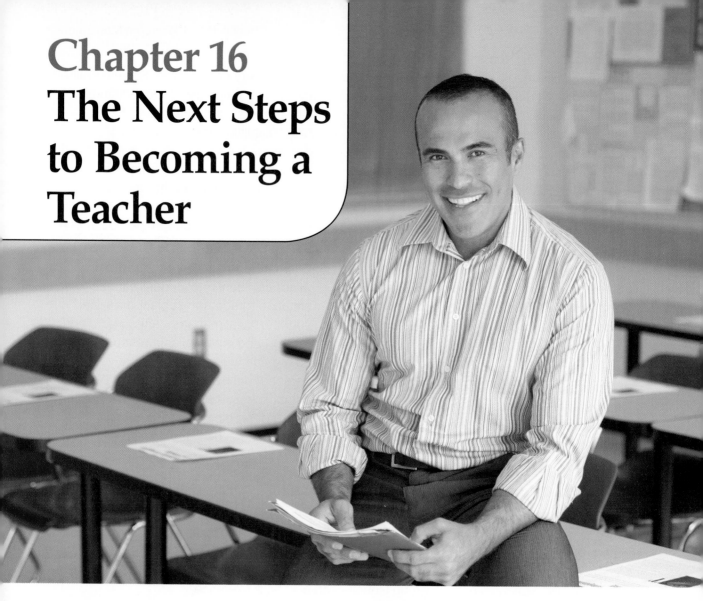

Content Terms

résumé
headline
career objective
accreditation
advanced placement courses
dual-credit courses
work ethic
professionalism
in-service training

Academic Terms

adhere
mediocre
advantageous
jeopardize
rapport

Objectives

After studying this chapter, you will be able to

- **present** a completed personal portfolio, including a résumé.

- **develop** a personal career plan.

- **utilize** effective techniques for comparing potential colleges and universities.

- **summarize** ways to maximize the high school experience.

- **apply** time-management skills to life and career success.

- **explain** the importance of leading a balanced life.

- **identify** the benefits of participation in professional associations for students and teachers.

Reading Prep

Take two-column notes as you read the chapter. Fold a piece of notebook paper in half lengthwise. In the left column, write the main ideas. In the right column, write subtopics and detailed information. After reading the chapter, use the notes as a study guide. Fold the paper in half so you only see the main ideas. Quiz yourself on the details and subtopics.

At the Companion Website you can

- **Practice** terms with e-flash cards and interactive games

- **Assess** what you learn by completing self-assessment quizzes

- **Expand** knowledge with interactive activities

www.g-wlearning.com/teaching/

Study on the go

Use a mobile device to practice terms and review with self-assessment quizzes.

www.m.g-wlearning.com/0094/

Case Study

As a class, read the case study and discuss the questions that follow. After you finish studying the chapter, discuss the case study and questions again. How have your responses changed based on what you learned?

What a day it has been. But then, so was yesterday and the day before. Shenequa has been applying for colleges, trying to succeed in school, doing family chores, babysitting, trying to help her younger brother who has been getting into trouble, and worrying about her dad's potential job loss. Today, Shenequa received a low test score at school, and one of her favorite teachers suggested she involve herself with Family, Career, and Community Leaders of America (FCCLA), a student leadership group.

When Shenequa got home, all she wanted to do was collapse in bed. Her responsibilities seem endless and she is concerned about pleasing others and getting into a college of her choice. *Why did my teacher want me to join FCCLA?* Shenequa wonders. *What can she be thinking? I don't even have time for my homework.*

Let's Discuss

- Why might Shenequa's teacher be suggesting yet another activity? How might joining this group benefit Shenequa?

- If Shenequa decides that joining FCCLA is a good idea, what can she change in her schedule to accommodate that decision?

- How might Shenequa's involvement in student organizations during high school benefit her in the future?

This text has given you insight into what being part of the teaching profession involves. Along the way, you have had opportunities to try some of the roles, responsibilities, and activities of teachers. You have considered the challenges teachers face and the satisfaction that can come with helping students learn and grow. Most importantly, you have reflected on these experiences to help you decide whether a career in education is right for you.

If you have decided to pursue a career in education, you can continue this quest on your own in many ways. You can take advantage of opportunities to observe what you see around you and you can look for examples of effective teaching and learning. You can observe and ask questions, such as: How do teachers form nurturing relationships with students? How do teachers meet the needs of individuals? Which classroom management strategies are most effective?

To prepare yourself for a career in education, look for opportunities to gain experience working with children and teens. Familiarize yourself with different age groups and observe how they interact, how they learn best, and what interests them (Figure 16.1).

Also talk to people who work in different capacities within the field of education. Although this text focuses primarily on the role of teachers, education relies on caring and qualified people in other roles as well. Find out more about what principals, early childhood educators, speech and hearing pathologists, school librarians, guidance counselors, and other education workers do. By investigating these roles, you will better understand the big picture and may find an alternative role for yourself if you decide not to pursue teaching.

In this chapter, you will learn more about specific steps that you can take to move toward a career in education. You will build your confidence in making realistic plans and preparing yourself for success in college and your career.

Figure 16.1   By observing teachers and students and interacting with children, you can learn about effective teaching and learning.

Polishing Your Portfolio

Throughout this course, you may have been developing a portfolio, either as a class requirement or on your own to help document your progress. As you know, a *portfolio* is a collection of materials that showcases your learning, accomplishments, strengths, and best work. It also contains your reflections about these materials and their importance to you.

Beyond this course, your portfolio has a variety of practical uses. Reviewing your portfolio can help you grow as you think about what you have accomplished and learned. Reflecting on your experiences can give you a clearer perspective about teaching and your possible role as an educator. You may use material from your portfolio to gain admission to a teacher preparation program or to apply for a job. You may find other uses as well.

For example, by keeping an accurate record of all work and volunteer or service-learning activities, you will have the details available whenever you need them.

After developing a portfolio, the next step is to *prepare* your portfolio in a final format. Your teacher may give you more specific guidelines, but generally, you should **adhere** (follow) to the following steps as you prepare your final portfolio.

Select Items

Remember that a portfolio should display your best efforts. This means being selective about what you include. Choosing items to include becomes increasingly important as you gain more experience and accumulate more material for your portfolio.

Choose pieces that show the breadth of your experiences related to teaching and to the skills needed for a teaching career. Include personal information about your education, volunteer and work experiences, and achievements. Select papers, projects, and reflections that represent your best work (Figure 16.2). Your teacher may help you decide what to include.

If you encounter materials that you decide not to include in your final portfolio at this time, do not dispose of them. Rather, store them for possible later use. Be sure to clearly identify each piece you store (what it is, how it was used, its significance, and the date). Store all your items in an organized manner. You may consider preparing a master list of all your portfolio items, including a brief description of each piece and its location.

Figure 16.2   After you have prepared your portfolio, keep it updated and organized.

Include a Résumé

When selecting materials for your portfolio, you will need to include a résumé. A **résumé** is an outline of your education, achievements, and experiences, including volunteer work and work experiences. A well-crafted résumé is necessary when applying for employment, and may be necessary when applying for college or scholarships. Résumés can be either chronological or functional. *Chronological résumés* focus on your work experiences, listing each in reverse chronological order. *Functional résumés* emphasize your qualifications, skills, and achievements. A résumé generally includes the following information:

- **Name and personal information.** List your name, complete address with zip code, telephone number (or cell number), and your e-mail address on your résumé.

- **Career objective or headline and summary.** The **headline** (a set of introductory words to capture attention) and summary are beneficial for people who have experience and expertise or for those who want to highlight their qualifications. A **career objective** is a one-sentence description that aligns you and your skills with a specific position (teacher). Career objectives are often used by recent graduates or those with less experience.

- **Education and degree type.** Under this heading list the schools you attended, beginning with the most recent in reverse chronological order, including the city and state. Identify the type of degrees you earned, such as an *Associate of Arts (AA)* or a *Bachelor of Arts (BA)*, and highlight your program of study.

- **Work experience.** Employers are especially interested in information under this heading. It is important to document and maintain a record of all work experiences for your résumé. The best résumé describes your job functions that showcase your skills and achievements.

- **Honors, awards, and achievements.** This section highlights your special achievements, such as graduating with honors or other awards.

- **Memberships and professional associations.** Include a list of your memberships in education-related organizations. List your memberships in order of importance, putting the most relevant first.

- **Additional skills and interests.** In this section, list any other skills you have that you think enhance your job performance. Employers especially look for computer and other technology skills. Also, mention your ability to communicate in a language in addition to English if not mentioned earlier in your résumé.

Make sure your résumé is precise and without errors. Many employers will request your résumé via e-mail, or you may need to upload it to an employer's website. In such cases, keep the formatting simple and make sure that lines and headers break properly. For employers that request your résumé via traditional mail, print your résumé on high-quality, neutral-colored paper such as white, gray, or cream. For more information about résumés, visit a college and career counselor at your school or research résumé layouts online. Figure 16.3 shows a typical résumé layout.

Write a Cover Message

A cover message (or letter) should always accompany your résumé whether sending it to a potential employer or using it as part of your college application. Use your cover message to introduce yourself and summarize your reasons for your message, such as college or job application, without revealing the details in your résumé. Your cover message should be positive and entice the viewer to read more. It should include an introduction, body of the message, and a conclusion.

Whether a traditional print message or an e-mail message, your cover message should utilize Standard English—correct grammar, punctuation, spelling, and usage. A cover message should be brief and to the point, whether you are using it to apply for a job or for college entrance. Be sure to include the following:

- the reason for your message
- your strengths, skills, and abilities
- reasons why you should be considered
- when you are able to begin
- a request for an interview

Prepare Selections

Once you have made your selections, prepare your portfolio for use. First, check to see if any items require updating. For example, you might revise your *philosophy of teaching* statement based on your experiences. Be sure to keep the original version. You might include both to show how your thinking has evolved.

Your portfolio must look professional. Begin by carefully proofreading all material, preferably several times. Ensure that pages are neat and well organized and clearly identify each portfolio item. If you are using a binder for your portfolio, consider placing bulky items in clear plastic sheet protectors or envelopes. You might include photos of larger items. If you are creating an electronic portfolio, ensure that your portfolio items are clearly identifiable and backed up somewhere reliable.

Lettie Ortega

12322 NE 135th Street
Woodyville, WA 99999
(Cell) 425.555.1234
Lettie.Ortega@e-mail.com

TEACHER QUALIFICATIONS
- Extensive hands-on experience in the classroom.
- Excellent communication skills, detail-oriented, organized, and highly motivated.
- Broad multicultural experience, including volunteering at children's camps in urban settings.
- Strong computer skills: *Microsoft Word, Excel, PowerPoint, Outlook, Publisher.*
- Proficiency in Spanish language—ability in speaking, writing, and listening.

EDUCATION AND CERTIFICATION
Bachelor of Arts, Language Arts—Pacific University, Woodyville, WA—June 2016
Washington State Residency Teaching Certificate, K–8

HONORS
Graduated *Magna cum Laude*—June 2016
Dean's List, 2013–2016

TEACHING EXPERIENCE
Elementary Teacher Intern (4th Grade), North Beach Elementary, Oceanside, WA *January 2016–June 2016*
- Effectively managed 27 diverse students including many who were gifted or on IEP's.
- Implemented a variety of lessons and units centered on state standards.
- Developed unique unit plans in science, art, and reading.

Elementary Intern (1st Grade), Peak Preparatory Academy, Mountaintop, WA *March 2015–June 2015*
- Provided one-on-one tutoring and assessments.
- Conducted reading and math lessons for a highly diverse group of students.
- Successfully managed 21 students with various needs.

Elementary Intern (3rd Grade), John Wheat Elementary, Mountaintop, WA *January 2014–June 2014*
- Worked one-on-one to provide student support in reading and writing.
- Assisted with classroom activities.

Teacher, Summer Camp, Compassion for Kids, Manila, Philippines *July 2013–August 2013*
- Created curriculum for and conducted week-long camps with a team.
- Responsibly managed up to 25 K–1st grade children in classroom settings.

RELATED EXPERIENCE
Au Pair, Private Employer, La Paz, Mexico *September 2016–Present*
- Oversaw and monitored two elementary-aged children at least thirty hours per week.
- Supervised daily homework and provided English language instruction.
- Achieved solid knowledge of the Spanish language through course work and utilization.

Counselor, Camp Firstwood, Ruralwood, WA *June 2012–August 2012*
- Supervised five to nine students weekly at a residential summer camp.
- Taught various classes on recreational activities.

ADDITIONAL EXPERIENCE
Resident Hall Student Advisor, Pacific University, Woodyville, WA *September 2014–June 2015*

Lifeguard, Firecreek Daycamp, Woodyville, WA *June 2011–August 2011*

MEMBERSHIP
Washington Education Association, Active Membership, *June 2016–Present*
Washington Education Association, Student Membership, *August 2013–May 2016*

Figure 16.3   This résumé example highlights this teacher's key qualifications, education, and experience.

Organize Your Portfolio

If your teacher does not specify how to organize your portfolio, brainstorm ways to divide portfolio items into logical sections. For example, you could place information about relevant volunteer and work activities together. You could group examples of teaching materials you have developed and place personal information near the front of the portfolio.

Once you have decided how to organize your items, prepare a table of contents. This will give those looking at your portfolio an overview of what is included and help them find materials of particular interest. Any time you revise your portfolio, update the table of contents (Figure 16.4).

Figure 16.4 Keeping your portfolio organized makes it easy for those who review your portfolio to locate items.

Developing a Personal Career Plan

To prepare yourself for college and career, also develop a career plan. A *career plan* is a tool that outlines how you will reach your career goal. It helps you map your way to achieving the future you want and identifies the concrete steps you need to take. By taking the time to develop a plan, you can focus your efforts most effectively. You will know where you want to go and how to get there.

Step 1: Define Your Career Goal

A *career goal* is a clear, concise statement about what you want to become in life. An example of a career goal might be, "To become a high school math teacher." If you wrote a career goal earlier in this course, take another look at it. In light of what you have learned about teaching and about yourself, you may decide to revise it. It is good to review the range of opportunities that fit your interests and strengths. Your goal should reflect your best assessment of what you think you want to do. You can change or refine it at any time.

Step 2: Identify Career Requirements

Career requirements are the education, skills, and characteristics a person needs to succeed in a career. If you are aiming for a career in teaching, the minimum educational requirement in most states is a bachelor's degree.

(Some states require a master's degree, so check the state where you intend to teach.) Throughout this book and course, you have learned about skills and characteristics teachers need. For the purposes of your career plan, identify six to 10 characteristics that seem to be most important. Examples might be management skills, interpersonal skills, and technical skills.

Step 3: Evaluate Your Accomplishments, Skills, and Interests

What are your accomplishments? What do you do well? What are your interests? Honestly assessing your accomplishments, skills, and interests can help you consider how to reach your career goal. For example, one of your accomplishments might be membership in the *National Honor Society*. Selection as a member of this organization acknowledges your scholarship, service, leadership, character, and citizenship. This honor will help you gain acceptance at a college or university, and those characteristics can aid your success in many careers. Skills at expressing yourself verbally or bringing a team together to achieve a goal are valuable in school and the workplace (Figure 16.5). Perhaps you are a top soccer player in your league. This might earn you a college scholarship. It would also be an advantage if your career goal includes coaching soccer, as well as teaching. When you identify your skills, interests, and accomplishments, you can turn them into assets.

Figure 16.5   As members of a debate team, these students are developing research, verbal, and leadership skills that will help them to reach career goals.

Step 4: Identify Possible Obstacles

Think carefully about what may impede you from reaching your career goal. Once you are aware of potential obstacles, you can determine ways around them. Obstacles may range from limited financial resources to lack of leadership experience, *mediocre* (not exemplary) grades, or difficulty writing well. Regardless of the obstacles on your list, you can plan ways to overcome them. A guidance or career counselor can help you find out more about financial aid. You might join a club or organization at school that will help you use and improve your leadership skills. You can commit to studying harder and asking teachers for extra help. You might take an extra writing course or ask if you can become involved in the school newspaper. Develop workable solutions and ask for help, when needed. Working to solve these problems now will make the road ahead much smoother.

Step 5: Determine Steps to Reach Your Career Goal

Although starting your career may seem years away, the path begins now. Identify six to ten steps or goals you need to achieve in the next three to five years to make your dreams happen. What concrete activities do you need to do this year? next year? as you start college? Do you want to graduate in the top 10 percent of your class? Do you need to improve your math skills in order to do well on college entrance tests? When do you need to apply for college admission? The next section of this chapter may give you additional ideas about what steps to include. Put your steps in order, starting with those you need to act on first.

Preparing for College Success

A career in teaching requires additional education beyond a high school diploma. Nevertheless, now is the time to prepare. Much like training for a competition, getting yourself ready can help make success in college a reality.

Choosing where you will go to school is an important decision, so you will want to allow plenty of time. Deadlines accompany various aspects of the application process. There are many steps that you can take now to increase your chances of success during college. You can use your remaining time in high school to help make your transition to college easier.

Choosing a College or University

You may have already begun thinking about where you will continue your education after graduation. If not, begin to explore possible colleges and universities. Search for schools that best match your needs and wants. Consider your expectations about academics and college life. Even if you are thinking about a particular college or university, take time to evaluate others (Figure 16.6). Here are some aspects to consider:

- *Size*. Would you prefer a large school environment or a smaller campus? Large schools offer more options. Smaller colleges and universities may have fewer students per class and more opportunities for involvement with faculty.

- *Reputation*. Look at a school's reputation in your area of study, not just its overall reputation. If you plan to teach, ask your school counselor and teachers about which schools are renown for teacher education. Middle and high school teachers usually specialize in one or more subject areas. Check what schools offer in those areas, as well.

Figure 16.6 Touring colleges of interest is one way to gather information about where to continue your education.

- ***Accreditation***. You may want to verify that schools of interest have accreditation in your area. **Accreditation** shows that an educational institution maintains standards that qualify graduates for professional practice in a career or career area.

- ***Location***. Do you want to attend school in another part of the country or closer to home? Would you prefer a school in an urban environment or in a smaller city or town?

- ***Admission requirements***. Some schools are highly selective and accept a small percentage of applicants. Other schools accept a broader range of students. Check information from schools that interest you to see if you are likely to meet admission criteria.

- ***Cost***. A college education is a major expense. Tuition costs vary from school to school. (In general, state universities have lower tuition for in-state students than private colleges and universities.) Books and living expenses also add to this cost. Most students rely on a combination of methods to cover these expenses. Students may receive help from family, personal savings, scholarships, grants (which do not require repayment), loans, and part-time jobs.

  Some colleges and universities offer financial aid directly. Students can also apply for and gain scholarships and grants that do not link to a particular school. Some scholarships may require involved applications. When you are considering the cost of a school, your school counselor can help you determine financial opportunities. Many websites and books can also guide your search if you need financial aid.

Do not rule out schools immediately because of their tuition costs—some may end up more affordable than they initially appear. Schools usually do not award scholarships until after you apply and gain acceptance to the institution. Apply to several schools that you are seriously considering and then compare your options. (Note that most schools have nonrefundable application fees, and these can add up quickly.)

Gathering information about colleges and universities can help you identify ones that seem to meet your needs and wants. Check schools' websites to learn about information posted for possible applicants, as well as degree requirements and campus life. Attend college fairs or similar events in your area. These give you an opportunity to talk to representatives of various colleges and universities. Contact the admissions offices of schools of interest and ask for informational packets. Talk to people about the schools they attended and find out as much as you can (Figure 16.7).

Figure 16.7 Many colleges expect applicants to have completed a course of study similar to this one. Your guidance counselor can advise you about what courses to take.

Some students start their college education at a *community college* (a two-year college) and then transfer to a four-year college or university to complete their bachelor's degree. This can be ***advantageous*** (beneficial) since tuition at community colleges is less expensive than at four-year schools. In addition, many students can live at home to save on housing costs. Class sizes at community colleges tend to be smaller, and schedules more flexible. Students who have jobs can more easily schedule their classes around work schedules.

Studies show that students who complete their first two years at a community college and then transfer fare as well academically as students who spend all four years at a college or university. Most community colleges work to coordinate coursework with four-year colleges and universities in their states to facilitate transferring. In such cases, community colleges are a way of getting your first 60 hours at a lower cost than at a major university. Make certain that your credits transfer to the university from which you plan to receive your degree, or you could lose the financial advantage of going to the community college.

Late in your junior year or by early fall of your senior year of high school, you should narrow your choices. Continue your research on schools of interest and try to visit your top choices. You can arrange for a guided tour through the school's admissions office, but also plan to spend some time on your own. Sit in on a class and eat in a dining hall.

Walk around the campus to get a feel for the school's learning and social environment. Talk to a professor and to several students. Also, watch people and ask questions. Visiting a campus can help you assess what a school is like.

Submit college applications in the fall of your senior year. When it is time to make your final choice, discuss your options with those people whose judgment you value. If you have done your homework, there is an excellent chance that the college or university you choose will be a good match. Often, there is no one "right" choice—every school has advantages and disadvantages.

Remember, too, that you can get an excellent education at almost any school. Your success depends mainly on choosing challenging courses, putting effort into your classes, and taking advantage of the many opportunities a school offers. Commit to make the most of what is available.

Maximizing Your High School Experience

Even though you are looking ahead to college, be sure to make the most of your time in high school. Your choices and performance during your high school years—especially your last semesters in high school—can affect whether or not you gain admission to the college or university of your choice to work toward the goals you set in your personal career plan.

Choosing Courses

Early in your high school years, make an appointment with your high school counselor to review the program of study for your *graduation plan*. First, check what high school courses the colleges and universities that interest you expect applicants to have completed for college acceptance and entrance. You will want to ensure you have enough credits in the right courses for your chosen career path and to meet the requirements in your state and for your school of interest by the time you graduate. In addition, many colleges and universities look at any special certifications, service-learning experiences, or endorsements you earn while in high school. Figure 16.8 lists some college expectations of applicants.

Also, explore the possibility of taking advanced placement or dual-credit courses, if these are available. **Advanced placement (AP) courses** are more difficult than regular high school courses and include content comparable to beginning-level college classes.

Figure 16.8	College Expectations of Applicants
High School Courses	**Number of Years**
Math	2–3
Laboratory science	2–3
English	4
Social studies	2–3
Foreign language	2–3
Visual/performing/practical arts	1

At the end of these courses, students take a standardized *advanced placement (AP) test*. A passing score on this test may give a student credit at the college level or advanced standing in college for completion of that college requirement or subject area course. **Dual-credit courses** are college- or university-level courses in which high school students enroll, and on successful completion of the courses simultaneously earn both high school and postsecondary credits. These courses may be taught in a high school or at a college or university by a college qualified instructor, and generally require use of specific textbooks identified by the college or university. These credits *may* be transferrable to another college or university the student chooses to attend after high school graduation. Both options require a high degree of dedication and maturity, but they give students a head start on college (Figure 16.9).

Figure 16.9   Taking on the challenge of dual-credit courses gives you a head start on college and shows your commitment to success in college and career.

Joining Student Organizations

Participating in student organizations at the high school level can broaden your experiences and polish your skills. Commit to being actively involved in any organization you join. This will give you opportunities to practice teamwork, leadership, planning, organization, service, and other key skills that link to success in college, in the work world, and in other aspects of adult life. Most colleges and universities evaluate applicants' involvement in activities and organizations, as well as their academic records and test scores—all of which help determine acceptance for enrollment.

Most school organizations provide opportunities to build key skills. Two are worth special consideration by students interested in teaching:

- *Future Educators Association (FEA)*. Future Educators of America (FEA) groups are active in many high schools and colleges. They bring together students who are interested in pursuing teaching as a career. FEA seeks to attract students to the teaching profession, promote teaching as a career, and provide resources and programs related to the profession.

- *Family, Career and Community Leaders of America (FCCLA)*. Family, Career and Community Leaders of America (FCCLA) is an organization for high school and college students. It aims to promote personal growth and leadership development in students preparing to enter the adult world of work and family. In FCCLA, student groups complete projects that require them to apply knowledge, interact with others, adapt to new technology, and logically think through problems.

  FCCLA focuses on areas related to family and consumer sciences and education in general, including child development and teacher preparation. These areas have practical applications regardless of a person's specific career goals. For example, all adults must manage multiple roles, including the roles of family member, wage earner, and community member. FCCLA seeks to improve the quality of life for students and their families and to prepare students for the adult world.

Staying Focused

It is easy, as your time in high school winds down, to lose your focus. Choosing where to continue your education can distract you from the present—and it is natural to be excited about upcoming graduation and college life ahead. Spending time with friends may seem more important than classes and homework.

Some students experience *senior slump*, a period of unfocused and unmotivated behavior before graduating high school. Along with lost learning, students' grades can drop significantly. This may leave some students unable to graduate and *jeopardize* (risk) others' class ranks and even admissions to colleges.

Senior slump may indicate that some students are unable to handle the shift to more independence. This shift involves self-discipline and good personal decision making, replacing the rules and structures imposed by parents and others. Once out of high school and into college or the working world, those who cannot stay focused on their goals are unlikely to reach them. College professors do not issue constant reminders about homework and studying. Students having difficulty in a subject must seek out help. Failure to keep up means failure of a course. Employers do not tolerate unreliable workers. They simply replace them.

The period of high school before graduation is a good time for students to establish and practice their work ethic. **Work ethic** reflects a person's dedication to completing important tasks. Work ethic indicates that you possess the maturity needed for college and career (Figure 16.10). There, you will face more choices, distractions, and independence. Remember that reaching your goals is worth the effort and that establishing a work ethic early on will benefit your future for years to come.

Managing Your Time

Sometimes you may feel that a typical day is not long enough for you to accomplish all that you need and want to do. Demands on your time will steadily increase in the years ahead. In college, you will be juggling challenging

Figure 16.10 Developing a strong work ethic early in life displays maturity and dedication to your future.

courses, significant amounts of homework, extracurricular and social activities, and other responsibilities. Many students also have jobs to help offset college expenses. Life as a teaching professional will be even busier.

The best strategy for coping is to develop good time-management skills now. Doing so will pay real benefits—immediately and in the years to come. There are plenty of books and articles on time management, but these basic steps will put you on the path:

Professional Tip

Dependability

Who do you depend on in your life? When asked this question, you probably reviewed the qualities of people in your life and chose those whom you can count on most. These are the people who will come to your aid when needed. In the workplace, dependability or reliability is highly valued. Dependability in the workplace includes showing up at the time agreed on, consistency in temperament and reactions to situations, and willingness to help where needed. Dependable people contribute to team projects and respect fellow group members. Teachers who are dependable are reliable and steadfast. They are trustworthy, loyal, and faithful to their students and the school. Sometimes teachers are the only people in their students' lives who are dependable.

Dig Deeper

As you consider a career in teaching, think about how others view you in regard to dependability. What qualities do you think you possess that show you are dependable? Cite examples that support these qualities that you think are observable by others. Then, write a short essay summarizing your qualities and examples. Ask your instructor for feedback and discuss your analysis of your dependability.

- **Write down what you need and want to accomplish**. This both keeps you from forgetting important tasks and serves as a reminder to tackle them. Find a system that works for you—low-tech or high-tech. You can use anything from a simple index card to an electronic version. When your list gets long, divide it into categories.

- **Prioritize your list**. Decide which items on your list are essential, which are important, and which you will do if you have time. (Some people use *A*, *B*, *C* or *1*, *2*, *3* to designate priorities.) Homework, team practice, and a part-time job schedules might be *A* priorities, for example.

- **Use a planner or calendar to schedule your time**. This will help keep you on track and accomplish more but does not mean that you must schedule every minute. The purpose of a planner or calendar is to prevent important tasks from slipping through the cracks. When you have a big project, start early by scheduling segments of time to work on the project over days or weeks. You will do a better job and feel less stress than if you try to do everything at the last minute.

- **Get organized**. Inability to find what you need is one of the biggest time wasters. At best, you spend time looking. At worst, you have to do work over because you cannot find what you already did. Start with simple techniques like putting objects in specific places. Organize documents and information in files, on paper, or electronically. Identify organizational trouble spots and devise solutions to improve them.

- **Establish routines**. When you do tasks automatically, the tasks get done, and you do not have to worry about them. Consider doing your homework right after school or dinner (Figure 16.11). If you always pack up everything for school before you go to bed, you will be ready to go in the morning, even if you oversleep. Establishing routines can help you manage time and avoid forgetfulness.

When you first try out steps such as these, they may seem awkward. Give them a fair trial. It takes at least several weeks for new habits to become comfortable and automatic. If you make the effort to use your time efficiently, you will be ahead of many of your classmates. These are habits that will serve you well over a lifetime.

Figure 16.11 Having a regular routine for completing your homework is a benefit in managing your time well.

Keeping Your Life in Balance

Like that challenging point of balance on a playground seesaw, it is difficult to arrive at a balance in life. A *balanced life* is one in which there are no extremes. Rather, all components of life have a place, and a person's focus remains on his or her goals.

Leading a balanced life is important—it is all too easy to get off track in one direction or another. You may know people so obsessed by grades that they have no time for family, friends, and activities. You may also know people whose primary concern is sports or partying. By neglecting their schoolwork, they jeopardize their futures.

Think about your own life by looking at the big picture. How much time do you typically spend on school, work, family, friends, and other priorities? Does this seem like a reasonable balance? If not, what changes can you make to become a well-rounded person?

Stress throws life out of balance and, when a person's life is already out of balance, stress increases the impact on all aspects of life. Everyone feels stress from time to time. They may be overwhelmed, anxious, frazzled, trying to make deadlines, affected by unexpected events, or struggling with relationship issues. A bit of stress is not all bad—it can motivate you to get things accomplished, even to think more creatively. With too much stress, however, the human body reacts as if it is facing a physical threat. Constantly being in a stressful state has many negative long-term effects. If you learn strategies to cope with stress in high school and college, you can apply them to the day-to-day challenges and stresses of finding balance in life as a teacher.

As with demands on your time, you can expect stress to increase as you start college. It makes sense to improve your skills for coping with stress and maintaining your balance.

Eating Well and Staying Fit

One of the best ways to strengthen your ability to withstand stress is to stay in great physical shape. When you feel well, you have more energy and are better able to cope with challenges.

Adequate nutrition and regular physical activity are the building blocks of good health. If your eating habits need improvement, start to make changes now. Beginning each day with a good breakfast can give you the fuel you need to revive your body. Making smart food choices for the rest of the day can help you feel your best. Also, build physical activity into your daily routine (Figure 16.12). If you need to boost your activity level, consider joining a sports team. Even if you are not a star player, the conditioning will help you get in shape. Working out or a simple walking program are other options. Remember that you can start with small changes and build on them. The results in how you will feel are well worth the effort.

When you get to college, make a point to eat well and exercise right from the start. It is easy to let good habits fall by the wayside when you are in a new environment. Today, colleges and universities make it easier for students to incorporate healthy habits into their lives. Many offer on-site fitness centers and other programs to promote wellness. As you visit schools, investigate this aspect of campus offerings.

Figure 16.12 Adding physical activity to your daily routine is a healthy way to deal with stress.

Coping with Stress

Learn how you react to a buildup of stress. Some people develop headaches or neck pain. Others find themselves developing short tempers or eating more. When you are attentive to your own signals, you can take appropriate action.

The first step is to identify the true source of your stress. It is easy to misidentify the source of stress. For example, if you oversleep and do not have time to polish your class presentation, you may feel stress as you run to a college class. You may think your stress is due to oversleeping, but more likely your stress is over not having time to practice your presentation. On an even deeper level, you may feel stress because you are anxious about presentations and about how others perceive you. Often, stress levels rise when you feel pressure from a number of situations. Perhaps, in addition to the presentation, you are worried about your mom's health and you are not sure you will make the final team cuts.

The second step in coping with stress is to make what changes you can to reduce pressure. Stress develops when the demands in your life exceed your ability to cope with them easily. Often, perceived demands are self-established and may be unattainable. In this case, oversleeping may be a sign that you are not getting enough sleep on a regular basis. You can do something about that. You might also adjust your attitude about the team cuts, and remember that you have done your best and have no control at this point.

Third, remember that you have some control over how you react. If you stay calm, your presentation will go better. If you do not make the team, you will be able to join another extracurricular activity, such as the on-campus Big Brothers Big Sisters group.

Fourth, consider long-term strategies for reducing stress. If you often leave assignments until the last minute, working ahead can help relieve many stressful situations. That way, when something unexpected happens, you will more likely be able to cope. Find your own ways to manage stress. Some people find that regular physical activity helps, while others find a friend to talk with when they feel overwhelmed (Figure 16.13). Try out several techniques and use the ones that work for you.

Figure 16.13 Taking time to talk with a friend is another healthy way to cope with stressful situations.

Figure 16.14 Observe the professionalism of educators you encounter and work to develop those characteristics.

Succeeding as a Professional Educator

Look into your future, imagine that you are now a college graduate and are a certified professional educator. The term *professional* implies someone who is educated and takes on significant responsibility. Professionals must show personal integrity, make complex decisions, model decisiveness, maintain commitment, and promote community awareness. Effective teachers exhibit all of these qualities.

As you move forward on your career path, pay particular attention to the ways educators act as professionals. How do they handle difficult situations? How do they show commitment to becoming better teachers? How do they become involved in their profession and their community? Professional qualities do not automatically accompany a college degree or a teaching job. Rather, you will develop them over time.

Professional Ethical Standards

Teaching involves more than helping students learn information. Teachers help to shape their students' lives. They model the roles of learner, professional, and citizen. Because of this influence, teachers are held to high ethical standards. Their behavior in the classroom and the community must live up to that responsibility.

Common sense is the foundation for many aspects of ethics. Teachers must obey laws and they must be honest. For example, it would be unethical to change a grade so that a student can qualify for sports. It would be dishonest for a person to provide inaccurate information about his or her educational background on a job application.

Other aspects of ethics deal with **professionalism**—conforming to the conduct, aims, or qualities that mark a profession. A teacher should dress and act in a professional manner (Figure 16.14). A teacher may have a friendly *rapport* (harmonious relationship) with students, but still must maintain professional teacher-to-student relationships at all times. As a professional, a teacher keeps personal information about students confidential.

Unfortunately, not all situations present clear-cut ethical issues and thus, a teacher must use good judgment that keeps the best interests of students in mind. In these situations, the teacher might consider, "How would I want a teacher to act if this were my child?" The teacher may also involve the principal or other school personnel to help clarify the best course of action for some situations.

A teacher's effectiveness—and even ability to find a teaching job— links to the teacher's personal reputation. Communities trust teachers with what is most precious—their children. A teacher who violates that trust through inappropriate behavior breaks that bond with the community.

Ongoing Professional Development

Today's world is characterized by constant change. To keep pace, employees must commit to being lifelong learners. This is especially true for teachers.

Professional development is learning linked to improving a person's professional expertise. For teachers, this can take various forms as long as the goal of development is to become better educators.

Most teachers engage in professional development by taking additional college courses after obtaining their bachelor's degree. Many school districts give salary increases based on successful completion of graduate-level courses (those beyond the bachelor's level that can lead to a master's or doctoral degree). Sometimes districts also partially reimburse teachers for the costs of such courses.

As with a bachelor's degree, a master's degree requires a specific course of study. Some teachers just take courses they feel will help update them in their subject areas or improve their teaching skills. Since many courses are now available online, it is easier for teachers to access graduate-level courses. There are also courses specific to other areas in education, such as those for being a counselor, a librarian, or an administrator.

Many school districts and groups offer other opportunities for professional development. For example, a school district might arrange for an expert on curriculum development to speak to all the teachers in the district or conduct a training session (Figure 16.15). Education, or **in-service training** such as this, is a type of ongoing professional development the school provides for its staff while on the job. Professional groups may offer workshops on topics of interest, such as using the newest technology to enhance learning. Conferences related to teaching may also contribute to professional development.

Figure 16.15 In-service training is a form professional development schools often provide.

State teaching licenses are usually valid for a limited number of years, and then teachers must renew them. Most states require that teachers meet specific professional development requirements in order to renew their licenses. This ensures that teachers continuously update their knowledge and skills.

As lifelong learners, teachers use every opportunity to increase their knowledge and skills. Such learning can come from many sources besides formal classes. Teachers also learn through work experiences, self-study, travel, and hobbies. Continual learning helps teachers keep their teaching fresh, interesting, and relevant.

Professional Associations

One of the best ways to stay updated on education issues and practices is to join one or more professional organizations. Many organizations are available for teachers and teacher education students. If you have an opportunity to attend a professional meeting as a student, be sure to do so.

Professional associations vary in their purposes. Some focus broadly on education. Others concentrate on some aspect of it, such as teaching social studies. Figure 16.16 lists just some of the professional organizations for teachers. You can check the websites of associations to find out more about them. Look for information about the goals of the groups. The sites should give you a good overview of the activities, resources, and opportunities for members, as well as the costs of membership. Check whether the organization has affiliated state or local groups.

Membership in a professional association can offer real opportunities for teachers. Through newsletters, journals, online postings, and conferences, teachers can keep up with current events and future trends. Most associations hold conferences and meetings that offer sessions to keep professionals up-to-date in various aspects of their field. These conferences and meetings also provide opportunities for both formal and informal interactions, creating valuable networking contacts. Teachers can serve on committees or take on other leadership positions within organizations.

Community Involvement

Effective teachers are good citizens. Many become actively involved in making their communities better. They put their knowledge and skills to work helping others and their communities (Figure 16.17). In the process, they often have opportunities to work with parents and other community members, strengthening those bonds.

Figure 16.16   Examples of Associations for Professional Educators
The American Council on the Teaching of Foreign Language
American Association of Family and Consumer Sciences
American Federation of Teachers
Association of American Educators
Association of Childhood Education International
Association for Career and Technical Education
The Council for Exceptional Children
The International Reading Association
Music Teachers National Association
National Art Education Association
National Association for the Education of Young Children
National Council of Teachers of English
National Council of Teachers of Mathematics
National Council for the Social Sciences
National Science Teacher Association

Figure 16.17   Active involvement in the community is another way teachers use their knowledge, skills, and strengthen relationships with parents and others.

As a college student, participate in community service opportunities. On-campus groups often work to be a positive force within the community. Such activities will help you gain experiences that can be helpful in your future. You will also have the satisfaction in knowing that you have made a positive difference in the lives of others.

Chapter 16 Review and Assess

Summary

- If you decide to pursue a teaching career, there are many steps you can take now to begin preparing yourself.

- Your portfolio showcases your accomplishments, strengths, and work related to a possible career in teaching.

- To polish your portfolio, select the materials you want to include. Then, prepare the selections for your portfolio in a professional manner and organize it for ease of use.

- Creating a personal career plan is an excellent way to help you reach your career goal

- Choosing a college or university to continue your education is one of the biggest decisions you face. Research and analysis can help you make an appropriate choice.

- Make sure your course schedule and graduation plan includes the classes you need for college, including advanced placement or dual-credit courses, and commit to doing well in them.

- Stay focused during high school, even if you feel unmotivated. This is a good time to develop your work ethic.

- Work to improve your time-management skills and learn to keep your life in balance. This may include eating well, staying fit, and coping with stress.

- Success as a teacher requires demonstrating the qualities of a professional, as well as teaching skill.

- You can begin to develop professionally by knowing professional ethical standards and joining student and professional organizations.

Review and Study

1. Describe two practical uses for a portfolio.
2. Identify and briefly explain the three steps involved in polishing a portfolio.
3. What is a *résumé* and when might you use it?
4. Contrast a career plan with a career goal.
5. List the steps for creating a career plan.
6. Name an obstacle a student might identify in reaching his or her career goal. Give an example of how a student might overcome that obstacle.
7. Name four aspects to consider when choosing a college or university. Which is most important to you and why?
8. Contrast advanced placement courses and dual-credit courses.
9. What are the benefits of joining student organizations in high school? List two that directly apply to teaching.
10. What is *work ethic* and why is it important to college and career success?
11. What steps can a person take to cope with stress? Give an example.
12. Why is professional development important for teachers? Give an example.
13. Identify at least two opportunities professional organizations offer teachers.
14. How do effective teachers display citizenship?

Vocabulary Activity

15. Classify the *Content* and *Academic* terms on page 402 into the following categories: *portfolio, career plan, college success,* and *professional*. Then pair up with a classmate and compare how you classified the terms. How were your lists similar or different? Discuss your lists with the class.

Critical Thinking

16. **Make inferences.** Early in the text, you learned about developing a *philosophy of teaching*. In this chapter, the author stresses the importance of reviewing and updating all materials for your portfolio. As part of this process, make inferences about how your philosophy of teaching or education has changed since the beginning of this course. What factors, such as formulation of a personal set of beliefs relevant to education, have influenced this change? Write a summary of your inferences.

17. **Analyze criteria.** Review the criteria in the text for evaluating a college or university— size, reputation, accreditation, location, admission requirements, and cost. Identify several technical or community colleges of interest to you that relate to the education and training and career cluster programs of study. Then identify and compare university programs and institutions that align with your interest areas. Analyze and compare each against the criteria for evaluating a college or university. Use the college or university websites to gather information. Write a summary of your analysis identifying which items are most important to your college decision.

18. **Draw conclusions.** Review the steps for effective time management on text page 420–421. Analyze your personal time-management skills against these steps. Draw conclusions about two areas that you feel could use improvement. Cite specific, objective evidence. Which of the specific techniques identified in the text might you try? Why? Write a short essay summarizing your conclusions.

19. **Analyze behavior.** The text cites that professionalism means conforming to the conduct, aims, or qualities that mark a profession. A teacher's reputation is important for success as a professional. Analyze types of behaviors you observe in high school and college students that could potentially affect their reputations in the future, positively or negatively. Discuss in class how students pursuing a career in teaching can begin to conform to the characteristics of professionalism. Use the text and other reliable resources to cite evidence about specific characteristics of professionalism.

Core Skills

20. **Writing and speaking.** Use the text guidelines and such Internet sites as CareerOneStop or O*NET in writing your initial résumé. Remember, your résumé is a continually evolving document. As you gain experience, update your résumé on a regular basis. After drafting your résumé, ask your instructor for feedback and discuss ways to improve your résumé if necessary. Save a copy in your portfolio.

21. **Writing and speaking.** Write a cover message following text guidelines to accompany your résumé, making it adaptable for college or career. Pair up with a classmate and proofread each other's cover messages. Give constructive feedback as necessary and discuss any questions with your instructor. Save a copy in your portfolio.

22. **Research and speaking.** Check online to find the admission requirements for several colleges or universities you are interested in that align with your areas of interest in teaching. Identify and compare the requirements for acceptance into the teacher education program at the schools. Prepare an oral presentation and share your findings with the class.

23. **Research and writing.** Use the websites of colleges or universities of interest to investigate scholarship opportunities. What types of scholarships are available?

What are the application requirements? Write a summary of your findings and post it to the class discussion board or website to exchange ideas and information.

24. **Speaking and listening.** Make an appointment to speak with your high school counselor to discuss choices for high school and dual-credit (enrollment) courses that relate to programs of study for education and training. What options are available and what are the qualifications for taking these courses? How will these courses benefit you as you pursue your teaching career? What adjustments might you need to make to your high school graduation plan?

25. **Technology Application.** Create a list of relevant websites or other digital resources for students interested in teaching, corporate training, or other education related careers. Include teaching resources, professional organizations, university programs, or support services. For each resource, write a one or two paragraph description and include the address. In addition, include your reflections about the usefulness of the resource. Save a copy of your descriptions in your portfolio for future reference.

26. **CTE College and career readiness practice.** Imagine it is five years in the future and you have started your first full-time teaching job. The work is demanding. You have watched family members and friends suffer the negative effects of workplace stress. Your goal is to maintain balance in your life and develop a plan for handling work stress. Investigate and evaluate resources from the Centers for Disease Control (CDC) and other reliable resources. Then write your plan for handling job stress.

College and Career Portfolio

Throughout this course, you collected items for your portfolio from earlier activities. Now is the time to organize and assemble your basic professional portfolio (both print and e-portfolios). It should include such items as your basic résumé, samples of your best work, a log of any service-learning or volunteer activities, results of assessments, and a sample scholarship application along with a list of items your instructor has provided throughout the course. Your instructor may have portfolio examples that you can review for ideas. Continue to add and remove documents as you complete assignments and learn new skills.

- Review your collection of documents and work samples, and choose those you want to include in your college and career portfolio. Make copies of certificates, endorsements, diplomas, and other important documents. Keep the originals in a safe place.

- Update the table of contents. You may also want to create a title page for each section.

- Place print items in your portfolio container and save your digital items in your e-portfolio.

- Present your completed professional portfolio to the class and your instructor for evaluation. Keep in mind that it should show a clear purpose, reflect your uniqueness, show your progress, and reflect professionalism.

Photo Credits

Chapter 9

Figure 9.0 Monkey Business Images/Shutterstock.com; Ch 9 Case Study Monkey Business Images/Shutterstock.com; Figure 9.1 Andresr/Shutterstock.com, Monkey Business Images/Shutterstock.com, Monkey Business Images/Shutterstock.com; Figure 9.3 Fuse/Thinkstock, bikeriderlondon/Shutterstock.com; Figure 9.5 Monkey Business Images/Shutterstock.com; Figure 9.6 Tyler Olson/Shutterstock.com; Figure 9.7 Fuse/Thinkstock, forestpath/Shutterstock.com; Figure 9.8 Fuse/Thinkstock; Figure 9.9 Jaren Jai Wicklund/Shutterstock.com; Figure 9.11 Rawpixel/Shutterstock.com; Figure 9.12 Digital Vision/Photodisc/Thinkstock; Ch 9 Professional Tip Fuse/Thinkstock; Figure 9.13 Christopher Futcher/Hemera/Thinkstock

Chapter 10

Figure 10.0 wavebreakmedia/Shutterstock.com; Ch 10 Case Study Stockbyte/Stockbyte/Thinkstock; Figure 10.1 wizdata/Shutterstock.com; Figure 10.2 Dean Mitchell/iStock/Thinkstock; Figure 10.3 Tyler Olson/Shutterstock.com; Ch 10 Professional Tip Fuse/Thinkstock; Figure 10.4 Anton Gvozdikov/iStock/Thinkstock; Figure 10.5 Goodluz/Shutterstock.com; Figure 10.6 michaeljung/iStock/Thinkstock, Purestock/Thinkstock, Tyler Olson/Shutterstock.com; Ch 10 Perspectives on Teaching Goodluz/Shutterstock.com, aetb/iStock/Thinkstock; Figure 10.7 Matej Kastelic/Shutterstock.com; Figure 10.8 Monkey Business Images/Shutterstock.com; Figure 10.10 Lucky Business/Shutterstock.com; Figure 10.11 Brand X Pictures/Stockbyte/Thinkstock; Figure 10.13 Jupiterimages/liquidlibrary/Thinkstock

Chapter 11

Figure 11.0 wizdata/Shutterstock.com; Ch 11 Case Study Hasloo Group Production Studio/Shutterstock.com; Figure 11.1 Monkey Business Images/Shutterstock.com; Figure 11.2 Monkey Business Images/Shutterstock.com; Figure 11.3 monkeybusinessimages/iStock/Thinkstock; Figure 11.4 Monkey Business Images/Shutterstock.com, Volt Collection/Shutterstock.com, Fuse/Thinkstock; Figure 11.5 Purestock/Thinkstock; Figure 11.6 Ariel Skelley/Blend Images/Thinkstock; Ch 11 Professional Tip Fuse/Thinkstock; Figure 11.10 moodboard/moodboard/Thinkstock; Figure 11.11 petrograd99/iStock/Thinkstock; Figure 11.12 Vitchanan Photography/Shutterstock.com; Figure 11.13 Monkey Business Images/Shutterstock.com; Figure 11.14 wavebreakmedia/Shutterstock.com

Chapter 12

Figure 12.0 wavebreakmedia/Shutterstock.com; Ch 12 Case Study larry1235/Shutterstock.com; Figure 12.1 Jupiterimages, Brand X Pictures/Stockbyte/Thinkstock, Monkey Business Images/Monkey Business/Thinkstock; Figure 12.3 Digital Vision/Photodisc/Thinkstock; Figure 12.4 moodboard/moodboard/Thinkstock; Figure 12.5 Monkey Business Images/Shutterstock.com; Figure 12.6 monkeybusinessimages/iStock/Thinkstock; Figure 12.7 Dawn Shearer-Simonetti/Shutterstock.com; Figure 12.8 Monkey Business Images/Shutterstock.com; Figure 12.9 Ints Vikimanis/Shutterstock.com; Figure 12.10 Tyler Olson/Shutterstock.com; Figure 12.11 Jupiterimages/liquidlibrary/Thinkstock; Figure 12.12 Jupiterimages/BananaStock/Thinkstock; Figure 12.13 Nick White/Photodisc/Thinkstock, Fuse/Thinkstock, Ryan McVay/Photodisc/Thinkstock; Figure 12.14 racorn/Shutterstock.com; Ch 12 Professional Tip Fuse/Thinkstock; Figure 12.15 Monkey Business Images/Shutterstock.com; Ch 12 Perspectives on Teaching Goodluz/Shutterstock.com, Intellistudies/iStock/Thinkstock

Chapter 13

Figure 13.0 monkeybusinessimages/iStock/Thinkstock; Ch 13 Case Study Dragon Images/Shutterstock.com; Figure 13.1 Syda Productions/Shutterstock.com, Rob Marmion/Shutterstock.com; Figure 13.2 Dmitriy Shironosov/iStock/Thinkstock; Figure 13.3 Angela Waye/Shutterstock.com; Figure 13.4 Terrie L. Zeller/Shutterstock.com; Figure 13.5 tmcphotos/Shutterstock.com;

Ch 13 Professional Tip Fuse/Thinkstock; Figure 13.6 wavebreakmedia/Shutterstock.com; Figure 13.7 Images used with the permission of SMART Technologies ULC (www.smarttech.com). SMART Board® and the SMART logo are trademarks of SMART Technologies ULC and may be registered in the European Union, Canada, the United States and other countries.; Figure 13.8 Rob Marmion/Shutterstock.com; Figure 13.9 michaeljung/Shutterstock.com; Figure 13.10 Monkey Business Images/Shutterstock.com; Figure 13.11 oliveromg/Shutterstock.com; Figure 13.12 moodboard/moodboard/Thinkstock, Pixland/Pixland/Thinkstock; Figure 13.13 mady70/Shutterstock.com; Figure 13.14 Creatas Images/Creatas/Thinkstock; Figure 13.15 National Oceanic and Atmospheric Administration and the Department of Commerce; Figure 13.16 Sergey Nivens/Shutterstock.com; Figure 13.17 Goodluz/Shutterstock.com; Figure 13.18 racorn/Shutterstock.com

Chapter 14

Figure 14.0 gece33/iStock/Thinkstock; Ch 14 Case Study Bruce Stanfield/Shutterstock.com; Figure 14.1 Tyler Olson/Shutterstock.com; Figure 14.2 Monkey Business Images/Shutterstock.com, Fuse/Thinkstock; Figure 14.3 Chad McDermott/Shutterstock.com; Figure 14.4 Goodluz/Shutterstock.com; Figure 14.5 AVAVA/iStock/Thinkstock; Figure 14.6 Orange Line Media/Shutterstock.com, Goodluz/iStock/Thinkstock; Figure 14.7 Monkey Business Images/Shutterstock.com; Ch 14 Professional Tip Fuse/Thinkstock; Figure 14.9 ngkaki/iStock/Thinkstock; Figure 14.10 Purestock/Thinkstock; Figure 14.11 wizdata/Shutterstock.com; Figure 14.12 Africa Studio/Shutterstock.com, Jack Hollingsworth/Digital Vision/Thinkstock

Chapter 15

Figure 15.0 Monkey Business Images/Shutterstock.com; Ch 15 Case Study Edie Layland/iStock/Thinkstock; Figure 15.1 Cheryl Casey/Shutterstock.com; Figure 15.2 Mike Watson Images/moodboard/Thinkstock; Figure 15.3 monkeybusinessimages/iStock/Thinkstock, Monkey Business Images/Shutterstock.com; Ch 15 Professional Tip Fuse/Thinkstock; Figure 15.4 monkeybusinessimages/iStock/Thinkstock; Figure 15.5 bikeriderlondon/Shutterstock.com; Figure 15.6 Comstock Images/Stockbyte/Thinkstock, Monkey Business Images/Shutterstock.com, Zurijeta/Shutterstock.com; Figure 15.7 Creatas/Creatas/Thinkstock; Figure 15.8 Syda Productions/Shutterstock.com; Figure 15.9 Hannamariah/Shutterstock.com; Figure 15.10 Cathy Yeulet/Hemera/Thinkstock; Figure 15.11 michaeljung/Shutterstock.com; Figure 15.12 Fuse/Thinkstock; Figure 15.13 Jupiterimages/liquidlibrary/Thinkstock; Figure 15.14 Purestock/Thinkstock; Figure 15.15 AVAVA/Shutterstock.com; Ch 15 Perspectives on Teaching Goodluz/Shutterstock.com, SZE FEI WONG/iStock/Thinkstock, Dusan Jankovic/Shutterstock.com; Figure 15.16 Alexander Raths/Shutterstock.com

Chapter 16

Figure 16.0 Chris Howey/Shutterstock.com; Ch 16 Case Study OLJ Studio/Shutterstock.com; Figure 16.1 Purestock/Thinkstock; Figure 16.2 ViktorCap/iStock/Thinkstock, Wavebreakmedia Ltd/Wavebreak Media/Thinkstock; Figure 16.4 Suprijono Suharjoto/iStock/Thinkstock; Figure 16.5 Ammentorp Photography/Shutterstock.com; Figure 16.6 Joy Brown/Shutterstock.com; Figure 16.7 Monkey Business Images/Shutterstock.com; Figure 16.9 michaeljung/Shutterstock.com, michaeljung/Shutterstock.com, Marcelo Rodriguez/Shutterstock.com; Figure 16.10 James Woodson/Photodisc/Thinkstock; Figure 16.11 Wavebreakmedia Ltd/Wavebreak Media/Thinkstock; Figure 16.12 lzf/Shutterstock.com; Figure 16.13 Martin Novak/iStock/Thinkstock; Figure 16.14 michaeljung/Shutterstock.com, Ermolaev Alexander/Shutterstock.com, Jack Hollingsworth/Photodisc/Thinkstock; Figure 16.16 Robert Churchill/iStock/Thinkstock; Figure 16.17 Monkey Business Images/Shutterstock.com, Monkey Business Images/Shutterstock.com, jdwfoto/Shutterstock.com; Ch 16 Professional Tip Fuse/Thinkstock

Glossary

A

abdominal thrust. The Heimlich maneuver or an action to dispel an object from a choking victim's throat. (10)

abstract thinking. In-depth thinking about ideas and concepts, such as justice or love. (1)

acceptable use policy. Specific policies regarding use of computers by students. (13)

accommodations. Modifications to the environment, learning strategies, or materials that are made to help students with particular special needs succeed in the classroom. (9)

accountability. Measurable proof that schools and teachers are providing high-quality education. (4)

accreditation. Recognition showing an educational institution maintains standards that qualify graduates for professional practice in a career or career area. (16)

accredited. A school that has passed a quality assessment. (13)

achievement gap. The differences in learning and graduation rates among schools; often correlates to differences in school populations and funding. (5)

active listening. Involves asking questions and restating ideas to discover the true message of the sender. (10)

adhere. Follow. (16)

advanced placement courses. Courses that are more difficult than regular high school courses, and include content comparable to beginning-level college classes. At the end of the course, students take a standardized advanced placement test. A passing score on this test may give a student credit at the college level for having completed that college requirement. (16)

advantageous. Beneficial. (16)

advocate. People who support or promote the interests of others. (1)

aggressive communicator. People whose verbal or nonverbal communication aims to hurt or put down other people and show disrespect. (10)

alternative assessment. A method of assessing learning other than through testing. (14)

amygdala. The part of the brain responsible for emotional reactions such as anger. (8)

analogy. A comparison of two unlike things for similarities. (2)

apprentice. Someone who learns a skilled trade by watching and helping an expert in that trade. (3)

arduous. Hard to accomplish or achieve. (9)

articulate. Put thoughts into words. (2)

artifacts. Physical items that are part of a portfolio, such as projects or papers, examples from a related volunteer activity, and academic and other awards. (2)

assertive communicator. People who freely express their thoughts, ideas, and feelings respectfully and allow others to do the same. (10)

assessment. A form of evaluation that involves determining how much a student or class has learned or is currently learning. How the teacher evaluates whether the learning specified in the objectives has taken place. (10, 11)

asynchrony. The lack of simultaneous occurrence as occurs when body parts grow at the different rates. (8)

at risk. Students or groups that have characteristics or experiences that make them more likely to fail academically. (5)

auditory learners. People who learn most easily by hearing or listening to information. (9)

authoritarian style. A management style that seeks to control students' behavior through many rules, procedures, and consequences. (15)

authoritative style. A management style that seeks to shape students' behavior through setting high expectations, explanations, and consistent application of consequences. (15)

autonomy. Independence that includes personal responsibility and decision making. (8)

B

baby boom. The great increase in births after the end of World War II. (4)

back-to-basics movement. A reform movement which emphasized the need for more reading, writing, and math in schools for students to succeed in a complex world. (4)

behaviorism. A theory based on the belief that individuals' behavior is determined by forces in the environment that are beyond their control. (6)

bilingual education. Classes taught in two languages. (4)

Bloom's taxonomy. A theory for establishing educational objectives as a basis for understanding and teaching various levels of thought. (11)

C

career and technical education. Prepares students for the many career opportunities in specific trades and occupations. (3)

career goal. A clear, concise statement of what you want to become in life. (2)

career objective. A one-sentence description that aligns you and your skills with a specific position. (16)

case study. A description of a realistic, problematic situation that requires a solution. (12)

certified teacher. A teacher who has met the state requirements for teacher preparation. (2)

chain of command. The official organizational structure that tells who reports to whom. (10)

charter school. A public school that operates with freedom from many of the regulations that apply to traditional public schools. (4)

checklist. A simple list of items to note, check, or to remember when evaluating learning. (14)

civil rights movement. A social movement in the United States led primarily by African Americans and their supporters who sought to gain equal rights regardless of race. (4)

class rules. The guidelines for student behavior specific to a class or teacher. (15)

classical conditioning. The theory that behaviors can be associated with responses. (6)

classification. The ability to sort items by one or more characteristics they have in common. (7)

classroom management. The steps teachers take to organize their classroom for optimal learning, engage students in that learning, and minimize behaviors that disrupt it. (15)

classroom procedures. Specific guidelines that translate the class rules into concrete actions expected of students. (15)

closure. A process that helps students draw conclusions based on what they have learned. (12)

cognition. Processes involving thought and knowledge. (6)

cognitive development. The way people change and improve in their abilities to think and learn throughout life. (6)

cognizant. Knowledgeable and mindful. (6)

Cold War. A decades-long standoff that began in the late 1940s after World War II, when tensions and competition increased between the Soviet Union on one side and the United States and its allies in Western Europe on the other. (4)

collaboration. Working cooperatively with others. (10)

collaborative learning. Offers a way for students to work in groups and solve problems together. A form of group learning in which assignments involve a task or problem students must solve using their complementary and interdependent skills, experiences, or opinions. (1, 12)

common schools. The first public state-supported schools that gave the same education to people from different levels of society. (3)

competency-based education. Schools teach toward students demonstrating mastery and achievement of specified knowledge and skills in subject areas. (4)

concrete thinking. Thinking that focuses on facts and actual experiences. (1)

conflict resolution. Skills that can help students learn how to state their needs, negotiate, and collaborate. (5)

consensus. A general agreement that requires analysis and negotiation to reach a solution on which the majority agrees. (12)

conservation. The ability to understand that something can remain the same even if the way it looks changes; for example, a simple change in the shape of an object does not change its amount. (7)

constructivism. Taking new knowledge and interacting with it by forming hypotheses, testing it, and making decisions on whether or not to add it to one's learning. (6)

context. Includes past experiences, knowledge, and current reality. (6)

controversy. Discussion marked by opposing views. (11)

cooperating teacher. A classroom teacher who supervises and mentors the student teacher. (2)

cooperative learning. A form of small-group learning in which students work together to achieve a common goal. (12)

copyright. The body of exclusive rights granted by laws of the United States to copyright owners for protection of their work. (13)

corporate trainers. Teachers who provide education to the employees of businesses and industries. (1)

corporate-education partnership. An expanded and more formal relationship between schools and businesses, especially large corporations, in which the businesses "adopt" the schools to help in a variety of ways. (5)

course evaluation. Making judgments about how well a course meets its goals and what improvements would make it better. (14)

course plan. A detailed outline of what a particular teacher will teach throughout a course or year based on curriculum but adapted to the characteristics of the teacher, students, and teaching circumstances. (11)

critical thinking. Allows people to gather information, evaluate its quality, and use it effectively. Also called *higher-order thinking skills*. (12)

curriculum. The courses taught in a school, what is taught in each course, and how the courses are sequenced. (1)

curriculum developer. A person who helps develop course content in a program of study or specific course; also known as an instructional coordinator. (1)

curriculum development. Determining what to teach in each course and at each level. (11)

cyberbullying. Intimidation through e-mail, social networking sites, and texting. (5)

D

dame schools. Schools in the colonies where students were taught by women in their own homes. (3)

development. The gradual increase in skills and abilities that occurs over a lifetime. (6)

developmental delay. A noticeable lag in a particular aspect of development. (7)

developmental disabilities. A group of conditions (physical, intellectual, or behavioral) that can severely impact learning. (1)

developmental theories. Explanations formulated by researchers about why people act and behave the way they do and how they change over time. (6)

dexterity. The skillful use of the hands and fingers. (7)

differentiated instruction. Different modes of instruction to match a student's preferred mode of learning, disability, or background. (9)

differentiated instructional method. Using different techniques of instruction to match a student's preferred mode of learning, disability, or background. (12)

direct learning. A method of teaching in which a teacher tells students what to learn and provides all the structure for the learning to take place. (10)

disposable income. Money to spend on things people want, not just need. (3)

distance education. A learning situation in which the teacher and student are not in the same location. (13)

diversity. The distinct and unique differences among people. (1)

dual-credit courses. College- or university-level courses in which high school students enroll and, on successful completion of the courses, simultaneously earn both high school and postsecondary credits. These may be taught in a high school or at a college or university. These credits may be transferrable to another college or university the student chooses to attend after high school graduation. (16)

E

educational standards. Guidelines defining what students at various levels should know and be able to do. (4)

educational standards. Statements about what students are expected to know and be able to do at certain points in their education. They are set by national organizations, states, and many school districts. Sometimes called *instructional goals*. (11)

egocentrism. Self-focus. (8)

empower. To give authority to. (12)

English language learners (ELL). Students that must learn English while also mastering the content of their regular classes. (9)

ethics. Conduct based on moral principles. (10)

ethnicity. Refers to a particular racial, national, or cultural group including that group's customs, beliefs, values, and often language and religion. (9)

exceptional learners. Students that require special educational modifications and, perhaps, other services that align with their abilities and potential. (9)

executive strategies. Skills used to solve problems. (7)

experiential learning. Learning that takes place when students actually experience and then reflect on their learning. (6)

experimental lab. Uses a formal process to research a problem. (12)

expulsion. When a student loses the right to attend school for a specified period of time. (5)

extracurricular activities. Activities that take place before or after school. (1)

F

facilitator. An educator who creates situations that help students learn by developing activities that actively involve students in learning, rather than just presenting information. (10)

fine-motor skills. Skills that depend on development of the small muscles such as those in the hands and wrists. (6)

formative assessment. An ongoing part of instruction that provides feedback about students' learning as it occurs during instruction; generally not graded. (14)

formulaic. An expression of facts, rules, or procedures in mathematical symbols. (11)

G

genetics. The traits, abilities, skills, and tastes people are born with. (6)

global economy. Finance, international corporations, and trade link the economies of nations around the world—particularly those of major countries. (4)

grants. Money that is given for a specific purpose, such as educational expenses, that does not have to be repaid. (2)

gray matter. The cells of the brain that actually make a person think. (8)

gross-motor skills. Skills that depend on development of the large muscles, including those in the arms, legs, back, and shoulders. (6)

growth. Physical changes in size, such as gains in height and weight. (6)

growth spurts. Rapid increases in height and weight; marked growth that occurs during *adolescence*. (8)

guided practice. An activity designed to reinforce and apply learning that includes feedback from other students or the teacher. (11)

H

hand-eye coordination. The ability to move the hands precisely in response to what the eyes see. (7)

headline. A set of introductory words to capture attention. (16)

Holocaust. The mass slaughter of European civilians, especially those of Jewish descent, by the Nazis during World War II. (4)

hornbook. A flat wooden board with a handle. A sheet of paper—usually containing the alphabet, a prayer or two, and Roman numerals—was pasted on the board. A thin, flat piece of clear animal horn was attached to cover and protect the paper. Used during the Colonial Period. (3)

hypocrisy. Acting in contradiction to a person's stated beliefs or values. (8)

I

illiterate. Unable to read or write. (4)

inclusion. When students with special needs attend regular classes with the requirement that they will receive some benefit from the classes, even if they are not able to keep up academically with class requirements. (9)

independent practice. A personal activity outside of class that students complete on their own. (11)

individual accountability. A way to assess each student's participation and learning. (12)

Individualized Education Program (IEP). A written plan for providing a student with the most appropriate opportunity for learning. (9)

Industrial Revolution. A period of complex economic, technological, and social change in America and worldwide. (3)

in-service training. Education that is a type of ongoing professional development the school provides for its staff while on the job. (16)

instructional method. The basic techniques used to promote learning. Often called *instructional strategies* or *teaching strategies*. (12)

instructional objectives. Clear statements of what students will achieve as a result of a lesson that they exhibit in an observable way. Also called *learning outcomes*. (11)

instructional technology. The application of technology to enhance teaching, learning, and assessment. (13)

instructional units. Related topics that are grouped in a logical order and taught together over a period of time. (11)

insubordination. Disobedience to authority. (15)

intangible. Abstract and less concrete. (10)

interactive whiteboard. A versatile type of teaching equipment that connects to a computer and projector to allow the board to become an extended computer touch screen. (13)

intimidation. Real or implied threats. (5)

invincibility. Feeling incapable of being defeated or having anything bad happen. (8)

J

jeopardize. Risk. (16)

job shadowing. Following a person on the job for a few hours, a day, or even longer to experience what the person's career typically involves. (2)

K

kinesthetic-tactile learners. People who learn best by performing hands-on or physical activities. (9)

L

learner-centered method. Teaching strategy in which the teacher acts as a facilitator, or guide, for learning, and students more actively engage in directing and achieving their own learning. (12)

learning activities. Learning experiences that help students learn the content and achieve the outcome of the instructional objectives; the second major component of lesson plans. (11)

learning diversity. Differences in learning based on abilities, interests, or experiences. (9)

learning styles. The methods individuals prefer and find most effective to absorb and process information. (9)

lesson plans. Detailed outlines of topics to teach, how to teach them, why they are necessary to teach and learn, and how to evaluate learning. Sometimes called *instructional plans* or *teaching plans*. (11)

lifelong learner. People who commit to staying up-to-date in their knowledge and skills. (10)

limited English proficiency (LEP). A person's difficulty communicating effectively in English because English is not his or her native or primary language. (9)

M

mainstreaming. When schools place students with special needs in one or more regular classes based on their expected ability to keep up with the standard curriculum. (9)

McGuffey's Readers. The first widely used textbooks published during the American Common School Period. They included moral lessons along with science, grammar, and other subjects. (3)

mediation. Process in which a mediator tries to help those in a dispute reach a peaceful agreement. (10)

mediator. A neutral third party. (10)

mediocre. Not exemplary. (16)

mentor. An adult expert who commits to a long-term relationship with a student to provide support, guidance, and help. (5)

mentor teachers. Experienced, skilled teachers paired with new teachers to help them improve their skills, solve problems, and become comfortable in their new roles. (14)

metacognition. Thinking critically about a person's own thinking processes. (8)

mission statement. The official version of an organization's purpose and goals, along with policies and procedures. (10)

mixed message. A discrepancy between verbal and nonverbal messages. (10)

model. A real example that shows the characteristics of excellence. (13)

moderator. Leader. (12)

Montessori Method. The teaching principles developed by Maria Montessori, an Italian doctor, emphasizing self-directed learning through sensory experiences. (3)

motivation. Personal incentive or drive to succeed. (9)

multimedia. A technique for combining several forms for media to express an idea. (13)

multiple intelligences. The theory that individuals have a broad range of types of intelligence, each to a different degree. (9)

multitasking. Trying to do many things at the same time. (8)

N

national standards. Performance standards for knowledge and skills to be mastered in specific subject areas. (4)

neural connections. The links between brain cells that can be strengthened through activities that repeatedly stimulate the brain. (8)

nonsectarian. Private schools that are not based on or affiliated with any religion. (1)

nonverbal cues. Communication without words using techniques such as eye contact, body language, gestures, and physical closeness. (15)

normal schools. Teacher-training schools that prepared men and women with the necessary skills to become teachers. (3)

O

online learning. A learning situation in which students complete assignments, participate in discussion boards, and may even take exams online. Also called *virtual education*. (13)

open-ended questions. Questions that require more than a few words as an answer. (12)

operant conditioning. When people tend to repeat behaviors that have a positive result or are reinforced. (6)

optimism. The inclination to see favorable outcomes. (10)

Oregon Trail. The only practical route for people to emigrate from Independence, Missouri to the western United States, primarily Oregon and California. (3)

organizational culture. The "personality" of an organization based on the assumptions, values, standards, behaviors, and actions of people, as well as the tangible signs of an organization. (10)

P

pacing. Refers to the rate at which a teacher moves through the components of a lesson or the lessons throughout the day. (12)

panel discussion. When a group of people present and discuss a topic. (12)

paraprofessional. A person who works under the supervision of a more highly educated professional. (1)

parent educators. Educators who come from a variety of backgrounds and offer training and encouragement to parents. (1)

passive communicator. People who are unwilling to say what they feel, think, or desire, wanting to avoid all conflict. (10)

peer evaluation. Students' assessment of each other's learning. (14)

permissive style. A management style that sets few expectations and rules for students and enforces them inconsistently. (15)

perseverance. Steadfast persistence in an undertaking. (15)

personal portfolio. An organized collection of materials and information that shows how personal knowledge, skills, and attitudes have developed over time. (2)

philosophy of teaching. A personal statement about your thoughts, views, and values as they relate to teaching. (2)

physical development. Involves advances in physical abilities. (6)

plagiarism. The use of someone else's original words or ideas without giving that person credit. (13)

postsecondary education. Education that takes place after high school. (1)

prefrontal cortex. The part of the brain that regulates emotions and impulse control. (8)

prerequisite course. A course that students must complete before entering a program or prior to taking a higher-level course. (2)

proactive. Anticipating the need to find solutions to future problems, needs, or changes. (10)

productive lab. Focuses on producing an end product. (12)

professional development. Involves taking part in professional organizations, attending seminars and conferences, pursuing an advanced degree, or other activities meant to improve professional knowledge and skills. (10)

professionalism. When a person conforms to the conduct, aims, or qualities that mark a profession. (16)

proficiency test. A test that measures skill and knowledge in a subject area. (2)

proficient. Able move forward in accomplishment. (7)

program director. A person who oversees the mission, goals, and programs of an organization, such as a child care center. (1)

programs of study. Rigorous sequences of career and technical and academic courses to prepare students for successful transition from high school to postsecondary education/credentialing and employment. (4)

Progressives. Members of the reform movement during the Progressive Era. (3)

Project Head Start. A federal government program designed to help preschool children from low-income families develop the skills they need for success in kindergarten and beyond. (4)

psychologist. A person who studies human behavior and mental processes and develops theories to explain why people behave the way they do. (1)

puberty. The physical transformation from a child to an adult capable of reproduction. (8)

Q

quotas. Limits. Immigration laws set limits for people coming to the United States from other countries. (3)

R

rapport. Harmonious relationship. (16)

real time. All students are online for class at the same time. (13)

reciprocal agreements. In teaching, agreements between states that allow teachers certified to teach in one state to teach in another state that is part of the agreement. (2)

reflective response. An activity in which students think deeply about an issue or something they have learned. (12)

reliability. A characteristic of an assessment that measures the same over time—meaning the results will be similar with different learners and under different circumstances. (14)

repertoire. Your list of skills, activities, and methods or strategies for teaching. (12)

resilience. The ability to bounce back after a defeat or setback. (8)

résumé. An outline of your education, achievements, and experiences, including volunteer work and work experiences. (16)

role-playing. A learner-centered simulation that involves students in acting out a role *without* a script. (12)

rubric. A scoring tool that lists the criteria for judging a particular type of work. It also describes levels of quality for each of the criteria and is often organized as a chart, with the *criteria* (characteristics that count for scoring) on the left, followed by columns that describe different levels of quality for each characteristic. (14)

S

salary schedule. A chart or table that shows the progression of employee wages over time. (1)

school funding gap. Challenge that occurs in school districts with lower levels of income from property taxes; tends to be in urban areas that often have a higher proportion of students who are from low-income families and need a higher level of services. (5)

school policies. Overall guidelines that generally address major issues such as attendance and dress code. (In some districts these are called *rules*, *regulations*, or *procedures*.) (15)

school-based curriculum. A set of curriculum standards where teachers are involved in making decisions about what is taught in their classrooms and schools. (1)

scorecard. A tool for evaluating alternative assessments that lists the characteristics or factors to use when evaluating learning and a maximum point value for each criterion but does not describe levels of quality. (14)

self-concept. A person's own assessment or view of himself or herself. (7)

self-contained classrooms. A situation in which the same teacher and group of students remain in one classroom for most of the day, with one teacher teaching most or all subjects. (1)

self-evaluation. Students' assessment of their own learning. (14)

sequence. Steps that occur in a predictable and orderly manner. (6)

seriation. The ability to place objects in order by a characteristic, such as smallest to largest. (7)

service-learning. A special type of unpaid volunteer effort that combines classroom learning with meaningful hands-on experience to meet community needs. (2)

simulation. A way to put students in situations that feel real, even though they are not—eliminating any harmful risks. (12)

skit. Learner-centered simulations that involve students in acting out stories based on scripts. (12)

social-emotional development. Development that includes the areas of relationships and feelings. Individuals must learn social skills and how to care about others. (6)

Socratic learning. Sharing dialogue between a teacher and students so students can discover new learning for themselves. (6)

special education. Provides adapted programs, extra staff, and specialized equipment or learning environments or materials to help students with special needs to learn. (9)

special needs. A broad range of physical, mental, social, and behavioral challenges that affect learning. (9)

spending per pupil. The average amount of money a school district spends to educate one student for one year. (5)

standardized tests. Tests designed to give a measure of students' performance compared with that of a very large number of other students. (4)

stereotype. Preconceived generalizations about certain groups of people. (9)

student portfolio. A collection of a student's work selected to show growth over time, highlight skills and achievements, or to show how well the student meets standards. (14)

student teaching. Culmination of the teacher education experience that involves placement of student teachers in public or private school classrooms to immerse themselves in the practice of teaching. (2)

subjective grading. Grading on opinion rather than fact. (14)

summative assessment. An evaluation of students' learning after instruction has taken place. It measures results, assessing whether learning objectives have been met; often scored or graded. (14)

T

Teach Act of 2002. Allows some use of copyrighted material for educational purposes. (13)

teachable moment. Unforeseen teaching opportunities. (10)

teacher education programs. University or college programs that prepare students to become teachers. (2)

teacher-centered method. Teaching strategy in which the teacher's role is to present the information that students are to learn and to direct their learning process. (12)

teaching academies. Programs that help high school students to explore the teaching profession through classes, observations, and hands-on experiences. (2)

teaching license. A license or certificate a certified teacher receives from his or her state. (2)

technical schools. Schools that offer programs that teach the specific skill requirements to begin working in a trade. (1)

transitions. Smooth ways to move from one part of the lesson to the next. (11)

transitivity. The ability to understand that relationships between two objects can extend to a third object. (7)

V

validity. An important characteristic which requires choosing an assessment that actually measures your learning objectives. (14)

viable. Reasonably successful. (11)

virtual school. School that exists only online. (13)

virtue. Commendable moral qualities or traits such as kindness and honesty. (6)

visual learners. People who learn best by seeing. (9)

visual-motor coordination. Involves matching body movements to coordinate with what the child sees. (7)

W

wait time. A brief period of silence between asking a question and calling on a student; allows all students to mentally process the question and formulate their replies. (12)

WebQuest. Inquiry-based learning projects utilizing information from preselected websites. (13)

work ethic. A reflection of a person's dedication to completing important tasks. (16)

Z

zero tolerance policy. The prohibited behaviors and actions that schools will not tolerate—no exceptions. (5)

Index